Voices From Home

•

The North Carolina Prose Anthology

Edited by
Richard Krawiec

Avisson Press, Inc.
Greensboro

First edition
Printed in the United States of America

Library of Congress Cataloging-in-Publication Data

Voices from home: the North Carolina prose anthology/edited by Richard Krawiec. — 1st ed.
p.   cm.
ISBN 1-888105-29-1 (lib. bdg.). — ISBN 1-888105-30-5 (pbk.)
1. American prose literature—North Carolina. 2. North Carolina -
-Social life and customs—Fiction. 3. American prose literature—
20th century. 4. North Carolina—Civilization.
I. Krawiec, Richard.
PS558.N8V65 1997
818'.5080809756—dc21   97-27446
                              CIP

Acknowledgments: "After Revelation," Copyright © 1991 by Fred Chappell, from *More Shapes Than One* by Fred Chappell. Reprinted by permission of St. Martin's Press Incorporated. "Paths of Glory" by Hal Crowther, from *Unarmed But Dangerous* Copyright ©1995 by Hal Crowther. Reprinted by permission of Longstreet Press, Inc.; "The Holly Pageant" Copyright © by Lavonne J. Adams. Used by permission of the author. "Shell Island," Copyright ©1993 by Ellyn Bache, from *The Value of Kindness.* First published by Helicon Nine Editions. Reprinted by permission. "Lise: Her Hands" Copyright ©1996 by Rebecca Baggett. First published in *North American Review.* Reprinted by permission of the author. "Ten Rabbis Eat Cake," Copyright © 1995 by Jeff W. Bens, first appeared in *Vignette* magazine. Reprinted by permission of the author. "Wallpaper," Copyright © 1997 by Sally Buckner. Reprinted by permission of the author. "Love in the Middle Ages," Copyright © by Kelly Cherry, first appeared in *Georgia Review.* Used by permission of the author. "The Hunt Fund," Copyright ©1997 by Michael Chitwood. Used by permission of the author. "Angel," Copyright ©1995 by Jim Clark, first appeared in *The Nightshade Nightstand Reader.* Used by permission of the author. "Jailhouse Religion," Copyright ©1997 by Mary E. Drew. Used by permission of the author. "Fear Kills," Copyright © by David Guy, first appeared in *The Sun.* Used by permission of the author. "Porch Sitting as a Creative Southern Tradition," Copyright © 1996 by Trudier Harris, first appeared in *Southern Cultures.* Used by permission of the author. "Touching What Remains," Copyright © by Virginia Holman, first appeared in *The Independent.* Used by permission of the author. "Private McKinney Died in France July 9," Copyright © 1996 by Elizabeth C.

Contents

Introduction

This book isn't meant to be a "Best of North Carolina" anthology. Neither is it meant to be limited by regionalism. Although the writers included in VOICES FROM HOME are current, or former, residents of North Carolina, the stories aren't always set in North Carolina, and not every piece features a distinctly "Southern" style.

When discussing writers, people often forget the other half of the equation—readers. In making selections for this anthology, I wished to compile a miscellany of prose that would appeal to the diversity of readers in this state.

Think of VOICES FROM HOME as a loosely-organized literary buffet, a place to browse and sample. In these pages, you'll find serious fiction, humor, creative non-fiction, satire, columns, essays, memoirs, meditations—even a folk tale.

Read what you like, and leave the rest for others. As you go through these selections you'll notice they aren't identified as fiction or non-fiction. That's intentional. With the blurring of lines in prose writing these days, some of the questions raised by this book are these—What is true? What is real? How do we tell the difference? Should we?

My one regret is that I didn't have space to include everyone whose work was strong enough to deserve publication.

By arrangement with the publisher, a portion of the sales of this book will be used to fund writing workshops for at-risk children and adults in homeless shelters, literacy classes, housing projects, prisons, and elsewhere.

Richard Krawiec
— May 1997

Condolences to Every One of Us

•

Allan Gurganus

For Brett Singer
and for Marianne Gingher

Dear Mrs. Whiston,

I was in Africa on Father Flannagan's Tour of the World with your parents when they were killed. I want to tell you how it happened. My son-in-law is a doctor (eye, ear, nose and throat) at Our Lady of Perpetual Help outside Toledo, and he says I should write down all I know, the sooner the better, to get it out of my system. I am a woman of sixty-seven years. I have a whole box of stationery here. If this doesn't turn out so hot, I'm sorry. My mind is better than ever but sometimes my writing hand gets cramped. I'll take breaks when I need to. I've got all morning.

I blame the tour organizers. They should be informed about the chances of a revolution happening while one of their buses is visiting some place. When I first looked at Father Flannagan's literature, I got bad feelings about Tongaville. I'd never even heard of it, but on these package deals you just go where the bus goes. You take the bad cities with the good.

Your parents were the most popular couple on our tour. They always had a kind word for everyone. They'd made several other world trips, so your mother knew to be ready for the worst. She shared her Kaopectate with me when I most needed it outside Alexandria. I'm sending along a picture I took with my new camera at the Sphinx. It's not as sharp as I expected but here it is. Your mother is the one in the saddle and your father's holding his baseball-type cap out like he's feeding her camel. He really stood about ten feet in front of it because

9

we were told they bite. The woman off to the right is Miss Ada McMillan, a retired librarian just full of energy and from Winnetka, Ill. She is laughing here because your father was such a card, always in high spirits, always cheering us up, keeping the ball rolling in ways our tour guide should have. I hope knowing more about your parents' death will be better for you than remaining in the dark. I think I'd want the whole truth. What I've read in American papers and magazines about the revolution is just plain wrong, and I believe that using the photograph of your poor parents lying in the street was totally indecent and unforgivable. I pray you have been spared seeing it. That started as a Polaroid snapshot taken by my neighbor and ex-friend Cora White. She was along on the African tour. I hear she sold the picture to a wire service for 175 dollars. I will never speak to her again, I can promise you that, Mrs. Whiston.

I'm rambling already, so I will begin to sketch out what I remember. If you choose to stop reading here, I can understand that. But I'm going on anyway. If I don't get this Africa business laid out in the open, I know my dreams and housework will stay like they are now, a big mess.

My memory is one thing I've always been proud of. I can rattle off restaurant menus from lunches I ate with my late husband in 1926. Till now, the only good this ability has done me is not needing to keep grocery lists and never forgetting any family member's birthday.

The bus had to wait for sheep to cross the road just outside the capital city. I was putting on my lipstick when we heard the explosion. Tongaville is made of mud walls like what's known as stucco in America. The town was far off, all one color on a flat desert so it looked like a toy fort. One round tower blew into a thousand pieces. The shock waves were so strong that sheep fell against the front of our bus. They got terrified and were climbing up on each other. They don't look like our American sheep but are black and have very skinny legs. Their coats are thick as powder puffs, only greasy. Seeing how scared they were scared me.

Some of us tried talking sense to our tour guide. He wasn't any Father Flannagan. We'd all expected a priest, even though

10

the brochure didn't come right out and promise one. This guide was not even Catholic, but some Arab with a mustache. He spoke English so badly you had to keep asking him to repeat and sometimes even to spell things out. We told him it would be a mistake, driving into a town where this type of thing was happening. But he said our hotel rooms were already paid for—otherwise, we'd just have to sleep on the bus and miss the Game Preserve the next morning. We were so tired. Half of us were sick. Somebody asked for a show of hands. Majority ruled that we go in and take our chances. But my instinct told me, definitely no.

Mrs. Whiston, we'd been in Egypt earlier. It is dry and outstandingly beautiful but as far as a place to live and work, it lags way behind Ohio. But, maybe that's just me. Thanks to Egypt, I had the worst case of diarrhea I have ever heard of or read about. You cannot believe how low a case of diarrhea can bring a person's spirits and better judgment. Because of it, I voted Yes, enter Tongaville. In my condition, a bus parked on the desert, where there's not one blade of grass much less a bush for fifty miles, was just no place to spend the night. So, like a pack of fools, we drove into Tongaville, right into the middle of it.

The bus was air-conditioned, and we couldn't exactly hear what all of them were shouting at us. Then Miss McMillan, who's in your parents' snapshot and at seventy-nine is still sharp as a tack, she said, "CIA, they're yelling CIA," and she was right. First it sounded like some native word but that was because they were saying it wrong. Miss McMillan was on target as usual. The only ones who'd voted to skip Tongaville were her and the three Canadian teachers who often acted afraid of us Americans, especially the Texans, and who wore light sweaters, even in Egypt. "Father Flannagan's World Tours" was spelled out in English all over the bus. Some of our people said it had probably tipped off the natives about our being Americans. But after three weeks with this group, I knew we weren't that hard to spot. I never thought I'd be ashamed of my home country, but certain know-it-all attitudes and rudenesses toward Africans had embarrassed me more than

11

once. This might have been my first world trip, but wherever I am I can usually tell right from wrong. the Texans especially were pushy beyond belief.

Hotel workers came out and joined hands and made two lines for protection, a kind of alley from the door of our bus to the lobby of the Hotel Alpha, which was no great shakes but, by this time, looked pretty good to me. Your father, I remember, was the last to get off because he kept photographing rebels through the big tinted back window. They had already started rocking the bus and he was still inside it running up and down the aisle taking pictures of their angry faces near the glass. Your mother just plain told him to come out of there this minute and he finally did. I made it upstairs to my room and looked out the balcony window. The crowd had climbed up on our bus and pried open the door. They swarmed all over it, about a hundred half-dressed people, so skinny it hurt you to look at them. The bus's sunroof was glass and I could see them in there scrambling over every seat. The street in front of our hotel was just crawling with people. One group waved brooms. A few boys had found golf clubs somewhere and were throwing these up then catching them like majorettes would. A naked man and a woman danced around, holding a vacuum cleaner over their heads. He lifted the body of it and she'd slung the hose over her shoulder and kept shaking the wand part at people. Even from the second floor, I could tell it was an Electrolux. The crowd didn't seem to know what a vacuum cleaner was. They kept staring up at the thing. Seeing this scared me more than anything so far. Then our bus drove off. Most of the Africans ran after it, all cheering. I stood there at the window thinking, Well, there our only hope goes. This is probably it, what could be worse for us? That's when I noticed our tour guide. He went sneaking across the street, looking left and right, guilt written all over him, and carrying a red Samsonite makeup case exactly like Mimi Martinson's, a rich divorcee's from St. Pete. That little Arab turned a corner. I knew then we were on our own, with this mess out of our control.

I decided to build a barricade in front of my door but realized that the rest room was out in the hall. We had to share.

Father Flannagan's leaflet said in big printing, "Rooms with private baths at the best of the earth's four-star hotels." I went to find the bathroom but somebody was in there and four more of our people were waiting in line.

Old Mr. McGuane, one of the Texans, stood around, real casual, holding a pistol. He was telling the others how he'd brought it along just in case, and somebody asked how he'd gotten it through customs and the hijack inspections and he said he didn't know, it had been right there in his bag all along, but he could tell them one thing, he was mighty glad to have it with him now. Other people asked, just in case, what his room number was. I had to use the bathroom so much but I knew it was going to take forever. Seeing people from our tour had depressed me even more. So I walked back, locked my door, and just sat down on the bed and went ahead and had a good cry. I thought of Teddy and Lorraine, my son-in-law and daughter, who'd given me this trip to get my mind off my husband's death. I couldn't help believing that I'd never see Toledo again. I kept remembering a new Early American spice rack I'd hung in my kitchen just before leaving. It's funny, the kind of thing that gives you comfort when you're scared.

I told myself that if I just lived through this, if I got to go one more time to the Towne and Country restaurant near my home, and order their fantastic blue-cheese dressing, and then drive over to the Old Mill Little Theater and see another production of *Jacques Brel Is Alive and Well,* I'd give five thousand dollars to the Little Sisters of Mercy Orphanage. I vowed this and said a quick prayer to seal it. I found some hotel stationery and sat down and wrote out my will. I already had a legal one back in our safe deposit box, but it soothed my mind so much to write: I leave all my earthly goods to Teddy and Lorraine. I leave all my earthly goods to Teddy and Lorraine. Sitting there, I fell asleep.

I know I'm rambling worse than ever. But in emergencies like this, little things bunch up and get to seem important as the big facts. So I'm putting most everything in.

I woke up and at first didn't know were I was, then I remembered, Africa, and I thought, Oh Lord. Even in Ohio, sometimes this feeling comes over me and I wonder, What exactly am I doing here? In Tongaville, it was that same question but about five hundred times as strong. I crawled to the end of my bed and looked out the balcony window and that's when I saw your mother and father wandering around down on the street. Frankly, Mrs. Whiston, I thought they were pretty foolish to be out there. When our bus was hijacked, its spare fell off, and now the street was totally empty except for your parents and the tire and a beggar who was propped up in a doorway down the block. I think he was only there because the mob had carried off his crutches as two more things to wave around.

Your dad was taking a picture of the tire and your poor mother was looking at the light meter. You probably know how your father asked her to help by testing the brightness of the light. He pretended to include her in his hobby but, in my opinion, he never really listened to Lily. Many times I'd hear her say, Fred, it's way too bright out here. Without some filters, every shot is going to be way overexposed. This is Africa, Fred." He'd nod and go on clicking away. She acted like she didn't notice this, but after forty years of a thing, you notice. It made me remember my own marriage to one basically good man. I wondered, Is it wise or crazy to put up with so much for so long. Your dad was mostly kind to her and he didn't mean any harm, but this once he'd told her not to bother, to just go on upstairs and take a nap or something. Instead, there Lily was, two stories down, the poor thing holding out a light meter of no earthly good to anybody, squinting at it and wearing her pretty yellow pantsuit. I should have called to them. If it had been just her I definitely would have, but when a woman's husband is along, you often act different.

Then they both looked down the street. By leaning out the window, I could see a whole parade, this whole mass of people carrying signs painted on sheets stretched between green bamboo poles. The writing was a foreign language, foreign to me, at least. Groups came down the street and sidewalks, pushing, waving scrap lumber and garden tools. They all moved together. They looked organized and almost noble, like they knew just what they wanted and deserved, and, right now, were headed there to get it. I expected your parents to run straight back into our hotel. They had time. But instead, your father changed cameras. He wore about three looped around his neck and he crouched down like a professional and started taking pictures. The Africans were shouting something hard to understand except I think the CIA part was still in there. The chants got louder and echoed between buildings. Your dad stayed put. Lily looked confused but tried to make herself useful anyway and held out that light meter toward the crowd, like she was offering it to them. Lily kept glancing at the hotel doorway. But she didn't budge, she stuck out there in the open with your dad. He hunched down facing them. I just stood upstairs and watched. I kept believing he knew things I didn't.

His camera had a long black lens and this was pressed up against his face, and I don't know if people thought it was a gun or what, but along with their chant, I heard this one pop, no louder than a firecracker, and your poor father fell right back. It was as fast and simple as that. It seemed like he did a backflip he'd been planning all along, or got more interested in the sky between buildings than the crowd, because he was lying there staring right up at the sun. He tried to toss the camera to your mother, like the camera mattered most. She caught it and looked down at the thing for a minute. Then she seemed to wake up and she took two shaky steps toward him. But that moment the people shoved past our hotel. There were hundreds of them and they were running fast. Some were banging on pots and garbage-can lids. They carried things along over their heads. A phone pole on its side, people hanging onto the loose wires like these were leashes. Along came what looked like a huge snake held up by dozens of black hands, but it was just the vacuum hose. I could see flashes of her yellow suit down there. The last of the parade went rushing by, women, children, and some bony dogs hurrying to catch up. Your mother was face down on the street, way beyond your dad. People had taken her blouse off. All the cameras were gone but one that had been trampled. They'd carried off the tire, and your poor mother's yellow blouse.

I just fixed myself a cup of coffee, Mrs. Whiston, and ran

15

cold water over my writing hand. I'm in such a state trying to get this down. I plan to start forgetting just as soon as this letter is done. But I think it's important to face the hard facts at the time, and not let yourself off easy.

My Willard died at the cement works where he'd been their employee for thirty-five years. I drove out a week or so after the funeral and talked to the boys he'd worked with on his last morning alive. They told me little things they remembered from that day. One man, a colored fellow named Roy, he'd been with Diamond Cement as long as my husband. He said Willard told a joke just before lunch hour, which is when he passed away. His heart went. The joke was about the three priests trying to catch a train to Pittsburgh. Willard must of told that one about five thousand times. He'd got it down to an art, this priest joke and some other favorites. I asked Roy, Which joke? like I'd never heard it. He probably guessed that in the twenty years Willard had been telling that corny thing, I'd have to know it by now. But he started up anyway, understanding that I needed it. Roy went through the whole thing, waiting in the right places, adding all Willard's extra touches. When he finished, I laughed out loud like it was new to me, and not just for show but from the heart. Hearing it helped me so much. I'm not sure why I started telling this. I think it's to show why I'm not holding one thing back, not sparing you anything, no matter how bad it sounds.

I tore the sheets off my bed and unlocked the door. People had stacked their luggage as a barricade across the stair landing. I shoved through this, and some fell down the stairwell but I didn't care. I ran into the lobby. A black bellhop tried to stop me but I got past him through the revolving door. Out in the sun and heat, seeing them stunned me all over again. I bent down beside your father and felt him. One camera had been stepped on, lens glass was shining all around his shoulder. Then I ran down the street to your mother and put my hand on the side of her face. Both your folks were dead. Her back looked so bare and white, and the bra strap seemed to be cutting her. I spread the sheet over Lily and then I lifted it up and undid the clip of her strap. The beggar had leaned out of his doorway to stare at me. For some reason, this made me feel guilty, like I could have saved them or was stealing their watches. I stood up dizzy but made it back and called the bellboy to come out here and help me carry your folks inside. I kept waving but he'd just press up against the glass and shake his head no. Then he crooked his finger for me to come back in. I saw something move upstairs and I looked up there, and it astonished me. There were three guests in every balcony window, our whole busload all lined up in rows and staring down at me with your poor parents.

Cora White peeped over the grillework on the third floor. When she saw me looking up, her head jerked back. But one of her arms stayed there holding the Polaroid, then her other hand came out and poked the button. Many people were taking pictures. The whole group from Texas was, every last one of them. I put a hand over my eyes for shade and called, "Come help us, come help us. The Madisons are dead," and I pointed to your folks. But nobody budged. It was a scary and terrible sight, Mrs. Whiston. Most windows were closed, so I called louder. Some of the women would look at each other and back at me, but not one soul up there moved. So then, when I saw what was going on, I started screaming names. I'm not a young woman, Mrs. Whiston, but with all my might I hollered upstairs, especially to my friends who, like me, had signed up for this at Holy Assumption. "Deborah Schmidt, Cora White, LaVerne and May Stimson, I see you, and I know you, so you all come right down here and help us." But as I called their names, they'd ease back into the rooms or let the drapes fall over their faces. I was out in the sun, feeling totally lost. I was starting to shake. People weren't even looking at me or your folks any more but along the street in the other direction, and when I saw a crowd headed here even bigger than before, I stooped down and ran right back inside. The bellboy jammed a baggage cart half into the revolving door, then the two of us ducked under the front desk and we stayed there.

I'd turned into just as big a coward as the rest, so who am I to point the finger? All the same, I won't forget how it is to be

17

the person who needs help, and to look up and see your group, your people, lined up like in a department-store window, and every one refusing you. Your dearest friends on earth doing that.

I never figured out how the Marines from the U.S. Embassy knew where we were, but all of a sudden they showed up in a truck, carrying rifles. I was so concerned for my own safety I hardly gave your parents' bodies another thought, Mrs. Whiston. The Marines looked very young, like they couldn't be old enough to drive, and here they were rescuing us. I asked if the Embassy had maybe picked up your parents, because by this time, they were both gone, nothing left but broken glass on the pavement. The Marine said, "No, Ma'am." I wish you could have heard him say that. He was tall and had a sweet pink healthy face. Like all of them, he seemed to talk in a Southern accent, and when this boy told me, "No, Ma'am," it was so full of politeness, so old-fashioned and American in the good way that after what our busload had just done, I broke right down in the lobby. Nobody on our tour would come near me now they'd gathered downstairs, all shy to see me still alive. The Marine looked embarrassed. I thought if he would just put his arm around me for a minute, I'd be all right. And I'm sure he was going to, but when he saw that no one else was rushing over to help, not even one of our women, he said, "Excuse me," and hurried off. He was just shy, a man's body and this little boy's face.

Up drove the Embassy's four black cars to rush us to the airport. American soldiers and government secretaries were driving anything they could lay hands on. They said to leave all the luggage we couldn't carry in our laps. Mimi Martinson asked everyone but me if they'd seen her precious makeup bag, so why should I have told her where it went? More officials arrived, two sports cars and a Buick that looked bigger than ones at home but was a lot like Teddy and Lorraine's, only yellow. That's how crazy I'd turned. By this time, I didn't know Africa from around the block.

A Volkswagen camper with Delaware plates pulled up in

front. I rode in that. It belonged to the Ambassador's daughter. We unloaded food from the little refrigerator to take on the plane with us. The freezer was full of Stouffer's Lobster Newburg dinners, and more of these were waiting at the airport in ice chests from the Embassy Commissary.

We'd started for the plane when we heard the biggest explosion yet. An oil refinery, this row of tanks went off like bombs and in one minute the entire sky got black. We had to keep low in the camper, but at an intersection near the refinery I heard something and looked out and saw two sheep running through the empty streets. I think oil had spilled on them and their coats were on fire, Mrs. Whiston. They both ran down the center of the road right along the dotted line. Smoke came blowing off their backs and real flames and they were making noises so human, so terrible I cannot describe it. When I was a child, I was sick a lot and had nightmares full of horrible sights, and this was like some dream from then but worse.

The Embassy man tried to tell me that these sheep were headed toward some river and would be all right. But, if there was a river through the desert, how could it stay a desert and dry? We flew to Athens then to Brussels then home to Kennedy. We were treated like royalty, except by the reporters, who were rude. The Ambassador and his wife acted just like everybody else and weren't a bit stuck up. He said he'd known there was some trouble brewing, but as for a revolution, he guessed he'd been caught napping.

Now, I am home. I'm safe and sound at my own kitchen table. When I walked in here for the first time last week, my new maple spice rack looked like an altar to me. I'm tired and never plan to leave the security of Toledo again.

Mrs. Whiston, it's hard for me to believe that our earth has gotten this bad this quick. I'm not saying your dad was right in doing what he did, rushing outside without understanding how dangerous things are now. He just forgot his place and took way too much for granted. He thought all people on earth were as

19

good-natured as himself, and with as much free time, and would pose for him. But he overlooked hunger. That is bound to make terrible changes in people's dispositions. White or black, people are more miserable and less willing to be scenery than the *National Geographic* would like us to think. Every fact I once held dear has swung around and turned into something else.

As one example, Teddy says there probably *is* no Father Flannagan. It's just a name somebody thought up to suck people in. Anyway, I contributed a gift in honor of your folks and my late husband to the Little Sisters of Mercy Orphanage. I found I had less of a nest egg thanks to the bite the money crunch has made in our economy, so I only gave half of what I promised, but the Sisters seemed happy and Teddy told me I was crazy to do it.

I feel that knowing what I know now, I should start life over. If you asked what Africa taught me, I couldn't spell it out with words but in my heart, I think, something serious has switched. Chances are, my life is too far along for any last-minute change in plans. However, I've been thinking. Maybe we should give up what we own to feed the hungry? But at my age, an old white woman and spoiled like this, I wonder how much I could do without. It shocks me to understand how greedy I am. Really, I've learned so little.

As a result of being long-winded like this, I am very tired. So listen, across the miles, Mrs. Whiston, I just offer you a hug. I do hate to hit the end of this letter. I would like to buck you up in your time of sorrow but my place, I think, is still here in Toledo in the old neighborhood. This afternoon I'm tending my grandchildren who are way ahead of others their age. They're final stars in whatever crown I'm going to get on earth.

Oh well, so long. We all do what we can, don't we? We just hope that in the end it's worth the hard daily efforts and has been mostly for the best. We are really the lucky ones. The rest think they are outside looking in at happiness. If they only knew. When the highs and lows are so far apart, it's hard to stay in the middle and think of yourself as a good person. But I'm trying.

Teddy and Lorraine said to send their regards. I pass on my deep sympathy to you and, as far as that goes, to every one of us. I'll just sign this as coming from
          Yours truly,

Mrs. Willard Gracie- (Maria)

P.S. If you write back, wonderful. I don't get much mail.

The Leech in the
Chinese Rainhat

•

Charles Edward Eaton

I have known Jonathan Barley now for thirty-five years. In fact, I am his oldest friend, and I do not think anything would induce him to give me up. He lives in England. I live in Connecticut, and we do not see each other much more than once a year, but there is a viscous quality in our relationship which has been able to stretch across time and place, and if it were released or broken now, I think it would snap and thrash around me like the thick coils of some subliminal creature.

The metaphor of our friendship was provided long ago by the students at the university. Good ruddy North Carolina country boys, with here and there a sprinkling of more sophisticated types, they were conformists all, and Jonathan Barley was just the sort to make them feel they were right about everything. His name amused them. His totally unathletic build, poor coordination, the way he rolled the blue eyes in his enormous head shaped like an inverted pear, his general sloppiness, the slightly fermented odor of his body, gave these lusty, centrally focused young men the eccentric which made their world safe and wonderful.

Moreover, far from being hostile, Barley seemed to welcome their jibes, any form of notice that came his way. He employed his peculiarities the way most people use their most attractive qualities—I have never known anyone more intent on making friends by any means whatever. It was as though friendship were the greatest unknown in his life. Somewhere someone would tolerate him long enough to teach him what it is.

He let it be known that he spoke Chinese, and indeed he did

with much grunting and blowing from the nose so that one of the football players said he sounded like "an elephant farting through his trunk." It became a general indulgence to stop Barley on the campus for a session of China-baiting. He always responded with good humor, looking hungrily at his interlocutors, his loose mouth hanging open like a suction cup. It was the active submissiveness that finally earned him the nickname of "The Leech," and the country boys waded through him as if they did not have an extra drop of blood to spare.

I took several classes with Barley, and since my name happens to be Reed Rice, this in itself paired us together in the humor of the undergraduates. A fraternity man, a good athlete like myself, did not have to worry too much about his image. It did not bother me that the other fellows called us "the guys from the grainery," or sometimes, "the silo boys," and I began to think of it as a distinction to have Jonathan as a friend. After all, no one else liked me all *that* much, and youth easily settles into unequal relationships of admirer and admired.

As Jonathan became more obviously a protégé, I even encouraged his Chinese proclivities. He blossomed out on occasion in a coolie costume. But one spring day when it had been raining, I was not prepared for his emergence in a large, weird contraption which he had made himself and called a Chinese rain hat. It was lacquered a bright green on the outside and sat on his head like a parasol. If one had any imagination at all, it began to create a montage effect. Beneath it, Jonathan's large face seemed to swell in its proportions, more impressive than ever before, monolithic, like a carving under the eaves of a pagoda. This melted back, of course, when he bobbed his head too vigorously, and the hat slipped to one side, an enormous dripping saucer someone had crowned him with.

It began to rain again and when I joined him half-way underneath, I said, "You've done it this time, boy. You'll never get away with it."

"Why not?" he asked. "Much more practical than an umbrella. Leaves my hands free to carry my books."

"And to fight off the local gentry as well?"

"Now, Reed," he said, drawling heavily in a tone that

always made me feel the need to substantiate what I was saying. "Who would want to do a thing like that?"

I ignored his question, looked up, and saw that the inside of the rain hat was painted a vivid blue. "All this and heaven too?"

"Yes," he said shyly. "It makes me feel the sun is shining even when it's raining."

Two heads under a bright bowl must have been too much for one of our professors who passed us, and he never seemed easy with us in class after that. The rain hat, of course, did not get accepted as such. Some called it the "Green Pee Pot"; the football players, who began to avoid me as well, referred to it as the "Fruit Bowl." To accept an invitation in under the rain hat for a steamy little session was as good as posing for a caricature in the college *Buccaneer*. Once when I returned to the dormitory after dinner, I found on my desk a dead white rat on a plate with a knife, fork, and folded paper napkin beside it, the gift, no doubt, of some science major.

My conservative parents disapproved of the association, my older brothers threatened to take me down to the barber shop and have my head shaved and plaited in pigtails, and I might have yielded to their pressure, except, even then, I found the world so boring. Consequently, those college years which might have passed uneventfully are staccato with images: Jonathan driving our gym instructor to distraction with his pratfalls, trotting through the campus with books swinging from either end of a bamboo pole, Jonathan entangling his Chinese kites in the trees of the arboretum, or staying after class in Victorian Lit to sit in the lotus position like a late, late Buddha on the desk of Dr. Hooker, arguing some minuscule point with the fastidious, high-collared professor—Jonathan pulling his long face and saying, "Now Reed . . ." when I became too coercive or autocratic.

Summer was hard for us both since I was required to go home to Charlotte and he to the little mill town where his father was postmaster. It was a test as to just how stretchable a relationship like ours could be. I grew irritable and felt bloated with idleness during the long hot days, feral with tiger lilies in July, hectic with crepe myrtle in August, when the obscure psychic buildup of late adolescence had no outlet. Jonathan wrote regularly long ornate letters that looked as though they had been done with a brush, while I condescended with postcards.

Then came the first of his fabulous maneuvers, worthy of the intrigue of the Chinese Court. He persuaded his neurotic mother to invite me for a visit to Batesville. I was to be handled like royalty, called for and delivered by Jonathan's father, and a whole list of activities and entertainments were projected. It was clear that no one had ever visited Jonathan before, and since the protocol of the situation had no precedent, everything was overdone: special food they couldn't afford, a constant watchfulness for any sign of tedium on my part, and an almost suffocating deference from every member of the family, including Tom, the younger brother, a wastrel and a hellion, but, nevertheless, much preferred by his mother since he appeared "normal."

My background has taught me to be a master of pretense, and Mrs. Barley who tried to take me into her confidence was constantly put off by my unwillingness to cooperate.

"I do wish you would speak to Jonathan about his clothes," she said when he was out of the room. "I can't do anything with him. His father and I are so worried."

"You should see how some of the other boys dress, Mrs. Barley. No socks, no ties. They're all a bunch of Sloppy Joes."

"I didn't mean that, Mr. Rice. I mean *how* he dresses."

Though the Barley-Rice exchange seemed too ludicrous for words, I kept a straight face and said, "Well, at least Jonathan isn't dull."

"Oh? Perhaps not, perhaps not. I suppose college boys always have a whimsical turn of mind," she said unhappily. "I just don't know what will become of him in the long run."

Though I had my doubts myself, I was not going along and have her turn into a leech of another sort, one that fed on tears. I said more sententiously than I should, "Let the long run take care of itself, Mrs. Barley. Life is made up of a lot of little short runs that succeed, and your son hasn't been sent home from the university yet, has he?"

25

Jonathan, who as far as I could discover resented no one, did not even seem to dislike his mother. He treated her many moods with boisterous, irrelevant laughter or Chinese solemnity, staring at her as if he were trying to understand what on earth she was talking about. Only if her petulance was exceptional would his face grow pink, his loose mouth pucker up like that of a child about to cry, and there was something suctorial about his subjection as if, after all these years, there should be something more in her to extract than this.

Looking back now, it seems that the country boys and the football players were not as hard on Jonathan as they might have been, and I was perhaps closer to what he desired of me than I was ever to be thereafter. College boys, or so it could have been said of my generation at least, had no real power and tended to extrovert their latent cruelties in jokes and pranks. Jonathan did not have to be disposed of because he did not get in the way of anybody's vested social interests or encrusted view of life. Even in my case, he was mainly a diversion. I did not have to fit him into any permanent scheme of things. Jonathan in the sustained camaraderie and leisure of the campus was one thing, in the world, another, and I can see now that this was what his pathetic mother foresaw.

After we graduated there was a long interval in which Jonathan receded, becoming more or less spectral to me like a Chinese lantern bobbing in the dark haze of forgotten college friendships. I went to one graduate school, he to another where the Oriental studies were particularly good. Marriage and career loomed ahead—I must put away childish things, and Jonathan seemed of the most infantile I could recall, belonging to a time when self-love is able to avoid any contact that might sting or deplete it like a bee. Jonathan had flitted about me, bright, lacquered, zany and amusing, but I had kept most of the nectar as balm for future wounds.

But this was my idea, not his. Since a car was beyond his means, he bought a motorcycle and came roaring into Cambridge, crash helmet and all, usually around exam week or some equally inopportune time. His enormous head stuffed in the oversized helmet looked as weird, and a good deal less amusing, than in the rain hat, and, like many a hard-pressed graduate student, I suppose I had begun to lose my sense of humor.

Moreover, it became clearer and clearer that the modern world was too much for the dreamer from Batesville. On a rocking horse he might have been a winner, on a motorcycle he could one day be easily catapulted out of control. As he became mobile, he seemed more disturbing and irrational, and one wondered how much longer he would be able to land on his feet. His motorcycle broke down, he got lost constantly, and was stopped by cops for various infractions of the law. His leather jacket and baggy pants were packed with innumerable schedules, directions, and memoranda to himself, and, hanging on a long chain which ran from his belt to his pants pocket was a collection of keys that could have belonged to the warden of the unknown. The ecology of the rain hat was now as diffuse and vast as the sky itself.

It was about this time, I suppose, that I tried to construct another persona for Jonathan, or so I thought then, but now I wonder if he did not lure me into being a kind of paternal constructivist. Since I did not have too much time to devote to him, I thought in my ambitious graduate student way that we should make it count. Anybody studying *Beowulf* for three hours a day has had enough of monsters, and my approach to Jonathan became briskly clinical. He always brought me a large platter of problems and difficulties, and I cut them up for him as if I were feeding a child.

But then just as I was completing my graduate studies, the war came along and tossed up greater chunks of the unexpected and irrational than even my bright engine could handle. My dreams of pushing on were exploded overnight, and what homilies and exhortations still held water were sorely needed for application to myself. An eye injury in childhood put me in Naval Intelligence and kept me in the United States. Jonathan, however, was immediately drafted and shunted around the country as unreliably, I thought, as any explosive in our arsenal.

It turned out, however, ironically enough, that we managed the war about equally well at first. I took it seriously, whereas his approach was unintentionally comic. I recognized another kind of Establishment, adapted myself to it, but Jonathan, I am told, one day "sounded off" in Chinese. His habit of heaving his trousers unzipped earned the new nickname of "One Hung Low," and his sergeant found him one morning in the lotus position meditating by his cot. Long before the war was over, he was cashiered out with a pension as a psychological casualty. For the first time in our relationship, I was jealous of Jonathan. He had succeeded by failing.

Since we could not really meet and I would not write, he evolved what he called his "Continental Communication Service." He would compose letters to himself filled with blanks, and all I had to do was check alternatives, interpose missing words, and return the letters to him. It was surprising how clever he was at reproducing my tone, and I sometimes had the eerie feeling that more of my civilian life was in his keeping than in my own. I found this system of communication not only undemanding but curiously calming: the great fatigue of being Reed Rice was being handled by my former consultant. Somewhere sleeping in every man is the desire to be a leech.

But if war toyed with our relative positions, the armistice belonged to me. I had finished my Ph.D., married, got a good job at the University of Kansas in furious reassertion and reaction. There was nothing for Jonathan to do but reattach himself to the source of energy which was going to run the postwar world after all, and he came to me wanting a blueprint for peace.

Since I had always counseled persistence, concentration, and order, we talked things over and he decided to study Library Science at the University of North Carolina as something that would force him into methodical discipline. It took a load off my mind since Jonathan wanted me to "place" him, and I had put him somewhere comparatively safe for the next few years.

Meanwhile, Carolyn and I quickened our pace as young American couples are likely to do. It was the next bit of progress, the new acquisition, the next deal or plan that made us feel, at least kinetically, movers in our time, but there among his card catalogues, I could feel Jonathan growing heavier, lagging farther behind. Whenever I was feeling low, some memory of him would wriggle reductively past like a worm I had divided once too often. Again, in more resigned moods, I could sense him, always surrounding me, far off, vaguely comforting, like the serpent swallowing his tail.

But since American education adores the underachiever, Jonathan got his degree, or this was my judgment on the matter at the time. Recommended by me and the university he even got a job as head librarian at a little teacher's college in New England. That year very few letters with blanks to be filled in came from Jonathan, and those that did were Kafkaesque in their mystification. No one was mentioned by name, but there were hints of a plot to undermine him. Even at so great a distance, one could sense the tension growing in his large head as if a cistern had been called upon to handle the resources of a dam.

The following August when he turned up in Charlotte where Carolyn and I were vacationing with my parents, he looked like a figure of edema. Sitting with us under the raw sensuality of the crepe myrtles, his cheeks were hectically moist, there was sweat under his eyes, and he smelled of cancerous defeat.

Since it was clear he had come to be drained, I got right to the point. "How do you like New England? How's the work going?"

"Well, Reed . . ." He said and paused, staring at me like a doll whose eyes were stuck.

"You always wanted to live in New England," I prompted.

"Yes, I did." He shifted one large haunch and a squeak of gas suggested a slight puncture had been made somewhere.

"Must have been a good place for winter sports," dear Carolyn put in as she searched wildly for an entrée.

A blush started somewhere in Jonathan's shoes and flowered furiously as if his face were chameleonic beneath the crepe myrtles. "Yes, Carolyn, it was," he drawled and waited helplessly for her to proceed with the development of her gaffe.

29

The silence became engorged, empurpled, as they both looked to me as the only one who could lance it.

"When do you have to go back?" I asked, and Jonathan, with obvious relief, began to suppurate. "You are going back?" I plunged the scalpel into the heart of festering matter.

"Well, Reed . . ." Jonathan began again, and then mumbled his story like a patient under anaesthesia who could drift off in the calm belief that I would deal with him surgically.

He had had two assistants at the college, and this in itself presented a labyrinth of human relations since he had never in his life had to tell anyone to do anything. In his effort to initiate reform, he had gotten hopelessly entangled in trying to transfer the collection from the old-fashioned methods of his predecessor to the Dewey decimal system. By spring no one knew where anything was, and the library was totally inoperative. At the end of the term, the president had fired him in an excess of rage with the parting shot that "people like him ought to be locked up," and that "he had done twenty thousand dollars worth of damage to the library."

When the story was finished, stretched out like a new lake of sorrow on the New England landscape, I wasted no time reading the riot act to Jonathan. I explained his errors and misunderstandings to him, and, I suppose, explained them away. I sutured him with reproof, reproach, and advice for the future, and he got up from my ministrations like Lazarus. I still cared, I was still interested. That was enough for Jonathan. When he left, he had tightened up and actually looked ten pounds lighter, but I felt the heavy increment left with me. Had I any right to encourage him? Was I releasing into the world a victim or victimizer?

After that, Jonathan went back to the safer sphere of arts and crafts. He attempted pottery, but his hand had a quirk in it which produced little hernias of irregular modeling on all his pieces. He tried making tiles since he had heard they would sell, but insisted on decorating them with inlays of silver and priced himself out of the market. These failures were deposited in my lap, and I was called upon to tell him what to do next. Having been handed chunks of misadventure so often with no

30

instructions except my own as to how to rebuild the person Jonathan wanted to be, I felt that I put back together a somewhat smaller person each time and would one day end up like a wicked sorcerer with a toadish little mannikin at my feet.

Finally, however, since I had no ready answer for the first time in our long acquaintance, I forced myself to think about Jonathan rather than the next move I might suggest. Had he ever progressed in my imagination beyond that picturesque collegiate image of the kookie boy in the rain hat? Pushing ourselves and our possessions along in the world, we frequently let our friends accompany us as little more than counters of their former selves, but imagination saved only for oneself as we make the painful solipsistic thrust into the future is blind at least in one eye. What did I really have on my hands in the person of Jonathan?

I came to the conclusion that I did not know him and probably never had. What was he really like apart from our brief, pictorial encounters? He stank of loneliness but only like sulphur on a passing breeze. What was his experience of living entirely in its fetor? There is a time in youth when loneliness can be like a fresh lover in your bed, but it grows flatulent and flaccid with age, the slut who has pretended to you all your life that things will be better.

I had to admit that the flesh of our relationship was literally scythed with unanswered questions. What did Jonathan do for a sex life? Had he ever touched a woman? Did he have fantasies that filled the underworld with such passionate force he was aware in every social encounter that all of the meat of life was underfoot? Did Rimbaud's *la nuit seule* sometimes really give him the day on fire so that at least he had a hectic sense of existential extremes? Or were all of his powers consumed merely in the mechanics of living? Moreover, did he perhaps *prefer* to live like a figure of allegory? Were there, in fact, many people like him in the world who were nothing but pictured forms in the minds of others?

But it would not, I knew, do any good to go too far down the unused road of sentiment. I had been giving directions too long when I really did not know the way for Jonathan. No one can release another from the allegorical prison. Not once had he ever challenged me, shaken me up, forced me to think of him in any other fashion, demanded that I give him room to grow in my developing imagination. If one thought about him too hard, one could grow slightly sadistic about his passivity. He imposed a presence, but he did not want to inject himself with full vitality into the three-dimensional human scene. If Jonathan had meant all along to infect my life with guilt and obliquely turn the tables on his teacher, I did not need, no matter how picaresquely presented, a long, sustained instruction in how visible life can be flattened into a form of Loneliness.

So, after this latest series of fiascoes, I took a new tack. I did not try to change Jonathan. I did not advise him unless he absolutely forced the issue. When he came to see me, I listened without raising any objections to his latest proposals and ventures no matter how impractical they were. I simply blessed him and let him go. I pointed out the difficulties of my own life, pockmarked the idol as much as I could, let him know in many subtle ways I was not the person he seemed to think I was. It was a red-letter day for Jonathan if he could successfully attach his siphon and get the old warm flow of homily and solicitude which could make his future seem a matter of importance.

But, curiously enough, all this accomplished was to age our relationship in a manner I had not counted on. I was enjoying an extended physical youth—no gray hair, no paunch, few, if any, lines in my face, and I am fastidious in the extreme. So it was disconcerting that as I began to push Jonathan away emotionally, he became more physical with me. His fat, moist fingers lingered longer when we shook hands, he sat closer, got in my way, it seemed, so that I jostled against him. And, all the while, he dressed more sloppily, grew more obese, grayer, and could hardly sit still for an hour without farting like a man stuffed with stink bombs. Sitting before me like the portrait of Dorian Gray, he seemed to draw from me all the physical poisons my system refused to absorb. The old compulsive guilt and concern for his welfare mounted, and on one of his visits, I jacked him up about his appearance. He thanked me for my "long-playing advice" and went away like a man who had not had a good fix in a long time, leaving me with needle in hand and a criminal feeling about life in general.

I have spoken of the imagination as the propulsive force in life, and, up to a point, indeed it is. Think, plan, dream something, and, in part, it begins to exist until one reaches the wall of one's own future. We can dream for a long time, and this in itself provides enough kinetic thrust to give us the feeling that we are moving toward a goal. But at some point in the forties, except in very rare individuals, the imagination begins to weaken, and the wall of the future seems to come in closer, to jut toward us rather than stretch back before the momentum of our approach. One is not going to be president, become a millionaire, one is not, as in my case, going to be a Kittredge or a John Livingston Lowes.

It is then that people like Jonathan may begin to have their first illusion of catching up. They have survived too, and, ironically, with one-tenth of the effort of persistent dreamers. They have had their dreams as well, but have simply let them float along. Forced to come to terms with reality only occasionally, as Jonathan did in the New England library, they have learned the pure art of fantasy which bumps into walls but only as mists do.

This moratorium between stress and fantasy came later to us than it does to some, but there were a few years when my full professorship did not materialize and none of my critical books won the National Book Award that the distance between myself and Jonathan seemed largely chimerical. Carolyn and I began to accept him simply for what he was—avuncular in friendship, the ancestor of all my acquaintances, poignant in the long, drawn-out ceremony of sequential devotion. He had the grotesque glamor of one who had traveled all over the world in search of friendship. Carolyn even overcame some of her feelings of physical repugnance and began to speak of him wryly as our "Senior Eccentric."

It might have ended there—all of us waiting at the wall, subdued and patient, with Jonathan now having perhaps a slight edge on things, nice and goofy as an old chinese genie whose flesh could turn to smoke when it struck against stone.

He enjoyed those years like none since we were two boys standing under the rain hat.

But the wall suddenly shook itself free of the stalled imagination and took a giant step forward on its own. My father died, leaving me an ample income, and Carolyn, the children, and I moved to Connecticut where I could pursue my critical studies unhampered by departmental politics and the jealousy of colleagues. Imagination began to strain forward again, lean and leathery as its neck now might be, scanning that wall with the hardened, practical vision of the fifties. Not long after, Jonathan's bitch of a mother died and left him a considerably more modest income, but, combined with his pension, enough for him to don for good whatever kind of hat he chose to wear.

It put us back on the old footing immediately. What were we going to do about it all? If I were to proceed as before, but now with caution, where was he to live? What could a man of many parts not very conventionally put together do but circulate? After several sessions and proposals, he decided, with my blessing, to live in England since he had a distant cousin in Wales. There was also a London friend who was something of a Sinologue, others in Paris, Majorca, whom he had met in his travels, and one or two acquaintances more distantly placed. No doubt he exercised a certain canniness in choosing England, which has had a long and honorable tradition of offbeat characters.

In any case, he settled down to cultivate his garden on a farflung, world-wide scale in such a manner as would have amazed and perhaps amused Voltaire who originated the phrase on more intimist terms. Making his plans months in advance, he would go half-way across the world to have lunch with someone in Hong Kong or dinner with Carolyn and myself in Meadowmount. Perhaps the preparations, the logistics, the effort of the journey itself, made him feel that he was actually spending longer with his friends than he was. He always arrived heavily encumbered with baggage, cameras, equipment, as if for a lengthy stay, and invariably showed photographs, colored slides, and memorabilia of places where this or that person who still tolerated him lived. He was like a landscape architect who had to carry with him the evidence of all his constructions and plans. So many beautiful scenes, and here and there the shadow of a human being. It produced in the viewer the eerie feeling that there were perhaps only two or three people left in the entire voluptuously beautiful world and that Jonathan worked tirelessly at keeping them alive. One paused in the midst of furious activity to admit him like some mysterious doctor burdened with nostalgia over the imminent death of human contact. With his exquisite sense of place, attendant on "the world's body," he nevertheless diffused an anxiety of vacuity. Hopping from island to island, treading softly from one place to another in search of those who would agree to discount the abysses that lay around them, he seemed to be warily drawing together the rich contingency of nature and human nature that was stretched out of all proportion, limp, and full of holes like an old net of meaning of which too much had been demanded. It gave us a rarified feeling of figures in a rotted sieve.

It seemed curious that this mood should have come over us when the world, in fact, was becoming dangerously filled with people in the extremes of confrontation. But, most depressing of all, Jonathan pointed up the fact that the huge, meaty world had no spiritual center anymore. When so many were "freaking out," there was no way in which one could be gently and picturesquely off-center. Where any form of behavior was readily accepted and soon became conventional, Jonathan seemed now oddly old-fashioned — solicitous, even gallant, in his peculiarities. Compared with a bearded young man who strolled on stage nude or a girl who walked down the street in a black cape and hip boots like a spider with patent-leather legs, Jonathan had lost all status as an eccentric except in the eyes of a few of us — reliquary, shadowy, fragile figures who must somehow be kept alive.

The last time he came, loaded with the impedimenta of a call he had made most recently on Jorge in Majorca, he looked more heavily encrusted than ever before, like an Ivan Le Lorraine Albright "There Came Into The World A Soul Named Jonathan." His old dark blue suit was decorated with the

35

squama of soup he had spilled, things he had sat in, paint and ink stains here and there — a patina of persistence, the ontogeny of his faithful journey.

When he shook my hand, he lingered even longer than usual, as if he were taking my pulse.

"You're looking well," he said, and I wondered if I really were.

He embraced Carolyn as one might kiss a spoiled little girl who might not recover from some illness of which only you were aware. He gave her a package which contained a small, perky bird of blue crystal, exquisitely done, and then sat down heavily at the apex of our triangle so that he could keep us both clearly in view.

"I need your advice," he said, and I marveled at the way in which he reached for that persona as if it were still as delicate and lithe as a figure in a Chinese print.

Nevertheless, I brightened immediately like a man who had been given a benzedrine. Carolyn giggled and said quickly before I had time to come out with anything serious and ponderous, "Oh, Jonathan. You are priceless. You never give up, do you? How can we advise you about anything?"

Jonathan looked uneasy as if his visit had not taken effect, and I knew it was time to roll up my sleeve and extend the arm for puncture. "Let the man talk, Carolyn," I said.

"I am thinking of making a change," he plodded on. "I've stayed rather long enough in England. I'm looking around for another place to locate myself. What would you think of my setting down somewhere in Connecticut?"

If he had said Meadowmount, I think both Carolyn and I would have felt that we were in the hands of Svengali.

"I don't know about that, Jonathan," I temporized. "Would it be as convenient, I wonder, as a base of operations? We would love to have you closer by, of course, but you might find it rather slow after London."

"Then what would you advise?" he asked amiably, even, I thought, with relief.

"Connecticut looks greener than it is," I said as I gained

momentum. "There are nematodes in every soil. I don't know whether you would like it here."

"Well, Reed . . . ," he said with an old tired smile of gratitude. "You're always right. I can count on that." He turned to Carolyn expansively. "You know, there's nothing like having a friend you can turn to."

"And you are my oldest friend, Jonathan. You are indeed."

For a moment, the old tone was there. I had relieved us of the world as it threatened to be. The terror had been in the complex shifting around us of possibilities which had taken place lately. If I had yielded, if I had said, Come to Connecticut, I think Jonathan would have given up all hope. But he had to test us, reaffirm the fact that, as he experienced the term, we were still among the living. The trick lay in refusing to acknowledge the overpowering patchiness of things, in manipulating topography to defeat the desert. So far, so good. There were green spots in the great stretched view which a man of many parts could quilt together. The enchanted, shadowy garden had survived.

When he left that evening, noticing that it was raining lightly, I asked as I handed him his battered fedora, stained, empurpled with age, rococo in the associations it summoned up, "Whatever happened to the rain hat?"

Jonathan grunted, wriggled boisterously with laughter like an old fat snake dancing on his tail. "Now, Reed . . . ," he said. "Can't you see? I'm still wearing it."

So Jonathan was still with us, stuck, it would seem, not so much in our flesh as on the surface of the past as if for no other reason than to show us that the stony-seeming body still ran blood. In a very real sense he would not let the spirit of our youth calcify. He had the greatest gift for the vicarious of anyone I have ever known, capturing us long ago in a conclusive field of feeling — "Forever wilt thou love, and she be fair" — and I suppose our greatest failure had been in not seeing that he was the poet of our experience. We have always wished to conclude, to terminate, to arrive, but neither Meadowmount nor my father's money has prevailed against the modern world. If Carolyn and I have learned anything, it is how inconclusive life is when it does not carry with it its own radiant atmosphere of contained devotion. It has been heartbreaking to at least conclude that all along our methods may have been our motives. The trip was the treasure. Linear types like us may not necessarily get any further than those who visit in meandering fashion the corners of a sickened garden.

At this point we reach a conclusion of a sort, and I wish I could leave it at that. Plateaus, even with misty views around them, are more pleasant than always climbing or going down. One might say that we have gone as far with meaning as most of us would like to go, but plot has a way of wanting to drive in deeper as if to see if we have really hit the quick of the matter. So there is a postscript. Jonathan did come to Connecticut after all.

On a lovely afternoon last summer, Carolyn and I were sitting in our garden cherishing ourselves for having lived another day when a telegram arrived from Jorge in Majorca saying that Jonathan had died of a heart attack. The news overwhelmed us, for more than I think we realized we had counted on Jonathan as an unobtrusive fixture of the years ahead. It was as though we sat on a beautiful but flimsy piece of material which had suddenly become unstitched from everything around it. For the moment we had the feeling of floating in absolutely nothing. The point of the needle that patched things together, searching quietly through the further reaches of plot, had broken off in the hard flesh of time.

But the next day even these images were not left to us, for we came down from our detachment onto parts of the world which we had been persuaded were not there at least as far as Jonathan was concerned. A lawyer in North Carolina telephoned us to say that he had also received a wire from Majorca and had been instructed, in this event, to inform us of the contents of Mr. Barley's will. All of his material possessions were to go to Jorge in Majorca, but Mr. Barley had willed us his body.

No one else would have thought of this way of making a permanent visit. Even in our stunned condition we had to grant the wit, the originality of invention. No excuses, no evasions were possible now. We were going to have him on our hands for good. In one master stroke he had made himself into a real person.

So Jonathan is buried in our little cemetery in Meadowmount. We never opened the coffin when it arrived. We simply did not have the courage for that. But we have finally stopped resenting this final touch of black humor. It seems the right thing for him to have done. Jonathan saw that perhaps he had been too subtle, and we had missed the point. We temporize for the sake of the things we love. We use the powers of levitation to moor a magic carpet here and there, make every connective gesture at our disposal, will an idea or an obsession for as long as we can. But one cannot conclude by leaving the world suspended in a dream.

Red Horse
Running Through Water

•

Melissa Malouf

Every night for forty-four nights, after the men and the women had taken their empty plates back to the kitchen and had returned with steaming cups of coffee to their usual places in the dining hall, Jack tried to tell them the story, and for forty-four nights he could not tell it.

On the first night Jack began at what he thought was the beginning that would carry him straight and smooth to the end, and he said: This is the story of the death of Raymond White Eagle—perhaps you have heard his name when it is carried here to our faded desert settlement by the winds from the valley that smell of eucalyptus and something close to freedom.

But he could get only that far. The remaining words refused to come forward. So Jack wrote down on a piece of paper that he felt as if a kumquat were stuck in his throat, and the piece of paper was passed from table to table, and the men and the women shook their heads in regret and nodded their heads in understanding, and tried not to stare at Jack's throat—where indeed something like a kumquat appeared to be stuck.

Over the next few nights, a few sentences at a time, Jack was able to tell them some of the details of Raymond White Eagle's background: how he had been taken to a government boarding school called the Harmen Institute when he was a boy, but not as pliable a boy as the supervisors of his re-education might have liked. The thing about Raymond White Eagle, Jack told his captive audience, was that he was never one to let them see that he was not pliable in the least. So once he got his formal education, they kept him on at the Harmen Institute for many years—a groundskeeper, they called him, since they did not know he was a teacher who showed us in secret how to listen to the voices of the Old Ones.

Ah, said the men and the women, and over those first few nights they began to forget how tiresome and salty their dinners often were because they got too busy thinking about the after-dinner story that Jack could not tell them from start to finish, and they got too busy wondering about the lump in Jack's throat, which had grown to the size of a lemon.

At the beginning of the second week, one of the men suggested that instead of trying to tell his story from the same spot where he had just eaten his dinner, Jack should move to the front of the dining hall and tell it from there, and everyone approved of this idea with whistles and nods and smiles. So two of the strong women picked up Jack's chair with Jack in it and carried it to the front of the room, whose old stucco walls did their best to contain and reverberate the laughter.

Jack told them that night, the eighth night of his trying, that after sixty-seven years Raymond White Eagle left the Harmen Institute, for he awoke one morning and found five albino eagle feathers on his windowsill, and they, or the voices they represented, or some new part of his old desire showed him the way to the burial grounds of his people. And he found that the graves were not covered by shopping malls or mobile homes but were deep in the valley beneath a green and white ranch where horses were raised and ridden for profit. And Raymond White Eagle became the fencekeeper at the horse ranch in the valley. Every day he walked miles of fence with a pail of paint and a hammer and nails, and while he kept the fence looking clean and straight and white, he spoke in old Shoshone to the Old Ones about all that had happened since they lost their land and died.

That was as far as Jack could get. It was not much, but he had made some progress, and the men and the women felt sure that Jack's move to the front of the dining hall had done him some good, that the lump in his throat was perhaps a little smaller—that in any case he had spoken to them like a storyteller for a longer time than he ever had. And they were glad, for they believed that soon, perhaps tomorrow, they would learn the rest of the story about the man whose name is carried through the desert by the winds from the valley.

But Jack had a relapse. The next night he walked to the front of the dining hall after the tables had been cleared and the coffee had been poured and all he could say was, A red horse running through water.

So he wrote down on a piece of paper that he was sorry, that he couldn't explain it, that he hoped to tell them soon what he meant, that he would not give up, no, and that he thought he ought to go to bed early. As this message was passed from table to table, Jack left the room almost unnoticed, but the others remained and drank coffee for hours and finally agreed on a way to help Jack tell the story he had come there to tell them, and someone was sent for the tools.

Late that night, the rhythms of sawing and hammering escaped from the dining hall and danced upon the cool desert air and made the crickets dream the words to an ancient Chippewa chant.

On the tenth night of his telling, when he stepped onto the platform that the men and the women had built for him, Jack thanked them all and waved to the people in the back of the room—he could see them better now, he said, now that he had a platform to stand on. Then he squeezed a swallow past the lump in his throat and began: Tonight I am going to tell you about the man named Johnny Johnson.

But the people moaned as if their voices were one, and Jack had to raise his hands, palms forward, in order to quiet the men and the women who had waited too long already, they said, to hear the story of Raymond White Eagle, and who had good reason, they said, to protest Jack's starting another tale about someone else. What about the red horse? one man asked.

Jack said, You'll see. And then he went on: One night, no, it was not night yet. It was close to sundown. I remember that it was not night because I remember that as I crossed the courtyard at the Harmen Institute where I too grew up and almost grew old, the chickens were one minute squawking and the next minute sleeping. And they did not even get up on their

42

roosts, as chickens must do, but plopped over like dogs and went to sleep before sunset with their ears to the ground.

Jack's audience responded to these details with audible oohs and ahhs that made him feel better than he had felt in a long time.

And then the watcher, he told them, whose job it is to watch whoever tries to leave or enter the Harmen Institute, took off his uniform jacket and his uniform pants and took a walk toward the red setting sun. And then the hot dry wind that had been making the bougainvillea scrape and scratch against the wall of the dusty chapel for ten days and ten nights suddenly stopped. And the scraping and the scratching stopped. Somewhere a train whistle stopped. And there was Raymond White Eagle, standing beneath the arched entrance to the Harmen Institute where there was once a gate that had locked him in when he was a boy.

I knew it was him though he had been gone for years and I had never seen him wear a hat like the one he was wearing—a cowboy hat, raven black, no, blacker than that, with a brim that curved downward in front, sharp, and a crown that is banded by an orange and yellow snakeskin. On one side of the brim are the five albino eagle feathers that are too white for a human being to look at for very long.

Jack stopped talking, but it was not clear whether he was finished for the evening or catching his breath or thinking about that hat, so the men and the women did not make a move—not until the oldest of the old women, who always sat at a table near the back with her seven daughters, came silently forward and handed Jack a glass of water.

And when he looked into her face, Jack said: I knew that it was Raymond White Eagle because his eyes were dangerous and holy and as gray as the underpaws of the mountain lion. And still he wore his sideburns down to the bones of his jaw. And still he rolled long cigarettes that were as long as cigars. And when he stepped into my room that had once been his room at the Harmen Institute, Raymond White Eagle said to me, Johnny Johnson is waiting for us.

Johnny Johnson, said the men and the women.

Jack stepped down from his platform feeling drained, almost dizzy, and ashamed of himself for feeling so drained without having come close to the end of the story. But he smiled despite his shame and despite the pain that throbbed in his throat, for he saw that his people were content, or at least hopeful, as they said, Good night Jack, sleep well.

But instead of sleeping well Jack wondered how much longer he could go on this way and he imagined, for a moment, the act of giving up. And when that moment was over he tried to convince himself that he could tell the whole thing in one or two more nights if he only put his mind to it and forgot everything else: forgot the thing in his throat that was getting to be the size of a nectarine, and forgot about telling the ending, and forgot about how his hands moved like fish in a stream when he spoke in public, and forgot about how he couldn't control his tone, and forgot about the splendid, resonant, unhesitating voice of Raymond White Eagle. Jack finally went to sleep saying to himself, I will do it, I'll do it tomorrow, and he dreamed of a red horse running through water, fast.

That same night the wind from the valley sailed into the desert and changed the minds of a pack of coyotes, who decided to leave their lonely arid hills and begin a new life among the people of the settlement. So they walked side by side toward the light that shone from the dining hall where the men and the women were again sawing and hammering and telling their dreams to one another until well after midnight.

From dawn until dark, every day of the week, Jack and the people of the settlement worked on the ditch that stretched toward the water that would turn their dry desert acres into a field of corn and beets. So Jack did not see until the next evening at suppertime that during the night they had built him a stage. There was no curtain, no backdrop, no props, no special lights—just three plain cedar walls and a cactus-bark roof with a fanciful pointed pitch to it. But a stage of sorts it was, and in its center was a lectern sculpted from a large piece of sandstone whose flakes of quartz made magic with the mundane lights in the dining hall. And when Jack finally did see the stageroomteepee that the men and the women had built for him, he was too filled with gratitude to say anything at all except, Thank you. He returned to his room even earlier than usual and was glad the coyotes had warmed his bed.

Then it was the twelfth night and Jack felt strong and eager after his long night within the calm of dog. So when the meal was over he stepped bouyantly up to the new stage — as the men and the women had hoped he would — and he leaned his elbows on the lectern as if he had leaned them there many times before, and he said: Raymond White Eagle sat in the room that had once been his room and he smoked a long cigarette while he told me that the horse ranch in the valley where his people are buried is not the sort of horse ranch we might imagine, but a kind of school where the daughters of the white men who own things learned to ride expensive horses, and not ride them as we might imagine, but sideways and backwards and crossways in a dance with no purpose they called dressage —

Dressage, the men and the women repeated —
and they rode the horses over high fences as well, as high as the walls of this stage, for contests and for money. The spirits of the Old Ones spoke to Raymond White Eagle about the many times they had helped the horses jump without harm the high piles of stones and logs, and they asked him why these horses had to leap so high for their keep. They are horses, said the Old Ones, they have no wings for flying. And Raymond White Eagle had tried to explain what little he knew about the white man's contests and taxes and investments, but the Old Ones did not see the reason.

And the daughters, Jack continued, the girls who were not quite girls and not women either, were not what we might imagine, for each kept to herself and thought only of winning and did not share secrets with friends for they had none, not until things changed.

Jack took a long breath that was meant to give him time to remember what came after "not until things changed." But he had forgotten the words or had dropped them somewhere, and he looked around behind him as if he might learn there what it was he was supposed to say next. Oh yes, he mumbled with his back to his audience. But he did not mean Oh yes at all — instead

45

he meant Oh no. For he had lost his story, that was clear, and he could not find it no matter how hard he stared at the floor or the walls or the fanciful ceiling above his head. It was gone. All Jack could find were some fragments, bits and pieces, here and there, eighteen of them altogether. I could spread them out over eighteen nights, Jack said to himself, thinking fast. Maybe by then I will find the rest, maybe by then I'll remember. So for the next eighteen nights Jack offered what he could, a piece at a time, and it went like this:

Johnny Johnson, horseman manhorse (That's all, Jack said, and the people said, That's all right).

Girls blond frowning private (and the people, after Jack was gone, elected the man with the most beautiful handwriting to write down the fragments Jack managed to tell them).

Eucalyptus trees undressing (Jack said twice, but the men and the women agreed that the repetition, in this case, did not seem to matter).

Flared nostrils, like deer (and Jack flared his nostrils in order to show the people what he meant).

Raymond White Eagle saw (and the people repeated *he saw,* and they gave each other understanding looks since they knew by then that if there were something to see Raymond White Eagle was likely to see it).

Manhorse whinnying pawing the earth (then Jack sat with a cup of hot chocolate while the men and the women demonstrated whinnying and pawing and talked about how a man with the name Johnny Johnson might do such things).

La Traviata Calypso King Red Thunder (at this the people threw up their hands and said, Impossible, until one of the seven daughters of the oldest old woman said to her friend that if she had a horse she would name it Red Thunder).

Circling pretending, the girls (and the men and the women said, Those girls again).

You lucky dog (Jack told them with a curious smile on his face).

Red horse running through water (said Jack, and he looked so tired that the men and the women did not try to keep him from returning quickly to his room).

Sunday morning (Jack began, and then he took a breath and added:) repudiation Sunday (and after he had spoken those words he leaned against the lectern for an hour and thirty-five minutes on the eleventh of the eighteen nights).

Raymond White Eagle saw (and the people asked the man with the most beautiful handwriting to put a special mark next to this fragment because this, they believed, was no mere repetition).

Leaning into his scent, picnics for grooms (and that night everyone, including Jack, ate a second helping of dessert beneath the bright desert stars).

Imported teachers of dressage (and again the people repeated in unison the word *dressage*).

Linking arms (Jack said to the men and the women with his arms outstretched).

What dream (said Jack, and then for a while he held his head in his hands).

The hat (he whispered, and the people knew which hat he meant, the black one, and some had even seen the hat when they visited Jack in his room).

The Old Ones, desire (Jack said on the eighteenth night).

Jack stayed later than he usually did in the dining hall that night and he listened to the men and the women discuss the bits of story he had told them thus far, and he felt the lonesomeness that has to do with missing oneself. But as he walked to his room around midnight he was able to make the sentence, *The Old Ones filled the valley with desire,* and he kept on repeating the sentence to himself so that he would not lose it and so that he would not have to think about the rest of the story that seemed to be lost forever.

But when he entered his room, he found it. It was sleeping there more than half-hidden among a pile of suckling coyote pups that had been born on his blanket nearly two weeks before. And Jack understood why his story had abandoned him for this, and he did not blame it since he would probably get in there too if he could.

Jack began the thirty-first night of trying to tell the story he could not tell by announcing to his people that the story had

47

been found, that their patience would be rewarded—but perhaps not right away, he added, especially since the thing in his throat was now as large as an avocado and it, or something else Jack could not name, was changing the sound of his voice, making it deeper, slower, older. So for tonight, he said to his audience, I can only tell you, I will tell you about—let me start over.

Jack went through the motions of clearing his throat that could not be cleared and then he said: Johnny Johnson came to the valley from the east and the west and the north and the south and he had no car and no watch and no money, and he had no desire for cars or watches or money, and he had no past and no present worth knowing. But he could talk to a horse better than some horses can talk to each other. And this horseman Johnny Johnson paid no mind to the daughters of the owners as they pouted and eyed him and then turned their eyes to the ground. But Raymond White Eagle saw it all from the first day Johnny Johnson showed up like a dandelion out of nowhere. He saw the noses of the girls flare like the noses of deer as they breathed in the scent of Johnny Johnson, and he saw how up and down the length of the barn the horses hung their heads out over the doors of their stalls and stretched toward Johnny Johnson as he read their names from the brass plates nailed to each door—La Traviata, Calypso King, Red Thunder, and all the other names. And he saw Johnny Johnson hug their necks and rub their foreheads and their eyes while the girls circled and watched and pretended not to watch or circle. And the girls pretended not to see that wherever Johnny Johnson walked the dust became pungent and wet, and they pretended not to hear him snort and whinny and then paw the earth and call himself a lucky dog. What a lucky dog I am, Johnny Johnson said to Raymond White Eagle. I'm home, said Johnny Johnson. And then—

Jack could not go on. Something pulled him back to the words *I'm home*. He wanted to go forward, to get to the next sentence and the one after that, but something else wanted him to go backward, to say *I'm home*. I will have to stop now, Jack said to himself, though he found that in fact he had spoken out loud, for he heard his people saying, Yes, why don't you stop now, do not tire yourself, we can wait. We have a present for you. And they handed him a blanket that was the color of the first desert sunset and that was embroidered with the eighteen fragments he had spoken on the eighteen nights he had tried to tell them the story even though it was hiding from him. That night and every night thereafter Jack wrapped himself in the bluegreenyelloworangepurple blanket and the sentences he could not make and he never had a bad dream again.

For the next seven nights Jack said to himself that it was all right that he was not able to tell the story as he had intended to tell it, the way Raymond White Eagle would tell it—without a breath, sweeping like the wind from the valley, gathering and embracing but never pausing, always moving toward the sea. It was all right, Jack told himself again and again. People are different. I cannot be him. I will tell the story a few minutes at a time. That is all someone like me can do. And the men and the women cleared the tables and brought in the steaming cups of coffee, knowing as Jack knew that it was not really all right, that it would not be all right until Jack could soar through each note of his story and wear the hat that was raven black, no, blacker than that, which he kept on a table in his room.

But the men and the women and Jack himself made believe that Jack's way of telling the story was the best way for him. And so for a week, a few minutes at a time, Jack told them about the turbulence of the girls, which no one saw at first except Raymond White Eagle; and he told them about the scent of Johnny Johnson, which was the scent of saddle and alfalfa and cheap cologne; and he told them that the girls and their mothers brought grand picnics for the grooms and the field hands and asked them to sit in the shade of the eucalyptus trees and eat; and while the grooms and the field hands ate, the girls and their mothers curried and brushed the horses for the first time, and they rubbed the horses' legs with linament and scraped manure from their hooves for the first time; they tied their blond hair in bandanas and cleaned the stalls and the saddles and the bridles and drove the tractors loaded with irrigation pipes for the first time; and Jack told them that the girls for the first time ever

49

opened the gates of the arenas and rode off into the hills at a gallop.

And he told them about the fathers who came to the horse ranch in the valley to look things over and to worry out loud about the land they possessed and the investments they had made in horses and arenas and imported teachers of dressage, and to ask out loud of the girls and their mothers, What has happened here to the Spirit of Competition? And Jack told them that when Johnny Johnson walked by he stopped to ask if any of them—the girls or their mothers or their fathers—had seen how the eucalyptus trees shed their bark in such large smooth pieces, It's kinda like they're taking off their clothes, don't ya think? And Jack said that when Raymond White Eagle spoke to him of all these things he was grinning the grin of one who knows where the thing is buried that he has been looking for for a long time.

Ah, said the people.

When that week was over, the men and the women came up to the stage and touched Jack's arms and squeezed his calloused hands in theirs and spoke words of praise and comfort. And though the lump in Jack's throat now looked to be the size of a grapefruit, Jack did not think to cover it, for he was more than a little elated by the approval of his people, and a flush came into his cheeks that remained there for days.

It was November—no one could have foreseen the coming of an awful heat that for the next several days fell upon the settlement like a proprietary giant who does not look about him before he lies down and goes to sleep. No one said that the heat that had never before paid them a November visit had anything to do with Jack's half-told story. The heat has simply lost its way, they said as they worked on their ditch that was now two miles long, only one half mile away from the mountain where the scouts had found a stream that would turn their dry desert acres into a field of corn and beets. Soon the heat will wake up and remember where it is supposed to be this time of year, the people said as they returned to the settlement scorched and exhausted at the end of the day, far too worn out to listen to any storytelling, especially Jack's kind of storytelling.

But Jack was too flushed and relaxed and dazed from the heat to recall his limitations. He was ready, he thought, to get to the end, to finish. I could tell it all, Jack said to himself, tell it all without a breath. But now they cannot hear me. So from the sandstone lectern he looked out upon the vague rounded shapes that the imperial heat had made of his audience and he spoke some words about the short half mile they had left to dig and he wished them a good night's rest, but they were asleep in their chairs before he finished even that.

For five days and five nights the heat lay heavily upon the settlement, making the people dizzy and furious and mute, until it finally awoke, as they knew it would, and left under cover of darkness without apology, as they knew it would.

On the next day, the forty-fourth day, the sky that framed Jack and his people as they dug toward the mountain looked like cool blue water, and the breeze brought them odors of pine and mesquite, which banished their aches and their silence. And they finished all but the last few yards of the digging before they hurried back to the settlement for a night of celebration and feasting, for the oldest of the old women had gone that day with her daughters into the forest on the mountain and had returned with dozens of silky rainbow trout, and with necklaces for everyone made of juniper and holly berries, and with pine boughs and ferns to decorate Jack's stage. (These adornments will raise expectations, Jack said to himself, and then he added, Don't worry. You'll do fine.)

But even before the special meal was over, long before the plates were returned to the kitchen and the coffee cups brought out, Jack found a piece of paper and wrote, The lump in my throat, it is worse. I may have trouble when it is time for me to speak. Remember that the Old Ones filled the valley with desire. And the men and the women handed the note from table to table and smiled encouragement at Jack, though they wondered how he would be able to get any words at all past the thing in his throat that was larger than ever, and they saw that Jack was wondering the same thing when later he stood on the stage strewn with pine boughs and ferns and said nothing for twenty minutes.

51

Then one of the women began to chant: The Old Ones filled the valley with desire. The Old Ones filled the valley with desire. Everyone joined in, gently, almost whispering, and when they were about to finish saying the words for the seventh time, Jack blurted out, *with desire*, yes: Johnny Johnson for the horses, the girls for Johnny Johnson, the mothers for they knew not what, for wind and pasture and work, Raymond White Eagle for a place beside his people, and all of them for the smell of the eucalyptus trees —

Yes, said the people, and Jack took a breath —
and when the fathers went again to the ranch to look things over and announce their worries, the wind from the valley began to blow and blow, and it blew the fathers up onto a ridge from which they could see all the land they owned for miles and miles. And then the wind blew them down so that they lay next to the earth on the graves of the Old Ones, who sang for them the ancient song of repudiation and munificence. And in the early evening when the wind finally stopped the fathers walked close together back to the barn where the others were waiting, and then the fathers relinquished the land and the horses and the arenas and the imported teachers of dressage. They relinquished and conveyed it all to the mothers who turned it over to the daughters who gave it all to Johnny Johnson who offered it to Raymond White Eagle who would not own it —

No, he would not, said the men and the women —
Raymond White Eagle would not own the land, Jack continued, but he wished to be buried there. Which is why he came back to the Harmen Institute and took me with him to the valley in the green truck that Johnny Johnson drove, and which is why he told Johnny Johnson the story of the Old Ones and their Dance of Life, and which is why he asked Johnny Johnson to tell it to the others so they would know what to do when the time came, and they did.

Jack took a deep breath and rubbed his throat and tried not to feel the gaze of the oldest old woman whose gray eyes were the eyes of Raymond White Eagle and whose gaze embraced him as if he were her child. Then he said: Raymond White Eagle told me that I would not return to the Harmen Institute and that

I would find my home in the desert near the mountain, where I would hear his name carried by the wind from the valley, and where I would tell you all—

Jack stopped. The oldest old woman, who was older than Raymond White Eagle was on the day he decided to die, came forward without a sound and stepped onto the stage and lightly kissed Jack on the mouth. Then she returned without a sound to her place beside her daughters near the back of the dining hall.

Where I would tell you all, Jack went on, that I saw in the valley on a Sunday morning, on the day after Raymond White Eagle could no longer tell his own story, I saw them all, arms linked in a ring, singing to the sun and to the eucalyptus trees and to the rich brown color and the sweet supple smell of the upturned earth on the slope of pasture where Raymond White Eagle is buried.

Jack gasped for breath. He could not continue. The lump in his throat felt as if it were moving. And Jack was so startled that he suffered almost no pain as the thing moved slowly into his mouth, and then he cried out once as it dropped into his waiting hands, which were ready to catch it even though Jack could not believe that there would really be something to catch. But there was, and he caught it, and he held it up for the people to see.

The next day the water came to the settlement from out of the stream on the mountain, and the first thing the men and the women planted was the seed that Jack had given birth to. There had been no debate about what it was: a seed of sorts, they were certain. But some said the seed was shaped like a watermelon, others that it was perfectly round; some said that you could see right through it, others that it was surely opaque; some said that it was silveryblue, others that it was yelloworange. Those who said that by springtime the seed will have become a tree that would shed its bark in large smooth pieces and bear fourteen different kinds of fruit for a hundred years or more were right.

When the people of the settlement linked arms and sang and danced around the spot where the seed was buried, they asked Jack, Is this how they danced and sang, the people at the horse ranch in the valley who learned from Johnny Johnson who learned from Raymond White Eagle how to listen to the music

53

of the Old Ones? Is this how they danced and sang? And Jack said, Yes, that is how.

And that night, after the tables had been cleared and the coffee had been poured, Jack put on the hat and leaned against the lectern, and he saw in the faces of his audience that he wore the hat of Raymond White Eagle as if he had worn it all along. And in his new voice, a voice that was resonant and unhesitating and splendid, he told them everything again without a breath from beginning to end, and he did not leave out the eighteen fragments, for they had become part of the story, part of Jack's way of telling it. And when he came to the last words, *where Raymond White Eagle is buried*, he paused. Then he said, There is more —

Yes, said the people. There is more.

And Jack told the men and the women, On the second day after Raymond White Eagle brought me to the valley so that I might witness the end of his story he was already awake and dressed when the fingers of the sun began to reach over the horizon and take hold of the sky. Good-bye Jack, Raymond White Eagle said to me in the language of the Old Ones. And I said to him, I thought you meant to go into the sleep last night that one does not wake up from. That is the usual way, according to the voices you taught me to hear. But Raymond White Eagle shook his head and smiled, and you would have seen in the way he shook his head and smiled and in the talking of his hands and in the darkness of his eyes that he welcomed his death even though he had not let himself go into the sleep that one does not wake up from.

Then in the peachpurple light of early morning, I walked with him to the barn and he asked me, What dream do you have that makes you want to leap into the dream and stay there? And I told him, I dream of riding a red horse running through water, fast. And Raymond White Eagle said, So do I. And that is what he did that day until his heart stopped.

And it was glorious, said the people.

Yes, said Jack. It was.

Nigger Fate

•

Richard Zimler

Almost a year ago, just before my dad died, when his bladder cancer had already spread through his body, he insisted that we go to the Metropolitan Museum. He wouldn't explain why. He flew up from North Carolina without my mother. At the museum, we stood in front of an ancient Egyptian relief depicting a ceremony presided over by the Pharaoh Akhenaton and his queen, Nefertiti.

"Well?" he said. He was rubbing his chest with both his hands like he used to when he was excited. By then, he had grown a scruffy beard to mask his gaunt cheeks and graying skin.

"Well, what?" I replied.

"What do you see?"

"Two Egyptian monarchs in profile. A lot of servants around them."

"Look closer at those profiles."

Then I saw what he meant; my mother looked like Akhenaton. They had the same almond-shaped eyes, high cheekbones and long, looping neck. We laughed. My dad said, "I first noticed the resemblance when I was a music student at N.Y.U. I'd seen your mother dance up in Harlem and was already madly in love." He held my shoulder and said, "I just thought you should know these things." As he took his hand away, he caressed my cheek. Time ceased its flow as we stared at each other; we were both aware that we would soon be separated.

My dad died when he was just 58. I'm an only child, so it's

just me and my mother now. I wasn't ready.

My mother had studied ballet as a girl growing up in Charleston, moved to New York when she was twenty and switched to modern dance. As the story goes, my father finagled his way backstage after a performance of the Harlem Dance Ensemble at the Apollo Theater. He presented her with a black silk rose. It wasn't love at first sight for my mother, but my dad was persistent.

My parents were married in Charleston in June, 1958. My mother was twenty-five; my father, twenty-three. They moved into an apartment on West 84th Street.

In 1961, my mother joined Alvin Ailey's American Dance Theater and my father started playing violin with the Brooklyn Symphony. I was born August 21, 1966 in Roosevelt Hospital, was given the name David after my father's grandfather. My mother resumed her dance career two years later and stayed with Alvin Ailey until 1970, then started giving private classes. In 1977, just after I finished fifth grade, the three of us moved to Durham, North Carolina; my parents had accepted teaching positions, my mother at Duke, my father at the University of North Carolina in Chapel Hill. My dad also played in the North Carolina Symphony until he started getting real ill in 1990.

When I was very small, I got to watch one of my mother's performances from the wings of the stage. Maximilian, one of her friends in the troupe, lifted me up onto his shoulders as she was dancing and told me, "Your mamma ruffles the air behind her when she walks. And when she jumps, she splits it open. You're a lucky boy."

After my dad died, my mother lost these powers. I'd never before realized that it was love which gave them to her. These days, she only leaves the house to give dance classes and go food shopping at Kroger's. At night, she boils up some pasta and eats it with canned sauces while watching television. She keeps saying to me, "Just give me time." She warns me not to give her encouragement. She says, "I just can't get used to anything less than the excitement I had with your daddy. When

I was with him, I felt that I was at the center of the world."

I managed to avoid depression myself until three months ago. It was then that my first novel was returned to me by my literary agent. He enclosed a two-line note saying that he'd shown the book to nine publishers and thought it hopeless to keep trying. Editors, he said, kept finding the novel either "too filled with complicated characters, like a Russian novel," or "too rough--too crude in language and tone." I was feeling abandoned and betrayed. I'd spent more than three years researching and writing the novel. It was the story of two slave families during the 1840s and '50s, one living in Arkansas and the other in South Carolina. I had based the book on twenty-seven letters written by a distant ancestor of mine on my mother's side named Evelyn Carter to an uncle of hers, George Washington Robinson. The letters had been discovered in a Gump's shoe box inside the linen closet of Charlotte Robinson Hilfer's house in Charleston, after her death in 1979. Charlotte was my grandmother Patricia's cousin several times removed. If our family oral histories are to be trusted, she was also the great-great-great-great granddaughter of George Washington Robinson. Since nobody else in the family was very keen on having the letters, my mother snatched them up. Before my agent's note had arrived, I'd been halfway through the first draft of a follow-up novel about my great-great grandmother's oldest sister, Cecilia. In 1893, when Cecilia was only twenty-two, she'd ridden in a covered wagon from Arkansas all the way out to Portland, Oregon. There, she'd married a white logger of Norwegian ancestry and had had four surviving children. Their descendents, distant cousins of mine, lived mostly in Eugene and Seattle. The Eugene half of the family had held onto the diary Cecilia had written on her journey. My novel was going to be structured like a Bruce Chatwin travel book, with vignettes about what Cecilia discovered along the way and how she felt. Now, I couldn't see any point in working on it if there was no chance that my first novel was going to be published. I hadn't been able to write a word in over two months. And I suddenly missed my father so much that all my emotions other than hopelessness seemed faked.

I'd kept all this from my mother, but finally told her because she sensed I was shutting her out of my life. She told me to come to Durham right away because she had something important to show me. "I don't know if it'll cheer you up or make you more upset," she said. "But you'll want to see it." She wouldn't tell me what it was. She and my father had always been nuts about surprises.

I work as a graphic designer for a small ad agency, and my boss is good about giving me time off when it's really necessary. So I got a week off without too much fuss. My mother picked me up at Raleigh-Durham airport wearing sweat pants and a Duke t-shirt. She smiled real big when she saw me. We hugged, and she started crying. We walked arm in arm to her car. She looked tired but good, had clipped her hair real short and stopped dyeing the gray patches in front. When we were ready to head off, she squinted at herself in the rearview mirror and wiped the tears from her cheeks. She sighed. "Lord, I'm getting old," she said, adding a Southern drawl to her words as if that might really convince me that she was over the hill.

"Cut the Carolina grandma act," I said.

She smiled like I was evil, then smacked my thigh. "That's for staying away from me for four months!"

At home, she sat me down on the sofa in the living room and said, "Wait here a second, baby." She went upstairs, and when she came down it was with one of the letters from Evelyn Carter to George Washington Robinson.

"Which one is it?" I asked.

"You've never seen this one," she told me.

"What? I thought you showed me them all. I sure as hell needed them all to write the book!" I was suddenly furious. "Why did you hold one back from me?!"

"Hush a minute! I kept only one letter from you. And for a good reason. But now you can read it."

"Why now?"

"Just read it and then we'll talk."

The letter, dated July 7, 1855, was one of the last Evelyn Carter had ever written.

****

Dear Uncle George W.,

Tragedy. Does it sneak up on you in South Carolina, too, or is it only like that in Arkansas? Hereabouts lately it seems that we got tragedy like stalking cats. First there was my daddy's sickness and death. Then Old Finley's accident. All of which you know about if you received my last letter. That's a hint for you to write, in case you finding yourself too trapped in your own troubles to look underneath the words I'm using for what I got hidden down there. Because I ain't heard nothing from you these past seven months. And now I got to tell you about Digger and Elvira. Sorry I got to tell you all this, because I know you liked Digger when you visited back in May, 1837. A little boy he was then, the proud-faced one who carried Little Henry's butterfly net like it was a flagpole, the one I chose for the reading and writing. I ain't had much reason to tell you about him these past years because everything seemed to be going along like a simple melody for him. Then, when things started going wrong and trouble done buried itself in him, I didn't have the heart to pass on his bad fortune to you. But now that the worst has happened, I ain't got no choice.

Anyway, it all began last Tuesday at the cookshack. You remember where it is — you walk down the oak pathway from the big house toward Christmas Creek. Elvira was serving up supper, and though the smell of her pea and porkfat stew was a powerful discouragement to even the hungriest laborer, the girl's face done lit up the place. You never met Elvira, because she ain't been even so much as a thought when you were here. But as I said to you before, she was a bright, honest girl. She was just seventeen when all this happened, skinny and healthy as a summer weed. Her step was quick with happiness and a smart answer was always hiding inside the pink of her tongue. She had big goldfish eyes, a long lean neck — the kind of neck the

59

purest singers always seem to have. Uncle George W., I tell you one thing, that child's voice just kept getting finer and finer. Of late, it could reach all the way up to heaven and grab the angel Gabriel by his hand and pull him right on down to our crooked old church before you could find time take a breath in astonishment.

The men said it felt good to pinch her behind when you passed, not because it was especially big—it was anything but that—but because you could always count on a yelp and then her unflinching warning, "You want this stew in you or on you?!"

This kind of boy and girl playfulness increased a bit of late because she finally started to get some meat on her in all the right places. And I seen more than one man covered with peas and porkfat. I liked the girl. I should have tried not to because she was beyond my help, but I did just the same. I remember you and mamma both used to say, "Never love anything beyond your protection." Only much later did I realize that that expression had to come down to you from your mamma or daddy and the times before slavery, because we all know that there ain't nothing safe inside a slave's or slavewoman's protection!

The row of men sitting at the table were enjoying Elvira dishing out the bowls of food, and the cruelty of our Arkansas sun and the future the white folk got planned for our children and our children's children were forgotten for a moment in the pleasure of a mouthful of food. Sometimes I think that if God ain't allowed us food, our lives would be one misery after another without no break at all. And don't you talk to me about love! Yes sir, Uncle George W., I still believe in God, but not love. And no, they ain't the same thing. Love is made for white folk and for slaves bred in fantasy tales. I ain't got much patience for either of these the older I get.

While Elvira was serving up lunch, Digger came up behind her real quiet like and had both hands around her waist before she could jerk away. You of all people know how men are when they want you but ain't about to declare themselves, but Digger was sweet on her, that was one thing I knew for certain.

"Get them killer hands off of me before I dunk you in the stew!" she shouted at him.

The men laughed, but Digger got upset, just how upset I only realized much later. Weaver said he done seen it in the young man's face. Weaver, as you know, is a hunter, and he notices little movements that other men ain't able to see. And I know why Digger felt so bad—because of his hands, you see. They were his fate. You know the first time he ever realized he had hands bigger than a normal man rightly should? He was working in the fields, just a boy of eleven. Mr. Arthur Broadman, a mud-minded slavetrader and friend of Big Master Henry's from Charleston, had been riding through the fields and made him come up to him and hold them up in the air. He said to Big Master Henry, "The hands on this nigger boy could choke the life out of a horse."

I was stooping over some cotton nearby and heard that. Yes, I did. And I know the worry that creased that boy's face, because you can bet he was thinking, *I'm a slave and I ain't even a normal one.* He was clever too, that Digger, and maybe he was even thinking, *Them white folk got plans for me.*

Even our babies know that bad things happen when white folk got plans for you.

The seed of his fate had been freed into the soil that day. A seed which would lay dormant for seven more years, but which he knew would come to grow and bud and finally flower. Because we ain't allowed love, as I say, but we sure as hell get a great load of fate. Nigger fate, my daddy's mamma used to call it. You never met her, but she still remembered Africa, and she was the one person I ever met who could spot fate the moment it targeted its falcon eyes on you.

Because of his hands, they turned the boy into a fighter. Little Henry trained Digger with his wrists tied to a trotting horse, and he'd run behind the horse up and down the road to Wynne mile after mile till he dropped like a discarded rag. Two years ago, he had his first bout, just eighteen he was then. I told you about them matches that Dr. Green sets up on his farm outside Helena, but I only found out Digger was one of them contestants because he came back one Sunday morning all bloody from a rip in his cheek two inches long, like he was cut open with a knife. Little Henry asked me to do my best to make it stop bleeding, and when I asked Digger how he got it, he told me that he was fighting in a stable and that the other boy had worn a special ring. That ain't allowed, of course. But white men like to see blood or the fight ain't worth nothing, and Digger and the other boy had skin too tough, so they gave some kind of iron ring with studs to the other boy for his middle finger. They ain't found a ring like that big enough for Digger's finger, so they let him keep a nail between his knuckles. He won the fight, but I ain't got the courage to even think about the shredded ribbons of skin that that other boy had to show to his mamma.

Digger began fighting the last Saturday of every month after that. Three years now, almost, and they say that he killed two men in the ring. He never talked about it. When he wasn't working or training, he was always reading. You know I recognized the light of a story-lover in him early, and I taught him well. Little Henry gave him the books. Digger used to read just about everything from travels at sea in sailing ships and white folk up in Boston to the history of France. Of late, he was reading over Mr. Francis Parkman's "Oregon Trail" and memorizing sentences from it like they were from the Bible. He told me just last week before church, "Mamma Evelyn, Mr. Parkman says that the West is all mountains in primeval sleep. Don't that sound just fine?" Digger told me that he was planning on buying his freedom someday, and that then he would fix it up so he could go live by the Pacific Ocean. Way out there beyond Texas and everything else, he said, he'd become a writer. "Mamma Evelyn, maybe the real reason God gave me such big hands is so I could be a writer," he told me. "After all, any writer who got big things to say must surely need big hands."

Uncle George W., ain't that a fine thought for Digger to have had?

Anyway, when Elvira shouted about his "killer hands," Digger must have thought: *Even Elvira knows I'm a murderer who ain't fit to be a husband.* It had to have twisted his heart into a knot because he was so sweet on her. When he looked at the men, they were laughing and telling him to pay her no mind.

I should describe Digger for you, so you can see what happened. He was short but broadly built, had legs and arms on which the muscles shimmied when he walked, like they were strings on a guitar. He had big moon eyes, a flat, broad nose and the darkest skin of anyone in his family. "Shade," his mamma Gloria had always called him, but when he was real little, he could dig for fishing worms in the soil better than all them other boys and the name "Digger" had stuck and ain't no one could get it off.

Lord knows when this letter is going to find its way to your hands, but July the 7th has come to Arkansas today, and when tragedy snuck up on us, it was last Tuesday as I already said. Big Master Henry was in Memphis to pick up some fabric ordered by Miss Caroline. She just had her 19th birthday, is real pretty and proper. Little Henry was in charge of the plantation in his absence, of course. And Miss Julia was at home, too, since she was jealous of Miss Caroline and ain't wanted to go to Memphis to see her new fabric. Miss Julia is going to be sixteen in September, and she begrudges her big sister everything that comes her way.

Little Henry had grown up with Digger, and they were as friendly as white and colored could get without breaking the law until all this happened. When Little Henry walked through the fields, he even shook Digger's hand like he was a man. It was funny to see the two of them together — Digger so powerful, Little Henry so lean, looking like a thistle because his thick red hair is cut real short by Mr. Brickman, the barber over in Forrest City who everybody says is a Jew. Little Henry has big white teeth like a rabbit and a laugh which people like, but which I ain't never trusted. The men think we all going to be lucky when he inherits River Bend, but the women know better. Big Master Henry may be hard, but he sticks to the rules and believes in God. He seems to me like a long long road you got to walk down in the midday sun before you get home and rest. What I mean is, you know just what to expect from him and can see the landscape coming up ahead. But Little Henry ain't got belief in nothing but dressing up fancy and dancing in

Memphis. And he ain't got rules. His road is all twisted and ugly with stones. If you can be patient another minute, you're going to know just what I mean.

Tuesday night fell and we ain't had no moon so it was real dark. Digger thought it was safe to sneak off and do some fishing in the creek that skirts by Big Master Henry's property and which rightly belongs to Mr. Morgan Davis who lives over in Clarendon and who ain't had nobody working on his land since I don't know when. The wind was blowing hard from the west. Ain't that interesting? Because if it was blowing from any other direction, the girl's screams would never have reached Digger. Somebody else might have heard them, but that somebody ain't likely to have had the urge to do anything about them, and this letter would be talking about something else entirely. That's nigger fate for you. It does things like change the direction of the wind.

Little Henry asked Elvira to come to the house because Miss Julia was going to play the piano and needed a singer. But it ain't worked out like that.

So Digger heard screams. Even if the house slaves ain't heard, we'd know that for sure she done screamed because how else could Digger have known that she was in trouble inside the house? And we'd know that she screamed something fierce because she had that voice of hers that could tug the angel Gabriel from heaven right down to Arkansas. As I say, we ain't heard nothing because of the direction of the wind, but Crow was polishing the furniture in the sitting room and said that she let out a couple of shrieks that were enough to wake the dead.

Digger came in through the back entrance and snuck through the larder. We know that because they had me cleaning up the mud from his boots the next day. And he walked right up them stairs to Little Henry's bedroom, all the time with Crow telling him, *You better not, you better not because if you do you's going to end up in a real bad way.*

At first I thought that Digger had to have thought he was invincible with those big hands, that he considered himself a colored boxing champion who was going to save the girl's honor and make it out to Oregon to be a writer. Only just before

I decided to write you this letter did I realize what he was truly thinking and what he did.

So he marched right up the stairs and found Little Henry lying on top of Elvira and lifted him up by his scrawny neck. Little Henry was struggling and shouting, *Let me go you damn fool nigger!* And Crow kept screaming, *leave him be, Digger, leave him be!* Elvira was reaching for her clothing and crying.

The first shot hit Digger square in the chest and before he could bleed to death in the house, he held up his hands, looked at them for a real long time and shook his head like he was wondering why they'd been given to him. Then he walked on out onto the verandah and jumped down into the yard. Do you suppose he preferred to die outside than in a white man's house?

Anyway, what I realized for certain just before I started this letter is that Elvira's words about his killer hands had to have upset him more than I originally thought. He had to have realized that no one, not even the innocent little girl he loved, could see him anymore as anything but a murderous prizefighter. That was what his white master had wanted, and that was what he was.

That boy had to know it would be the end for him when he decided to walk up the stairs. Because even if he done succeeded in killing Little Henry and running for his life, he was not so foolish to think that he was going to make it even as far as the Mississippi border. Not with the whole of Cross County out hunting for him. So dying had to be what he wanted, ain't that what you think? Or maybe not what he wanted, but the only way out of his predicament that he could rightly see.

It was Miss Julia who fired the shot. Big Master Henry made sure his children knew how to shoot since they were little. She was standing in the doorway in her nightgown with her daddy's pistol. Crow and Little Henry were so surprised by it all that they ain't gone over to her, and she got off a second shot that hit Elvira in the hip. The girl fell backward with a kind of surprised expression on her face, never said another word and bled to death on the way to Dr. Morgan's slave infirmary in Wynne.

I don't know where this leaves me. I mean, I counted on Digger being the one to read and write for the next generation, to pass on the gift just as you passed it on to me before you were sold and left for Carolina. I guess I'll pick another of the young ones, one like Digger, with the light of curiosity shining from his eyes. But I'm an old lady, and I ain't got the patience I once had, and I confess, Uncle George W., that I ain't looking forward to

When Big Master Henry got back from Memphis, he was real angry with Little Henry because he done lost him a cook and his champion prizefighter, and a big match for Digger against some Cajun champion all the way down in New Orleans had been set up for the first week in August.

A bullet is so small, but I figure it might as well be the biggest wall in the world. Because no matter how big your hands may be or how well you can sing, you just ain't ever going to get past it.

Digger's hands and Elvira's voice. One thing's for certain, Uncle George W., the white folk use our joys against us and turn them into nigger fate.

Your niece,
Evelyn

P.S. Wren, Martin, Crow, Lily, Weaver, Thomas and Martha send their love. Write!

***

My mother was in the kitchen making tea when I finished the letter. I was moved by Evelyn Carter's writing, as I nearly always was. This letter also put some peripheral puzzle pieces into place; it explained why she had never written anything again to Uncle George W. about Digger or Elvira. Also, it was clear now why she suddenly began teaching her little niece, Tillie, how to read and write. Her last three letters are filled with her frustrations and joys with the girl. Tillie was my great-great-great grandmother. She'd had three children, and her eldest was Cecilia, the central character in my second book. And now, of

66

course, I thought I knew why Cecilia had chosen Oregon for her destination; probably, she'd read Digger's copy of Francis Parkman's "Oregon Trail." I, too, had read the book, and it pleased me that she, Digger and I had similar taste. But I was still puzzled why my mother hadn't shown me this letter earlier. When she came into the living room with two steaming cups of tea, she said, "Well? Are you still angry with me? I hope you won't have to change the first book now." She sat down next to me, sat up real tall as she always does, and handed me my cup.

"No. There's nothing I need to change. Digger and Elvira are both just minor characters. I could go back, add a chapter if I want, but not for now."

"So you're not angry?"

"Just puzzled. Why didn't you want to show it to me before?"

"This is the letter that makes it clear that in every generation of our extended family, one child was chosen to learn to read and write. There was George W., then his niece, Evelyn Carter, then Digger. When he was killed, Evelyn had to teach little Tillie. Then Tillie passed it on to Cecilia. When she went out to Oregon, I don't know who she trained."

"Her middle son, Randolph," I said. "When I went out to Eugene, I was told that Cecilia taught him how to read and write even before he got to school."

My mother stared down at me over her nose and nodded like she does when she's impressed with someone's professionalism. "That's good to know," she said. "Anyway, your daddy and I were both worried that until you decided for sure that you wanted to be a writer that this letter would make you feel that you had no choice—that you had to be a writer in order to make up for Digger's death. Or to carry on some tradition. Your daddy and I didn't want you to feel burdened. We couldn't risk that."

"But weren't you both sure that I was serious about writing when I had my first few stories published? That's already four years ago now."

My mother rested her tea cup on the arm of the sofa. She brought her hands together into a gesture of prayer like she does when she's angry at someone's stubbornness. "Was Evelyn Carter a serious writer?" she asked.

"I think she was a great writer."

My mother frowned. "I didn't ask that. I asked if she was serious."

"I don't know what you mean."

"I mean, if Big Master Henry had forbidden her from sending letters to Uncle George W. or anyone else in her family, would she have gotten desperately depressed."

"She'd have done everything she could to get letters to him."

"And if she couldn't?"

"She'd have been very upset. Obviously."

"Well then, I'd say she was serious. And yet, she didn't have any stories or letters published, did she? Not a damn thing. Baby, publishing doesn't make you a serious writer. From those stories you had published, your dad and I knew you were good. And that first novel of yours proved to us that you were damn good. But there's a difference between damn good and serious." She ran her hands down the long curve of her neck; she was gathering her thoughts. "This depression of yours, this inability to write—that's that difference. You can only tell if a person is serious about something when there's big trouble. If he moves on to something else, he isn't serious. Depression happens when people can't move on, when they're dedicated to something that's getting away from them. It can be a woman or a man. It can be dance or music . . . or a child. Most anything you love. Maybe I'm crazy, but it's precisely how bad you now feel right now that's convinced me that you're really dedicated to this writing of yours. I couldn't show you the letter before I knew that. I just couldn't. But now I know that Digger and Evelyn won't make you feel any extra burden, because the truth is, you're already burdened. You love writing. And love is the biggest weight you'll ever carry. It changes everything. And it can't be replaced." She brought her hands over her mouth suddenly, as if she'd said too much, and started to cry. I sat on the floor at her feet like when I was a kid. I put my hands in her lap. She closed her eyes. Tears were trapped in her lashes. She whispered, "The bastard left me all alone."

We locked hands. Then she started rubbing my fingers, and I was sure she was remembering when I was a baby. "You always had real big hands. And because of Digger, I guess I've been afraid that you'd be forced to do what you don't want. Maybe that was the real reason I didn't want to show you the letter."

"I'm not about to become a boxer at this point," I said to make her laugh.

She let go of my hands, took a sip of tea, wiped the tears from her cheeks. "No, but those publishers might take your books and make you shave all the rough edges from them so that they can get neatly packaged. What they don't understand is that Evelyn Carter, Uncle George W., Digger — all of them are complicated people. Just like in your book. If you shave their black edges off so that they can fit into a nicely printed white page up in New York, all you're going to have left for both them and you is 'nigger fate.'"

When she said that, it was like some bell had tolled. Neither of us talked. I'm sure that my mother was remembering my father. I was looking at her, wondering how much she resembled Evelyn and Tillie and Cecilia. She said, "Just give me time, baby. Evelyn Carter and Uncle George W. needed to wait a hundred and forty years for their story to be told. I need a few more years myself before I'm ready to go on with my own. People have to simply coast along sometimes."

"I understand," I said.

After that, I started picturing Cecilia in the middle of the Utah desert. It was a scene that I hadn't written yet. She was sitting on a sand-colored boulder, a young woman of twenty-two, all her future in front of her. She had dark dark skin, my mother's almond-shaped eyes, was as lovely as midnight. She was reading Digger's copy of "Oregon Trail." It was July of 1893. Her mother Tillie was back in Arkansas, still living at River Bend, but now as a freed servant. Evelyn Carter had been dead for thirty years, was buried in an unmarked grave near

Christmas Creek. I wouldn't be born for another seventy-three years, the great-great-grandson of Cecilia's youngest sister, Nellie.

Gratitude for all this history made me kiss my mother's hand. She kissed the top of my head. The sun was setting out the living room window, and for no reason at all, I was as happy as I've ever been.

New Orleans, August 1988

•

Kim Church

Author's Note: This is a work of fiction inspired by actual events. Certain characters—Ronald Reagan, Thomas Kean, George Bush—are real, and the statements attributed to them are from their convention speeches. All the others are fictional.]

GABRIEL DuMONDE, project coordinator: It wasn't me who came up with the elephant, or James. It was that girl James hired, the Flynn girl.

James Toussaint, my boss, James's idea was to put up bleachers on a bank beside the highway. Fifteen-by-thirty-foot aluminum bleachers, with potted plants in rows of red and white, and a corner section in blue—a flag.

JAMES TOUSSAINT: I thought having the Republicans in town would be a good excuse to do some sprucing up, make the parish look nice and give the workers something to do. I ran the project out of Public Works, but we got our crew from all over: Levees, Streets and Highways, Bridges, Drainage. I asked Gabby DuMonde to coordinate because he'd worked in almost every department in the parish and was a good liaison; he knew how to get things done. Plus he knew engineering.

What we still needed was a plant person. I called my friend Merlin Staines in Metairie to see if his firm wanted to be involved—Merlin runs a consulting firm, you know, landscapers, planners, transit people—and he sent me a girl named Parris.

Parris never gave you a chance to decide what you thought of her; she literally came in talking and never took a breath. I mentioned the flag and right away she goes, "Salvia. We'll use salvia. It comes in red, white and blue, and it'll take the heat."

We could grow it a foot high, she said, and let it bush out, and it would give us a nice big American flag. She liked to show you with her hands, always gesturing and framing things out.

PARRIS FLYNN, landscape architect: The project happened the way things always happen in New Orleans. At the last minute, the city decided it needed a monument for the convention, so it started collecting money from the parishes. Jefferson Parish chipped in the lion's share because James Toussaint, who had been the Director of Public Works down there just about forever, wanted something in his parish. James was into flowers. His vision was to have a flower monument to honor the Republicans.

RONALD REAGAN: It's our gift to have visions.

PARRIS: The problem was, everything was *so* last-minute. The convention was starting in August, and it was already the middle of June, just sixty days out, and by then the big flats of bedding plants were gone from the garden centers, and the growers had stopped growing their warm-season annuals from spark plugs. "Spark plugs" are what you call the little fingerling plants before they get put into cell-packs. A few growers had already started on their cool-seasons, but it was still about a month early and not much to choose from—a few mums, pansies, calendula, mostly yellow blooms that wouldn't work for a flag.

So in other words, there weren't any plants we could just go out and get. Whatever we got, somebody would have to grow for us.

GABBY: You ever work with a woman landscaper? All they do is worry about what's gonna go wrong. Soon as you say you want to do something, they'll figure out why it won't work.

PARRIS: And I started to think, and I thought about things like wind—you know, things that could happen to plants that were just sitting on bleachers. And I thought about all the spaces you'd be able to see through if the plants weren't just the right size and if they didn't stay in exactly the right places.

Gabby thought I was being fussy. I had to demonstrate to him with sample pots how there was no way you could stabilize them on bleachers unless you built a big canvas sling with holes in it that you could suspend the pots through, and you'd have to paint the canvas red under the red plants and white under the white plants and keep the whole thing watered down constantly, and it would just be too hard to do.

I said, Why don't we do this? Why don't we use a real flag, a big thirty-by-seventy flag draped across the bleachers, and plant an elephant in the ground? I sketched it out, the Republican elephant in a semi-circle under the flag. Of course we'd have to tack the flag down and box it in behind, make it airtight so it wouldn't turn into the world's largest parachute, because all of this was out by the interstate, so it had to be ultra-stable.

GABBY: All the talk about a real flag sounded like we were giving up on the bleachers, because what would we need bleachers for? I didn't know what James would say, the bleachers being his idea in the first place.

PARRIS: The bleachers were going to be an anchor, a frame for the flag which would be back behind the elephant in a gorgeous, all-American display. It'll be really big, I said to James. Really Republican. You're going to love it.

JAMES: One of her ideas was to use a real flag, and I suggested that they use Harry Marslander's flag. Harry was the sheriff, and this flag was worth about fifteen hundred dollars, so I told Parris she'd have to be careful not to ruin it.

PARRIS: James was always more interested in flowers than a flag—really, the flowers were the thing from the beginning—so we ended up trashing the flag altogether and going with just the big flower elephant.

One of the things I've learned about design is, nothing ever stays the same.

My little assistant never could understand that. At this time I got my first professional assistant, a fifth-year landscape student at L.S.U. named Lydia Havermeyer. She was sort of shoved on me because she was dating the son of the parish finance director, Winnie Chocteau. When Winnie heard what we were doing she came up and uncasually asked me did I think it would be possible for her future daughter-in-law to work with us on the project. So I got Lydia. As it turned out,

Lydia was an okay worker, but she could never understand the principle of centered skiing.

I read this book about snowskiing that said if you had your feet squarely on the ground underneath you and somebody came along and pushed you to try and make you move, the way to keep your feet planted is to flex your knees, bend and shift.

Lydia never could understand that. Every time we came up with a new plan she thought it was going to be the final one. She irritated the life out of me.

LYDIA HAVERMEYER: Disorienting. That's how I would describe this project from the word go. Because it was just constantly changing. We went from salvia to petunias—which I've never liked, they're too sticky and garish. And we went from a flag to a flag and an elephant to finally just an elephant. We were going to do a big red elephant with a blue dome on its back, for the Superdome, and three white stars, and a white border all around, which I actually thought would look nice. But then we had to stick in that sign.

GABBY: I asked James shouldn't we work in something about Jefferson Parish, since that's who was paying the bill.

JAMES: Parris said we needed to switch to petunias because it was too late to get salvia, and as it was we'd still have to have the petunias grown for us and they might not be ready on time. She was extremely worried about time; for Parris, every minute of every day was somehow critical. She was always reminding me how *pressed* we were, that was the word—don't get me wrong, she was respectful, but whenever she talked it sounded like her voice was about to break into pieces. I said to her, Parris, I was never wedded to salvia; just go ahead and order what you need to.

Hell, I was never wedded to any of this.

CAMILLE MINYARD, historian: New Orleans never belonged to the United States, or even to the South, other than technically. It was never *assimilated*.

PARRIS: I had called up some of my friends over at Orleans Parkways to get an estimate of how much time they thought it would take per plant, because I knew they had done a lot of these massive plantings. I told them I was doing some work for the convention and the whole story—well, not the elephant part, but that I was thinking about planting some petunias—and they all thought I was crazy because it was an odd time of year to plant petunias. Which it was, but, you know, theoretically it would work, provided they had enough sunlight and water. Water was the big issue.

LYDIA: Originally Parris was going to have Blaine Kern paint the sign—you know, the Mardi Gras artist? But then she decided it would take too long. The sign we ended up with, well, all I can say is, it was big.

PARRIS: We commissioned a sign thirty-five feet wide by four feet high with red and blue letters on a white background: "Republican National Convention" in red letters on top and "Jefferson Parish" underneath in blue, the way James wanted.

While it was being made we were out working at the cloverleaf—the Clearview interchange on I-10, the first big one past the airport—building this humongous hill so you'd be able to see the display from a distance. The face of it was an enormous flat semi-circle, thirty-five feet in diameter and sloped back about thirty degrees, like this.

GABBY: I got forty truckloads of dirt from a levee that was coming down on the west bank, a sand-clay mix.

I'll say this: James got his money's worth on that hill.

PARRIS: The budget for the whole project was fifty thousand dollars, but I don't know where it all went because the plants were less than five thousand, and mostly we were using parish labor, and we even got free dirt. The only dirt the parish had to pay for was the topsoil, four dumptruck loads.

LYDIA: Mr. DuMonde was amazing—a skinny, leathery little man who smoked a thousand cigarettes and never had much to say but he could make his crew do anything.

PARRIS: Gabby only ever talked to me in bits and pieces, never the big picture. Like saying, "Let's go," and when I'd say, "Where are we going?" he'd say "Just follow me" and take off in his truck.

He called every last one of the workers Bubba. "Bubba, come over here." "Bubba, I want you to plant this petunia and I want you to do it right now." "Bubba, you've had enough Coca-Cola.

Don't ask that lady to get you any more Coca-Cola."

LYDIA: You could tell him apart from everybody because he wore a gray outfit with his name on the shirtpocket and a huge safari hat that nearly swallowed his head. The other men, the workers, just wore jeans and t-shirts and workboots. And they carried strips of white sheet or towel or something that they doused in water and draped over their heads when they got hot, with their baseball caps on top. I thought they looked like Egyptians with those white things hanging down their necks. Like Egyptians building pyramids. Only, can you imagine, what if the design for the pyramids had gotten constantly changed?

JAMES: They laid the Jefferson Parish sign into the face of a big dirt hill, and because of how it was tilted back it caught the sun just so. Within half an hour after that sign went up I got three complaints in my office from motorists who said it was shining in their eyes. I called Parris.

PARRIS: We had to completely reshape the hill—change the slope of the face and make it more of a bulkhead so we could set the sign in vertically.

GABBY: The sign had to be trimmed down.

PARRIS: I asked Gabby to take over the sign because he did better with something of his own to be in charge of, so he was getting it moved around, and in the meantime I was going back over my petunia order and realizing it was wrong. I had ordered too few of the reds and too many blues. It was one of those things I'd had to rush on—you know, coming in on Saturday after my first meeting with James and calling around to the big color growers and finding out we couldn't get salvia, number one, and number two, we might not be able to get anything. But then one grower in Texas offered me petunias, so I went ahead and made a rough count and placed the order without sitting down first to draw the location of every single petunia, which I should have done.

And every conversation I had with the grower, he made a point of how he was growing these plants special for us, and I had been telling the parish people that it was a feat of the greatest magnitude that I could get petunias for them at all, much less the exact colors they needed.

So at this point I had to sketch out a new design for the petunias I'd actually ordered. I made the top of the elephant's back solid blue instead of blue and white, and instead of a solid red body I thought I would just do a red trunk and a red outline, and on the inside I would mix in some whites and bicolors. I was hoping from a distance your eyes would blend the colors when you looked at the body, and it would seem kind of dark pink.

THOMAS KEAN, keynote speaker: I don't know about you, but I believe Americans, Republican and Democrat alike, have no use for pastel patriotism.

LYDIA: I told her the elephant wasn't going to show up right.

PARRIS: The petunias were scheduled to arrive on July 28th, a Thursday, two weeks before the convention. Sixty-one hundred petunias—two thousand white, forty-one hundred red, blue and bicolors, with names like Red Magic and Telstar Blue and Midnight Madness. The Madnesses are supposed to be the hardiest—they can take heat and drought and heavy rain, and they're the most disease-resistant. Plus they bloom like mad, which is how they got the name.

So the day comes, and we're all out at the hill waiting when the petunias come rolling off the truck, the red and white ones first. We've got about seventeen Manpower guys in a big chain from the end of the semi to the underpass, and they're stacking off colors and I'm counting flats. And then they come off with the plants that are supposed to be blue, I'm supposed to have nineteen flats of blue, but after nine flats these plants aren't blue any more, these are Burgundy Madness and they're purple—and not even a blue-purple, a red-purple. They're really pretty but they're not blue.

Well, I'm having a fit. They had also promised me we'd be the first stop but they'd made us the last stop, and when I asked them where they'd been, they said down in Orleans Parish. They gave Orleans my blues.

LYDIA: Parris had been acting like she was about to perform a miracle. She had all of us standing out there holding our breath for those petunias, even the Director of Public Works.

PARRIS: They unloaded the purple ones last because they wanted to make sure, you know, that they had me feeling good before they started bringing out the wrong color. I was so embarrassed—James Toussaint was right there. I gave the driver heck and then I jumped in the back of the semi to see if I could find my plants myself. There were rollers on the floor for rolling the flats out, so it was a little bit dangerous.

LYDIA: It was horrifying how she went rolling through the back of that big truck, yelling at everybody, looking for plants that weren't there.

But that was Parris, always rushing around and talking loud. I think a lot of short people are like that.

PARRIS: There was nothing I could do. I knew I couldn't get any other plants, so I couldn't not take the purple ones. I thought maybe I'd use them around the trees, and in the elephant I'd arrange the colors in a different way and spread the plants out more—I'd been planning to go six inches so they'd look full and lush, but you can space them as much as a foot apart, so I figured if I had to go to eight or ten inches it wouldn't be so bad.

Or maybe I wouldn't try to make an elephant at all. It was hard to tell if these colors would work, and as far as I knew nobody had ever planted an elephant in petunias so there was nobody I could call to check and see.

In the meantime Lydia is going on about how she can't believe I'm going to change the design *again*, making me feel just awful. I said okay, we will make an elephant out of what we have. I figured as long as we outlined the body with the bright reds it would show up and look like an elephant.

So I counted out the rows and we started planting.

LYDIA: It was like plantation days out there, with twenty guys shuffling plants around and this little woman yelling at them, "Seven red! Four white! Three blue!" And them dropping on their knees to plant.

DELANO CAGE, workman: When we first started out she had us digging trenches by a string line, but then when she saw how much digging that was and how long it was going to take, she told us just to line up the plants and dig holes.

PARRIS: We worked straight through the weekend and Monday and Tuesday all day long getting those flowers planted. And every day the fire department came out to water.

DELANO: Some of us thought she would be going off looking for shade to sit down in and drink her iced tea. But she was in the field every day slutching those plants around, and if one of you wasn't doing a thing the way she wanted it done she would step in and show you how. And if you stood back a little too long she would just do it herself.

LYDIA: When the plants first came they were full of flowers, but after they got planted all the flowers dropped, and at the end of Tuesday there wasn't a bloom in sight. Parris said she wasn't worried, that this always happened.

DELANO: Not like that girl that always followed her around asking questions. That girl never planted the first petunia, far as I know. I never saw her get dirty. I never saw her on a Saturday or a Sunday, either.

PARRIS: Everything was fine, we had the little plants in perfect diagonal rows and we were keeping them watered—we upped it to a thousand gallons a day as soon as they were in the ground—so they were green and healthy and covered with buds, buds galore, and everything was going to be great. At the unveiling, which was a big media event, Bob Brunelle from the main news station said to me, "You must be sweating bullets," and I said, "Oh, no, they'll flower, just give them another day or two"—which I knew was overly optimistic, but I figured by the weekend they'd be all right, because they had buds all over them.

Then we got the tropical depression.

RONALD REAGAN: What times we've had!

PARRIS: It had been so hot—of course we have this hideous heat down here, and the whole time we were planting it was just blistering hot. So when the weather changed I thought, Good, wonderful, I've had petunias screaming at me for a week, and now this front's coming through and the heat will break.

But the depression wouldn't turn into a hurricane and it wouldn't blow away; it sat over the city for six days.

BEATRICE MOORE, New Orleans poet: Our city is like the

79

great slow-thighed beast of the Second Coming, crouching alongside the river, chugging the brown water.

DELANO: It started to rain and it kept on raining.

PARRIS: And the petunias — by the next Thursday, which was three days before the convention, they had started to bloom, but they were having serious problems. My biggest concern was the red border.

LYDIA: On the Friday before the convention, when Parris's picture came out in the paper, the petunias were looking absolutely terrible. Parris was frantic, trying to find somebody to spray, but it couldn't be just anybody, she said, it had to be somebody who was licensed, and offhand the only licensed person she knew was a tree-trimmer who charged a fortune, so she had to get somebody else. Anyway, by the time the truck came to spray for the fungus it was too late.

I just thought of something. You know how the Nile sort of looks like the Mississippi, only it flows upside down, south to north? On the Nile, the cut bank is on the west, which is considered the place of death — that's where they put all the tombs. But here on the Mississippi it's reversed, and the east bank, the side we were working on, is the death side.

PARRIS: The plants were diseased when we got them from the grower — the ones that went to Orleans Parish got the fungus, too — but I doubt they would have succumbed if it hadn't been for all that rain.

Actually, the white ones did extremely well. They never got the fungus and they never lost their flowers the way the other ones did. But the colored ones, midweek I noticed a couple of them looked bad, then the next day it was four, and by the weekend it was twelve hundred. And it wasn't like they were out on one corner, either; they were all right in the center of the display, shrivelling up and dying. The blight spread through them like a prairie fire.

RONALD REAGAN: We lit a prairie fire a few years back.

PARRIS: There were a lot of things I didn't know at the time, like how to pick varieties of petunias that would cycle well together. I'd pick a whole different set of plants if I had it to do over again, which I hope I never do.

JAMES TOUSSAINT: I supported this effort because I believed it would foster inter-departmental cooperation in the parish; in that, we succeeded.

PARRIS: They never truly recovered. We used a fungicide and also a liquid fertilizer, to try and push them out a little. But the first treatment didn't bring them completely around, and by the time they needed to be treated again the convention was already over and nobody wanted to pay sixty dollars to have petunias sprayed any more. So I just quit going out by the hill.

GABBY: The black-haired girl, Lydia, went to the convention. She was the only one I knew that got to go. She brought us all back some pork rinds and hot sauce, George Bush's favorite. Some of them got a kick out of that.

GEORGE BUSH, accepting the nomination: Thank you. Thank you very, very much. Thank you so much. Thank you so very much. Thank you very, very much. Thank you all. Thank you ladies and gentlemen. Thank you very, very much. Thank you.

PARRIS: Actually, there was one time when you could tell it was an elephant, and it just happened to be the time, I swear to God, the time that Merlin, my boss, drove out there. It was the Sunday of the installation period, when we filled in the trunk with red. Up until then it had just been a big square, with a little hump on top for the Superdome and a couple of cutouts on the sides. But the trunk — the trunk went slipping out of the corner like this. The trunk was the only thing that distinguished it as an elephant instead of, you know, a box.

And so when the red flowers were still flowering and we lined them all up and started planting and filling in around them with cypress mulch, and the little red trunk was sticking out, there was that one fleeting moment when it looked like an elephant.

— With thanks to C.

The Hunt Fund

•

Michael Chitwood

When his gun went off, I jumped, bumping against the tree. Then the deer was crashing down the hill toward me. It sounded big as a cow. Just as it got to the creek bank 25 yards in front of me, it disappeared behind a tangle of honeysuckle vines and saplings. I had the gun raised, and the safety off. The deer would probably step out in a moment. From the blast of adrenaline my body had given itself, I started to shake.

* * *

"When did this get planned?" my wife asked as we dressed for work one morning, a week before season opened.

"Back in the summer," I answered.

My father and brother hunt the entire opening week of deer season. They go to the grocery store together to buy supplies and fill the back of Dad's Bronco with food, clothes, a Coleman stove, pots, plastic dishes and utensils. It's a family joke now that Dad stashes money away all year for the Hunt Fund, and he pays for everything during the week out of the fund.

I explained to my wife that I just wanted to get my share of the Hunt Fund. She pulled a towel from the closet and shut the bathroom door.

* * *

In late October and early November, whitetail deer become very active. They show up in odd places. The local paper will probably have a story about a terrified deer rampaging through a shopping mall parking lot or breaking its neck trying to leap a backyard privacy fence in a well-populated subdivision.

They aren't frightened by hunters. In most places, deer season doesn't open until the middle of November. The deer are in rut. The males will follow the females wherever they go. The males will also try to run other males away from their tract of woods. It makes for recklessness.

Because deer now have no natural predator other than man, the population, in many parts of the country, has outstripped the available territory. Deer have moved into the suburbs.

Any hunter who says he hunts to keep down the deer population, to maintain nature's balance, is a liar.

* * *

I grew up hunting, mostly rabbits. Every Saturday during rabbit season, from the time I was about 12 years old until I was about 17, my father and I would join Franklin Furrow, Dad's friend, and his son Rodney, my good friend, for a day of hunting. Many times other men and boys would come along.

My father and Franklin Furrow both had beagles. Most of the dogs were related. Our best jump dog was the daughter of Franklin's best jump dog. Sally and Dixie would sniff so hard inside a brushpile that they actually snorted. If there was a rabbit in there, he was coming out.

There were rules. You didn't shoot a rabbit on the jump. We wanted to hear the dogs run. You never shot in the direction of a person or dog. If the dogs jumped a deer, you didn't continue hunting until all the dogs came back. Rabbits run in a circle and won't go very far from where they are flushed. A deer will leave the voting district. Sometimes we had to stop the rabbit hunt, get in the truck and go find the dogs. We'd drive along back roads with the windows down. Two men and two boys packed in a truck cab, listening.

* * *

My brother was working his way down the hill from his

stand, toward the creek. Either his shot had hit the deer, and it had died behind the honeysuckle or it would flush very shortly.

I walked toward the tangle with my rifle up. The deer broke away from us, heading up the creek. Picking them up and putting them down, as my father says.

How can you be so surprised when fully prepared? I swung and fired. I don't know where the first shot hit. I know it wasn't the deer. The second shot hit a pine tree square in the middle. The deer disappeared into the woods.

My brother and I walked to the tangle of honeysuckle the deer had hid behind. The leaves were splattered with bright blood. It was crimson, almost unnaturally red.

"Damn it, damn it, damn it," my brother said, taking off his cap. "I thought I hit that deer. Damn it." He walked up the creek a little way then walked back. He looked in the direction the deer had gone as though he might be able to see it. "Damn it," he said. "I hate that."

* * *

I work in an office in the Research Triangle Park, North Carolina. My wife works in an office in the Park. About 34,000 people come to work each day in the Park. It's one of the largest concentrations of Ph.D.s and engineers in the United States. We all work in offices or laboratories—8, 10, 12 hours inside each day. When we have finished working, most of us drive home and go inside our houses. Maybe we go to the mall or catch a movie.

More than likely, you're inside right now. When was the last time you were seriously cold? Which direction was the wind blowing today? Was it cloudy when the sun came up this morning? If you stood in your yard would it be quiet enough to hear a leaf striking bare branches on its way to the ground?

The company I work for has just purchased equipment for research in virtual reality. The engineers tell me that eventually you will be able to drive through a town, walk through a house or rearrange the furniture in a room without moving from in front of the computer monitor. You can even have virtual sex, and it's much safer than the real thing.

* * *

Our best jump dog was an escape artist. She was a master hunter and hated the confinement of the dog lot. I would watch from my sister's bedroom to discover the latest escape route. Sometimes she found a soft spot and tunneled under the fence. Other times it was over the top, climbing by hooking her fore paws over the wire and pushing with her hind legs.

After she was almost hit on the highway during one of her breakouts, Dad rigged a leash to slide on a wire inside the lot. It gave her run of the place and still kept her safe.

It was my job to feed the dogs each day after school, a chore I did with varying degrees of promptness. Sally's body was stiff when I found it dangling halfway down the outside of the fence. She must have come over sometime that morning. I cradled her cold rigid body to free one hand to unsnap the leash, her noose. Her awkward stiffness and my tears made it a difficult task.

* * *

"We'll have to track it," my brother says, still pacing up and down the creek bank. He has been spanking his leg with his cap. Now he puts it back on and starts off in the direction the deer went. He's crouched, scanning the leaves.

"Here," he points to a few splotches of blood. "You stand here," he says. He moves ahead. "OK, here's some more," he says, pointing to where he wants me to stand. I wait while he scouts the forest floor. If he doesn't see anything after twenty yards or so, he comes back to me and heads in a different direction.

* * *

Dawn in the woods is slow motion. The light soaks in like a drizzle. The landscape forms out of the darkness like the images

85

on a Polaroid. Christmas morning, and there, materializing, is the happy boy with his new shotgun.

* * *

The squirrel was working a pine cone. My father whispered in my ear, so close his Saturday stubble scraped my face.

"Take a deep breath and squeeze the trigger; don't jerk it."

He braced me with his chest at my back, his arms around me in a light hug. All during church the next day, I touched my shoulder, proud of the tenderness.

* * *

Our stands are homemade. I had helped my father and brother set them up a week before the season opened. "This is a good place," my brother said as he tightened the chain that held the stand to the tree. "I got that big one here two years ago."

The stand is a ladder with a small platform on top. The platform has a semi-circle cut into it, which fits around the trunk of a tree. You find a tree the correct size and lash the stand to it. It's best to choose a smooth tree because it will be your back rest.

You should get to your stand before daylight. You climb up, keeping your rifle pointed away from you. You turn carefully and sit down. Your feet rest on the topmost rung. Settle in, you're going to be here awhile.

Still-hunting is our native Zen. You must remain as quiet as possible. You must be absolutely alert. You can scan about 200 degrees of the circle of surrounding landscape without straining unduly. You must listen into the other 160 degrees.

* * *

I stopped hunting during my college years. I was the first member of my family, my extended family including grandparents, aunts, uncles and cousins, to attend a residential college, which meant I was away during most of hunting season. Also, thanks to some courses I had taken, I had

86

questions about hunting. Mostly, though, it was just because I was away.

My brother did not go to college. His hunting experience is seamless. My education, which my parents paid for, allowed me to get a good job, inside, at a desk far from my home county.

My brother is a heavy equipment operator, by all accounts one of the best in the county. He lives four miles from my parents on land purchased with money my parents gave him, the equivalent of the sum required for my college education. Which is more real, an idea or an acre?

* * *

The week before season opened a deer was killed at the mouth of our exit onto Interstate 40. It must have been hit by an eighteen wheeler because it was reduced to fairly small pieces that were scattered along the highway, on the shoulder and in the middle of the road.

All week long, the commuters, speaking into cellular phones, sipping their coffee from wide-bottomed mugs, catching up on the world with National Public Radio, rendered the chunks of meat into a long red stain.

* * *

There was a scooped out place in the leaves and a large splash of blood at the center of it. "He lay down for a while," my brother said. We tracked the blood trail for about a mile. "It shouldn't be much farther," my brother said.

Three hundred yards more and we saw the deer standing in the woods. Some of his intestines were dangling in the leaves. My brother dropped to one knee and brought the cross-hairs of his scope to bear. The deer fell with his shot. When we got to the deer we discovered that the first shot had broken his right hind leg.

"I'm glad we found you," my brother said to the deer as he pulled intestines and lungs from the chest cavity. He was field dressing the animal so the meat would be in the best shape possible. He was up to his elbows inside the deer. "I would have felt terrible if we hadn't found you."

* * *

When the breeze stirs, the stand sways with the tree. You sway with the stand and the tree. It's a gentle dance because the roots have a solid hold.

* * *

My father had a business meeting he couldn't skip on the second morning of deer season, but he came home at noon to see if we had any luck. We had my brother's deer in the back of his pickup.

We told my father the story of the creek and the tracking. My brother and I told it in tandem, each breaking in to add details or mention landmarks we knew our father would know.

"I hate it, but I've got to go back to work," Dad said after we'd finished. He handed me a twenty dollar bill.

"Y'all get some lunch. This week everything's on the Hunt Fund."

* * *

We've thrown a chain across the biggest limb of the maple at the side of the house to hold the buck while we skin it.

"You'll have to lift him up until I can get the chain hooked," my brother says. I hook my hands under the buck's front legs in a kind of hug and strain to lift him.

"A little higher."

I have to get a better grip. I pull the deer to me, brace him against my chest. My face is buried in the brown, black and grey of his shoulder. It's all I can do to get him high enough.

Twist 'n Turn: A Memoir

•

Susan Weinberg

I carted my school books up the hill, following Stacy through the woods behind her house. I could hear the slow whine of cars around the cul-de-sac below and the rocky bubbling of the drainage creek where Stacy's family was allowed to wade, even without sneakers. It was a Saturday afternoon, October, and Stacy had promised to help me crack the mystery of long division. Up away from everybody, where we might also share the secret pages of our spiral notebooks. Our sketches of "naked ladies," to be exact. That was what she'd called them too, using the same words the boys choked to each other behind closed fists.

Stacy scuffed leaves away from a circle of ground and pointed. "We can lean up against these trees." She smiled and the sun sparkled off her braces. In this light, her gold-flecked eyes looked green. Stacy was in sixth grade, I was in fourth, the same class as her brother John. On weekend days like this one, he'd pretend he didn't know me.

Stacy shuffled her books into a pile and set her Barbie carrying case down beside them. She opened the top notebook and surveyed it. "Wanna see some Playboy pictures?" she said and thrust the book at me.

After all the hints we'd passed back and forth to arrange this, I'd somehow expected it to take a little longer. To draw out the shame, and the sense of ceremony.

"Where's yours?"

I looked down the hill, then glanced around behind me. "Maybe we could do some homework first?"

Stacy shook her head, whisking her bangs around.

I set down her book and started riffling through mine. Pages and pages of smeared equations—but where were my drawings? I started from the back and flipped forward. Had my mother discovered them while searching for a permission slip? Had my math partner torn them out when I was in the bathroom and passed them around for the whole class to see? But no—I started to breathe again—my pictures were hidden behind the spiral's third divider—a border the steady march of fourth grade math would not cross until spring.

Stacy grabbed my notebook and snuggled down against the trunk of her tree. I couldn't stand to see her looking at my ladies—I'd made them hideous purposely.

Stacy's sketches began right inside her front cover. "Hey, you're a good artist," I said, but Stacy only nodded, studying my drawings, tapping a pencil. Her ladies' breasts were shaded into angular planes; their groins narrowed to precisely pointed V's. The pubic hair was sketched in feathery wisps, and one woman held an arm akimbo, showing the grainy stubble of her shaved armpit. Mine had cherry nipples topping monstrous breasts; the shadow between their legs was an angry scribble. Stacy's brothers were whooping below, coming closer; lost in their own game, they could stampede right through our secret circle. Stacy traced one figure's curves, then cross-hatched in a few corrections.

As she did this, something inside me began a sickly pounding, but I couldn't fix the source. It felt like I was about to be tickled by an invisible hand, and the muscles of my stomach rolled and bunched beneath my corduroys' elastic.

If I could only draw like Stacy, I thought, I'd do more than naked ladies. I'd do hairstyles, fruit bowls, horses running with their manes in the wind. Just one more reason I envied Stacy, just one more reason I thought I wanted her life for mine. She had, for instance, a training bra you could see through the back of her white blouses, and a mother, a normal mother, who understood that this was a necessary thing. Stacy had a little sister and two cool younger brothers, whereas I had only one sulky younger brother, cursed with a mathematical mind. All the Stevens kids got to sleep in one big room, in two huge beds pushed together. They had curving headboards and a blue dust ruffle, fancy as a dollhouse dream. And between the curtained windows, the kids got their own 36" TV. A year before the Waltons came on, this was my picture of what family life should be.

I must have paged through Stacy's notebooks for a good 20 minutes while she examined mine. Both our sets of naked ladies faced front, arms obediently fixed to sides, highlighting the hourglass cinching of their waists. Now I'd say they looked like a police line-up, but more likely the image came from field trips to the natural history museum. There we'd beeline to the Hall of Man, where the evolution of anatomy was displayed in a wall of photo panels. Naked against a dark background, pale bodies (how did they ever consent to this?) stood shoulder to shoulder, facing front, black strips taped across their eyes, as if before a firing squad.

But it was not just the naked bodies of adults that made my stomach chill. It was the charts tracking the development of a generic boy and girl, as if they were simply specimens of another category of living things. The idea of fixed stages was reassuring up to a point—larva, pupa, chrysalis, winged—we'd been prepared for metamorphosis since kindergarten. Now you are a girl; now you are a young lady: the stages seemed clear and distinct. But when did you become an aunt with tobacco armpits and a smothering bosom? When, like your own parents, did you start locking the bedroom door and taking naps in the middle of a Saturday, like a 5-year-old, again?

On the Wonder Bread commercial you basically shot up, while your silky sheet of hair shot down. In Girl Scouts they'd shown us a movie the month before, where beneath your unchanged bob of hair, your cartoon outlines flexed and flowed into an hourglass frame. There seemed to be no still points along the way—no place to say stop, slow down.

For a long time, the Girl Scouts had made development look desirable. Right up front in the Girl Scout handbooks, they showed the uniformed stages of what was to come—Brownie, Junior, Cadette, Senior—with shapelier bodies and accessories

91

to match. From the dollar green of the Junior's tunic to the peaked wedge of the Seniors' cap, you could see that better things lay ahead.

That promise changed the day the leaders showed The Movie we'd all been whispering about.

It all started with the permission slips our mothers had to sign for us to see it. We read them outside before the car pools came, puzzling out the smears of purple mimeo ink. "Min-is-tra-tion???" Was this about the Sunday School that also met in this church basement? Was it something else like caroling I'd be forbidden to take part in?

Shy Kim, who lived next door to Stacy, had to admit she knew that word. Her uniform always fell in perfect creases; her stainless bow tie never drooped. She wouldn't tell us what it meant, but simply shrugged, hunch-shouldered, with an uneven grin.

When the lights finally went out and a familiar paintbrush stroked the title across the screen, I could have sworn it was a Disney film. Oh boy, we said, and settled in. There were no tweeting bluebirds or doe-eyed heroines, yet the blood that pooled in the cartoon organs, then drained through the long, hollow canal was white. Disney-fied. Some girls came away insisting it was urine.

Kim watched, her arms and legs twined around the seat as if she'd been handcuffed there. At least we were hearing this all together in our pack, but Kim's mother must have cornered her to explain it one-on-one. It was awkward enough when mothers tried to spell out something easy, like where dandruff came from.

The leader clapped her hands. "Girls! Girls!" She introduced Dr. Keene, the county's public health official and the mother of Tammy, the troop captain.

Wide and calm in her white coat, the doctor stood before us and tore open packs of pads and sanitary garments. A belt was passed from hand to hand, drawing giggles: the tiny keyhole slots that dangled off the front and back looked just like the girdle snaps that had locked my grandmother's garters. This was two years before the peel-off strip, or any gradation of mini to maxi. The possibility of tampons was never mentioned. In the old days of pioneers and World War II, Dr. Keene told us, women used to wash their own cloth pads out by hand. We girls, squirming in our metal seats, had no idea we were so lucky to live in modern times.

That was all the truth they told us that one afternoon, as if the horrifying news, like our changing figures, must be broken and dispensed in distinct stages. As we filed out to the waiting carpools, I looked for beautiful Tammy, the doctor's daughter, in the crowd. She was right there in the middle, not even trying to skulk away. In gymnastics, Tammy's arms sliced the air; her leaps were pointed and precise. She wore leotards instead of shorts, and her shag hair layered perfectly. Hers was another life, like Stacy's, I would have traded for my own, were it not for the mother who would put on such a display in public.

Stacy had promised to show me long division. She had also promised we'd play Barbies. So what if she was a little old for that? But up here on the hill, someone was sure to find us soon. I wanted to continue with the plan.

"Wanna play now?" I asked, tapping the pink case she carried her dolls around in. Stacy shrugged and rolled to her stomach, then took back her own notebook and started to look through it.

I flipped open the metal tabs to find Barbie and Ken lying in side by side compartments. (Stacy had a Midge doll too, but her little sister had bitten off the chin.) For Barbies their clothes were pretty ratty—a striped tank top and polka dot pedal pushers and one elbow-high evening glove for her; some bland slack/shirt combo for Ken. If it couldn't be a white prom tux, who cared what he wore?

Still, the one Barbie I'd owned and treasured for her old-style bouffant helmet had worn only the tennis outfit she'd come in, and even she'd been lost when we moved houses. Her tennis shoes had disappeared early on, I remember, and I couldn't make her stand up, much less run, tottering on those bare arched feet.

Even before the big move, I'd wanted more, and what girl

didn't back then: Barbie, Skipper, Midge, and Tutti—with hair that flowed at the push of a belly button—one set of dolls in pale and one in summer tan. I knew what I wanted, and it was not until my teens that I learned Malibu was a place and not a word for orange skin.

Stacy was fumbling with Barbie's clothes, trying to peel off the top and shorts.

"What are you doing that for?" I asked and she thrust Ken into my hand.

"Make him strip," she commanded.

And so I did.

"Barbie," she yoo-hooed, "your date is here."

Ken looked even more foolish, smiling that smile with his body peeled. I glanced between his legs. A nub, a kind of squarish projection. What, did they think we'd had no baby brothers who needed help to pee?

Stacy looked out from beneath her slipping bangs, then shook them back again. "Do you know what fucking is?"

I felt the hot glob of my breakfast oatmeal gluing my lungs to my ribs.

"F-U-C-K?" she repeated.

I'd seen that word scratched onto desks and inside putty-colored locker doors. "It's something you really hate. Or someone."

"Nope. Look." Stacy took the Ken doll and laid it sideways against Barbie in the leaves. She rubbed them up against each other, plastic limbs clacking. Barbie's elbow-length glove was getting smeared with dirt.

Sweat was pricking out over my skin. "You're a liar," I said when she explained it. Other kids were always trying to fool me, but I'd thought Stacy was my friend. "Boys' things are way too wobbly for that. Ask anyone, just try it."

Grown-up Ken's square nub sure couldn't plug into anything. And with Barbie's fused bosom between them, how could they get close enough lower down? The idea was clearly stupid. This whole game was sickening.

"Moms and daddies do it," she insisted.

And like every other child since history's dawn, I said, "Not mine."

She nodded. "Yuh-huh."

Well, maybe Stacy's father and mother did. Suddenly, training bra or no, I was glad for a mother in cashmere skirts and airy perfume, instead of a mother like Stacy's whose flowery housedress hung half-open through the day; a mother who was always sick and wore Listerine as a heavy cologne.

I wanted to get away.

"Look," said Stacy. "It goes like this. They snuggle up in bed together and hug and kiss."

I felt my nose and eyes pinch shut.

"Then Barbie says 'Hey, Ken, you wanna fuck?' He says 'okay' and then they go like this."

Stacy bumped the dolls together, guiding them by their rumps. I smelled smoke and charcoal fluid, steak smells wafting up from a barbecue. "I never will," I said, feeling my voice crack and quiver.

She set Barbie and Ken on the ground and smiled down at me. "Don't worry," she said. "Fucking feels nice. I do it with my brother every day, practically."

A month after Christmas, when things had turned gray again, my mother gave me a book to read. It was red and black, had "questions" in the title, and crinkled with library cellophane. She'd bought me stationery I didn't use, blouses I wouldn't wear, but somehow from her tone I knew I had better read this one. "If you have any questions, you can ask," she'd said, handing it through the car window when we got home from the library.

It was all in there, except for the word Stacy had used. Complete with drawings, all the bad news together in one place. I couldn't trust anyone anymore. Not my best friend, not the Girl Scouts, and not even my own mother, who'd somehow taken this as permission to have another baby.

So it was true, what I'd heard, piece by piece and stage by stage. From AA training bras to the thing that was like a sneeze. My very own body was soon to betray me: I'd be wearing blouses under T-shirts—a poor excuse for the layered look—to hide the heavy jog of my breasts by the time 7th grade rolled around. Underneath my kelly Cadette uniform, I'd find hair and padded belts and ladies' bazooms; and then after Seniors, past the age of uniforms, much worse.

But what did this have to do with actual boys? Real, actual fourth-grade boys whose faces I pictured during the swooning Cola ads on Thursday night TV? The boys whose bony shoulders I felt when I shut my eyes and hugged my kneecaps close? Nothing, nothing at all. The bad news all came from mothers, sisters, nurses, girls; the bad news was written on and hissed under the doors of bathroom stalls. But with the boys, I still longed to buy the world a Coke and hold hands on top of a hill. No matter what new horrors the girls' room graffiti announced, Greg Whitaker's face still glowed the color of buttered toast; Len Schmidt made me shriek and run, but not too fast, from his multiplication riddles; Mike Bean's invitation to search for iron filings with magnets in the playground sand still filled me with the shivers. Out on my cola nut island, where life would be sweet as soda pop, I could marry all of them and not go past the kissing part.

I can't remember what I said to Stacy then. I think we must have just slid the clothes back onto Barbie and Ken and packed them away again, must have flipped our scribbled notebooks back to the starting point and walked on down the hill. All I remember is the shouting of boys in the woods that day and the sound of Stacy's murmuring.

I do remember that after I learned her secret, Stacy's hair still whisked around as neatly; the faces she drew still had the same hollow-cheeked perfection; the orange safety patrol belt she wore still cut across her breast like Diana's quiver. But I no longer envied her green-gold eyes and sparkling braces or yearned for her queen bed's pink dust ruffle.

The Wonder Bread commercials disappeared, but ads for a new kind of Barbie took up the Saturday morning slack. Her ponytail grew, but that wasn't all: she turned at the waist, twisting from girlhood into puberty and back

Come junior high, come seventh grade, it was twist 'n turn city. I was surrounded by girls who sprouted breasts and bras and cute mix 'n match wardrobes overnight. The locker room sinks were mobbed by girls who had It, and sponged with paper towels instead of taking the mass shower.

I had twisted and turned, gone from pupa to moth, but the bras, the bodysuits, the yoo-hoo dates did not rain down. I'd cut my long hair and it had been a bad mistake. I wanted only to twist back the other way again.

But junior high was a swarm of girls twisting faster and faster in the same direction. In the first quarter of Family Life, they stuffed the question box with slips asking the teacher if she was still a virgin. By December they were cracking up over rubber factories in World Geography films; by the New Year they were making cryptic comments about missed periods. "I'm so relieved," the girl behind me in Homeroom must have sighed three times that spring.

But I was more uneasy all the time.

Stacy's brother John was now the soccer team's blond star forward. Stacy herself smoked, wore two-snap Viceroys, and had long forgotten we were bus stop friends. The time was coming when I'd realize that the hourglass would never be my form; that blowjobs weren't something done to a car; that three and a half beers could make the world turn upside down. But I still wanted to corner Stacy, in the Girls' Room or the woods, to confront her brother John, their parents, Dr. Keene, and the dumb librarian who'd set those "a doctor talks about" books for parents on the Children's Desk. I wanted to make them swallow every single last word.

Lise: Her Hands

•

Rebecca Baggett

The woman I loved told me she was going to shoot her
dog, and I didn't say a word to dissuade her. I'd been in love
with Lise for six months—*in love*, I say, as if I could give the
situation more dignity than it possessed. I was infatuated,
crazed, obsessed—I both sought and dreaded opportunities to
use her name, because speaking it aloud felt like confession; I
faltered in mid-sentence when I heard her voice in the crowd
behind me at parties; and my fingers stuttered across the
keyboard if I thought of her while I was working, so that I tried
never to think of her, which was clearly impossible, spent large
portions of my day staring blankly out of windows, head
propped on my hand.

So when Lise said she *had* to shoot her dog, that the dog was
clearly crazy, that she couldn't deal with her destructiveness
any more and couldn't leave her chained outside all day,
because what kind of life was that? when Lise said no one
understood, that her lover, her coworkers, her friends all
thought she was cruel, so she'd have to do it alone, and she
dreaded it, I said of course she wouldn't, I'd help her, I'd go
with her, I'd do anything. . . . We were in a downtown cafe,
exchanging poems. We met there twice a week, ate lunch,
critiqued each other's work. My poems lay beside Lise's plate,
with a smear of marinara sauce on the first page. Hers were in
my shoulder bag, which hung from the back of my chair. I was
sipping a lukewarm cup of Earl Grey tea; Lise had Red Zinger
and Mexican beer.

She leaned across the table, put her hand on mine. She had

square fingers, close-cropped nails, callused palms. She had worked as a horse breaker in Arizona, on a shrimp boat off the North Carolina coast, and roofing houses in Texas and Louisiana. I dreamed about those hands, imagined they could do anything. I wanted them to do it all to me. I was twenty-three and had had exactly two love affairs. Lise was thirty-one and said that she'd had dozens. She and Celia had been together for four years.

I'd never know, Lise was saying, in her voice like whiskey, her husky, caressing voice that sounded like making love even when she was passing on a recipe, I'd never know how much better that made her feel. She didn't want to put it off too long, thought she'd do it Saturday, would call me then. I turned my hand in hers, clasped it for a moment before she took it away, and wondered what she thought of my smooth palm, my shaped and polished nails.

Lise finished her beer, unzipped her backpack, slid my poems inside. We left a big tip and parted on the corner, hugging each other good-bye. Her flannel shirt stroked my palms; wisps of her curly hair tickled my ear. I thought of turning my head, brushing my mouth against hers, so quickly that it might seem an accident, but she had already taken her hands away. I stood blinking as she strode to her truck and slung the backpack onto the seat, then lifted her hand in farewell.

I woke early Saturday morning. Lise didn't call. We met on Monday, at the cafe, and she explained that she and Celia had spent the weekend quarreling, most of Saturday debating whether they should break up. She tapped an unlit cigarette against the table edge and sipped from a bottle of Heineken. I watched her hands and clenched mine in my lap, hoping there was nothing but concern in my face, my voice.

Lise raised the cigarette to her mouth and lit it, cupping her hands around the flame. She shook the match and dropped it on her saucer, inhaled, blew smoke toward the ceiling. Did I think—she began, then shook her head.

Making up, she said, had taken all of Sunday.

Friday at lunch I had a beer myself. Lise drank two and told me earnestly that we'd have to take the dog out to the country in the morning, that her mother would be coming up next weekend, so it had to be tomorrow. She would call me, early.

The brown bottles sweated against our hands. I watched her fingers, curled around her bottle's side. We ate two baskets of chips and salsa and talked about my poems. Lise told me she hadn't been writing.

I want to read this one aloud, she said, and read my own poem to me, leaning against the table. I didn't dare look at her, stared instead at my hands, knotted on the table, while that astonishing voice slid inside me, through my veins, leaving me open and aching. Lise stopped reading, then talked about the last lines. I nodded, scarcely knowing what she'd said, and her fingers brushed mine.

You mustn't just agree with criticism, she said. You have to have a sense of what you want to do with your work. Defend it. Fight for it.

I stared into her hazel eyes, counted flecks of green and gold.

I do know, I said. Exactly what I want.

Good, she said. That's good. And looked away.

Saturday I waited for her call until eleven-thirty, then gave up, went to the laundromat and grocery. I returned at two and from the porch heard my telephone ringing. I hurried into my bedroom, snatched up the receiver, and a woman's voice, a stranger's, impatient, demanded if her order was in *yet*, didn't we know she needed it right now, today? I said it wouldn't be in for a month, slammed down the receiver, then picked it up again and dialed Lise's number. Celia answered on the second ring. I listened as she said hello? hello? hello? her voice rising a little with each repetition, then set it down, quite gently, and turned away.

Lise called me just before midnight. I thought she would apologize, explain, but instead she told me that she and Celia had quarreled again; she'd needed to hear my voice; I was the

100

only person in the world whose voice she could bear to hear. Her words slurred slightly at the ends, a gentle sound, almost like the sea.

Should I come over? I asked, reaching for the jeans I'd tossed across my desk chair an hour before. Or would she like to come here? Or we could, if she preferred, meet somewhere?

Her breath came roughly across the wires, as if she were crying, or on the verge of tears. She couldn't, she said, couldn't see me now. She just wanted to hear my voice. She'd sleep now, and call me in the morning.

Of course she never called. Despising myself, I scarcely left the house, dialed her number four times, hung up before the ring. Monday we met at the cafe. She drank black coffee, iced, and spoke in monosyllables. She gave me two new poems, said she hadn't had time to read mine properly, and could we skip this Friday's meeting? She wouldn't have time, she said, with her mother coming.

She hooked an arm across the back of her chair, lit a cigarette, and stared at me across it, as if daring me to mind. I forced my voice to coolness, told her Friday was no problem, I was busy, too. A lie, of course, and I was sure she knew it.

She drew on her cigarette, exhaled, and said that she'd been thinking we might want to scale down to one meeting a week. Two seemed a bit much. Didn't I agree?

I said of course, if that was what she wanted, then stopped and drew a deep breath and said no, I didn't agree at all, that I would miss the second meeting, that it helped my work, I'd like to think it helped hers, that once a week was not enough for me. My voice trembled, and I could not read her eyes, though she didn't look away. Besides, I added, this wasn't only business — there was friendship. I'd thought that we were friends. I stopped myself again, before I could cry, and stared at my fingers, curved round the thick white mug of China tea.

She jabbed out her cigarette with quick, sharp movements and put her hand over mine. We were friends, she said. She didn't mean it. She was tired and worried about Celia and her mother. They didn't get along, and the dog had been wild again, all week. Next weekend, she said, she'd definitely call me. And we could meet for lunch on Monday, when her mother had gone.

The next Monday we talked first about our poems, and Lise said that one of mine had gone through her head all weekend, that she'd heard my voice whenever she closed her eyes. I'd wanted to like her new work, hadn't, and had spent two hours Sunday deciding exactly why. She listened while she sipped her second beer and said that she agreed, had known even while typing out the poems that they were weak, but hadn't wanted to acknowledge it. She said her whole weekend had been maddening, that the only thing that kept her sane had been the thought of lunch today, that she hadn't realized how much she needed this time together, needed me. She hoped she hadn't been too harsh last week. It was only that she felt safe with me, she said, could trust me to forgive her darker side.

I shook my head, murmured something, and abandoned my tea, knowing I couldn't swallow if I tried. Outside, Lise put her arms around me, held me tight. I felt her heart beating against mine.

Friday, she said, and let me go. Till Friday.

Friday she was late. I stalled the waiter, drank wine I didn't want, and bitter coffee, knowing I'd have to go from lunch to work. I was ordering when she came to our table, her backpack dangling from one shoulder, a cigarette already in her hand.

Dos Equis, she told the waiter, and taco salad. She hadn't thought she'd make it, she told me, drawing on her cigarette, staring across the room at someone I couldn't see. Work had been a madhouse. She hadn't rewritten the poems. Mine weren't bad, but she hadn't read them carefully. She ate half her taco salad, gulped her beer, and left before I'd finished, saying she had to get back to the site. I finished my meal carefully, forcing myself to chew, and before I left the table picked up her beer bottle and drained the last sip. The mouth of the bottle was cool.

The phone woke me, early the next morning. I fumbled for it, pressed the receiver to my ear.

Hey, said Lise. I woke you, didn't I? I mumbled something and stared at the clock face: 6:15.

I'm sorry, Lise said.

I said it didn't matter.

I'm going out this morning. With the dog. If you don't want to go, I'll understand. I've been awake all night, thinking about it. If I don't do it now, I never will.

I'll come, I told her and put down the phone.

She picked me up twenty minutes later. She had a thermos of coffee in the truck, which she handed to me as I closed the door. I put in cream and sugar, she said, just the way you like it. Unless you'd rather have a beer.

Oh, no, I said, my stomach churning at the thought. She nodded, raised the can she held to her mouth, and tipped back her head. I watched her brown throat move as she drank.

There was a shovel on the floorboard. The dog was in the back. She whined against the window until Lise pulled away from the curb, then stood with her head over the side, ears blowing. She was a larger dog than I'd remembered, with a pointed face, long ears like a spaniel's, and golden fur. Three years old, her former owner had said, and housebroken, but she chewed everything in sight, pissed all over the house, shat under the dining room table and in a dim hallway, whined night and day, and had at least two seizures a week. The vet said it wasn't anything he could repair; she might have been mistreated at some point, there might be brain damage. A healthy animal otherwise, and Lise should fence the yard, keep her outside.

We drove out of the city, into the country, where dirt roads branched off from the blacktop every mile or two and kudzu strangled trees. We drove and drove until I dozed off, then woke with a start to Lise's hand on my thigh. I blinked at her.

Celia and I split up last night, she said.

Again, I said, as lightly as I could. But come tomorrow. . . .

No, she said softly. This time's for good. She turned the truck abruptly into a field. I clutched at the door as we jounced

103

across old plow furrows, then came to a stop beside a stand of trees, stranded like an island in the sea of red clay. This looks like a good place, she said, and opened her door.

I opened mine, more slowly, and stepped into knee-high scrub. Lise was leashing the dog, murmuring, Good dog. Good dog.

The dog whined and wriggled, licked at Lise's face, then pissed a stream across the tailgate. Jesus, Lise muttered and tugged her down, then turned to me. Can you hold her? I have to get the gun.

I took the leash. The dog's nose pushed against my palm. I smoothed the fur between her ears. *The dog*, Lise had called her, for so long that I had forgotten her name.

Good girl, I said. Good dog. The truck door slammed. Lise walked around, her left arm angled behind her.

Can you tie her over there? she asked me, gesturing to the trees. There's rope in back — hope it isn't wet.

Lise —

I stopped, picked up the rope, led the dog away, and tied her to the nearest tree. I watched my pale fingers fumble with the knots. They felt icy cold, though my face and neck were hot. The dog whined again and nudged her head against my thigh. A little trickle of piss ran across the tree roots.

I looked back toward the truck. Lise set a beer can on the tailgate, cocked the rifle, then lowered it again.

Okay, she said. You need to come back here.

I looked at the dog, swallowed hard, and went to her.

Stay behind me, she said. I raised my cold hand, closed it on her shoulder, and said, Wait. Lise, wait.

Jesus, she snapped and lowered the gun again, shrugging my hand away. What is it?

I'm sorry, I said. Lise, I'm sorry, but surely there's something else — some other way you could —

I've been *through* this, she said. Goddamnit. The Humane Society says they'd euthanize her — but maybe she'd spend a few days in a cage first, miserable. She hates being tied — I can't afford a fence. And who would take her? You want her? Sure — she's yours.

104

I shook my head, stared down at the grass.

All right, then, damn it. Get out of the way.

She stepped past me, walked toward the dog, who whined and wriggled her hindquarters, tugging at the rope. Lise stopped about a foot from her, her right arm holding the rifle against her side.

Good dog, she said. Good dog, and raised the gun. It cracked, and her shoulder jerked with the recoil. The dog slumped without a sound into the grass. Lise stumbled to the truck, laid the gun in back, then braced her hands on the side.

Oh, God, she said, as if she were truly praying, oh, God, and put her hands across her face. When her shoulders began to shake, I looked away, toward the clump of trees. The dog lay stretched as if asleep, her golden fur shining from the scrub and weeds.

Lise uncovered her face. I think I wanted you to stop me, she said, and stretched out a hand to me. I stared at it, feeling everything inside me halt, then turn to ice.

I'll get the shovel, I said, and turned away, glimpsing, from the corner of my eye, Lise's hand lowering again to grip the side of the truck, remembering how I'd dreamed those hands on me.

Shell Island, 1985

●

Ellyn Bache

Eban's wife, who had left him, would eat anything but reds. Stayman, Jonathan . . . occasionally a Golden Delicious. Most apple people felt that way. After Alex was born they had moved from Washington to Smithsburg, Maryland, because Lila's brother had died and she wanted to take over his job in her father's orchard. Autumn weekends she stood on the loading docks selling bushels of reds to people who drove up from the city. "They think you can use them for pies and sauce, but you can't. Reds get an ugly taste if you heat them," she'd say. Not Red Delicious, just reds, the way Communists were reds in the '50s.

Eban knew nothing of the apple business. He taught some classes in town and drove into D.C. two days a week for his research. Alex had just turned ten when Lila announced she was moving in with her father's foreman, Larry. "I don t know why, Eban, I cant give you a clear explanation," she said when he demanded one. "Maybe it's because he can tell a red from a Macintosh and you can't. Honest to goodness, maybe that's why."

So it was that at the age of forty-seven Eban came to take a job on the coast of southeastern North Carolina, where there were no mountains and no apple trees and, except in the fall, brought to the grocery stores from great distance and at great expense per pound—no reds.

He took Alex with him. "When you're young, it's good to have all the different experiences you can," he explained to the boy. "We've never lived by the sea." Alex shrugged his shoulders. He had fallen into a state of lethargy and could register only indifference. Indifference to Eban, indifference to his mother, indifference to leaving the school he'd attended since kindergarten. They went at the end of August, before the new term, driving the eight-hour stretch south with only two brief stops for gas and lunch.

The land was flat along the coast, and sandy, with squat houses and scrubby trees. A real estate agent greeted them. Alex had always lived in a house and Eban did not wish to make a drastic change. The agent drove them around under a bright sky she described as Tar Heel Blue, blasting her air-conditioning against 93-degree heat. Tall stands of pines lined the roadways, shedding needles onto exhausted Southern grass. She showed them tiny ranch houses on flat lots, dwarfed by the pines. Eban found them depressing. Alex did not react. The humidity was overpowering.

"Or you could rent at the beach until May," the agent finally said. "People let the houses by the week in summer, but they like long-term tenants after that. September and October are really the nicest months."

She drove them across the drawbridge toward Johnnie Mercer's Fishing Pier, where the evening before they had sat on the beach after swimming. She showed them an apartment jammed between graying frame houses, then a claustrophobic condominium overlooking the marsh. Finally she brought them to an oceanfront house at the uncrowded north end of the beach, which looked like a shack on stilts from outside, but inside was spacious, well furnished, and clean.

"Of course out here you'll have all the little problems of living on a barrier island," she said as they stood on the deck looking out at the water. "They'll evacuate you every time there's a hurricane warning." Alex perked up at the mention of hurricanes. The woman had anticipated that. "Don't worry, these places have been here for a while. They've withstood a few storms, they don't blow down that easily." Alex glowed. Eban himself was beginning to like the idea.

To the north and south were other, similar dwellings, facing the dunes and the sea. In town, the sad little houses had been landscaped with pampas grass and myrtles, but here even grass did not grow on the lots, only weeds and burrs. There was not a single tree. It suited him. Alex was watching the ocean curl toward them in the late-afternoon light.

"We'll take it," Eban said.

The section of beach on which they lived was called Shell Island. The streets were named for shells—Sand Dollar, Conch, Cowrie, and Scotch Bonnet. Scotch Bonnet? Eban bought shell books at the souvenir store on Johnnie Mercer's pier, and was surprised to find shells he'd never heard of occupying so much space in his illustrated paperbacks—160 species of cowries alone, commoner than he would have thought.

Except for Eban's job at the university, and Alex's school—a private school Eban had chosen because of the small classes and Alex's emotional state—they had nothing to do but explore the island. Each morning they drove over the drawbridge into the town of Wilmington, where Eban arranged his schedule to coincide with Alex's, picking him up at three each afternoon. They bought Styrofoam belly boards to float on in the ocean—Alex at ten, Eban at 47—learning to catch the breakers just so. Alex—lighter braver, more indifferent—repeatedly skinned his belly on the drifts of shells which washed onto the shore with each tide. He didn't complain. The sun remained intense through September, the weather stayed hot; and all around them was water—ocean to the east; to the west, the Sound.

Alex spent hours fashioning sailboats out of cardboard milk cartons, narrow creations using straws for masts and Kleenex for sails. Holding the boats delicately in his hands, he crossed the narrow road that ran the length of the island and set his creations afloat in the Sound. Eban's passion was not boats but the sea itself. He stood on the deck putting off housework and laundry, making note of the colors as the ocean changed from green to deep blue in the late afternoon light. He watched the gulls circle and dip in the breakers. He searched for the dolphins that sometimes came leaping by, breaking water with their fins. Peering through the set of good binoculars Lila had given him early in their marriage, he charted the ships that floated against the horizon. Finally weary of staring, he hiked up a new road that had been built to the northern tip of the island, where construction had already begun on rows of condominiums and a hotel, but where for now there was still an unobstructed view of long-legged water birds in the marsh to the west, and pink-and-gold sunsets over the reeds. Many days, after work, Eban spoke to no one but Alex. In the evenings fishermen lined the shore as the tide came in, casting out in the areas where the gulls were feeding. At first Eban and Alex only watched, peering into buckets filled with ice and bait and the day's catch. Finally Eban, whose fishing experience consisted of a day on a bass boat in Western Maryland, bought surf fishing gear at the marine store across the drawbridge. "All right, I'm going out to catch our dinner," he said — and by luck or stubbornness he did.

It didn't happen again. He tried different baits — shrimp, which slipped off the hook, bloodworms, which bit, and cut mullet. "You could try for spots off the pier," Alex suggested, knowing his father had a weakness for small panfish. But Eban, thinking use of the pier was somehow cheating, refused. He gave up fishing and returned to his study of shore life, identifying birds in the marsh and shells on the beach. He watched the boats. He bought their seafood at the strong-smelling fish market just across the drawbridge, where mako shark and swordfish steaks were placed on ice and the cheaper fish dumped unceremoniously into bushel baskets. At night, glutted by sight of brown pelicans and sand sharks, by talk of spots and whiting and blues — at night he often slept.

Mornings, he woke from dreams of Larry and Lila together, touching, or of his inlaws having the two of them over for dinner. He had liked his inlaws, before. Country people, they had deferred to his better education, his maturity (compared to Lila's), his lack of impulsiveness. He in turn admired their pulling the orchards through four years of recession. Only their speech, dotted with colloquialisms and bad grammar, embarrassed him. When Lila left, they claimed to be bewildered by her behavior, but they never fired Larry. A long-time foreman, they said, the only one familiar with the work. It had never occurred to Eban that he — the scholar — would become the embarrassment. Waking from dreams of that, he looked out to ocean sunrises rather than blue mountains—red sky, white breakers, hungry gulls. The scenery struck him as exotic, and eased his pain.

They were often stopped by the drawbridge on their way into town. The bridge opened every hour on the hour to let the boat traffic through. Bearing down on the Intracoastal Waterway at 45 miles an hour, they became accustomed to seeing red lights flashing in the distance and wooden barriers coming down telling them without question that they were going to be late.

Neither of them minded much. Stopped in traffic, waiting for the steel girders to rise, Alex got out of the car and ran up for a closer look. Eban was pleased to see him taking an interest in the boats heading south on the Intracoastal for the winter. For himself, the appeal was being locked on the island seven or ten minutes longer, caught in view of the reedy growth from the bright water, fishing rigs unloading at the market, unfamiliar island life. He rather liked the bridge blocking passage so effectively—making the island a barrier from the mainland as well as the sea: impermeable: safe.

Alex often returned to the car disconsolate—for what rea- son, Eban could not decide. Perhaps the southbound boats unsettled the boy, traveling so freely while he was due at school. Later Eban realized Alex was not watching the boats at all, but rather the shore itself—shelves of sand rising from the shallows, long stretches of marsh grass, clusters of reeds. Alex had been seeking something there and was disappointed not to find it. But as to the object of the search, which disturbed his son so, Eban had no clue. Then one evening as Alex walked toward the Sound with the day's newly completed sailboat, Eban understood with sudden insight that *his boat* was what his son expected to see morning after morning. Alex thought somehow that the sea would carry it from Banks Channel into the Intracoastal and give it back to him the following day. Perhaps he believed that the same law would also bring back his mother.

Eban, helpless, began to buy milk in large plastic gallons, unsuitable (he hoped) for fitting out with sails.

110

They had been there less than a month when a hurricane warning came. For days there were reports of a storm moving northwest from this coordinate to that coordinate, packing winds of 120 miles an hour, but so far away. A momentary bleep of excitement in Alex's eyes, followed by indifference.

Then one day they woke to a metal-gray sea, churning. All the schools had been closed. If the storm continued on its present course, it would make landfall at Wrightsville Beach sometime the following night. Its power, coupled with the evening's high tide, could make for untold damage. The beach communities were to be evacuated. "All right," Alex sang, dancing. Eban pulled the porch furniture inside from the deck and tacked boards (left by the landlord) over the sliding glass doors facing the sea. Alex helped him, having abandoned altogether his previous indifference.

Inside, the phone was ringing. Lila, Eban thought. She had called once before at an awkward moment, to check on Alex when classes began. Hearing that the boy was in private school, she'd said bitterly, "Trying to get around that bussing order for racial balance, aren't you, Eban? Don't tell me it never entered your mind." (In fact, it hadn't.) "I never thought you had it in you to be a bigot."

Since she'd left, she'd made a point of lacing their conversations with whatever wounding comments she could. Eban wondered if she was trying to insulate herself against the accusations he might make otherwise, or if the insults had been stored up all the time they'd lived together — directed, in those years, against the reds instead of Eban. He believed that now, secure with Larry, she might have managed to be kind.

"Well, I never thought you had it in you to be an adulteress," he'd replied.

A shriek of wind, shearing over the deck. Eban envisioned Lila wrenched from her distant bliss by a momentary pang of conscience at abandoning her son to storms. The phone rang a fifth time, a sixth. He was annoyed that she'd choose just then to call, when Alex seemed to have recovered a measure of normality.

"Eban?" The woman's voice startled him because it wasn t Lila's, surely: but reedier, and more Southern, a Carolina voice.

"Dennie Mattson," she said. It was a moment before he placed her: the middle-aged departmental secretary whose car sometimes occupied the parking spot next to his, adorned with a bumper sticker that read: "If God isn't a Tar Heel, why did He make the sky Carolina blue?"

She was always inquiring about his adjustment, suggesting sightseeing trips, offering to help. She might have annoyed him except that she seemed so sincere. Once, to make conversation, he'd mentioned the salt-spray glaze that stuck to his windows—a housewifely detail—and she'd said: "We had a place out there once with the same problem, and the only thing we could ever get to cut that stuff was Softscrub"—looking almost triumphant at being able to offer a solution. Now she wanted to know how they had taken the news of the evacuation, what he was going to do.

"We're getting ready to go over to the high school, I guess," he said. "They say it's the evacuation center for this area."

"I was calling to invite you here instead," she told him. "Last year the centers were just misery. Babies crying, and you couldn't get into the bathrooms." Hurricane Diana had hit Wilmington the previous fall, sweeping through the center of town, spawning tornadoes which uprooted masses of trees. "I've got some other people coming, too. We'll have a hurricane party."

"We couldn't really," he said.

"Bring some sleeping bags, and flashlights if you have any. Last year the electricity was off a couple days." She gave directions to one of the flat, pine-woods developments where a month before Eban had refused to rent a house. She sounded—in her Southern way—as if she expected them.

To the east, the sky had grown darker, and the wind had begun to rise. The sea, whitecapped, came almost to the dunes. Hurricane. Alex was watching with glittering eyes. On the drawbridge, police in slickers stood in the rain, allowing people

112

off the island but not on. Eban felt suddenly displaced, as he had in the days preceeding his move from Maryland. What if the beach house should be ruined? A vision rose before him of the evacuation center some days hence, in the sticky aftermath of storm: a high school gym dim from lack of electricity, filled with the anxious sweat of unbathed families, crowded bathrooms smelling of urine. And Alex, indifferent. Eban headed not to the school, but to the woman's house.

"I'm so pleased you decided to come," Dennie Mattson said, opening the door to a small beige living room full of people. Introductions all around: an elderly aunt and uncle who lived out on the beach; their son; a fat X-ray technician and her daughter from the house next door.

They all behaved as if his joining them were normal. The adults watched the weather reports on TV, drank beer from cans, ate Cheese Nips out of a box. At some point hamburgers and chips were served for dinner. Alex perched himself by the window to chart the storm, which so far wasn't much. No danger, the broadcasters said, until night. The others talked of the eye of the terrible hurricane last year, a perfectly calm and yellow eye. "There were ten people staying with us, and I'll tell you, that's something you don't forget," the X-ray technician said. Eban had nothing to offer on the subject except the fogs that haunted the Maryland mountains. Driving up from town in the rain, he came to know exactly at what altitude the zone would change, above which the clouds would close in, leaving him to cling to the white line at the side of the winding road. He'd been more wary of fog than Lila had—she had grown up with it, after all—and she had held him (he realized now) in contempt. Her own terror had been of lightning on the mountain, which did its damage, he supposed, but was, after all, in contrast to the fog—light.

He didn't speak of Lila aloud. He drank yet another beer, waited for them to ask. No one did. He realized that, from their perspective, he was merely a man alone, with a school-aged child. . . he might have been divorced for years.

The announcer said the storm had begun to turn north. Perhaps it would hit Morehead City, or even Cape Hatteras farther up the coast. The Wilmington area would see only heavy gales. In the dark, with rain slashing and wind whipping, the X-ray technician announced that she'd better go home and feed her cats. Her daughter went with her. Eban heard himself saying (he was a little drunk by then), "And all the rest of us can go out for a walk."

Dennie clapped her hands — a blond, middle-aged cheerleader. "Oh. wonderful!" The elderly aunt and uncle declined, but Dennie and the cousin and Alex went, wrapped in slickers, into the night. The wind buffeted them, less (they all noted) than it would have during a typical afternoon thunderstorm. Even so, Alex's color was high. The hurricane might yet hit. Last year it had changed course several times before making landfall. A few blocks from Dennie's house, a man, watching the storm from his porch, asked as they passed: "Do you need shelter?"

"No, we're just walking." But they were pleased.

Back in the house Dennie and Eban and the cousin watched the news and had a final beer after Alex went to bed. The storm was definitely heading north. Loose and slightly dizzy, Eban realized that he had not tasted alcohol since Lila's departure. In the aftershock of her going, he had stopped drinking altogether — had disciplined himself, rather, to prepare regular meals for Alex, to go to bed (though not always to sleep) at normal hours, marshalling his forces, as it were, to survive the hardship. He had no sense that his difficulties were over. But for the moment, sitting in a stranger's living room in a circle of light, talking of innocuous matters like winds and tides, with the buzz of alcohol between his ears, he felt, mind and body, like a tense muscle that had suddenly unclenched — one of those absolutely still moments he had not known for some time, when life breaks and pauses before it goes rushing on.

By morning the wind was calm; the evacuation order on the beach had been lifted. Dennie wanted everyone to stay for pancakes, but Eban was anxious to get back. The newspaper reported that the ocean had overreached the dunes during the night on parts of the beach. The speed limit was an absurd twenty-tive miles per hour, but he observed it. Arriving home, he found everything intact. They removed the wooden boards from over the sliding glass doors just as the clouds blew off and the sun came out, giving them a clear blue holiday, because in anticipation of damage, most schools and businesses had been closed. He and Alex wandered the beach in the dry sunny air. Alex gathered the large, conical shells the high stormtides had washed in. Eban looked them up in his book. "Whelks," he said. Normally whelk shells did not reach shore, he supposed, because they were too large for the ordinary tides to propel them in. The specimens Alex had gathered were mostly broken and worn down to gray, but he lined them up on the picnic table on the deck. So: the hurricane had brought whelks, but no damage. Eban walked the house, testing faucets and outlets. All of them worked.

That was Friday. By Monday the heat had returned and Alex was tired of the whelk shells. "Some hurricane. This is what they give two days off of school for. Big whoop. I'd like to show them a big snow on the mountain."

After that Alex's mood stayed grim. "It's too hot for fall," he whined, as they slid into October and it was. He wanted crisp mornings, gold and auburn hills. He made no more sailboats. Eban could not, or did not, try to offer a defense. He had no wife, no dignity, no mountains and no apple harvest. He watched the sea.

Three days a week he had early classes, so he tended to his students and then brought his research materials back to the beach house. Positioning his desk to face the ocean, he worked until it was time to get Alex, his binoculars by his side. He allowed himself a session of bird-watching instead of a coffee break, gazing at brown pelicans flying in straight lines close to the shore, casing the surf for fish. He lunched to the sight of dolphins, noticing that they almost always traveled south. Perhaps they liked the warmer waters. He did not investigate further. The dolphins cheered him, and he preferred they keep their mystery. He was beginning the draft of his first new paper since the move. The heat was no longer stifling, though Alex thought it was. He turned the air-conditioning off and opened the sliders to the breeze.

Dennie, by virtue of their spending the hurricane together, now considered herself his friend. Days he lunched at the university she wandered into his office with her own brown bag, filled with sensible egg-on-pumpernickel sandwiches and carrot sticks, much like the lunches he packed for Alex and himself. Had she reminded him in any way of Lila, he might have minded, but Lila was only 35, dark and flirtatious, while Dennie was as old as Eban—a pale, straightforward woman with spindly limbs and a cumbersome bust. Eating her nutritious lunches, she seemed not a woman at all—in the sense that Lila, who lunched on Diet Pepsi, had been— but simply a companion, which Eban could accept.

She read his horoscopes from the newspaper and told him about astrology. "Once we got audited by the IRS and ever after that we mailed the tax when the moon was void of course, and we never got audited again," she asserted.

"And what does that mean exactly—void of course?"

"All I know is, it happens every other day. And any project you start then you'll never hear anything more of it."

Eban raised his eyebrows. "You have that superior look on your face," she said. "But I bet right now you're making a note to yourself to mail your tax next year when the moon is void of course." And, in fact, Eban was.

She told him the departmental gossip and enthused about Wilmington's building boom. Later, she told Eban about herself. Her son was at college in Chapel Hill; her husband Edward (she pronounced it Ed-wood) had worked for Corning glass when he wasn't fishing, and died of a heart attack at the age of 53. She spoke of him cheerfully enough. He'd had a boat which she'd finally sold, and had entered the King Mackerel contest every year. "Ever taste King Mackerel?" She made an unpleasant face.

"I've seen the steaks in the fish store. Look kind of dark."

"Terrible, if you ask me." He liked her frankness, coupled with her soft North Carolina drawl. Much better, he thought, than the country quality Lila's speech had. With Lila it was:

"Don't wear that it needs washed," always dropping the infinitive, and once, when Alex was small, "It's new, but I wore it on him once," which annoyed him disproportionately. "I suppose out there at the beach you do some fishing yourself," Dennie said, biting into a pickle.

"I gave it up," he said, looking at the pickle. "I felt too sorry for the fish."

"Fish don't have feelings."

"How do you know?"

"You eat them, don't you?" That seemed to settle it for her. "I even feel a little sorry for the worm," he said.

She broke off a piece of the pickle and handed it to him, having noticed how he was staring it down.

It was the middle of October and the temperature had not gone below seventy degrees for a week. even at night. There were occasional cool spells, but the tendency of the air was always to heat up. "It's not normal," Alex said.

"We have no way of knowing what's normal. We've never been here before in fall." Eban rather liked the idea of a climate without autumn. At any rate, they had nothing by which to judge it; normal didn't exist.

"Well, I hate it," Alex said.

In the increasingly angled light, the sea was blue-green, fading to darker blue in the depths. "It doesn't look like itself," Alex asserted. But the ocean *was* itself, Eban argued; what else could it be? What did they know of North Carolina waters in the seasons? Yet when he looked at the aqua shallows, he was reminded less of the Atlantic than of the Caribbean, where he and Lila had been on the company trip that ended his marriage. His inlaws had hosted an early December vacation—after the harvest—on which most of the employees had come with their wives. Larry had been alone.

It was then that Lila's affair had begun. She had bought three new bathing suits, one of them a bright turquoise which set off the darkness of her skin. He thought three suits was excessive for a five-day trip. He said she would always have the figure of a young boy, regardless. That was a joke, but Lila glared at him. She looked good in clothes and knew it—everyone said so. There was something lyrical about her appearance. She spent hours preparing for the trip in a tanning salon. She didn't want to burn, she said. She never burned.

The group rented a boat and went out to the reefs to snorkel. Under the water, plants waved tendrils at him and colorful angelfish wiggled by. In the distance, just visible from where he swam, a barracuda lurked with all its shadowy menace. Surfacing, he was so absorbed by the experience that he barely noticed Larry staring at Lila's turquoise bathing suit and approving, and Lila looking back. He'd always felt his failure to observe them just then had left him, later, responsible.

"The boy is bored," Dennie said, "Living there on the beach. That and the adjustment." Most of the houses on Shell Island were empty now, not having been rented for the winter. Their little lane housed a group of college students next door and a retired couple across the way, but Alex was the only child. The bathers and surfers and fishermen that had given the beach its festive quality had deserted. Alex's one friend from school lived twenty minutes away in town. "At least shoot a few baskets," Eban urged, pointing to a basketball goal at one of the abandoned houses nearby. "That's something you can do by yourself."

But Alex would not. "I miss grass," he said, looking at the lot below: weeds and sand. He spent hours watching "You Can't Do That on Television." It was a pastiche of one-liners and throwup jokes: *Mother, I think you love Tommy better than you love me. – Oh Alistair, I never loved you.* Sometimes Alex laughed out loud.

"Just the adjustment," Dennie said. On weekends she invented outings for them, inviting herself along. "Remember, he's been through a lot," she admonished, though Eban had not once offered up the details of his broken marriage. They took Alex to a surfing competition and a chowder tasting at Greenfield Park. "Are you going to marry her?" the boy asked. "Of course not. We're just friends. I don't even find her attractive."

"Me neither," Alex agreed. But Dennie had adopted them, swept them up, was out of their control.

She insisted they go to the aquarium at Fort Fisher, where there were slide shows, nature walks, and a shark in a huge tank. A sign announced that it was a nurse shark, one of the species known to attack man. Alex stared at the beast swimming around in circles, its huge skin like pinkish sandpaper, its small blue eyes lashless and mean. "So that's it," he said flatly. "Big whoop."

In the newspaper, the fishing columns lamented the lack of autumn fish because of the warm waters. The speckled trout hadn't come in and only a few mullet were being caught at night. The ocean was ten or fifteen degrees warmer than usual. "God, do you believe this?" Alex said. Eban reminded him of the bare bones of trees on winter mountains, the cold. the death. Alex said he'd never minded. The week before Thanksgiving, the paper ran pictures of azalea bushes beginning to show bloom.

Then there was a spell of dark, rainy weather, spawned by a late hurricane in the Gulf. The first day was cool, like the sober end of the apple harvest. and they thought the season would change. It didn't. Trying to write in the rainy, humid heat, Eban felt distracted. He spent hours sitting on the dunes with his binoculars, watching the frothy gray-green sea, the pelicans dive-bombing after fish. When the hard rains came, he slept. He dreamed of the mountains. From their house he and Lila had had a clear view of the valley — neat rectangular fields, other orchards, other houses — and then more mountains on the other side, a perfect oval around the perspective. He woke to a rainy flatland: of the beach, the sea, his soul.

A terrible dank fishy smell sometimes rolled in from the ocean, the odor of decayed seaweed and rotting fish. Eban slept his afternoons away. He stopped dreaming of Lila and dreamed instead of Todd, Lila's dead brother, whom he hadn't thought about for years. In his dreams Todd walked beside him on the beach. They walked for miles, for hours, and Eban woke exhausted, as if they really had.

119

Todd was a dark, rangy man who worked in the orchards but whose first love was flying. He was a student pilot at first, then licensed, and finally instrument-rated. He flew in winter when there was no work to do, and in the growing season when there was. One day when a fog rolled in, Todd flew his rented Cessna into the mountain. He was 27 at the time. Lila, pregnant with Alex, wanted to name the baby after him.

Eban refused. They'd be saddened every time they looked at a son named Todd, he said. But he begrudged Todd his dying and Lila her orgy of mourning; he begrudged the waste of a life for sport. A few months later, when Lila's father suggested she take over Todd's job, she reacted with surprising emotion. She hated the city; orcharding was the only work she knew. Eban could have his career anywhere. Having refused her on the matter of the name, he was reluctant to say no again. They moved from Washington, where Eban had been happy, to Smithsburg, where he was not. In a way, Eban had blamed Todd for that, too.

But now, ten years later, dreaming, he and Todd walked the beach with no resentment between them. Together they looked out at the sea, at fish and plants which seemed to be visible under the water—the same plants he had seen in the Caribbean—and at gulls and pelicans above. "It wasn't just for sport, you see," Todd told him. "I was in search of another element." Eban nodded, understanding. Todd had no more expected to conquer the air than Eban did the ocean; it was too unfathomable—but just, somehow, reaching, to cope.

Dennie had invited them for Thanksgiving dinner. Her son would be home from Chapel Hill. "Billy will love it," she insisted. "The thing he always hated when he was younger was if we didn't have a lot of people for the holidays. It'll be good for Alex, too." Eban tried to refuse but in the end they went, just as they had gone during the hurricane, because the other alternatives were even less attractive.

The day was hot and sunny—eighty-three degrees by noon—abnormal, as Alex pointed out. Billy turned out to be blond and nondescript and just as cordial as his mother. Seeing

120

Alex lose interest in Dennie's shell collection, he brought out an obviously new and complicated camera, which he taught Alex to use. At one o'clock they ate turkey and gravy and potatoes in the stifling dining room, getting up from the table overstuffed and irritable. Alex might have sulked except that Billy suggested they drive out to the beach, to Eban's house, to try the camera .

"We should shoot you swimming in the ocean," Dennie said when they got there. She'd changed into shorts which showed the fine varicose veins in her legs, under the bright sun. "You can take the pictures up north to your friends." She often spoke of people going "up north," whether they came from Virginia or Maine. It was as if all places north of Wilmington were cold and gray and identical, and could not be distinguished from one other.

"It's not really up north," Alex said quickly. "Maryland is south of the Mason-Dixon line. You can see some of the stones that mark the Mason-Dixon line not far from our house."

Our house.

"I'm getting dressed," Alex told them. "I hate this sand."

Inside, the phone was ringing. Eban had no time to reflect that it might be Lila before Alex grabbed it. Eban heard him saying, "Yeah, grandma — turkey and stuffing and the works. Then we went swimming, believe it or not." His mother-in-law. Eban imagined for an instant that she'd called to apologize for not firing Larry; perhaps even to say Lila had left Larry and wanted Eban back. A lightness bloomed in his chest, where before had been a dark weight. Then Alex handed Eban the phone and his mother-in-law said: "Eban, I know how awkward this is, but I'm calling to ask if you'll let Alex come up here for the Christmas holidays. I know it's not in the agreement." She paused. "It isn't for Lila I'm asking," she said. "It's for me."

Dennie and Billy were in the living room, pretending not to listen. "I'll ask Alex." And Alex danced, shaking sand off his bare legs onto the rug, waving a fist in the air: "All *right*."

121

The drawbridge schedule had changed. Instead of opening at hourly intervals, it went up on demand, whenever a boat needed to go through. In the warm, sunny weather boat traffic was heavy all through early December. Sometimes, running an errand into town and coming back, Eban was stopped by the bridge on both legs of the trip. One afternoon, late on his way to get Alex, he found the bridge closed, with an interminable succession of boats passing underneath. Alex hated him not to be waiting when the bell rang. Lila had left him too long at a birthday party once, and he had feared ever since being the last one to be fetched. Minutes passed, the car was hot. Eban had to pull the collar of his shirt away from his neck and wipe his sweating palms on his trousers. Boat after boat: sailboats, fishing rigs, cabin cruisers. Eban's heart beat rapidly, an uneven rhythm. His breath came short and fast. (Lila had hyperventilated during labor, and swore the labor would be her one and only.) Chest aching. Breathe slowly, he told himself. The bridge began to open. His hands were trembling. Wooden barriers rising. Foot on the accelerator. Moving now. But it was as if he had been cut off forever: from the mainland, the town, his son.

A gray sky, cooler weather, coming back from a shopping trip for Alex's winter clothes. He would need them for his trip up north. "Don't call it *up north,* Dad. It sounds like you're from here." Dusk was falling, night coming earlier. A line of brown pelicans swooped by them, eerie against the darkening sky. "They're creepy," Alex said. "They look like pterodactyls."

Looking at the ocean, Alex said: "I hate the way the land ends right there, and the water closes you in." Eban thought of mountains ringed by other mountains, deceptive, as if at the end of those hills, everything stopped.

The morning Alex left was blinding-bright with sun, but really cold, for once. Alex was tense with excitement, anxious to get on the plane. Eban hugged him goodbye, but the boy pulled away, embarrassed to be embraced in public. Then he was gone, down the little chute that led to the plane. Eban was sure he'd refuse to come back and had said as much to Dennie over the past weeks. But she'd replied: "Maybe not. Maybe the trip north will get it out of his system."

Driving back through town from the airport, Eban saw there'd been a hard freeze. The first? He didn't know. On the beach the landscape was always the same: sand and weeds; no green, no bushes, no trees. In town the grass was crusty from ice and the tender plants had wilted. It looked surprisingly normal. He was visited by a vision of his Smithsburg house against a muted sky: bare orchards, violet and gray winter, masses of birds. Returning to the beach, he noted that the reedy dune grass was now brown and beaten down by salt spray. The sand was interminable. Except for the ocean he might have been living on a desert. That had been Alex's view of it all along. He imagined his mother-in-law phoning, pleading Alex's case, begging him to leave the boy in Maryland. He'd been imagining such an outcome for three weeks, and now that he was finally alone, after all that high emotion he couldn't sustain it. He felt drained, empty. If Alex came back, they would move into town.

Dennie insisted he come for dinner, because otherwise he would brood. She cooked an elaborate meal, wore a silky dress. "Lila wanted to name Alex for her brother," he said. "I wouldn't let her." He had not spoken of such things before and now could not make himself stop. Perhaps insisting on Alex's name had been a mistake; perhaps it had something to do, all these years, with Lila's working so hard in the orchard and Eban's raising their son. Dennie nodded, not disagreeing. "I still think after Christmas he'll be ready to come back," she said.

Sitting in the living room after the meal, she smiled at Eban in what he recognized as a come-hither way. He was vaguely surprised. He saw that she expected him to make love to her, and supposed he would. There was no hurry. In the meantime they gazed at the shells that filled her knicknack shelf, gathered during her husband's fishing days. Among the conchs and the olive shells and the cowries was a long strand of flattish beige disks, almost like segments of a sand-colored lei. He could not identify them at first, and then recognized them from a drawing in his shell book. "Whelk egg casings," he said.

"Yes. Though sometimes I have trouble imagining whelks laying eggs."

She raised her eyebrows and he tried to picture whelks mating; he couldn't, of course.

"These things wash up onto the beach in the summer," she said. "Here, let me show you."

He picked up the papery necklace and handed it to her where she sat. With a long fingernail she slit open one of the compartments and emptied it onto the coffee table. Hundreds of tiny, whitish whelk shells fell out, perfectly conical, perfectly detailed miniatures even to the spiky nobs near their tops.

"You can imagine how many eggs there must be altogether," she said. "I mean, rows and rows of these casings washing up onto the beach. And each one has — what? Maybe a hundred of these little compartments?"

He touched his index finger to his tongue and then to the table, so that several of the little whelk shells adhered to it. He raised them to his eyes. They were small and white, each one capable of a new life, and they struck him as distinctly hopeful.

Ten Rabbis Eat Cake

•

Jeff Bens

Simon Finkel was having trouble, or at least his mother thought he was, and that prompted the thirtieth phone call of the week and I'd have sworn to you his problems were nothing compared to mine. I taught high school at a Yeshiva, a school for orthodox Jews. I had tried to keep my office number from Reviva but our school secretary, Mrs. Lubitch, threatened to quit, said Reviva's calling was driving her to drink. And I could sympathize. The very instrument through which Reviva Finkel sang like an off-key violin was the instrument which 364 days earlier had clubbed me into the blackness of loss. The fucking telephone, I'd have ripped it off the wall if I'd only listened to the phone company and bought that jack-insurance they assured me I'd someday need. And who knows more about love than the phone company, how many hearts have been broken or made to sing through Alexander Graham Bell's infernal machine?

Something about having two tests on his birthday, Reviva said. About how she had spoken with Rabbi Mandelbaum, who pointed to Tu Bi Shvat and how he couldn't possibly, and how I, then, as a non-believer the assumption went, might have a little more secular leniency. Mostly she just wanted an ear for her voice, an ear which I was increasingly providing against what in sturdier times I might have called my better judgment. An enormous woman, Reviva barreled through life with the delicacy of a longshoreman, moved with the subtlety of an ox. Sometimes I would set the receiver down, in a snake-plant, in a file cabinet drawer, picking it up occasionally with a uh-huh or maybe a mmmph. Other times I'd pull the plug, tell her the lines were down; once I told her in no uncertain terms to never call me again, which she didn't for two days at which point we carried on like nothing had happened. Insane, she sometimes brought her husband Morey onto another line to have someone to argue with. They'd fight and I'd listen, occasionally egging them into Yiddish with a few choice terms I'd picked up, other times responding with a series of non-sequiturs: Nixon, polyurethane, suppository. It made no difference; the calls came, a dozen a day.

Reviva stole Simon's weight. Of this I'm sure. While Simon was not anorexic—I know anorexia, Kara had it, I sometimes blame her leaving me on my own thinness, too much a reflection of her disease, I stand six foot and weigh 135 pounds—Simon was more smothered. Simon didn't so much have a negative body image, I'm convinced, as no body image at all. He lived, it seemed, solely to receive the queer looks of his classmates, to remind us all of how an undertaker should look, just as Rabbi Mandelbaum, ironically, reminded us all of Santa Claus. Shoulders stooped, an oily blackness forever beneath inwardly focused eyes, Simon would sit off to the side, not observing, not deep in a daydream of Rosie Stein's forbidden ripeness, but in a personal darkness, a place without feeling, a place defined by absence.

The way Kara said it to me was this, "Let's meet at the Reynolda Cafe, I was there last week and I think you'd like it." Over the phone, Reviva was onto the Holocaust, a subject she knew might draw me back into our conversation as it is the focus of my graduate studies, and I thought about neighbors turning away when all involved knew it was murder.

"But Reviva," I finally said as Morey had begun wheezing over some other extension, a wheeze in the darkness, and I thought I saw a chance to refocus and maybe get on and out, "the Holocaust has absolutely nothing to do with Simon's test date." She has a master's degree in biology and, like the other nuts I have met in my life, is capable of profound clarity.

"The holocaust has everything to do with Simon's test date—" Reviva spoke gravely, earnestly; for a moment that voice moved through me like a wrong number in the nighttime, at once irrelevant and personal, a call to wake up, " — the holocaust has to do — "

Micha Mandelbaum oozed into my office. He pressed his fingers to the mezuzah, kissed them. He picked up a history book, smiled falsely at me, his eyes searching I believe for horns on my head, the horns that my Jewish father was asked if he had at training camp in Kansas in 1952, kissed the mezuzah again, and left. Micha had brought me the mezuzah in September, hung it like a warning on my door. " — with everything," Reviva said.

"He doesn't understand," whispered Morey.

We dated for three months before we made love. For twelve weeks we'd rolled on top of each other in my torn-up Toyota, bodies pressed together like flowers in a thick book, moaning, hands up her blouse, biting, she screaming and then we'd go home. The afternoon when we finally did it, I was feigning an interest in one of the Brontes when she said, "Let's fuck." Sun crossed her floor stacks of Victorian literature, passed through a rack of pastel dresses and shoulderless shirts, wedged through the front spokes of a customized racing bicycle, and fell across the dried flowers I had brought and put on the floor in the still-damp bottle of domestic champagne. We made love. She said she saw colors, fields of poppies and roses, it had never happened before; I breathed her in, my tears on her face. When she washed, she had to run, I could stay, listen to the Al Green CD I had brought, but she had to go, a party, I wouldn't like it; when she washed I watched the fury with which she doused her face, not meeting herself in the sink mirror, and when I put my hands around her from behind, pressing my chest to her shoulders, she jumped.

The Holocaust was made simple. The test day, about which Rabbi was being so inflexible although Reviva could understand as you can't just change celebratory days although this was only an arbor day even if it was for Israel so she thought he might make an exception, was also Simon's birthday and was also the day on which Simon's grandfather had died, thrown out a fifth story window by a drunken German draftee.

127

Simon's birthdays were spent in black, in a Kaddish, a gathering of ten men, remembering the dead.

At the Reynolda Cafe I felt it coming. Kara sat in a great red velvet chair and when I arrived she had a look on her face so exquisitely pained that I fell in love with her a thousand times more. She stood to hug me and like a fool I accepted although I knew what held her thoughts. My body felt frail in her bared arms; a roomful of graduate students had bowed down to me in reverence when they heard we were dating. We jogged together once, and she breathed as hard as I, and then proceeded to run three times my distance later telling me I never had enough to eat. I sat on the arm of her chair. She said, "I'm leaving you."

Micha Mandelbaum was President of the junior class. In the high school where I was a junior, back in 1980, the class president was the casual athlete and gentleman drug user who got all the girls. Micha was not that. What he was was the Rabbi's son and there was constant discussion at the post-election lunch that something other than the cabbage had been stuffed. I disliked his inflexibility, his insistence that God's name never be used in vain, the way he averted his eyes when I told a dirty joke. Once, during a fire drill, he sat entranced, reading pages of the Torah tucked inside a history book, sat motionless but for a slight rocking as the room sped around him. I slammed shut his book and he looked up with such an expression of innocence and purity that I made a mental note to lower his next test grade by a third. Another time, he announced to the class that he felt the necessity to ask his father, the Rabbi, if he could sit in a lecture where I planned to discuss the Quaker response to the transformation of Puritanism, informing me that any discussion of Christianity was grounds to have me killed.

Morey was on about his back and how I had to come to the club to play golf once it was better. "It'll be an experience," he was saying in a way that burned me, like I didn't grow up in a town that was a third Jewish, like I had never shtupped any but Presbyterians, like my father didn't count. And I was about to tell him this, grateful for the focus really, when I realized I had never heard Morey speak for more than a minute and a half. And here he was, wheezing on about lumbars and discs, five irons and turf, and here I was trying to remember back to Sarah Saperstein, my first love, trying to feel the fullness of her breasts, trying to feel again and feeling nothing, eroticism and anger dead in me, and softly, into the blackness came a noise of such delicacy that it touches me even now. It was the soft cry of the Battleship Reviva sinking.

In Los Angeles, when the lights go down and the exteriors diminish, there is very little there. You walk along the sea and smell nothing. And I'd do that, dragging home from graduate classes, staring out into black, stepping around drunks passed out for the night, avoiding the deep tire tracks of police vehicles which had carted others off not to prison but to Van Nuys or Palms or Panorama city. Dragging home, searching for solace in Thomas Aquinas or Merton, trying to feel my solitude, but feeling instead a rubbery casing, a sarcophagus of waiting. I'd try to avert my eyes, from Orion and Cassiopia, from the stereo with our music, from the answering machine with the light that broke me open with each hopeful blink, a blink I came to revere, grateful for anything with a beginning, middle, and an end. On her birthday I played the ninety minute message tape straight through, a year's worth of her rising, then falling. On the last message I had picked up, the tape ending with a cough, a beep, and then silence.

Reviva clicked off, her softness ending not as it had begun, ending quickly, her tears swallowed deep into her gut. "Goodbye," a coping back in place. Morey ignored it, asked if I ate meat which I told him I didn't, told me that was why I was so skinny, that life was short and you should enjoy. "So many people have so much misery," he said.

I slept with Kara once after our break-up. It was my birthweek and she wanted to take me out. We ate on her expense account. By the way she ate I knew she hadn't really for days, she'd laugh how she'd out-eat me, but it was four meals to her one, nails chewed away, I wondered if the Pill had ever restored her cycle. She wore a floor length black dress and her skin shone like silver. I tried. I spoke in a voice that almost held meaning, that almost pulsed in my heart, told her I missed her, tried to stay clear, I knew I couldn't play games and the food sat

129

there, requiring consumption: socially, biologically, to be a man is to eat, to be a human is to kill other things and she touched her cheek and I told her that I loved her so. We went to her bed and I kissed her and we made love and I dreamt that she told me she loved me and in the morning her alarm was set for five and it rang and she told me what we had done was wrong.

Reviva drove a big Chevy Wagon, an avocado green bomber with a dent in the side the size of Massachusetts. She drove it like a sea captain, weaving through traffic as through troublesome waves, blaring the horn as if in a perpetual fog. Inside, she stowed provisions, bags of kosher chips, soda six packs, big bowls of vinegar potato salad or kugle — the car was in a state of perpetual picnic — fabric bolts, catalogues responsible for the clear-cutting of at least one national forest. And every morning from that traveling barge, Reviva would step ashore, assess her port of call with a consistently disappointed eye, and tow her Simon to the Rabbi. Her trust was in God, but since God wasn't teaching in the Los Angeles area, she'd settled.

In black pants, jackets, hats and white shirts my class would study history. The school was uncharmingly old, in a part of Los Angeles that seemed unchanged from the 20's, the 20's of immigrants and workers. The wood rotted and stank. The plumbing bled lead into the water. Once, when the school was ransacked with swastikas and broken glass, the Baptists up the road bought us new paint.

I had ten exams stapled and collated, my ability to do mundane tasks surprising me: I never bounced a check after she left, I exercised four days a week. Each morning was the same. Yaron Nicoll would be late and would blame it on his sister, someone — usually Aaron Barak — would comment on what he'd like to do to Yaron's sister, Micha the Rabbi's son would avert his eyes, and I would make small talk about the Dodgers or the Intifada depending on my mood and the lesson I hoped needed teaching. It was my politics that turned her on. Forest retreats to her were exotic. A soup line was a place of vanguard romance. The night that I typed the exam, the eve of our little anniversary of pain, I had an exam myself. At 4 PM I wrote the test for my students. I asked: "Why were the American Indians killed?" At 7 PM I typed an eleven page response to the question: "What role might Heaven serve in everyday life?" At ten-thirty I returned to my barred-in apartment to find that the heat had gone out. Upstairs, the couple above me fought, made love, and switched on the local news.

At midnight, I thought about Reviva. Street lights brushed the blinds. Her father flat in his blood on a rose quartz terrace. Cleaned up by Jews, or Poles, or gays. Trash. Her mother, her sister. The television above me switched off, their bed gave a settling creak. I slipped the last photo of Kara and me from my wall, laid the picture in an ashtray I used for change. A minor photo, taken by her mother, Kara and I arm and arm on the edge of Bryce Canyon, I liked it for the way she held me close. With a match from a red-boothed restaurant where she told me she loved me, I lit the photo, the surface curling and burning out, lit it again, and still again, held the match until my fingers burned. In the fire we melted into one. A friend once threw an ex-fiancee's photo into the ocean only to have it wash up ahead, into the path before him. A single ash floated up to the bedroom ceiling. I lay back in my bed to receive it.

On that anniversary morning, I focused on the tasks at hand, performed life with a utilitarian competence. Driving to school I bought a newspaper, forgetting the name of the news agent whom I saw every morning. At school, my class was waiting. I didn't risk a smile; I greeted them with a series of nods. Simon was there, gaunt, his desk pressed to the wall, but Micha, for the first time, was late. Their faces staring at me, I knew if I went to the men's room I would never return. Rabbi ran by, nervous, had no idea where Micha, his son, could be, wasn't in prayers, they had bicycled in together as always. The Rabbi's hands ran through his snowy beard, scared. My eyes feeling like I was punched, the room wavering. Waiting. Waiting: little Ory Melish, seventeen going on puberty, and Oscar Malik, two sandwiches shy of a delicatessen, his girth so large that his father had bought the school special desks; Aaron, leering, peeking out the window, hoping to catch a housewife bending over to pick up her morning paper, the kind of guy that would put mirrors on the tips of his shoes if anyone ever really did such a thing; and Simon folded in on himself, alone, holding the secrets of this day from all of us.

When the candles came in I was deep in a dream of her dragged to a pit's edge, naked. The dream flickered like newsreel.

I swallowed back bile and shook. Micha stood still in the doorway, holding a cake. Tu Bi Shvat, I remembered. Arbor day, a day of celebration. What the hell. I waved him in. He balanced the cake, kissed the mezuzah, pushed up his snotty round glasses and began to sing. It wasn't about trees. It was "Happy Birthday." He had bought the cake for Simon. The class joined in, their voices falling across Simon like petals.

Simon moved fast, uncoiled like a spring, his long legs hurtling him out the classroom door. His classmates scrambled to the windows to see, pressed around me as a horn blared, tires bit, and we charged out after him into the street.

A blonde, pinkish girl screamed out from her convertible Cabriolet. The frame around her license plate read "A D Phi or Die" and Simon lay across the blacktop, his hat thrown, a launched USC football bear face down at his side. "It's a rabbi!" she screamed. "I've killed a rabbi!"

We rushed out, ten of us, in black, charging across the street in a herd, Micha still holding the cake. Yaron held back traffic, Aaron rushed to Simon's side. Ory ran for an ambulance, Avi took down the license plate and make of the car. "I never saw him," she was shaking, her hair falling across Simon's face.

"Get away," Micha hissed. He set down the cake. "Somebody call my father."

Simon opened his eyes, wide, looked at the cake and smiled. "I'm OK." She screamed and kissed him. Micha pried her off. She kissed him, too. Her shoulders were bare in the sun. They lifted Simon to his feet, hugging him, patting him on the back. His jacket was torn, his tallith dangled. She began to cry, short spasms of fear belching out. She stood alone, unable to be touched.

Simon looked back at her. "Don't bother the Rabbi," he said.

At the curb, he sat. The others joined him, lined in a row.

The girl pulled her car to the side. Hip-hop still pounded from the speakers. Micha cut eleven cake pieces, passed them down the curbside.

She stood beside me. "I didn't know what happened." I thought of the singing. "I never saw it coming." I thought of the dream. "I couldn't help it. I couldn't stop." I thought of Kara and I wrapped between blankets, a human burrito on Del Mar beach, I thought of fire and gas and sunlight. I took the melted photo from my pocket and gave it to her. Ash streaked my hand. I felt ice cracking. A milk truck flattened the USC teddie. Mascara ran down her face.

Micha put his arm around Simon, the curbside buzzing with laughter as they sat in the LA sunshine, ten rabbis eating cake, a makeshift Kaddish for the living and the dead.

Aunt

•

Rebecca McClanahan

Maybe some of us were meant from the beginning to be aunts. Maybe we are too weak to bear the full weight of a child. How many times have I had this nightmare—a baby being sucked from my hands out an open window, and me left holding the sack of its nightgown. Maybe the powers-that-be give children to women who can survive the love, who know when to let go, who won't die if they suddenly find themselves holding an empty nightgown. My mother must have known from the start that I would never have children. I needed a guide for that other road, the road my mother had not taken, so she sent for Aunt Bessie.

Bessie was my grandmother's older sister and she arrived on schedule each time my mother gave birth. She wasn't particularly good with babies, but she was available. Grandma had the farm to keep up, chickens and geese and corn and cows and beans and horses to feed. Aunt Bessie was portable. Since she belonged to no one but herself, she could easily pull up stakes and join us for as long as my mother needed her. The way I saw it, she was created solely for our convenience. The night she arrived to help out with my baby sister, I was sitting cross-legged on my bed, reviewing the events leading up to World War II for the test the next day. When I heard gravel in the driveway, I walked to the window and lifted a slat on the Venetian blind. Dad was opening the door to the passenger side and from the light of the porch, I saw her emerge. In a few minutes she stood in the doorway of my room holding a brown suitcase, layered like an exiled Jew from the pages of my history book, her navy blue wool coat stuffed so tight that the buttonholes squinted. And as I watched, an amazing thing happened. She started out plump, then sweater by sweater, blouse by blouse, skirt by skirt, she shrunk until she stood before me, a humped scrawny sparrow of a woman in a brown taffeta dress with glittery buttons.

I ran into the kitchen where my mother was stirring a pot of stew, balancing my baby sister on her hip. "Why me?" I screamed. Mother just shrugged and smiled, as if that were answer enough.

"Why me? Why not Claudia or Jenny?"

"They're night owls, honey. Aunt Bessie's an early riser like you."

By the third day the battle lines were drawn. I divided the dresser. Lining the mirror on my side was a row of eight dolls which I dutifully dressed each morning, a three-tiered jewelry box that played "Around the World in Eighty Days," a cache of plastic pop beads and initial bracelets, a pair of clip-on earrings I was not yet allowed to wear, and a grainy five-by-seven of Ricky Nelson which I had scissored from Teen Magazine. On her side, under a yellowed doily, was everything she had unzipped from the satin pouch of her suitcase—a gold pocket watch, tweezers, a box of Polident, a framed picture of Lord Byron, a huge black purse with a clamp like an alligator's jaw, and a photograph of a sad young woman. My mother said it was Aunt Bessie's wedding picture, but I didn't believe it. I had seen plenty of wedding pictures—the bride radiant in a flouncy veil and pearls, her white-toothed groom bending over her as they cut the cake together, hand over hand, grinning into the camera.

No, I decided, the woman in this picture could not possibly be a bride. She was standing alone in a shapeless gown. Her head was bare, her hair yanked into a knot—not the silky chignon the women in Wagon Train wore—just a tight thin knot, without ribbon or other adornment. She was turned sideways, her head bent low, and she was holding—not a bridal bouquet with streamers—but one rose, drooping as if it were falling from her hand. My mother assured me there had been a husband and that he loved Aunt Bessie so much he built her a home in Stockwell, Indiana, with an oval window embedded in the front door, a home filled with beautiful things, like linen napkins pressed just so in the drawer of a heavy chest that stood in the entry hall. I didn't believe that either. "If Aunt Bessie was really married," I said, "where are the grandchildren?"

"She had one baby," my mother answered. "But it died a long time ago, long before I was born. " I could not imagine history that ancient.

By the third week I was wishing Aunt Bessie dead, or at least transported to my sisters' room. I hated her oldness — the swish of taffeta down the hall, the clonk of heavy heels, and the mechanical clack of her loose dentures. Over the years many dentists had tried, but Aunt Bessie had a crooked jaw, and when my father finally located a specialist and paid hundreds of dollars for two sets that actually fit, she lost them both — one in a field in Pennsylvania where we'd stopped to pick blackberries and one at sixty-miles-per-hour, in the cubicle bathroom of a Greyhound bus. Finally in desperation my father settled for an economy set. Every night I'd pull the covers over my head and try to sleep as she propped up a pillow, turned on the night light attached to the headboard, and clacked her way through National Geographic, Browning's last duchess, seed catalogs, fairy tales, detective magazines, Reader's Digest, whatever she could find. She always ended with Byron. She didn't read silently with her eyes like normal people, but she didn't exactly read aloud either. She simply moved her crooked jaw a little and whispered, just enough movement to set her dentures clacking. That was the last sound I heard at night.

And in the morning I'd wake to the fizz of Polident in a glass by the bed. I'd look up through bleary eyes for my first sight of the day — Aunt Bessie leaning at the waist and pouring her powdery breasts into a stiff brassiere. She'd stand by the mirror and pluck a stray whisker from her chin. This disturbed me: a woman with whiskers. And not only whiskers. All over her body, hair sprouted in unlikely places — from her nostrils, her ears — migrating from the places where I judged it should be, the places where it was just beginning on me. She never shaved her legs, yet they were smooth as the legs of a rubber doll. The pits of her underarms were hairless. Even her eyebrows were missing. She'd sketch them in each morning with a small black pencil that she kept rolled in a hankie. Old maid, I'd hiss beneath the covers. When she was gone, swishing down the hall, I'd crawl from bed and dress for school, where girls with real eyebrows were gathering in the halls.

I had long since given up my dolls, but every Sunday I volunteered to dress Aunt Bessie for church. She was the only grown-up small enough and old enough to be under my control. Looking back, I wonder why she let me use her. Maybe she liked the attention. Maybe the feel of young hands was so comforting that she bore the humiliation. I started with her hair. It was gray—not the silver floss of my grandmother nor the spongy blue-gray of widows whose hair is constructed each Saturday morning. Hers was the muddied gray of leftover snow. She'd lean over the kitchen sink and I'd lather up the Prell. Wet, her hair was fine as a baby's. Her scalp beneath my fingers was pink and exposed, and I could hardly stand to look at it. I'd squeeze the wet hair into a towel, then coerce a rattail comb through, making parts for the yellow rollers—a row down the center from her forehead to the nape of her neck. Then pin curls on each side, above her ears.

It was the year of dryer bonnets—my mother had gotten one for Christmas—so next she would be put under. I'd slide the plastic daisy bonnet onto her head and it would fall toward her eyes, over the scratchings of what was left of her eyebrows, their shapely arches having long since swirled down the drain with the Prell. I'd set the timer for ten minutes. With each minute, her face reddened and chapped and she talked louder and louder as if it were my ears that were covered. When the timer went off, I unrolled the curlers one by one and for a minute she was a Shirley Temple doll, the ringlets tight and shiny from the heat. Then the artistry, the teasing and back-combing at the crown to give her the fullness I'd seen in Ladies Home Journal. Then two curls on either side of her forehead, swirling inward like a ram's horns. "Cover your eyes!" I'd shout, and her hands would jump to her face while I sprayed Aqua Net until she choked and begged "No More!" I'd pat her hair, shoot one final spray, and she would smile. A little blush on her cheeks, a little pink lipstick. She'd replace the eyebrows herself while I held the mirror.

Her hands were strong and fearsome, the yellowed nails like talons curving in. The manicure was the final challenge: the taming of a wild thing. First I clipped the thick nails, then filed them into ovals. I rubbed cream into her hands and fingers. Her skin was thin, stretched over knuckles knotty as roots, nothing left but bone and gristle. I'd choose Avon, some childish pink or coral, and begin painting the nails. Two coats. Blow on them to dry. Then the dress. The black crepe or the navy blue taffeta? Maybe the white blouse with a cameo pin. I chose for this Sunday a flowery chintz my mother had made—pale green with yellow zinnias and a ruffled lace collar. "Fine," she said, and I slipped the dress over her head, over the safety-pinned strap of her brassiere and past her crooked hip. I zipped up the back and she was done.

I grew three inches that year, sailing past Aunt Bessie's lopsided shoulders. The waistbands of my dresses rose; saddle shoes that were fine one afternoon pinched my toes the next morning. I was Alice in Wonderland, a fever dream pulsing out of control. It didn't surprise my mother. "Kids grow at night," she said matter-of-factly. "That's why they wake up hungry. It's hard work." One night I woke with excruciating pain in my calves, as if my legs were being stretched on a rack. I kicked off the covers and grabbed my knees, pulling my calves in close. The night light switched on above my head and Aunt Bessie sat up, turning her face toward me. She was a drawing pad sketch, a gesture, a jot, the mere suggestion of a face. Eyebrows, teeth, the hair-sprayed pouf of morning hair, were missing. All that remained were her eyes, dark sockets that loomed huge and black without the softening frame of glasses.

She sighed a self-satisfied sigh, as if she'd been anticipating this moment all her life. "Growing pains," was all she said, yet even that was garbled, delivered, as it was, toothless. She creaked from her side of the bed and walked in the semi-darkness to my side. She rubbed her arthritic hands together. Carefully she folded back the covers and touched my shoulder, coaxing me to turn. Then she rummaged in the headboard shelf and I smelled wintergreen as she squeezed Ben-Gay onto her hands.

Why I gave in so easily, I still don't know. In daylight she was the last person I wanted, the last person I could have imagined touching me. I could have called for my mother; she surely would have come. But I was helpless in the pain and confusion of this newest trick my body was playing, and Aunt Bessie's hands went right for the hurting place. They kneaded and rubbed and tamed the pulsing muscles of my calves. Her yellowed knotted hands, the protruding veins, the fingernails I'd painted orange just that morning. She squeezed more ointment from the tube, warmed it between her palms, and began to rub my calves again. After awhile, the pain stopped. My tears stopped. And for the moment, at least, I stopped growing.

Nights when my husband is working, I drive across town to see my niece, delighting in the small hands running a brush through my hair or slapping red polish on my nails. "Walk on my back," I say, so I can feel her plump feet kneading the kinks. Sometimes at night I crawl into my nephew's bed and curl behind him, press into his warm back and touch his chest, feeling the heartbeat, holding my next breath until I feel his. Yesterday my niece called me into the bathroom to read her a "potty story" while she sat on the toilet. Her pudgy hands gripped the rim, and her training pants had slid to her feet. As I looked down, I saw that the skin of her thighs was translucent. Beneath it ran a fine river of blue vein. And last month when my nephew turned two, the outside world found him. It landed in dirt creases on the back of his neck. While I wasn't looking, he learned to sweat, and now instead of the powdery baby scent, his smell is the smell of a wet puppy.

This past summer I turned forty two. On my birthday, my

mother sent a leather diary marked 1897. It is Aunt Bessie's diary. In it are recorded the small moments of her seventeenth year. The handwriting is eccentric and unpredictable as she was, at times painstaking in its perfection, at other times scrawling and nearly illegible. There are entries of anger and self-pity, loneliness and disappointment, then sudden wild-geese flights of joy. She wishes for the words to come more easily. She longs for the power to express the sting of a sleigh ride, the red burn of sunset, the taste of oyster soup and apples. Usually she borrows the words of others, Longfellow and Byron mostly, only occasionally breaking into songs of her own, recalling the gleam of sun on a field "ridged with frost" or a sky "cloudless except for a few fleecy ones in the east." And as I read the diary, it begins to make sense—my hunger for words, my very choice of vocation. I want to thank her but she is not here.

The night nurse said she would call for us, the grand-nieces and -nephews, her voice down the hospital corridor unrolling our many names, beginning and ending with mine. She died alone, between shifts. A stranger dressed her and parted her hair and brushed rouge across her gray cheeks. She was buried on a muddy March afternoon, just a few miles from her birthplace. Now all these years later I hold her to me—a tribal instinct perhaps, to know our mother's sister, our father's sister, the sister of our grandmother. The bond without the bind. Or perhaps I simply want to give back some of the words to the young woman in the diary. I sit in my study where shelves of books line the green walls. I finger the dictionaries and search for what lies beneath: Aunt. From old French, *ante*, an offshoot, hall leading toward the main room. Latin root, *amma*: Mother. Or *amare*: to love. As in *amigo*, as in *amour*. As in amateur, one who works for the bare love of it.

The Holly Pageant

•

Lavonne Adams

Everything is ready. The fire trucks and ambulances have been moved outside, floors have been swept, chairs have been placed in orderly rows. At seven o'clock, the Holly Pageant is scheduled to begin.

Armed with a green metal cash box and a rubber stamp for the patron's hands, I take my seat behind the folding table to the left of the front door. I watch as the girls and their parents arrive, chattering excitedly, arms laden with garment bags, shoe boxes, makeup cases, curling irons. The mothers greet each other, size up the competition, push compliments from their tongues—"Oh, you look so pretty tonight!"—"What a beautiful dress!"—"I love what you've done to your hair!"

Barbara, one of the pageant organizers, arrives. She is in charge of acquiring the judges from the "Certified Judges List," a product of the judging seminars held every year in Raleigh. Each year, she assiduously sets the judge's table with a white tablecloth, glasses of water, and bowls of snack foods. When the judges arrive, she ushers them into the radio room where they remain sequestered until the pageant commences. She stands at that door, as anxious as a presidential bodyguard.

I have heard rumors of corrupt judges, bribed by overanxious mothers at other pageants, yet have been assured that these judges are not told the names of the contestants until they are handed the programs.

Barbara's four-year-old son runs up to her, yanks impatiently on her arm, whispers something in her ear. She glances around anxiously, frowns as she takes his hand, then

141

disappears in the direction of the bathroom. The inner sanctum has been left unguarded. I take advantage of the opportunity. Unobtrusively, I walk toward the radio room, cautiously turn the knob, ease open the door, and slip inside. The judges look up, startled . . . perturbed. Once I explain why I am interested in talking to them, they smile, settle back in their chairs, obviously relieved. They agree to let me interview them after the pageant. I slip back outside.

The Holly Pageant is a tradition in this small North Carolina town, a social event rivaled only by the yearly parish "reunion" at the town's largest Baptist church. The Holly Ridge Volunteer Fire Department and Rescue Squad officially adopted the pageant a few years ago, after a group of local citizens abandoned it. There was much debate that night. Since I was a new member, I felt unsure of my social standing, so kept my mouth firmly closed. The other female members had stars in their eyes, the men had dollar signs. "This," one of them declared, "could be financially rewarding." He saw it as a means of breaking the endless cycle of barbecue dinners and bake sales. He was proven right: the department cleared approximately $1,400 that first year.

The theme for this year's program is "Rock Around the Clock." Mounted on the wall directly opposite the front door is a large black and white poster featuring a caricature of two "jitter-buggers," the male sporting a fashionable crew cut, the pony-tailed female wearing a poodle skirt, bobby socks, and saddle oxfords. The stage is done in a '50's motif, a reminder of an age of American innocence. Black 45-rpm records and oversized red musical notes are plastered on the white walls. All the props are surrounded with a gold tinsel garland, the kind used to decorate Christmas trees. Everything is supposed to shine in the harsh white glare of the spotlights.

I hear music, applause, the introduction of this year's emcee, a popular local disc jockey. The entertainment is beginning.

"Notice how carefully she walks—so ladylike," says the emcee. She is referring to Tiny Miss contestant number two, who is meticulously placing one patent-leather clad foot in front of the other. With every step, her fluffy pink iridescent party dress shimmers.

The Tiny Miss contestants are three to five years old—there are four of them this year. Glenda, another of the pageant organizers, told me that there was no contestant number one; she dropped out after the third night of practice—simply refused to continue.

"It's time for our former Tiny Miss Holly to present her portrait to Chief Duane Longo. Duane?" calls out the emcee.

Traditionally, each of the outgoing queens presents the department with a framed photograph—twinkling eyes, smile, and crown preserved for posterity. Duane walks toward the stage, bouquet of roses lying awkwardly across his left arm. Each footstep resounds from the plywood platform that functions as the stage. The Tiny Miss Holly is staring at his knee caps. He kneels. They look at each other uncertainly for just a moment, then swap the flowers for the photo. The little girl wraps her free arm around his neck, briefly buries her face against his shoulder.

"Awww," I hear from a woman in the audience, "isn't that sweet!"

Duane leaves the stage a flattering shade of crimson.

The four Tiny Miss contestants return to the stage. One is hiding behind the emcee; the rest are waiting expectantly, anxious smiles frozen on their faces.

"And your new, 1991 tiny Miss Holly is contestant number . . . three!"

The audience cheers, screams, whistles. A crown is placed upon a small head.

"When she grows up," the emcee tells the audience, "she wants to be a cheerleader."

I remember when they crowned last year's Tiny Miss Holly. One contestant, who stood to the winner's right, folded her arms across her chest, stamped her foot, eyebrows lowered over a fierce angry glare, bottom lip stuck out petulantly. For just an instant, I feared for the physical safety of the new little queen, afraid the other girl was going to hit her. As the twinkling crown was placed carefully upon the winner's blonde curls, her competitor burst into tears.

"How embarrassing for her mother," whispered a voice in the crowd.

There is a brief intermission. I see one of the defeated Tiny Miss contestants standing next to the stage. She's surrounded by friends and family. Her father is talking softly to her as she hangs her head dejectedly. I move closer, catch the funereal tones of the adult voices as her parents pat her shoulder consolingly: "You looked real pretty, honey" — "You did a good job" — "You'll be ready for them next year."

The pageant continues with the introduction of the Little Miss contestants, ages six to nine, a bit older than the Tiny Miss contestants. These young girls appear on stage one at a time wearing incredible concoctions of satin, lace, taffeta, beads and rhinestones: fairy-tale visions from our youth. The women in the audience gasp, sigh, exclaim enthusiastically over the beauty of each dress. Contestant number one steps onto the stage wearing a stunning teal-green party dress, appliqued with a combination of rhinestones, pearls and sequins.

"Contestant number one," reads the emcee, "enjoys shrimping with her daddy."

I sit down in a chair recently vacated by one of the covey of visiting queens, winners of other local pageants. To my left sits a stately, composed woman who is scrutinizing the proceedings. I ask her if she is the mother of the queen whose seat I just appropriated. "No," she answers, pointing to yet another queen who is getting ready to entertain the crowd, "That's my daughter."

As we discuss pageants in general, I ask her about the cost of the clothing.

"You can't wear a sack, you know. This is based on more than talent and poise. You can put the most talented, beautiful girl up there, but if her dress is not competitive . . . well. . . ." She leaves the sentence unfinished, raises her eyebrows, looks at me knowingly. She then describes a dress she saw at another pageant: floor-length black velvet with white satin flowers, spaghetti straps, fifteen-dollar-a-yard rhinestone trim. Total cost, $2,500.

She points to the owner of that dress, who later entertains the crowd with a "Dixie/Battle Hymn of the Republic" medley. Tonight she is wearing a royal-blue sequined cocktail dress. I am disappointed that she has not worn the black gown, as I've never seen a dress that costs $2,500.

My curiosity piqued, I head backstage to track down the owner of the teal party dress. I walk into the combination meeting room and kitchen, now transformed into a massive dressing room; the smell of makeup, hairspray, perfume, and hot bodies hangs thick in the air. One teen contestant is in the kitchen area, practicing her tap routine on a sheet of plywood meant to protect the new linoleum floor, purchased with the proceeds from last year's pageant. I look around the room, searching for that particular child—or rather that particular dress—in the confusion. I spot her on the far side of the room. As I work my way toward her, I dodge the hyperactive contestants and the tense chaperons who dress the girls and have them on stage at all the appropriate times. Once I catch up to her, I ask the woman I assume to be her mother, "If it's not too personal, would you mind telling me how much you spent on that dress?" I pause to gauge her reaction, then add encouragingly, "It's absolutely gorgeous."

To the mother's right stands a woman who has been acknowledged periodically throughout the evening as being instrumental in helping several contestants with both their dance routines and their hairdos. She is dressed in a pink lace, pearl-studded tea gown, blonde hair and makeup flawless. The mother pauses uncertainly, looks to this woman for support.

"Why do you want to know?" the woman growls. A feral look comes into her eyes; her demeanor becomes aggressive, yet with an oddly defensive undertone.

I catch myself taking a step backward, totally unprepared for the hostility in her voice. I straighten my back, refuse to be intimidated, wonder if she thinks I'm a spy for a competitor. I explain. "I'm a writer. I'm working on a story."

I wait as she stares me up and down, then nods to the

mother before turning her back on me.

"Three hundred and fifty dollars," states the mother.

While Glenda stressed that this year's parents have not been as competitive as those in years past, by the time you figure in the costumes and the dance lessons, it's about a $2,000 per contestant investment. This year the pageant has a total of fifteen contestants.

Before the crowning of the new Little Miss, the former Little Miss makes her final appearance on stage. Tradition. With tears in her eyes, she waves farewell to their admirers. Well-wishers step forward with balloons and bouquets of flowers as a pre-taped message plays, "I want to thank God for giving me the opportunity to be Little Miss Holly . . . and to Uncle Roger for letting me use his Corvette to ride in the parades."

My daughter says that several years ago the winner of that year's Little Miss competition wore her full-length dress to school the first day after the pageant.

"And she wore her crown, too!" she adds emphatically.

"The sash?" I ask.

"Yep," she says. "Her Daddy stayed with her all day. He even spread out napkins across her lap at lunch. And her friends had to hold up her skirts during recess because the playground was muddy and the grass was all wet. But she still climbed on the monkey bars."

We have another brief intermission, then the visiting queens go up on stage one by one to introduce themselves. Our newly crowned Tiny Miss and Little Miss are allowed to join the throng. When the Tiny Miss steps up to the microphone, she says, "Hi, I'm . . ." She panics, has obviously forgotten what to say, looks around like a cornered mouse. "Mommy!" she calls out in a frightened voice. Her mother steps up to the stage with an indulgent smile and prompts her daughter. The little girl returns to the microphone and announces her name.

Glenda chuckles, "If that wasn't precious!"

Most of the older girls, the Pre-teens and the Teens, have been in pageants before. They're familiar with the routine, know all the ins and outs, understand how to play up to the judges, an art in itself.

146

Teen contestant number one, for instance, seems to be a house favorite. She does a clogging routine entitled "Texas Tap" that brings down the house. Her talent is undeniable, her exuberance contagious. I find myself smiling and clapping in time to the music along with the rest of the audience. Unfortunately, when it comes time for her prepared speech, this contestant forgets what she was going to say, stumbles verbally. She mumbles, "Oh God," then continues the best she can.

A young woman on my right shakes her head, turns to me and says with resignation, "She would have had a hard time, anyway. Her gown is red."

My face must reflect my bewilderment.

"With her red hair?" she adds with implied significance.

Obviously, the contestant is unenlightened. Redheads don't wear red. *Faux pas.* One just doesn't do these things.

Some rules in the pageant circle are even more specific. Wearing black shoes with the evening gown is forbidden, as are hats, parasols, and elbow-length gloves. Rules are rules. I have heard that one mother, in another pageant, tried to add an extra row of lace to her daughter's socks. It was specified that only two rows of lace would be allowed. The pageant's organizers solemnly handed this mother a seam-ripper.

According to Glenda, this pageant has done away with collective judging, the commonly accepted practice of simultaneously lining up the girls on stage, having them turn, pose in front of the judges. "We don't want them compared to one another. They stand on their own merit."

Teen contestant number one does not win.

The pageant over, I weave through the departing crowd toward the radio room, anxious to talk to the judges. There is a long line. Accompanied by their mothers, the contestants are each given the opportunity to discuss her performance with the judges, find out what cost her the competition, where she lost those valuable points. It is a quiet cluster.

To my left stands one of the winners. Her mother is not waiting with her, not monitoring her behavior. One of her friends walks by, teases, "Hey, you won this year. Why are *you* waiting to see the judges?"

147

This victor smiles, puffs out her chest with pride, swings her right hand up to her forehead. She nods toward the closed door. "I just want to tell them . . . (with a saucy salute) . . . thanks!"

A mother and her daughter, one of the defeated contestants, try to slip past unnoticed. Another mother looks up, asks, "Aren't you going to conference with the judges?"

"No, I'm afraid I might start crying," the first mother answers. Her daughter says nothing, but her eyes are red.

After a thirty-five minute wait, I am finally able to talk to one of the judges, a man named John. He's wearing a black tuxedo, sporting a diamond stud in his ear, has a red carnation pinned to his lapel. He's a hairdresser, has done hair for lots of the pageants — that's how he got "hooked." Most of the judges, he explains, become involved when either friends or their own children enter a pageant. These judges don't get paid for their work; instead, they receive a small gift.

"Why do you do it, then?" I ask.

"I like to see the girls have a good time," he answers.

Every year I'm asked if I'm going to enter my two little girls in the pageant. Every year I say no.

"Mommy," asks the younger, "don't you think I'm pretty enough to win?"

Angel

•

Jim Clark

"Call her Angel, for she is not of this world." The words are blurred and blue, from a long ago time when I inexplicably decided that using my father's leaky old pump fountain pen would somehow enhance my writing. It is a line of bad poetry, from a poem never finished, from sometime around 1974. Although I am constitutionally unable to keep an ongoing diary or journal, lacking the requisite discipline, or audacity, as it may be, to scrupulously chronicle my daily portion of trash and treasure, I have, through the years, kept "notebooks." These are random and chaotic affairs, a lot like life, really, begun and abandoned willy-nilly as the vice of writing alternately tightened and loosened its grip on me. Leafing through them I find, not unexpectedly, but nevertheless much to my dismay, that most of the entries now strike me as the mental equivalent of butt scratching, such as, for instance, this one, circa 1977: "Dental appointment today — still no cavities. I wonder what it would be like to lose all your teeth?" If I were inclined to be charitable, I might find in this whimsical commonplace some inchoate revery upon mortality and the betrayal of the body, but I think not. It is simply an idle thought, barely conscious. And I wrote it down.

What has driven me here, to my old upstairs room in my parents' house where the antique steamer trunk containing these faded notebooks still sits, solitary, below the dormer window, is a song. Not a new song, recently heard, but an old song. One my friend Ben and I used to harmonize on in the cramped but acoustically perfect kitchens of late night North Carolina parties as they wound down and dwindled to only the

149

faithful and the beloved. Old song, new circumstance. The song is Townes Van Zandt's "Two Girls," with its spare chorus:

I've got two girls
One in heaven, one below,
One do I love with all of my heart
But one I do not know

Growing up, I spent most of my summers at my grandparents' farm at Black's Fork, a green and hilly east Tennessee mountain community near the Kentucky border that had managed, for the most part, to escape the calculated catastrophe wrought by the Cove Hollow Dam in the early 1940's. Even though I lived in Hunter's Point, a small town about fifteen miles from Black's Fork, my childhood memories are almost all of Black's Fork. And of two girls: Sarah Meachum, daughter of an elder of the Amish community near Oneida, and Angel — Angela — Rivers, whom I have just learned has died, with her husband and his white supremacist group, in a shootout with the FBI somewhere in Idaho.

How can I tell you about Angel? "Not of this world," I said. True enough, but worldly, just the same. She possessed a sort of feral beauty — "Wild Child" I would sometimes call her, after a song by The Doors. Here we are, then, Angel and I, age thirteen or thereabouts, sitting on a hard pine pew at the Wednesday night service of the Black's Fork Church of Christ. I have the aisle seat, and she sits next to me wearing something simple and white and flowing (her mother's touch, who thought it appropriate for a young lady to wear white to church), her long brown hair with a cheap rhinestone comb at the side and smelling of corn husks and honeysuckle, as it always did. We are sitting about halfway back, and it is late June, the windows open, the ceiling fans slowly, silently mixing the smell of new cut grass and the rhythmic, wave-like whir of tree frogs, congregated along the banks of the Olney River, just fifty yards or so beyond the church's twin outhouses, on the side opposite the graveyard. Sterling Simpson, the song leader, has risen from the front pew, and, smoothing his silver hair, calls out a page

150

number from the hymn book. Amid the requisite coughing and clearing of throats, Angel whispers: "Between the sheets. Say 'between the sheets' after the song title." I look down at my lap, at number 74 of *Christian Hymns, Number Two.* "I Am Coming, Lord," it says. I glance up at number 73, "Let Him Have His Way with Thee." I can feel my face burning, my sides starting to heave. Thankfully, Bertie Simpson, Sterling Simpson's wife, is sitting a little ways down from us on our pew. Her ineluctable alto, a shade flat, soldiers on, hiding my snorts, chuckles, hiccups. Her bulk bulwarks our pew, which doubtless otherwise would be shaking. Hoping for some respite, I look at the facing page, number 75: "How Shall the Young Secure Their Hearts?" (between the sheets), I read. This is one too many for me.

I'm not even sure I'm laughing anymore. I'm not sure what I feel. I get up and make my way down the aisle and out the back door. My grandmother gives me a puzzled, concerned look as I pass. A few minutes later, the service over, Angel and I are sitting on the river bank, listening to the tree frogs, and the current, like always, sluicing down towards Hunter's Point.

"You shouldn't have done that." I poke her with my elbow.

"What?"

"You know what. That 'between the sheets' thing. I had to leave."

"That's your problem." She smiles, and I think her dark eyes glittered in starlight.

* * *

Throughout Junior High I saw less of Angel. We had attended the same rural grade school, but now, thrown together in the Corbin County Junior High School with students from the six city and community schools, we drifted apart. I made new friends, most from the Hunter's Point city schools, and spent much of my time practicing my bass clarinet with the Junior High Band, and riding bikes all over Hunter's Point with my new friends. Angel stuck with a small group of Black's Fork students which dwindled rapidly, some dropping out of school in the seventh or eighth grades, a few ending up in the regional juvenile detention center twenty miles away in Bankston. Her father never allowed her to attend many school or social functions. She was well-endowed for a girl her age, and her full, sensual lips and upturned nose, coupled with the crowd she ran with, caused people to talk. "She's easy," some said. Others, "She'll be rocking a cradle before ninth grade." Ugly rumors dogged Angel Rivers. Although I could never say with certainty, later, after she left town, what was what, I knew that these rumors were untrue, and I said as much. "Oh, lighten up, Carter," my friends said. "Don't take it so personal. You county people all have a chip on your shoulder."

One day, near the end of the ninth grade school year, Angel stopped me in the hall. "Bobby, I need to talk to you," she said. The words caught in her throat, came out in a choked whisper. That, and the jittery look in her eyes, made me think maybe it was something to do with Tommy Hagen, her boyfriend of nearly a year. I'd known Tommy all my life, and while he was still in school, and had so far managed to avoid the juvenile detention center, he had a bad temper and was often in detention for fighting. He had been held back in school a couple of years, and was older than us.

That Friday there was no school because of a state-wide teachers' meeting. My father, who was the county agent for Corbin County, said he had to drive out to Black's Fork that day on business and would give me a ride out to my grandparents.

* * *

The gray sky of this April morning is clearing, and, as I top the graveyard hill and walk past the church, down toward the river, pieces of blue sky appear, and fingers of sunlight stretch down away across the valley. Angel is already there, smiling, but still with that nervous and edgy look. She pats the dry pine needles beside her. "Sit down," she says, and I do.

We talk for awhile about nothing in particular, about ball games, and dances, about the few people we still know in common. Every time I look at her, she turns away, stares at the ground, and I'm trying to figure out what's going on with her, so I say, "What is it, Angel? What's wrong? Is it Tommy?"

"Tommy?" she says, startled.

" Well, I mean, he does have a temper. I thought maybe . . ."

"Oh, god, Bobby. No. No, it's not Tommy. I only wish it was something like that. Are you jealous?" she teases, and her face brightens, momentarily. She gives me a quick smile, and it makes me shiver. I hug myself, and now it's my turn to stare at the ground.

"So, what is it then?"

"It's . . . It's my daddy, Bobby. My daddy . . . he . . . he's took a shine to me." It came tumbling out, all jagged and full of holes, like she needed a breath after each word. "Me and Tommy's leavin' for Knoxville, next week, for good. I just wanted to tell you goodbye. That, and to ask if I can count on you to help us if we need you. Say you will, Bobby."

"Sure. Sure," I say again. I'm fifteen years old, and what I know of the world is how to fix a broken bicycle chain, how to pitch a curve ball, how to drive a Farmall Cub tractor, how to play a pattern of sixteenth notes on the bass clarinet in perfect time. I understand her words, but put together this way, I do not know what they mean. But I can tell you something about Angel's daddy.

* * *

"Ol' Fate Rivers, now *there's* a piece of work!" my grandfather would always say. He cherished the story of how Fate Rivers had come to be appointed to the Corbin County Rescue Squad, and he loved to mimic Fate's telling of the story.

"Ol' Fate, he come by here one Sunday afternoon," the story begins, "just a-grinnin' like a possum. He was so tickled with hisself he just couldn't stand it. So I asked him, 'What do you know, Fate?' And he draws up a long breath and commences to stutter and twitch, and he fairly hollers at me, even though I'm sittin' right next to him in this very rocking chair—that's just how he does, he don't talk, he hollers—anyway, he says 'Weeellll . . . I'll tell you, M-M-Mr. T-T-Terry . . . '—just like that— 'uh, I was uh out on the lake last night uh with uh Ch-Ch-Champ Cooper and uh Willy Malone a-drankin', uh, just a-drankin' and a-fishin' . . .' Well, anyway, they was out on Will Malone's flatboat, over around Thurmond's Cove, doin' a lot more drinkin' than fishin', I'd say, when all of a sudden, ol' Fate he begins to get sick to his stomach. Well, he leans over the rail, and like he says 'I t-t-tell you Mr. Terry, I m-m-most puked up my guts.' And Champ and Will they come over to him with their flashlights, to see if he's OK, and danged if Will don't look down and see some polka dot cloth hangin' on an old log floatin' out there. Turns out it's the little Johnson girl that'd went missin' a week or so before. She'd got down there to the lake and drowned. 'So, uh, Champ and Willy, uh th-th-they says to me uh F-F-Fate, how'd you like to be a f-f-full-fledged member of the C-C-Corbin County Rescue Squad? And uh they uh sweared me in uh r-r-right there in the b-b-boat!' Why, I reckon he's found two or three other bodies that way since then. Kinda like a water witcher, I guess, only he pukes when he's around a dead body."

* * *

LaFayette "Fate" Rivers and his wife Anna Mae lived (perhaps still do live, for all I know) in a one bedroom, tumbledown, wood-frame shack, set up on rock legs, at the top of the Fire Tower Road hill, between my grandparents' house and the Black's Fork Church of Christ, off highway 53. He was a small, stoop-shouldered, ferret-like man who spoke (as my grandfather's story amply demonstrates) with a loud, grating, high-pitched stutter. He bore a remarkable resemblance, both in features and in behavior, to the character of Ernest T. Bass, on the old *Andy Griffith Show,* a fact my father, especially, found endlessly amusing. Besides his talent for finding dead bodies, he was also a voracious, though entirely undiscriminating, reader, with, I suspect, something close to a photographic memory. He would read anything and everything he could get his hands on—someone once gave him an old set of *World Books,* and he read them, cover to cover, and would, with no

154

provocation whatsoever, send any gullible listener spiralling down a meticulous, factual, maddening, labyrinth of digression. He also read novels, science fiction, supermarket tabloids, religious tracts—all, equally, with the firm conviction that if it had found its way into print, it was true. He, unlike his wife and daughter, attended church only sporadically, and, usually about once a month, would "come forward" at Brother Lambert's invitation at the end of his sermon, and confess that he had, as he put it, "strayed from the straight and narrow." This became so irritatingly predictable that Brother Lambert finally had to gently insist that he decide once and for all whether he was going to do right or wrong.

Anna Mae, his wife, was a large, shapeless woman with coarse dark hair and a doughy face, whose few remaining teeth were crooked and black. She could neither read nor write, and was obscurely afflicted with "nerves," for which she daily swallowed a fair handful of pills and capsules, provided her by the doctors at the regional mental health center in Hunter's Point, where she was periodically a resident. At my grandfather's funeral, she collapsed into hysterics, taking down a whole wall of banked flowers and wreaths when she fell, kicking and moaning, and mightily upsetting both my mother and grandmother, as well as angering my father considerably.

They were both compulsive packrats—he, with his books and papers, she with various blankets and articles of clothing people had given them—and the couple of times I was inside their house, I wondered how anyone could live in such a dark, smelly, claustrophobic place. Angel was their only child; she slept on the couch, having no room for herself. Such as they were able, Fate and Anna Mae doted on her. They saw that she attended school, church, and despite their own personal appearances and that of their house, saw to it, in an almost obsessive way, that she always looked as though she had just stepped out of a 1950's *Glamour* magazine, and not their pitiful little shack. Angel never talked much about them, although when she did, it was with a kind of detached, bemused affection.

* * *

155

For about as long as Angel had been seeing Tommy Hagen, I had been deeply and clandestinely involved with Sarah Meachum, from the Amish community. Well, "deeply" in an adolescent sort of way—all pining and longing, our love was a ragged landscape of hormonal peaks and valleys that we willed into being instant by instant and sustained by the intensity of our combined imaginations. In reality, we had spent probably no more than a handful of hours together, owing to the insularity of the Amish and her highly visible position as the oldest daughter of the ranking elder. So, clandestinely, yes. Sarah was old enough, though, and her father trusted her enough, that she was allowed to run errands, some of which took her all the way into Hunter's Point. We would meet wherever and whenever we could, for however many minutes we had, and were aided and abetted in our assignations by Terry Stone, the rural mail carrier who delivered the mail to the Amish community, and who, although in his late twenties, loved to relive his glory days by attending the Junior and Senior High ball games, and generally hanging out with us and being our idol and mentor. Sarah collected the mail from him, and we could pass messages that way.

Although I was very nervous about it, she had been pushing me to take her out on my father's motorboat, which he kept in a slip at the Cove Hollow boat dock. For one thing, my father had only allowed me to take the boat out without him a couple of times, and for another, I simply could not imagine what Elder Meachum might do or say, to Sarah or to me, if he found out. Nevertheless, she would have her boat ride. Saturday, the day after my conversation with Angel, I was to meet Sarah at 2:30 in the afternoon at the restaurant of the Cove Hollow boat dock, where she would be delivering butter and eggs from the Amish community.

* * *

I am sitting in a red vinyl booth, vaguely nauseous from nervousness and the smell of spoiled milk and the grease they deep-fry the fish in. I look at my watch for the twentieth time in about as many minutes and distractedly flip through the

156

jukebox song selection box attached to the wall by the booth. As I try to slow down on my second coke, I debate putting in a nickel and playing either Creedence Clearwater Revival's "Green River," or the Rolling Stones' "Honky Tonk Women," but before I do, the door opens to sunshine, April wind, and Sarah, standing there a little tentatively, with a basket on her arm. She turns around and I follow her out the door.

My father's boat is a small, aqua runabout with dark blue trim and a 60 horsepower Mercury outboard. It will pull two skiers, if you know what you're doing, but compared to some of the speedboats in the slips, it's a fishing boat. We slowly head out of the dock, past the "No Wake" buoys, and I rev it up a notch or two. Sarah, still standing, almost falls backwards from the sudden acceleration, but defiantly regains her equilibrium and shoots me an irritated look, like it was something I planned to do. She sits down beside me and starts undoing the braid of her honey-colored hair, carefully putting the hairpins in her breast pocket. So this is it, I think, the motorboat, the wind in her hair, just like she's talked about so many times. I give it a little more gas and put my arm around her as we fly by the cliffs at Puckett's Camp on our right. God, this is great.

I know we don't have much time, so I head right over to Thurmond's Cove, which is pretty and quiet and not too far away. It being April, we are almost alone on this part of the lake. In the middle of Thurmond's Cove I cut the power and we sink down, drift forward a bit, and then stop, rocking on our wake. We're quiet for awhile, and I hear a crow caw and, straight ahead, see a buzzard circling above Baptist Ridge.

"What *would* your father do if he knew we'd been out here together?" I ask.

"Don't even think that, Bobby. I honestly have no idea."

"Well, I mean, we're not really doing anything *wrong*."

"H'm," she says, and wrinkles her nose in a way I love. "'Wrong . . .' Bobby, according to my father, this *motorboat* is 'wrong.' Much less me being here with you, an outsider. I don't know. I dearly love my father, and I respect him, but I just don't know. I've never told anybody this, but when I was younger, I used to halfway believe that I was an orphan baby someone left

157

with my parents to raise. That's ugly, I know."

She turns away and looks out at the lake, just as an army-green bass boat slowly rounds the point and cruises towards us. Even from this distance I can tell it's Champ Cooper's boat with its little blue rescue squad light revolving. A second later, and I make out the features of Fate Rivers, perched in the fishing chair, his knees up at his chest, peering down at the water like some bird of prey.

As they get closer, Champ Cooper's voice booms out, "Ho, there! Carter, ain't it? Who's that with you?" We're almost side-by-side now, and I see the look of disbelief on his face as he recognizes Sarah and says "God above and all his angels! Ain't you Elder Meachum's girl?" Sarah turns her face and looks away.

"Well, I reckon they's just no tellin' who you're bound to run into out here on a pretty spring day, eh Will?" The leer in his voice is unmistakable. The other man, whom I now recognize as Will Malone, lowers his head and chuckles.

"So, y'all seen anything out here?" Cooper says.

"Like what?"

"Well, seein' as how we're out here in the rescue squad boat, with our light a-goin', I'd say like maybe a dead body floatin' around?"

"I hadn't heard about anybody dead or missing lately."

"Probably not. But then you ain't on the rescue squad, neither, are you?" Even though I had never had any opinion one way or another about Champ Cooper, I was growing to dislike him more and more.

"No, we haven't seen anything like that. Who is it?"

"Well, I reckon I can tell you, since it'll probably be in the evenin' paper. We have reason to believe Tommy Hagen's drowned."

His words hit me like a stomach punch. Then, just as I'm about to ask how come they thought Tommy had drowned, Fate Rivers jumps up from his perch, and, glaring at me, hollers out, with not even a trace of a stutter, "You stay away from my Angel, boy! Don't you go puttin' no goddam ideas in her head. If you know what's good for you you won't come around no

158

more, you hear?" Both Cooper and Malone seem startled by his outburst. And probably, like me, amazed that he didn't stutter. Never in my wildest flights of fancy had I ever conceived of Fate Rivers as being even remotely dangerous. It seems, all of a sudden, like I have a lot to think about.

"Bobby, let's *go.*" Sarah is tugging at my jacket and crying, maybe, although it's hard to tell, what with the wind and the sunlight glinting off the lake.

"Well, you let us know if you see anything," Champ Cooper says, as I gun it toward the boat dock. Sarah looks scared and sad on the way back, and we don't say much as I call Terry Stone for a ride and leave her waiting there for one of the other elders who's to pick her up in his wagon in a little while.

I tell Terry about what happened, about Tommy, and we ride out to Black's Fork, to the Rivers' shack. Anna Mae is there, but she's having one of her spells and I can't get a thing out of her All she does is wail and blubber and say "No . . . Noooo . . . Noooooo!" I decide it's time to get the hell out of there before Fate shows up.

* * *

The next day they found Tommy Hagen's body, in the backwater near the cliffs at Puckett's Camp. Doc Walker, the county coroner, said he had a concussion, but he couldn't say whether he had died from that or from drowning. Most people figured he'd just hit a rock or something diving from the cliffs, which he and his buddies liked to do. I never was so sure. I talked with some of his friends, later, and they said he wasn't at the cliffs that day. They said he was working on his car, getting it ready for him and Angel to drive to Knoxville.

I tried and tried to get in touch with Sarah, but Terry said some other girl had started picking up the mail. Then, finally, a couple of weeks later, he gave me a note she'd given him. It wasn't much, and it didn't really sound like her, although it was her writing. She said she was OK, and not to worry, and that she was sorry but she couldn't see me anymore, and for me not to try to see her. I thought about it for a long time. I was crazy about her. In the end, though, I just let it go. I don't know, maybe if I'd been older, or braver, or something. It seems to me now that a lot of things in life are that way. Something terrible happens, and you never know exactly why, and it just turns you inside out, and you feel like you've got to do something, anything. But you don't know what to do. You don't know where to begin. And so finally you just let it go, and get on with your life. Choices and consequences were not clear to me then, and are no clearer to me now. I had hoped to find a certain wisdom with age, but what I've found is only more paradoxical choices, more inexplicable consequences. I wonder, do you finally reach a limit of how many things like that you can carry around in your head?

Angel had disappeared, too. I figured she had probably gone to Knoxville on her own, and, a few months later, I learned from some of Tommy's friends that that was so. Over the next couple of years, various stories circulated about Angel. That she was arrested as an accessory to armed robbery when the Knoxville police found her asleep in the back seat of a car belonging to two guys who had just robbed a 7-11 store. That she was arrested in a drug bust at a house where she had been staying. I suppose these stories were true, but I'm convinced that Angel had nothing directly to do with any of those things, just the rotten luck of being in the wrong place, with the wrong people. Or no, not bad luck, exactly. Some deadly, unerring affinity pulled Angel toward the violent, the careless, the destructive. And now this. FBI, shootout, white supremacists. Jesus. Angel Rivers is dead.

* * *

"Why is it I have the feeling I'm saying goodbye to a whole lot more than just my grandmother?" I'm sitting, cross-legged, in front of the open steamer trunk, a spiral notebook with a manilla cover with AUBURN UNIVERSITY printed on it in Old English letters in my lap. The page is dated February 12, 1987, the day of my grandmother's funeral. That was a hard day for me, I'll admit. But I'm OK with it now. I won't be going to your

160

funeral, Angel. I don't even know where it'll be. So I guess this is it. Goodbye, Grandma. Goodbye, Black's Fork. Goodbye, Angel. I'll see you in heaven. I swear I think we all get there eventually.

Riding in the cramped Chevrolet in the funeral procession that day with the other pall bearers—my father, my brother, my brother-in-law and two cousins—I realized that this was the first time I'd been back to Black's Fork since the North/South highway had opened. Nothing looked familiar. The big four-lane went straight over the hollers, blasted right through the hills. Occasionally I could see curvy, dilapidated sections of old highway 53 to the left and to the right. I looked to my left and saw a majestic, bare old sentinel of a tree standing atop a hill. "Where are we?" I said. And my father said, "That's the old sweetgum on the hill behind your grandma's house." We were behind my grandparents' farm; highway 53 ran in front. And that's when it hit me—Black's Fork didn't exist anymore. Not for me anyway. It was just a few rugged, hilly miles between Hunter's Point and the Kentucky border.

I sat up front that day, which I never did before, at the Black's Fork Church of Christ. Although it was a mild Sunday afternoon, and I'm sure everyone who was able, came, the church was barely half-full, and that included a lot of family and friends from elsewhere. When the time came for the processional before the open casket, Sterling Simpson, small and old inside a suit a couple of sizes too big, struck his tuning fork, gave the congregation their notes, and voices, old and cracked, but resolute, began the song my grandmother had requested: "Beyond this land of parting, losing and leaving,/Far beyond the losses darkening this . . ." And it seemed to me, as those old folks I knew so well slowly rose and shuffled by the casket, each with a downcast look of infinite tenderness for their sister, my grandmother, it seemed to me they were no longer human, had shed the wrinkled, saggy, bird-like skin of their humanness, and were passing, one by one, out into the dim, cold light of heaven.

Lovers

•

Richard Krawiec

I could just die, the girl said. She lay her head on the neck rest of the car seat, and opened her wide mouth to the scorching air. She was only fifteen, but her skin was drained-looking. Veins showed on her eyelids and at her temples. Her limp brown hair was trapped between her back and the vinyl seat. Sweat clung to her face and neck like another layer of skin.

Her boyfriend, a stocky sixteen-year-old as dull-eyed as a bulldog, looked at her with dim-witted fear, like a pilgrim watching a miracle fade. You bleeding again? he asked.

The girl moved her head lazily forward. Honey, what do you keep bringing that up for? I told you that stopped. She was wearing a tight dungaree mini-skirt, her legs bare, and she reached under the skirt, poked her fingers inside her panties, then brought them up before her face. She sniffed at them. I told you before, forget all about that. I'm all right, she said. It's just the heat.

She looked ahead. They were parked on the sandy shoulder of a straight, narrow state road somewhere in eastern North Carolina. The asphalt was a simmering white. Fields on both sides were full of cornstalks, brown and brittle-looking. They'd been driving for two days and the boy had no more idea how close they were to Florida than when they'd started. Maybe we should just go home, I don't want nothing to happen, he said.

It already happened. God, she said. When you talk like that I think maybe my mother was right, you are stupid.

He clicked the key to accessory to check the gas - 1/4 tank. Then he dragged the thin wad of sweat-dampened bills from his dungaree's pocket. When he cranked open the door, the girl slid across the seat towards him. She grabbed his arm and said, Where you going?

Check the ice, he said.

Don't leave me here, she said.

He gave her a crazy look, then slipped outside, leaving the door open. She leaned back and chewed on the nails of her left hand. Her fingers were already raw from chewing.

The boy watched the girl watch him out the back windshield until he popped the trunk open and the black underside of it blocked out her face. A blue Colman cooler sat in the bed of the trunk, surrounded by empty plastic bottles which once contained rubbing alcohol. The seams of the cooler were split. Yellow insulation showed through.

He held his head back as he opened the lid. Keeping his eyes closed, he craned his neck forward as slow as a slug extending and sniffed. The odor wasn't as bad as he'd feared. He decided to look. Most of the ice had melted and the thing was turning blue-black. It was her word; thing.

He shut the lid, hafted the cooler onto the trunk rim, and tilted the spigot side towards the ground. But the contents thudded against the lowered side, and the boy's stomach grew so queasy he couldn't move.

He heard a car coming. He turned and stared like an animal transfixed by headlights. An old gray pick-up truck approached and, through his fear, the boy wished it would stop, so this whole thing would be over. But the pick-up drove past, wisps of sandy dust puffing from its bed in a plumed wake. He watched it disappear into the shimmering horizon before he returned the cooler to the trunk.

We need to stop again, he said.

Honey, I been thinking, the girl said. She watched his arms tense on the wheel. I'm tired of this honey. Let's just go home. Let's just turn around and go home, or else rob someplace. She gnawed at a finger and spit a bit of skin onto the dashboard. I mean, somebody has got to owe us something and it's our right to take it. What was the point of going through all this for nothing? Her reedy voice rose hysterically and her bulging, egg-shaped eyes seemed on the verge of popping out of her delicately-boned face. She shifted in her seat, feeling her dampness against the vinyl. If we had some money we could celebrate something, she said. Despite the heat and the fact they were parked just off-road, she bent her head to his lap and did exactly what she knew she had to to get him going.

They parked on the dry clay drive behind the convenience store. The boy went in alone first. He returned with two bags of ice and six bottles of rubbing alcohol. The girl stood beside the trunk, opening the caps on the bottles while the boy told her the layout inside. He drained a minute's worth of murky, foul-smelling liquid out of the cooler, then shook the alcohol into the cooler and dumped in the ice.

After he locked the trunk, he urinated on the white-painted cinderblocks of the building. The girl pulled aside her panties and squatted beside him. He looked at the threads of blood in her rapidly-drying puddle as she scouted around for something to use as a weapon. But there were only empty cardboard boxes and small piles of garbage here and there among the weeds which grew against the foundation.

He had trouble pulling up his zipper, and she fixed it for him, saying, You got strong hands, we don't need no weapon. She took him by the elbow and led him through the blistering sunlight to the front. They were sweating so much it looked like they'd just been dunked in a baptism.

Oh Lord, she said, this is heaven. She stood just inside the door and spread her arms and legs as if floating on the cool air. She told the man behind the counter, If I could, I'd rob you of this air-conditioning. You oughtta bag and sell it.

He was a man of fifty, dumpy and unhealthy looking, though his skin was thick and red. His face was all lumps and jowls and on his head thin wisps of greasy white hair were combed straight back. He recognized the boy, who was shifting nervously from foot to foot. The man stepped closer to the register and reached one hand beneath the counter.

The girl pretended not to notice. She tossed her hair over one shoulder and smiled. Rolling each slim hip forward, she sauntered towards the register. She gathered her hair and rolled it into a bun atop her head. Then she let it fall and shook it loose.

A few strands fell across her eyes. She smiled at the man, and when he smiled back, revealing that he had two crooked bottom teeth and no more, the girl called to the boy, Now honey.

The boy stepped forward and threw a lazy, looping punch at the man. He missed and his forearm hit the counter. The man stepped back, hands raised before his face, and caught the boy's second punch on his arms.

Hit him, hit him goddamn it, the girl screamed. What's the matter with you? The boy stepped back and stared at her. She lifted a jar of pickled eggs from the counter and threw it into the man's stomach. The jar spilled, but didn't break, when it hit the floor, the pickled eggs rolling out as if with intent. The girl grabbed the boy's arm and pulled him to the counter. He swung at the man again and missed.

Here now, the man said, I ain't fighting ya. He punched open the register and started fumbling out bills. Here's the twenties, he said. Here's the tens, here's the fives, here's the ones. He piled everything on the counter and started pulling out rolls of coins.

The girl pushed the boy forward. This is a robbery damn it, she told the boy, now act like it. The boy braced himself with one hand and swung wildly with the other.

This is just a job, the man said, ducking back. Take it. He pulled out the register tray and dumped the whole thing on the counter. His face had darkened to purple and he rubbed at his heart. Finally the boy was able to latch onto one of the man's arms. He yanked the man forward, so that the man's face was on the counter, and punched him in the back.

The man raised his head and howled.

The girl ran around behind the counter. The boy held the man down with one hand and looked at her. Don't stop, she told the boy, we're still robbing him.

The boy and the man looked at each other and the girl stooped to look along the shelf under the register. She found the gun and stood up.

Oh no, the boy said, releasing the man, who stayed down on the counter and watched the girl over his shoulder.

Shut up, the girl told the boy. We're the ones in charge here.

165

She pointed the gun at the man, but couldn't move the trigger. She shook it. Then she poked the barrel in the man's face and said, This don't work.

He pointed out the safety to her and she thanked him.

She flicked off the safety and raised the gun again. She backed out of the aisle to the front door, where she stopped and fired. The kickback sent her flying into the plate glass window. She hit and slid to the floor and when she got up the man was moving his mouth like a fish on sand. There was a trickling sound and she looked past him, to see the shattered bottles of pop on the top shelf of the aisle behind the counter.

Her head felt dizzy, like it was full of smoke. Her body seemed to be spilling out of her. She started to cry, but pinched her nose to make herself stop.

The man swept the money into a brown bag. He helped the boy pull her up. Give him five dollars, she told the boy. When he hesitated, she said, for gas. She explained to the man, We may be crooks but we're honest.

The boy said, She thinks because her name is Bonnie she's supposed to be Bonnie and Clyde.

Well everybody has to have goals, she said. She grabbed the boy's arm and waved the gun at the man to get him to back away.

When they reached the car, they realised they hadn't put the gas in yet.

You dummy. You should've put it in first, the girl said.

I was just doing what you told me. You were the one told me to pull out back, he said.

She lowered her head into her hands and saw the blood on her thighs. The fear was a sheet of coldness moving through her. She shut her legs so the boy wouldn't see. There's only one thing for it, she told him. We got to rob him again. And grab some food while you're at it.

They were on a back-country road, passing parched fields and the occasional small white house. They'd chosen this road when the girl noticed a sign for a Ferry landing. She had to get to Florida, for herself, and to settle accounts with the thing in the trunk. She figured the ferry landing must be on the ocean. They could follow the water south.

Florida was where her father had run off to when the girl was a baby. The girl wasn't chasing him, had no intention of tracking him down. She just remembered her mother complaining all the time that he'd left them for better opportunities. The girl could use some opportunities, now that the plans she'd made with the boy had changed. She figured maybe she could hook up with a boat smuggling drugs. This was her idea, and she said nothing to the boy.

I love you, the boy said as they pulled into a two lane asphalt drive before a dock on the edge of a wide, brown river. The river's surface was sparkling and chalky beneath the noon sun. I love you Bonnie and I would do anything for you, but I can't shoot nobody, the boy said. I love you, he said, and waited because it was her turn to say it. I would die for you, he said, to spur her.

She looked out her window. A schedule painted on a white billboard showed they had forty-five minutes to wait. The glare from the sign gave the girl a headache. She turned towards the boy, into the momentary illusion of cool the darker interior of the car gave. But she couldn't look at his expectant face so she glanced at the back seat, the cans of beans and tuna, the package of bacon. No bread, she said, no pimento spread, and nothing to drink. He lowered his gaze. I can't lie, she told him, but I can't tell if I love you anymore or not.

She got out of the car, stood for a second until the dizziness passed, then headed off across a small picnic grove towards what looked to be a small beach area.

The boy chased after her. He fell into stride beside her and asked, Is it because of . . . ? He nodded his head back towards the car, the trunk. Because I don't see why that has to change things with us.

That was us, she said, and she headed straight for the water. About fifty yards off shore, half a dozen men wearing overalls and flannel shirts, their faces hidden by visored caps, waded in water up to their waists. They all had on earphones, and wore storage packs on their backs, and moved some sort of metallic tubes back and forth in the water before them.

No one else was in the water, although several mothers and a few small children lay on the pebbly beach.

I can't swim, the boy said as the girl paused to kick off her plastic sandals.

Look it, she said, pointing to the men. You don't have to swim. It's just to cool off.

She plunged in. The boy, without taking off his work boots, followed, setting his feet down in slow, tentative steps. His face lengthened in sorrow and fear and he said, Bonnie, what can I do to make it up to you?

Just shut up for now, she said. She felt another wave of dizziness. When she sat down, the river rose to her neck.

The water was tepid and smelled of muck. She soon saw why no one else was in it—it was full of jellyfish, small white stinging nettles. They brushed against her legs and the burning, numbing sensation caused by their tendrils scratched up her legs like fingers. She dunked her head backwards, felt the pain of water backing up her nostrils, and thought of opening her mouth to let it in. But she didn't. She snapped her face forward, breaking into the air with a gasp, and saw a white form burst before her like a vision.

Then she heard the boy's voice, carrying back to her across the water. He was up with the men, asking what they were doing.

Looking for treasure, one man told him.

She saw everything too clearly.

The cars were parked on the bottom deck of the ferry, with just enough room for a body to pass between them. The girl went alone to the passenger area on the second level.

She leaned against the hot railing, its green paint flaking to reveal rusted metal, and watched several passengers toss pieces of bread to the flock of black-hooded gulls which glided like demons in the ferry's wake. The birds shrieked and dove for food. The laughter of the passengers carried back to her.

She looked to the side, at their blue Plymouth Valiant, stolen from the boy's father. The sun glared off the trunk and hood and roof in wide, white swaths. The boy stood with his back to the car, his fingers touching the window of the car beside him. He had the radio tuned to a rock and roll station. The girl felt so sad she was numb.

As she felt the fluid dripping down her legs, knowing it wasn't just water, but her own blood loosened by water, she couldn't understand how just a few days earlier all they could talk about was their life together, and now she couldn't stand to look at him. When she thought about it, she realized she didn't care for herself very much anymore, either.

She descended to the lower deck, feeling nothing but heat. The boy watched in silence as she took the gun from underneath her seat. Open the trunk, she told him.

Here?

Open the damn thing.

He backed to it, but he didn't pull the keys out of his pocket.

She pointed the gun at his face. There was a gasp from someone at the rear of the ferry. On the edges of her vision, the girl saw the people back there move to the sides of the boat.

We are never making it to Florida, do you understand that?

The boy, mouth open, shook his head. His image blurred before the girl's eyes, but she kept on. It's over. It won't work. Open the trunk.

But I thought . . . he hesitated, confused more than scared. You said we should put him to sea, he said. Then it came to him and he whispered, There are people here.

There are people everywhere you idiot, now just open the damn trunk and give me a hand.

The boy carried the cooler for her to the back of the ferry. There was a scrambling, rattling sound as the passengers and attendants ran along the side railings then fled up the metal stairs to the second deck. The girl looked back at them, pressed together and watching cautiously from behind the railing. She felt like she was on stage, like she'd felt her whole life had been on stage, everyone watching her every move to see how she performed. She pulled open the lid to the cooler and tipped it to her audience. We didn't abortion it, she said, and this is what we got.

A few gulls screeched. One large bird swooped low and

169

cocked its head for a look into the cooler. That was my delivery room, the girl said, pointing her gun at the shore. Wasn't enough nobody wanted us in their damn house. Wasn't enough we couldn't go to school no more. She was screaming now. When she waved the gun, the people flinched back from the railing. She screamed louder, We couldn't even get in the damn hospital with no insurance.

You *are* bleeding again, the boy said. He pulled a damp handkerchief from the back pocket of his dungarees.

You were supposed to change my luck, she said, looking into the cooler. She aimed the gun and pulled the trigger. The recoil set her down on the deck, and she got up and fired twice more, holding her ground.

Is everybody happy now? she said and she kicked and tipped the cooler into the churning water of the wake.

The black-hooded gulls shrieked and dove as one, flapping and bickering, their beaks poking and tearing at the dead flesh.

On the boat the boy and girl held each other, crying. Here, the girl said, and she handed him the gun. If you really, really, really love me . . . .

The Blue Wedding

•

Lee Smith

Sarah can't keep her mind on the spoons. So she starts
over, counting right out loud, "one, two, three, four," pursing
her lips in that way she has, fitting each newly-polished spoon
carefully into its allotted space in the big mahogany silver chest.
Thirty-six spoons, all accounted for. Normally this is the kind of
job Sarah just loves but today it's so hot, hotter than the hinges
of hell in here, and Sarah is distracted because Gladiola Rolette,
who's polishing the spoons and handing them over to her one
by one, will *not* shut up, not for a single minute. Gladiola beats
all! She does not seem to understand it's her fault it's so hot in
here, that she should have called a repairman the instant the air
condition went on the blink. Gladiola does not even seem to
understand that it's her fault Sarah has to count the silver in the
first place. But Gladiola just let it all go during the last six
months of Daddy's illness, forks and spoons jumbled up
together, the butter knives scattered to the four winds. And
furthermore, it is perfectly clear that Gladiola has been giving
her trashy family the entire run of this house.

Sarah has seen the signs everywhere — unfiltered cigarette
butts in the flower beds, a beer can stuck in a planter on the
portico, a lipstick smudge on the drinking glass in the
downstairs bathroom — why, even the furniture has been
rearranged! Gladiola herself would never think of doing such a
thing. But her daughters, both of them hussies, *would.* They've
got ideas, Gladiola's girls. Sarah has watched them grow up.

Right now Roxanne, the younger one, could not possibly be
a day over 17 but could pass for 30, she looks so cheap and so
jaded with that spiky black hair and all those holes in her ears.

171

Gladiola's older daughter, Misty, is down in Atlanta getting certified to be a massage therapist, or so she says. A massage therapist, ha! Sarah can just imagine. Of course Misty has already had one baby out of wedlock, that fat little girl out there digging in the mint bed right now with a spoon. Probably a silver soup spoon, Sarah would not be one bit surprised.

Little Bonnie comes to work with Gladiola every day, and eats everything in the house. This is a pure fact. Sarah had no idea until she came back to bury Daddy and stayed on to clean out this house. *Somebody* had to! Oh, a lot has been going on here that Sarah didn't know anything about. These Rolettes have practically taken over.

But of course it is all Hubert's fault. Hubert is Sarah's brother, the district attorney, a rumpled, distracted man. All Hubert cares about is his job, and all his Northern egghead wife Mickey cares about is taking classes at the community college where she earns degree after degree, or claims to. So Hubert was perfectly happy to hire as many Rolettes as it took and close his eyes to the havoc they wrought, just as long as everybody stayed out of his hair. Hubert! Hubert has no standards.

Sarah practically slams the knives into the silver chest, thinking of Hubert, Hubert who talked *so mean* to her the last time she came home and tried to make some reasonable suggestions about what to do with Daddy. Hubert wears wrinkled suits and horn-rimmed glasses way down on the end of his nose. He looked at her over the rims. "Hell, Sarah," he said, "Dad's fine. Just leave him alone. He *likes* to pile up newspapers all over the house, he *likes* to have Gladiola's granddaughter around, it keeps him company. He likes to stay up and watch the talk shows and then sleep until noon, so what's the harm in it?"

"People ought to get up in the mornings," Sarah said. "A regular schedule never hurt anybody." Sarah herself has not slept past 7 a.m. in twenty years. She eats one-half cup of bran cereal with banana for breakfast every morning of her life.

Gladiola, on the other hand, fed her father Pop Tarts and instant grits. This is a fact. Pop Tarts and grits! Lord knows what kind of shape his bowels were in by the time of his death, of

172

course Sarah did not discuss this with Hubert.

But she did bring up the hat. "I just don't think we ought to let him go around looking like that," she said.

Hubert laughed. "Hell, he's 85 years old, I think he ought to wear whatever damn kind of a hat he wants to."

So Hubert had destroyed her influence with Daddy, Hubert having his way as usual, Hubert who was possibly even more spoiled than Nonnie, God rest her soul however.

Suddenly Sarah feels awful.

She sits down abruptly on a Chippendale chair at the dining room table. She's just so hot! Maybe it's a hot flash, maybe she's getting the change of life. "Is there any ice tea?" she asks Gladiola, who runs to get it.

Thank God! There *ought* to be iced tea in any decent household in the summertime of course, anybody knows that. Mama was nuts on the subject. And among the three children, Sarah is the only one like Mama, that soft pretty woman Sarah can hardly remember right now, oddly enough, sweet Mama who died of a racing heart twelve years ago.

Sarah left work the minute she got the message, and drove all night long to get home in time to see to every detail of Mama's funeral. Then she volunteered to stay home to take care of Daddy who was just lost without Mama, it was really the saddest thing. You can't imagine how he carried on.

But instead, here was Nonnie back from California, flat broke, to recuperate from the second of her two divorces.

So Sarah stayed on in Richmond where she is a buyer for the housewares section of Miller and Rhoads, a perfectly elegant downtown department store with branch stores in all the suburbs. In Richmond, Sarah has her book group, her bridge club, and a whole host of lovely friends. To be perfectly honest, Sarah was *glad* to stay in Richmond in her new condominium with its eggshell walls and its silk ficus in the foyer. Daddy was disorderly and always had been, not to mention his drinking. Drunk and disorderly, ha!

Come to think of it, they were *all* disorderly—Daddy, Hubert, and Nonnie—not to mention all of Hubert's and Nonnie's wives and children, a great straggling parade which

173

Sarah loses track of. *Lost,* Sarah corrects herself. Which she has lost track of, as Nonnie herself is lost.

The worst part was that Nonnie wasn't even married to the man who caused her last, fatal pregnancy. At the time, Nonnie wasn't married at all, and he was married to somebody else. But she was sure he *would* marry her, Nonnie had confided to Sarah that summer morning nine years ago. They were sitting in the kitchen after breakfast, drinking coffee. It was already hot. Mama's climbing rose was blooming like crazy all over the trellis. Sarah remembers that morning like it was yesterday. Nonnie leaned forward, so excited that spots of color stained her porcelain cheeks. She looked like a person running a fever. She spilled coffee on her flowered robe.

"He loves me so much," she said. "You can't imagine." Two weeks later she was dead of an ectopic pregnancy.

Sarah drinks her iced tea. She finishes with the knives: 36 of them, all accounted for. She smiles at Gladiola. "There now," she says.

Gladiola grins back. She's a fat, foolish woman, poor white trash if Sarah ever saw it, of course up here in the mountains this is common. People spill over from one social class into another all the time—it's hard to know who's nice. This is not true, of course, in Richmond, where all the help is Black and a proper distance can be maintained.

Sarah has been absent from her job at Miller and Rhoads for five days now, but she will be back on Monday. She can't afford to stay any longer. As it is, they will begin carrying three new lines of china during her absence, all of them informal: "Pietri," heavy painted pottery from Italy, covered with fanciful animals and fish; "Provence," over-size French china patterned in wildflowers; and "HaciendaWare" from the Southwest, all earth colors (terracotta, sagebrush, sunset, and dawn, Ha!) which looks like hell in Sarah's opinion. All of it looks like hell. So does that new girl they've hired to "help" Sarah with the expanded china department, a girl with rat's nest hair and dead-white makeup and some kind of a degree in "design." Sarah knows she will hate everything this girl likes.

What Sarah loves with all her heart is her mother's delicate bone china right over there in the breakfront, china so thin you can practically see through it. It will just kill her to split up the set with Hubert, who is totally unable to appreciate it. Well, a salad fork is missing, no surprise. Also two butter knives—no, *three* butter knives!

Out the window, Sarah sees Everett Sharp drive past in his little green car. Everett Sharp is the undertaker who buried Daddy two days ago. Sarah had lost touch with him since their high school days when he was President of the Tri-Hi-Y Club and she was Recording Secretary, but she was pleasantly surprised by his manner: respectful, attentive, but not unctuous. Not *pushy*. Everett Sharp is a tall thin balding man with a red beard and a little pot belly. Sarah has to start over on the soup spoons.

"Let's us stop for lunch now and I'll tell you about the wedding," Gladiola says. Gladiola knows how to get Sarah's attention.

"What wedding?" Sarah is a fool for weddings. She stops counting and wipes her face with a napkin. Actually she's so hot, she's *glad* to stop for a while.

"Let's us go on in the kitchen and I'll tell you," Gladiola says.

Sarah closes the lid of the silver chest and goes to sit in the old kitchen rocker while Gladiola makes pimento cheese sandwiches, Sarah's favorite ever since childhood.

"Well, you knew Roxanne was fixing to get married," Gladiola starts.

Sarah just stares at her. "You mean Misty," she says automatically. It's a shame how Gladiola's face has fallen in like spoonbread around her mouth. She used to be a pretty woman.

"No ma'am," Gladiola says emphatically. "I mean *Roxanne*."

"But Roxanne is only 17," Sarah says. "Isn't that so?"

"Yes ma'am," Gladiola says. "But can't nobody do a thing with Roxanne once she takes it in her head to do something. She's been like that ever since she was a little girl, ever since she was Bonnie's age."

As if on cue, Bonnie comes tracking dirt across the clean kitchen floor on her way to the sun porch, where she turns on the TV. Sarah sighs, bites her lip, says nothing. It is possible to say *too much,* she knows this, and really this pimento cheese is very good.

"Tell me about the wedding," she reminds Gladiola.

"Well, I don't know where Roxanne got this idea, mind you, but she took it into her head that she just had to have a blue wedding."

"A what?"

Gladiola hands Sarah another sandwich, then sits down and grins at her. "A blue wedding! All blue! See, blue is Roxanne's favorite color, always has been, why last year when she was head majorette she forced them to let her make herself a new uniform, blue with gold trim instead of gold with blue."

"Do you mean to tell me that Roxanne had a *blue* wedding dress?" Sarah fans her face with a copy of *Time* magazine.

"*Ordered* it," Gladiola corrects her. "We ordered everything through Judy's Smart Shoppe. You know Judy is real reliable, so usually everything comes in right when she says it will. We ordered a baby-blue wedding dress and veil, and baby-blue tuxedos for Eddie and his brother and the two groomsmen, and three baby-blue dresses with an Empire waist and puff sleeves for the bridesmaids."

"My goodness!" It is all Sarah can think of to say.

"But then Roxanne and Tammy—that's her best friend, Tammy Bird—had a big falling out," Gladiola goes on, "and so Tammy said she just wasn't going to be in the wedding after all, and Roxanne said that was fine with *her,* for Tammy not to be in the wedding, and so Roxanne called Judy up and canceled Tammy's dress. But Judy just happened to be out sick that day, well actually she was over at Orange County Hospital getting her tubes tied and her mother was keeping the store for her. You know everybody thinks she's got Alzheimers."

"*Who?*"

"Mrs. *Dewberry,*" Gladiola says. "Judy's mother. But I don't think she's got it. I think everybody just says that because its popular."

"What is?" Sarah manages to ask.

"Alzheimers," Gladiola says. "That's one of those diseases

that nobody ever heard of until it got popular and now everybody's got it, like that other one, you know the one I mean, the one where you diet until you die, nobody ever heard of that one until it got popular either."

"Anorexia," Sarah says weakly.

"Whatever," Gladiola says. She lights a cigarette.

"*The wedding,*" Sarah says.

"Well, so Judy's mother went and canceled the *whole order,* is what she did, instead of just the one dress, and forgot to say anything about this to Judy, so when Thursday before the wedding comes and Roxanne's whole order doesn't come in, Judy calls them up. It's this company in New Jersey."

"Can I have a coke?" Little Bonnie comes to stand in front of Gladiola, but Sarah gets up and gets it herself out of the refrigerator. She gives it to Bonnie, then pushes the little girl back out on the sunporch where "All My Children" is on TV. Sometimes Sarah actually watches that show herself, back home in Richmond on her rare days off, of course she'd never admit it to a soul.

"Well, what about the wedding?" Sarah asks, returning.

"They couldn't have it, of course," Gladiola says. "Judy had to re-order everything."

"But I would have thought that since the church was already reserved, I would imagine, and the minister all lined up, and the *invitations sent,* for Heaven's sake . . ." Horror crosses Sarah's face. "I should have thought that they would have held the wedding regardless, and just found something else to wear. Perhaps something more traditional," she adds hopefully.

"Not on your life!" Gladiola snorts. "Roxanne had her heart set on a blue wedding." Gladiola shakes her head. She acts like it was all out of her hands, every bit of it, like she is powerless in the world. But Gladiola was the Mother of the Bride! Sarah can't say a word, she just stares at Gladiola who goes right on with the story. "Well, Preacher Sizemore said he could marry them any time they took a notion to do it, so they set another date, and Judy re-ordered everything, and we got on the telephone and called up everybody we could think of, and so we put it off. But then, do you know what those rascals done?"

"Who?"

"Roxanne and Eddie."

"What? What did they do?" Sarah cannot imagine.

"They went ahead and moved in together just like they had gone and gotten married after all! I was mad as fire. But there wasn't nothing I could do of course, you can't do a thing with Roxanne, and they already had this trailer that Eddie's uncle had gave them after he built himself a new brick home out on the Bluefield road. It's got an above-ground swimming pool," Gladiola says, "which I think are so ugly."

Sarah unbuttons the first two buttons of her blouse and rolls up the sleeves. "Then what?"

"Well, so they move into this trailer, which is already decorated real cute, and Eddie buys them a new car which he's real proud of, that he bought cheap in a bankruptcy action. A black Trans Am, they were both just crazy about that car."

"How old is Eddie?" Sarah asks.

"Nineteen," says Gladiola. "So anyway they get all moved in together, and the wedding is set for two months off, and then Roxanne signs up for that nursing program at Mountain Tech. You know she was always so smart."

Sarah nods. *Too smart for her own good,* is what Sarah thinks.

"Well, this is when the trouble really starts." Gladiola lights a cigarette. "Eddie's just a real jealous person, it turns out. He can't stand for her to go anyplace without him, and he especially can't stand for her to drive off anyplace in the car without him. Eddie gets downright peculiar about that car. So anyway, on the day that Roxanne has to register over at Mountain Tech, there's a big thunderstorm, and the computers go down over there. So it just takes her forever to get registered, and it's nearabout dark when she gets back to the trailer."

"Can I have one of those?" Sarah reaches for Gladiola's pack of Salems.

Gladiola nods absently, her mind on Roxanne and Eddie. "All I can say is that Eddie Skeens went temporarily insane because she was over at Mountain Tech so long. Just as soon as she pulled up in the road, he came busting out of that trailer hollering all this crazy stuff about Roxanne going off in the car

178

to see other men, and such as that, and then you won't believe what he did next!"

"*What?*" The nicotine is making Sarah feel high, dizzy.

"He picks up this two-by-four that was laying right there, that they were fixing to build a deck with onto the trailer, see, they had them a big pile of treated lumber that they got on sale from Walmart, and Eddie's brother was going to help them build the deck."

Sarah leans back in the rocker and shuts her eyes. It crosses her mind that Gladiola is trying to drive her crazy. "Go on," she says. She blows smoke in the air.

"Well, Eddie Skeens proceeds to lay into that car something terrible. He busted ever window *clean out,* he was so mad, and then started in on the dash."

Sarah sits bolt upright. "But that's just terrible! What did Roxanne do?"

Gladiola is putting things back into the refrigerator now. "I'm ashamed to own it," she says, "but Roxanne picks up this *other* two-by-four and hits Eddie Skeens right upside the head, just as hard as she can."

"*Good heavens!*" Sarah is suddenly, horribly agitated. She feels like she has to go to the bathroom. Instead, she reaches for another cigarette.

"Yes ma'am. Broke his nose and one cheekbone and some little bone right up here." Gladiola points to her eyebrow. "I forget what you call it. Anyway, blood went all over the place, it was the biggest mess. Now they've got Eddie Skeens all wired up till he can't eat no solid food, he can't have nothing but milkshakes. He's still in the hospital. His mother, Lou Annie Skeens, has gone and charged Roxanne with assault and battery, and Roxanne has charged Eddie with destruction of personal property. I tried to talk her out of it, I said, 'You'll have to pay that lawyer out of your own pocket,' but you know how she is."

"So what happened then?"

"Nothing yet. They're all going to court next week." Gladiola wipes off the kitchen counters and spreads her dishrag out on the sink to dry.

"And the wedding is off?" Sarah feels a sudden overwhelming sense of loss.

"You're damn right!" Gladiola says. "They was too young to marry in the first place. Plus they was *too crazy* about each other, if you know what I mean. They would of wore each other out or killed each other, or killed somebody else. It wasn't no way they could of stayed together."

The front doorbell rings and Gladiola goes to answer it, leaving Sarah alone in the kitchen where she rocks back and forth slightly, hugging herself. Sarah feels like she is hovering over her whole life, somehow, in this rocking chair, she feels way high up, like a hummingbird. It occurs to her that the change of life might not be so bad. *No* change of life might be worse.

"What is it?" She struggles to her feet.

Everett Sharp has to repeat himself.

"I do hope I haven't come at a bad time," he says, "although no time is *good,* in such a season of sorrow. I just wanted to thank you for your business and tell you I hope that everything met with your standards, I guess we probably do things different up here in the mountains . . ." Everett Sharp trails off, looking at her. He has to look *down,* he's such a tall man; this makes Sarah feel actually small, a feeling she likes.

"*Sally Woodall,*" he says suddenly, with a catch in his voice. "Aren't you Sally Woodall from high school?"

And then Sarah realizes he didn't know who she was at all, not really, he hadn't even connected her with her teenage self of so many years before. Everett Sharp moves closer, staring at her. Everett Sharp's long white bony arms poke out of his short white shirtsleeves; his forearms are covered with thick red hair. Sarah feels so hot and dizzy, she's afraid she might pass out.

"My wife died last year," Everett Sharp says. "I married Betty Robinson, you might remember her. She was in the band."

Sarah nods.

"Clarinet," says Everett Sharp. Then he says, "Well, why don't I take you out to dinner tonight? It might do you good to get out some. They've got a seafood buffet on Fridays now, out at the Holiday Inn on the Interstate."

"All right," Sarah says, but she can't take in much of what happens after that. Everett Sharp soon leaves. It's so hot. Gladiola leaves. It's so hot. Sarah takes a notion to look for her father's vodka which she finally finds in the filing cabinet in his study. She pours some into her iced tea and goes out on the porch, hoping for a breeze. She sits in the old glider and stares out into the shady back yard, planning her outfit for tonight. Certainly not the beige linen suit she's worn practically ever since she got here. Maybe the blue sheath with the little jacket, maybe the floral two-piece with the scoop neck and the flared skirt. Yes! And those red pumps she bought on sale at Montaldo's last month and hasn't even worn yet, it's a good thing she just happened to throw them into her traveling bag. This strikes her as fortuitous, an omen. She sips her drink. The glider trembles on the edge of the afternoon.

Then Sarah remembers something that happened years ago, she couldn't have been more than seven or eight. Oddly enough, she was sitting right here on this glider watching her parents who sat out on the curly wrought-iron chairs beneath the big tree drinking cocktails, as they did every evening. Sarah was the kind of little girl who sat quietly, and noticed things. Actually she spied on people. Her mama and her daddy were leaning forward, all dressed up.

Mama's dress is white. It glows in the dark. Lightning bugs rise from the grass all around, cicadas sing, frogs croak down by the creek. Sally has already had her supper. She wants to go back inside the play paper dolls, but something holds her there on the porch, still watching Mama and Daddy as they start to argue (jerky scary movements, voices raised) and then as they stand, and then as Daddy kicks over the little table, moving toward Mama to kiss her long and hard in the humming dark. Daddy puts his hands on Mama's dress.

The force of this memory sends Sarah back inside for another iced tea and vodka, and then she decides to count the napkins and placemats, and then she has another iced tea and vodka, and then she realizes it's time to get ready for her dinner date, but before she's through dressing she realizes she'd better go through the whole upstairs linen closet just to see what's in there, so she's not ready, not at all, not by a long shot, when Everett Sharp calls for her at seven, as he said.

He rings the front doorbell, then waits. He rings again. He doesn't know — he couldn't even *imagine*! — that Sarah is right on the other side of the heavy door, not even a foot away from him, that she has sort of slid down the door and now sits propped up against it like a ragdoll, her satin slip shining out in the gloom of the dark hallway, with her fingers pressed over her mouth so she won't laugh out loud to think how she's fooled him, or start crying to think — as she will, again and again and again — how Eddie must have felt when his very bones cracked and the red blood poured down the side of his face, or how *she* must have felt, hitting him.

Love in the Middle Ages

•

Kelly Cherry

O saeculum, O literae! juvat vivere!
— Ulrich von Hutten

There had been in her life a time, now historical, that was dark with fear and superstition: her fear; the superstitions of psychiatrists and psychoanalysts. This was in a place where winters were long and hard, the streets a sibilant soup of slush, sand, and salt, or treacherous with drifting snow, drizzle of ice sugar-glazing the leafless lindens. People were always turning away from other people to cough or sneeze into cupped hands. They lingered in coffee shops, the hot liquid in their throats like a medicine. Outside, cars skidded sideways to a stop in a ditch. Drivers exchanged license-plate numbers and the names of insurance agents wearily, as if they had been through this before, as if they had been canceled years ago and were now in syndication.

Winter in the year of our Lord 735. Snow is sifting into the moat, a thousand swans doing swan dives; it featherbeds the inner stone wall that stands near Lindisfarne, known as Holy Island, in the north of Northumbria in Bernicia. A stockade surmounts the stone wall, for those who would attack and lay siege to the court are many, including the Picts, and also the Mercians to the south.

The wind quickens, hurling itself against the stones like a lunatic beating her head against a wall. The falling snow glitters above the windblown water, phosphorescing, a final, brave flare-up. Touching down in the moat, snowflakes are snuffed out like candles.

To Nina, in this impossible place, there now came the suggestion of a new personal happiness.

Except that she refused to believe it.

Except that she was afraid to believe it.

Except that she was used to the way things were, her routine of child-minding, teaching, writing, and walking the dog.

But especially, except that she was afraid to believe it.

Though Nina loved some things wholly, things such as art and life, always ready to put either before herself, men were another matter. She had been unconnected to any man for so long, now, that she did not believe connection was possible. And who would ask her out?

"Single mothers are the romantically challenged of the world," she liked to joke.

The first time he kissed her, he touched his mouth to hers and then stayed there, mouth on mouth, as if resting, perhaps taking a short nap. Perhaps practicing CPR. For a brief moment of alarm she thought he might have forgotten what he was going to do. It had slipped his mind that he was going to kiss her! He had planned to kiss her, but then he thought of something more important! Breathing, for instance! And then, given that pause during which her fear walked past itself and out the door, she felt her heart bloom, felt the rose of it warmed and open, and he kissed her and kissed her until she forgot everything she knew: her past, her phone number, her name, why she never slept with men anymore.

The king and queen sit side by side on the high seat at the top of the table. Their dinner companions raise bronze cups of spiced red wine, cheering and toasting from places on cushioned benches. Platters of cold meats and smoked fish and flat wheatcakes glimmer blood-red or gold in firelight flung on the table by torches ranged along the wall and logs crackling in the hearth. Through thin slits in the wall, all in the hall can see the snow fall, fall, fall, the sky strangely lightening as the day grows darker.

The night before, a new moon's horns had lain downward, frowning, and forecasting a month of storms and bitter weather.

Present at the table, but made to sit far down along the side, is the princess, who watches her distant parents — so kingly! so queenly! — as if they were in another room. (It seems to her that they have always been in another room.) Not present is the princess's brother – firstborn and heir and, it is rumored, a follower of Merlin – who is doubtless joyriding in a stolen car or drinking or in bed with one of the princess's friends from college.

She had met him on the Square in summer, during the Merchants' Parade. He taught in the history department. Like most academics, he was deracinated, a man for all locales. Pittsburgh, Charlottesville, Palo Alto had been some of the points on his trajectory, but weren't they all the same, intellectually homogeneous no matter how ethnically diverse, one big reading list? He had the pampered academic's exuberant desire to see the world benefit from his thinking. He was generous and ignorant, a middle-aged male in a preserve for middle-aged males, a place where middle-aged males grazed on grants or snoozed the afternoon away in endowed chairs, a place where they had a kind of mental sex in institutes (Esalens for the mind, these "Institutes for Research") and grew fat on footnotes—perpetrated by friends in other preserves—that cited the few articles they'd written. He was a wild beast who had never actually had to survive in the wild and therefore knew nothing of the world Nina had come from nor anything of his own capacity for destruction; he had confused destruction with deconstruction—he had confused death with anagrams!—and Nina was afraid of him. Yet when she tried to imply something of this to him, tried to sketch (but gaily, optimistically, as if she was, after all, talking about a very slight apocalypse) the disaster and despair she feared might be the result of any further meeting (there was history and then there was her personal history, which she was not about to repeat), he said, "You're very imaginative. I guess that's what makes you a writer. Do you want to go to a movie?"

In the ninety-nine-cent dark in Middleton he put his arms around her. Popcorn spilled down into the neck of her cotton men's-shirt, but if she reached after it she'd look as if she was trying to cop a feel from herself. It was a movie from the eighties, about murder among monks. The screen was thick

185

with symbology. Nina felt she already knew everything there was to know about sexual abstinence.

She shook his hand before unlocking her front door. Under the porch light his eyes were hazel, a nutmeat brown.

Inside the hot house—it could be suffocating in summer—she untwisted her daughter from the tangled top sheet, and let the dog run out in back and then back in, and then went to bed, letting her skirt drop in a sighing heap on the floor, taking the blue shirt off, her young-looking breasts bare. And buttery!

Torchlight dances over the woven tapestries and embroidered wall curtains and causes the swords and armor hung on pegs to gleam, a metal-plate and chain-metal mirroriness. The king has been inspecting the strength of his hold against invaders. It is late in November, "the month of blood": In November, people kill their animals, knowing the animals cannot survive anyway because there will not be enough fodder to last the winter.

Gleemen play pipes and fiddle and harp for the pleasure of the king and his queen. And beneath the music run these whispered words, making their way from guest to guest: Winds had swept a monk out to sea on his penitential raft, and only the priest's prayers had drawn him back, as if by the rosary's rope, to safety. Cain's gigantic progeny had risen from the whirling water, seas sliding from their shoulders, drowning sailors. People had reported seeing dragons on the heath, fires starting up first over here, then over there as if blown about by the devil's breath. Demons had been observed having intercourse at midnight. Infant demons grew to full size in a single day and played evil tricks on unsuspecting monks, loosing the mooring of rafts on the Tyne.

He took her to dinner at l'Etoile, an expensive second-story restaurant she did not often get to eat in. It was still summer. The lights from the Capitol, which the window looked out on, were as soft as candlelight in the aquamarine of early evening.

They talked about their jobs and former marriages. A waiter whisked glasses and plates away, returned with others. Nina listened as Palmer described his ex-wife: She had been

186

beautiful, accomplished, lesbian. He had doubted himself. He had slept with women—he would hang his head to say how many— confirming his manhood, reassuring himself, but he was past that now. He was HIV-negative. What about her?

"What?"

"Have you been tested?"

"This is so mortifying," she murmured, wiping her mouth with a linen handkerchief the size of her daughter's nightgown.

"You shouldn't be ashamed. There's nothing mortifying about a disease. Although, etymologically speaking—"

"No," she said. "It's not that. I'm mortified to admit I haven't slept with anyone in a decade. I don't think I need to go for a test."

"In a *decade*?"

She didn't look at him. "Yeah," she said. "Is that a surprise, or what. I was surprised!"

"A *decade*?" Oil from the dressed mushrooms had gotten on his chin, giving him a glow like makeup. "*Why*!?"

"I was too busy?" she asked.

His fork had stalled in midair. "But you're so pretty!"

She looked up at him and then away and then back again, flattered and confused, gratitude making her simultaneously bold and shy. "I think I took a vow of poverty, too. I mean, the university certainly seems to think I did, because otherwise they'd have to pay me a living wage. But don't expect me to be obedient."

You can be a princess and still be forgotten during the festivities in the Great Hall. You can be there, among the company, and still know that on another level you have been banished—were banished before you were born.

Yet, looking down the long table at them, the princess is proud of her kingly father and queenly mother, of the way the whole realm pays tribute to her parents. Her face is rouged with the warmth of the fire, the wine, her own royal blood. She bends her head to take another sip, trying to hold the cup so as not to acquire, as has happened on other occasions, a red-wine moustache, and manages instead to dunk a strand of her hair in the cup. She already had broken ends, and now

187

they are wet and clumped like seaweed and smell of booze. She adjusts her royal crown to hide the fact that she is having a really bad hair day — her parents hate for her to be anything less than a perfect princess! Of course, she thinks sadly, her mouth still fuzzed and grainy with the taste of hair and setting gel, she has to be careful not to forget she's not supposed to be anything more than a princess, either. God forbid she should outshine her brother, get grandiose notions about the throne, displace her mother the queen.

"I always wanted to write a comic strip," she said to him, *gaily, optimistically.* This was part of her strategy for letting him know that she was not so easily snowed, she was not a romantic — she was going to let him know this by telling him about her comic strip. "Not as a way of life. Just this one strip. In the first panel, there are two hilltops, and on each hilltop is a snail. On one hilltop there's a boy snail, and on the other hilltop is a girl snail. They spot each other and it's love at first sight.

"So they race down their respective hills, only they're *snails.* And the seasons pass: It's summer, autumn, winter. And they keep racing and racing to each other's arms. And it's spring again, and summer, and autumn. And they keep racing. At a snail's pace! And finally, one day, they really do meet, down in the valley, and their love has lasted all this time. He's got a cane now, and glaucoma, and she has a dowager's hump, but they get married. The last panel is headed: *Happily Ever After,* and it shows two tiny tombstones side by side."

"Writers," he said. "You don't get out enough, do you? You should join my volleyball team. We play the poli-sci department on Tuesdays."

Also absent, absent forevermore, are many friends, taken by plague. The princess has seen how they die: the skin blackening as if there is an eclipse of the blood, the painful, grotesque swelling, all the body's estuaries filling with sluggish fluids. Lymph nodes in the armpits and groin blown up like pig bladders.

And then that blackening, as if the skin were charred by burning fever. People with plague cried out, tossing on straw pallets all through the night, falling silent by morning. But the worst thing, thinks the princess, is the babies. She can't understand why babies should have to suffer like that. Babies, she thinks, all babies everywhere, should wear teensy crowns and romper suits, and when they get a little older they should be given velveteen dresses, and seersucker play-outfits and OshKosh B'gosh snap-on overalls, and be hugged and cooed to and get their chins chucked a lot and have the run of the court. And if they fall down, their mother the queen and their father the king should be there to put a Band-Aid over the sore spot and kiss the hurt away.

The reason the crowns have to be teensy is so they won't make the babies' heads lie uneasy.

Palmer wore her down. He wouldn't be put off. Nothing scared him—not her being a single parent, not her being in the public eye (of Madison, anyway), not her incredibly complicated past, lived in several countries (and a few psych wards, too). She thought sure the snails would do it, but he just smiled at her, a smile that squeezed his eyes into the canoe shape of Brazil nuts. There were lines in his face like snowmobile tracks, coming or going, depending on how he felt.

The more good-natured he was, the less she trusted him. What man ever pledged himself to a woman on the spot? In the Middle Ages, all right, but this was some fin de siècle folly. He might be a historian, but she could see what was in store for the future—the female graduate students; the return of that old sorrow of discovering she was not, after all, first in anybody's thoughts. She saw the emotional distance that would gradually develop, as if the house itself were expanding, the bedroom miles from his study, her study, how he would come home one day—in a year, five years, twenty—and ask for a divorce, his voice breaking a little as if he were going through puberty. Which would be pretty much what he would be doing. In a year, five years, twenty, he would take back his books and exercycle and say he really hoped they would still be friends. After he left, everything would go back to being exactly the way it was now, except that her heart would have stopped, when he said he was leaving her, just long enough for a little more brain damage to take place. She was already concussive with rejection! That's why she would be bursting into tears for no good reason—she'd have lost control over certain bodily functions. She'd have trouble breathing, the work of it almost more than she could bear. Give this woman an oxygen tent! She should go home and make out a Living Will, right now. For a time, she would be irrational and in pain, the bones of her body bright and cold and snapping off like icicles, and at night she would crawl around in the cave of her own cranium, that unknown, dank, cobwebbed place. All this, while her daughter needed her—needed her to praise a scribbled drawing or button the top button on the back of her jumper or arbitrate a dispute between Teddy the Bear and a mob of plastic dinosaurs. No, Nina could not have this. She refused to sleep with him.

"I can wait," Palmer said. He looked at her thoughtfully. "Maybe not a decade. I don't think I can wait a decade."

Monks on rafts may be frightened by whales or evil spirits rising from the sea floor; a son of Cain can raise a full-blown gale merely by seizing a monk by the hair and twirling him like a top.

Cormorants, shags, gannets, and guillemots are birds of the shore.

Monks of the time carry gospel books. Living in large groups, monks are in constant danger of infection transmitted by communal cups. Infectious diseases include smallpox, tuberculosis, and bubonic plague.

Stained-glass windows shatter light from church lamps, splintering it into stripes that paint the cornfields and countryside, sheep fells and cow byres. An angel approaches the boy Cuthbert, who later becomes a monk, and advises him to treat his swollen knee with a poultice. "You must cook wheat flour with milk," says the angel, "and anoint your knee with it while the poultice is hot." On another occasion, Cuthbert sees an angel whisk a soul off to heaven, and the soul appears to be in the center of a fiery orb, like a small wax figure in a paperweight.

The princess, a studious sort, has made herself a kind of home office behind a folding screen. She convinced herself that if she hid behind a folding screen her brother would not know she was there, or would forget to pay attention to her. Her brother the prince, who has absorbed all the Continental ideas of existential absurdity and artistic freedom from psychological and social convention and keeps telling her she is the only person in the realm who has ever understood him. Which confuses her greatly, because she doesn't understand anything, especially him. Most of all, she does not understand why her brother said it is a tragedy that they can't get married. And she does not understand why, on one hand, he said this and, on the other hand, he sleeps with her girlfriends from college.

At two o'clock every afternoon during the summer Nina walked over to Mrs. Kendall's house on Kendall Street — though, as Mrs. Kendall was fond of pointing out, she was a Kendall by marriage and her ex-husband's family had been from South Dakota anyway so God only knew where the Kendalls were that Kendall Street had been named after — and helped her daughter gather up her day's output of drawings and collages and cardboard cutouts and brought her home. Today Tavy was baking Play-Doh in the pretend oven. "What kind of pies are these?" Nina asked her, saying "yum yum" and poking a finger in one.

"They're not pies," Tavy said.

At this age, Tavy had long, straight, brown hair with bangs; eyes that sometimes seemed like cameras registering everything on a film not yet developed; and the cheekbones of her mother Babette, her great-aunt and adoptive mother Nina, and her late great-grandmother Eleanor — cheekbones already celebrated by three generations of men. She had on a pale yellow blouse that was like a slice of lemon and a skirt the smoky color of Darjeeling. My little tempest in a teapot! thought Nina. "What are they, then?" asked Nina. "Cookies?"

"Turd tortes," said Tavy.

After dinner — meat loaf, not turd tortes — Nina sat on the front stoop of her house with Tavy and their little dog. Tavy held Teddy the Bear in her lap. It was a beautiful, clear night, just late enough in the summer to grow dark before Tavy went to bed. The sky was cobblestoned with stars. Headlights hurried by in pairs, as if they were on their way to an ark somewhere. "Tavy," said Nina, "do you want to tell me what's bothering you?" She smoothed Tavy's hair back behind her ears. "You seem angry about something."

Tavy tried to smooth the little dog's hair back behind his ears. "Mommy's being silly," she told him.

Nina said to Teddy, "Well, Teddy, if Tavy won't tell me what's wrong, how am I ever going to make it right?"

"Teddy can't hear you," Tavy said.

"He can't?"

"He's just a *bear*," she said.

"Can he think?"

"I didn't say he was stupid!"

"Then what is Teddy thinking?"

"He thinks you should marry Rajan. He doesn't think you should marry Palmer."

"Don't you like Palmer?"

"He's okay. But Teddy likes Rajan better."

"Honey, Rajan *is* married, to Lucy, remember?"

"She might die. She could do like Grandma and go to a foreign place and get old and die. Then you could marry Rajan."

"I'm sorry, sweetie," Nina said. "It doesn't work that way."

"I don't see why not," said Tavy, leaning heavily over Teddy, her chin in her hands, her elbows on her knees, her feet in their brown wide-strap sandals planted firmly on the chipped and cracking concrete steps that cost too much to replace.

In her home office in the castle keep she keeps her personal library. Donatus on the grammar of Latin; De Arte Metrica, with its study of poetic scansion; Isidore of Seville's Etymologiae, *Pliny's* Natural History, *the poets Sedulius, Juvencus, and Paulinus of Nola. (Perhaps she borrowed some of these books from the local monastery and has never gotten around to returning them.) During the winter, scribes' scrivening slows down; their fingers freeze up like the pistons of old cars and stall on the page.*

The monks smear resin from cedars on the books; otherwise, worms make holes in the vellum and binding boards and swallow words, and to no purpose for who ever heard of a wise worm? Precious and semiprecious stones stud gilt bookcovers worked in intricate designs. The princess glances out the window — moonshine makes a

*glow of frost, the whorled crystals a wavy pattern on the pane: frost-
stars and frost-mountains. She hears wolves howling in the distance.
There were travelers who walked a hundred miles to find books for
their libraries; they carried the books in satchels, these backpacking
librarians. They were sometimes eaten by the wolves.*

*Everyone has gone, settled down in some secret corner on a straw
pallet or featherbed or sprawled on a cellar floor. The princess pores
over her books.*

*This is what the princess has always done. She has always pored
over her books.*

*A chill wind wickedly wriggles its way in around the edges of the
frosted pane. Wax pools at the base of the candle and hardens; she chips
at it with her nails. As she reads and writes, she stays alert to any
sound, any shift in shadow — whatever might tell her that he is near
and waiting. If her brother the prince is going to rape her, she doesn't
want to be taken — taken! — off guard. She tells herself she is nothing if
not regal. Even raped.*

Nina and Shelley and Jazz stopped to have coffee and cranberry
muffins at the bookstore. Palmer and three of his volleyball
cronies were already there in a corner, a guitar trio with
concertina accompaniment, knocking out "Whiskey Before
Breakfast" and drinking Blue Nun white wine.

Maybe some of the customers were playing *taefel*, rolling the
dice on the table, the cubes spilling out of a pewter cup. Once,
rosaries were made from dried roses, were bracelets or
necklaces of rosepetals, were a rose garden of prayer. Hence: the
name of the rosary.

Nina, Shelley, and Jazz took a table up front by the high
churchlike windows. Jazz was saying, about someone in her
department, "I think he lives on some other planet."

"Yes," agreed Shelley, who knew Jazz's colleague outside
the university, "but I always found it an easy flight to that
particular planet."

"Well, he's moved on into deep space," said Jazz.

Nina was listening to her two girlfriends, one older and one
younger, and watching their expressive faces, one white and
one black, and feeling the secret warmth of her involvement

with Palmer. How astonishing it was to feel, after being so long alone, this sense of an invisible but ideal geometry, as if he and she were dots that knew their destiny was to be connected in a picture that would come clear. ("But when?" he had asked her again that weekend, the snowmobile in his face returning, crisscrossing the skin around his eyes. "Connected when?" And she said, "It's this chastity belt. I seem to have lost the key.") Even with her back turned to him, she saw him with one leg outstretched and the other propped on a footrest. She could almost feel the consoling softness of his sweater — the raveled sleeve of care knitted up in a cable stitch by Bill Blass — and his chest like something strong that she could lean against, a wall. She had thought this affection for manliness, for a man's way of being in the world, had died out in her, was a thing that had been catalogued and stored in the museum of herself, an artifact of feeling. But here it was, pulsing with contemporaneity. She thought he was beautiful, and she thought this very much in the same way as she had once thought Bobby Kennedy and Dirk Bogarde were beautiful.

Jazz said, "Excuse me a bit, ladies, while I jive and jam," and went to sing with the guys.

With only the two of them left at the table, Shelley — who sometimes ran into Cliff, a geneticist, at the hospital where she worked — said to Nina, "He sure beats Cliff."

Cliff, not Rajan, was who Nina had been going with before she stopped going with anyone, ever. "Cliff doesn't even seem real to me now," Nina said. "And it's not just because it was so long ago. My ex-husband, for example, was longer ago, and he still seems real. But not Cliff."

"Some men really are unreal," Shelley said. "Oh! But, anyway, I mean, you know what I mean."

"You mean that some men don't leave a mark on the world. They don't go down in history."

Jazz's voice climbed over the music like a bird that flies in through an open window and out another, a bird like a famous metaphor for life.

"They can be all the rage for a time, though," said Shelley.

"Oh my god, tell me about it. A miniseries. Foreign rights

194

sold to eleven countries. Paperback tie-in." Nina frowned, remembering Cliff's brief appearance on her bestseller list, the rave reviews she had so uncritically given him at the beginning, his Avedon-should-photograph-it profile, elegant and arrogant.

"What I think," said Shelley, "is that it's time you went back to the classics. Palmer looks to me like literature that lasts."

At high tide the horizon is a silvered blue; at low tide it is gold, as if an angel had tipped his wings toward the earth. Cuthbert, on the verge of starvation, was saved by two freshly cut and washed wedges of dolphin flesh that appeared before him as on a plate of air. A pair of dolphins frisked in the distant sea, each lovely and whole except for a missing triangle into which one of the wedges would fit. They seemed to have delivered themselves to him, willingly, unnetted with tuna, a dolphin-pizza delivery service.

Boats are wrecked on whales, nosed into disaster and salvage, or sunk by small forms of marine life that pierce the sterns' covering of tanned ox hide. Survivors often enter monasteries, devoting the rest of their lives to worship. Monks on rafts, affrighted by whales, may paddle and pole furiously, churning the sea into a beerlike froth. Everyone has something to do – the wheelwright, the mason, the blacksmith, the baker, the brewer, the cook, the beekeeper, the weaver. Prostitutes advertise their calling with handworked linen and luxurious brocade on their beds. Soldiers are armed with swords, spears, and axes; some turn the skulls of their slain enemies into drinking cups.

Every age has its customs: When a dead rat is discovered in the cook's flour, the cook pitches out the carcass and brushes away a bit of the surrounding flour but uses the rest without a qualm. Frequently, women who have been wives leave the secular life for the monastic when they become widows. These are some of the customs of the age.

Meanwhile, strewn among the princess's books are her personal effects: combs and needles, buckles and pins and brooches of bronze and bone. She wears a bracelet of blue glass beads.

She writes on goatskin, using a goose quill pen dipped in black ink that smells as sweet as perfume. Riddles, puns, and codes are much admired by the people of the time.

When her brother the prince comes into the room, he is laughing

195

*but in a way that seems, to her, mocking. He has sucked in his cheeks
and raised his eyebrows and pursed his mouth in a skeptical* moue *and
he looks like James Dean but a brighter, harder version, a movie star
who reads books. A movie star who reads books by Nietzsche. He
shoves the screen aside and lies down on her bed, his hands clasped
beneath his head. She remains seated at her desk; perhaps she hopes
that if she does nothing, nothing will happen. He is talking about their
parents, the king and queen — their parents' failures and the contempt
he is forced to feel. Again, a wolf howls. The candle has burnt almost
to the end, its nub swimming in a hardening sea. The princess feels as
though she has forgotten how to breathe. She feels clumsy, stupid,
inanimate. She can't move. He rolls on his side and reaches out a hand,
grasping her by the wrist. "Come over here," he says, "so we won't
have to talk so loudly. We don't want to wake anyone." The world
(which, she knows, everyone knows, is round, though everyone also
knows that no one lives on the underside) has shrunk. It has gotten
ever smaller, and now the princess sees that she is trapped in the
middle of it, a world the size of an egg, a burning egg. A burning egg
that scorches her ovaries, that turns her womb to ash. Her cauterized,
useless womb. He doesn't kiss her. He just makes another quarter-turn
until he lies on top of her. Her crown slips off and falls behind the
pillow. He undoes the brooches of bone, of bronze. Her blue-bead
bracelet slips from her arm, a sly little animal escaping like a
salamander beneath a rock. It lies on the bed, a kaleidoscope on the
tapestry and scallop-edged linens.*

*When she had been a very young princess, say, five, her parents
had told her that if she could kiss her elbow she would turn into a boy.
She had tried and tried, all the while being terrified she might succeed.
She liked being a girl, she really did! She wanted to grow up and have
lots of royal babies. But already she knew that it was better to be a
prince. It was safer. Princes had things easier. They earned bigger
salaries for less work. This, too, was a custom of the age.*

With all these conflicting opinions swirling around her, Nina
often felt as though she could not see where she was going. Was
she, that is, going to go to bed with Palmer?

She still didn't trust him. Why *her*? she wanted to know.
And why was he so set on marriage, which, even if it made a

new sense in parlous times, remained a radical step?

"You've heard of the end of history," he began. They were in her living room, dog and daughter sleeping overhead. An ambulance raced past the house to the hospital, its air-raid siren like a blitzkrieg. A semi rumbled past, shaking the house on its foundation.

"I have," she admitted. Academics loved these catch phrases, the undangerous electric shocks of them, the semiotic therapy of them, administered to lift the black cloud of scholarly depression, give a drained brain a charge. The death of God, the authorless text, the end of history — you made a conjunction of a contradiction and the Guggenheim Foundation prostrated itself in admiration. But this had nothing to do with ideas; it was all grammar, as Donatus had known.

"I saw it," Palmer said.

Nina was wearing jeans and an oversized dark-brown sweater and a Hillary headband, also brown, and white socks. She was sitting on the rug. She stretched out her legs so the bottoms of her feet could feel the fire Palmer had built in the hearth. She could make a joke now, or she could be serious. She decided to be serious. "What do you mean, you saw it?" she asked, hoping she was not about to find out that Palmer was, after all, weird. But if he was, after all, weird, that would explain, wouldn't it, why he'd said that he loved her!

He got up from the floor, sighed heavily, and threw himself into the Green Bay Packers chair, which was worn thin where her dog had, day after day for thirteen years, pawed in a furious flurry and then wound himself up like a clock before settling down to nap.

"I was walking home from school along the lake. It was a typically brilliant October day, the sky buffed to a high sheen, the leaves golden and flashing and the lake silver and sapphirine, everything lit, as with drugs, and shining. I was looking, you know, truly looking, thinking about what I was seeing and finding the words for it. And then it just stopped." He rubbed a hand over his forehead. "It just stopped," he said. "It didn't get dark, it was all still glowing, glints in the lake like fish, but these fish of light weren't moving. They weren't even

197

bobbing. Nothing was moving, because everything was just repeating itself. The wind blowing and the waves breaking on the shore and the people jogging and the airplane, I remember there was an airplane, getting smaller, and all the other stuff—everything that was happening had finally happened too many times and now it didn't count anymore. It was pure repetition, and repetition is the opposite of history."

Nina, who had recently been experiencing flashbacks in which she remembered not just that her brother had come into her bedroom (she had never forgotten that) but how she had felt when he did, looked into the fire for a reply. The woodsmoke smelled cedary and dry, like a shelter for birds in the snow. She imagined her heart glowing like a little fire, the way she warmed to Palmer. Maybe even the way she was getting hot for Palmer! But her daughter was upstairs.

"History is over," he said. "Done with, used up, finished. Don't you see?" he begged, and there was, she saw, in him a kind of contagion no matter what the test had said. It could be a sickness unto death, but she knew a cure for it. "On the tomb of Bruni in Santa Croce are inscribed the words *History is in mourning*. All we have now is fiction," he finished. "On the other hand," he added, "maybe I'm just having a midlife crisis. I believe it would be my third."

"From a parent's point of view," Nina whispered, knowing that tenured professors had seldom heard a parent's point of view, "repetition is not the end of history. It's the beginning of history. Every child is the dawn of time."

The blue-bead bracelet slips from her arm, as if fleeing. . . .

Nina went on: "What you saw was the world *in imitatio*, the photocopied world, the world that is merely a shadow cast by a larger reality. But what you *didn't* see is the *smaller* reality, which can be mistaken, at first, for a duplication but then reveals itself as essentially and eternally itself. You certainly don't have to be a parent to see this smaller reality, but being a parent may make spotting it easier. It's what children are—smaller realities. It's too bad you and your ex-wife didn't have any children."

"Thank you," Palmer said. "I knew you would save me."

"Who *are* you?" Nina asked, feeling as if she were remembering the words to an old, old song.

She held her breath; she could not imagine what she might have to offer him that he couldn't find more of, and better, elsewhere.

His thighs pulled against the cloth of his pants as he sat, legs athletically apart, in the Green Bay Packers chair. A sunburst of creases radiated out from the upper inseam of each pantleg. She looked away. "I had a vasectomy," he said.

"You and who else?! Every man I've ever known in this city has had a vasectomy. This is a city of vasectomies! I wonder why?"

"My wife didn't want kids. Look," he said, "if you don't marry me, it's the same as if we'd never met. Or it's the same as if we both had Alzheimer's." He placed his hands on his legs, cupping his knees in his palms as if hanging on but all he had to hang onto was himself. Or maybe he'd gotten mixed up and thought he really was a Green Bay Packer and was crouched to block and tackle. He looked so defensive, Nina thought, and so vulnerable, too. "I don't want to be forgotten," he explained. "Not again. I need to live with someone who is not going to forget who I have been to her." He let go of his knees, turned his palms up. "I can't keep doing this over."

"Tavy's the one you have to persuade." She was still whispering, as if not saying it louder would keep it from being too true. "I can't marry you if Tavy won't let me."

The bracelet is sliding from her arm, pale-blue beads spilling like ampules over the coverlet and onto the floor. . . .

After the fire burned down, he left and she went upstairs to undress for bed, but first, as she always did, she glanced in on Tavy. Tavy looked like a pinwheel in sleep, arms and legs flung in four directions, her soft blue nonflammable flannel nightgown in a windmill splay. The little dog was sleeping beside her, on his back, all four legs in the air.

It was well into winter now, the medicine cabinet in the bathroom cluttered with half-used bottles of cough syrup, cards of twelve-hour time-release Contac punched out except for one or two remaining tablets, the basement laundry sink plugged with lint from months of washing Tavy's thermal undervests, the maple floor scarred with salt near the front door. Municipal snowplows packed the snow in at the entrance to driveways so citizens couldn't get out without shoveling all over again. Four-wheel-drive vehicles splashed mud and grimy snowmelt on passing pedestrians, who, in down parkas, looked bulked up, as if they were on steroids. This was life in an unfriendly clime. It hardened you, toughened your character, caused you to blow your nose and fix yourself a cup of hot cocoa to take to bed with you, where you lay propped up against a pillow, dreaming, a little bit feverishly, of a wedding even at this late date, with this late date, this date late in the millennium.

The bracelet drops from the bed to the floor, glass beads shattering bluely, a waterfall of pale beads. . . .

Nina talked to Tavy. Tavy listened. Then Tavy wept. She wept from somewhere deep inside herself, her small back bent and heaving, the flexible spine outlined under her pullover, shoulder blades trembling as if something were pushing against them to get out—something like wings. When Nina put a hand under Tavy's chin and turned that fierce face toward her, it was a whole small area of turbulence, a storm, a tornado watch. Tears blurred Tavy's eyes and dripped down her cheeks, her nose ran, she swallowed tears and hiccupped, she used the back of her fist to wipe the tears from her face but more kept coming.

Already Nina could see the beautiful young woman her daughter would grow into, and she worried, knowing that beauty is often perceived as a form of power and that people seek, therefore, to prove their own superiority by subjugating it. (How many times, Nina remembered sadly, had men—in the days before she began to live like a nun—slept with her merely to establish for themselves the fact that they could. And each time, of course, she remembered ruefully, she had thought they loved her, and she had waited for them to ask her to marry them but they never did.) "Sweetheart," she said, beginning. But what she wanted to say was, *Get thee to a nunnery.* "Sweetheart," she said again, "do you really miss Rajan so much? We hardly ever see him anymore. Palmer is the one who does things with us now. And Palmer likes to do things with us. He cares about you very much."

"Is he going to live here?"

"I don't know. Maybe. Or maybe we'll all move to a bigger house. Would you like that?"

"Do you love Palmer?" Tavy asked.

"Well, I—"

"Do you love him more than you love Teddy?"

"Well, I—"

"Do you love him more than you love me?"

"Oh, no! Never never never!" Nina cried, amazed to realize what grownup fears a child can harbor. Or maybe she meant, What childish fears a grownup can harbor.

She is falling, too, slipping out of time and shattering into all her selves, so blue, so blue. . . .

Nina had noted that the older she got the faster time went. She had a metabolic explanation for this: When you were a kid, you had so much energy that your internal mechanism was going faster than real time, so real time went by slowly. But as you got older, you slowed down inside, your brain, your nervous reflexes, even your heart—which became cautious and invalid, an old lady holding onto the wrought-iron railing for fear of falling on ice and breaking a hip: that was your heart—and now time sped by you, you couldn't keep up with it. Eventually it outstripped you and was far up ahead somewhere, out of sight.

You had been left behind forever.

But that wasn't the whole story. There was a Darwinian advantage to the way time worked. If time didn't go by faster and faster as you got older, you would always be in mourning for those you had lost—your parents, your alcoholic brother, your ex-husband who died too soon, before you both had a chance to turn ninety and meet again and get married all over again and get it right this time, the way it was meant to be. As you got older, the movie stars started to die, the politicians who had shaped your world, the writers who, even if you'd never met them, had been a part of your literary landscape. And the friends, too, including the girlfriend you'd been twenty-two and on lunch break with, and including the handsome male friend you'd gone to Luchow's with and laughed with all afternoon while the band played polkas. They were gone too. If time were still as slow as it had once been, you couldn't endure it, feeling that pain for a thousand years every day. But time wasn't that slow anymore; it had gathered up enormous speed. It was only yesterday you broke for lunch, only yesterday your family were alive and problematic, only yesterday that you had been a new wife, shy and scared and deeply in love with a man who would break your heart before he died. Time had changed so that the past was almost present. It was the only way the fittest were able to stand surviving. Nina called this her Theory of Evolution.

Inside the fiery orb that was the size of a drop of blood the princess lived in a miniature village, where the huts had thatched roofs and there was a well in the town center, and there were neighbors and livestock. And then soldiers bore down, out of the hills, setting fire to huts and lopping off heads and arms and legs, and burning the cows and horses locked in barns. She felt her wine-dark hair burst into flame, the seed pearls sewn into her gown glowing red hot, like miniature coals. She felt herself gutted, nothing left to her but bricks and roof beams, a smudge of ash, a last smoulder of smoke. This was what it was like to be raped and pillaged, the Bosnian minority of yourself driven out and made a symbol. A symbol of something.

A grammar of contradiction.

History deconstructing itself.

She felt despair and recognized it as destiny, a sad song she was born knowing the words to. It rang in her body like a death knell, or the theme music for the nightly news. Wars and death, wars and death — they had happened before. By the time her brother thrust himself into her, she felt cynical and exhausted, as if this was old news, something that had already happened. That was the nature of doom — to be a rerun, repetition, the end. History? What history? There had never been any history, only a screen with moving pictures.

But there had been a time — she remembered now, weeping from deep inside herself, her back bent and heaving as he rolled off and she turned on her side away, shoulder blades trembling as if something were pushing against them to get out, something like wings — a time before history. It was so long ago; it was when she was younger, even, than Tavy was now, when everything still remained to be discovered for the first time. Tears burned her eyes. The betrayal at the center of her life was like a trap into which she kept falling, over and over. She had become a prisoner of expectation.

As if her brother had cared. As if anyone had cared. Her mother the queen and her father the king — they had had their minds on matters of state. She knew better than to bother them. She knew that as long as you still had your arms and legs you had nothing legitimate to complain about.

As if her brother had ever cared. He had confused her with anagrams, a game.

The students stuck suck-up notes into their end-of-semester folders: *Professor Bryant, I really liked your class*. Or, *Dear Professor Bryant, I feel I have learned a lot*. Nina tried to harden her heart against these not very subtle pleas for attention, but her heart grew soft anyway, the cheese spread of it, the cream cheese and crackers of it. Perhaps she was a woman with a deep need to be entertaining, to bring out food and drink and serve her friends.

Palmer was at the same table, reading blue books from his honors section. After a while he capped his pen, put it down on the table, leaned across to her, and said, "Let's make history." And after he said that, he rose from his chair and held out a hand to help her out of hers, and he led her, chivalrously, upstairs to her own bedroom, and she followed.

But she was afraid!

But she was afraid not to follow.

But especially, she was afraid, and she mumbled, "Tavy—"

But he said, "Tavy is sound asleep. Kids can sleep through anything. And she might as well get used to my staying here."

"The dog—"

"That's an old little dog, believe me. He'd rather sleep than watch us have sex."

"He's never had sex."

"Wake him up!" Palmer said. "Let that old dog turn a new trick!"

Nina looked at Tavy's closed door, and part of her wanted to open it and look in on her daughter. *'Night, princess,* she would say almost aloud, brushing Tavy's hair off her forehead. But another part of Nina reminded herself that her daughter had gotten over her cold, and also over her hurt, and would be okay.

As they entered her own room and shut the door behind them, she looked out the window and saw that fresh snow had fallen, arbor vitae wearing long white gloves on their limbs, like women at the opera. Frost-mountains sloped down the windowpanes into the valley of the sill. He lay down on her bed and, still holding her by the hand, pulled her down next to him. She was too embarrassed to look at him and ducked her head against his chest. He gripped her head with a hand on either side and lifted her away from him and looked her in the eye. It was like alchemy, the way the base metals of her brain became as bright as gold. She felt, suddenly, rich, as if she were the most fortunate woman in the world, and she wanted to give everything to him.

He undid the buttons of her shirt, the zipper of her jeans, the hook of her bra, the catch of her bracelet. Pale-blue glass beads sprawled like a rosary on the quilted comforter. Monks lost at sea could be tugged back to shore by people praying, if they prayed well enough.

There was always that fine print.

The wickedly cold air—despite the rope caulking! and Madison Gas and Electric made heating seem like something only a king could afford!—made her tingle, or maybe that was his hand. He got up for a moment and, in what seemed like a single swift movement, divested himself of sweater, shirt, slacks, socks, shorts. His naked body, white from months of winter living, was like a statue in Florence, hard-smooth and cool-warm as marble, a masterpiece, the human form in all its democratic beauty, freed from preconception and dogma. "You must work out a lot," she said weakly.

"Not really," he said, lying beside her again. "I just try to ride the exercycle every day." He kissed the dainty wrists and ankles that proved she was a real princess, the vein in the underside of her wrist where blue blood ran (she knew from a grim night long ago) ruby-red. She smelled his disinfectant smells of drycleaning and deodorant, toothpaste and soap, a slap of shaving lotion, a flourish of cologne, going down, down, down through all the layers of discovery to the Trojan base.

"You have an exercycle?"

She felt surrounded by him as by a Parthenon, a Colosseum. She put her hands on his shoulders, the rounded bones of them like amphorae, or well-wrought urns. A decade! she thought, disbelieving. Almost! As if she were encountering, in a way that would compel her to rethink everything she had been taught, an idea of antiquity, a belief in the dignity and excellence of Man, she caressed his neck and arms and calves. Touching him was like relearning some knowledge she had had and lost, knowledge of the world as a place that made sense. A place that could be studied, a place in which she could study without fear of interruption. A place like a science, rational and with laws. She felt his back under her hands like a revival of classical literature. She felt him in her like a kind of wisdom, humane, not dictated by the powerful God of superstition.

The next morning she woke late, Palmer already downstairs in the kitchen, with Tavy, pouring dogfood and cereal into bowls. She got up and threw on jeans and a T-shirt. She stopped to look out the window, before she left the room, and saw that spring was on them, or almost on them, like a new age. The snow was melting, and the sun shining like the Renaissance.

Fear Kills
A Memoir

•

David Guy

There is a centuries-old Zen koan, our teacher once told us, which has accumulated any number of answers through the years: How does the Buddha meditate when he is too hot, or when he is too cold? The ancient zendos made few concessions to the weather, and the climate was severe; you were given maybe one blanket, and wore the same garment winter and summer. One answer was, Buddha hot, Buddha cold, which meant: when you're hot, sweat; when you're cold, shiver. What's the problem? Another seems at first glance to say the opposite: heat *kills*; cold *kills*. It is not heat and cold themselves that kill, our teacher explained, but our ideas around them. Heat and cold are not problems. They are just facts. It is what we do with them that creates problems.

Which reminds me of a story that I heard years ago. At a scientific lab where he was working late at night, a man walked into a stand-up freezer and mistakenly pulled the door shut behind him. There was no way to open the freezer from the inside, and there was no one else in the lab. He slowly realized, to his horror, that he wouldn't be able to get out until the door was opened in the morning, and he couldn't possibly survive those frigid temperatures for that length of time. Barring a miracle, he would die in the freezer that night. It was a terrible realization, and he spent some time trying to figure a way out. But he was a scientist, and eventually decided that his death could be of some use to the world. He had a notebook with him, and could record the symptoms of a man who was freezing to death. He began to do that, writing down times and the physical sensations he was feeling. Eventually he wrote that he was starting to lose consciousness. He couldn't hold on much longer. He was going to lie down now and accept his death. That was the way his colleagues found him in the morning, lying beside his notebook, dead.

They also found that the temperature wasn't nearly cold enough to kill a man. It was barely below freezing. There had been plenty of oxygen to support someone through the night. The conditions in the freezer hadn't killed him. They couldn't have. He had just died.

II

When I was ten years old I passed through a period when I couldn't sleep. Probably on the first night I wasn't tired when I went to bed, or maybe the first two, but after a while I began to worry about not sleeping—I didn't see how I could go to school the next day, how I could possibly do any work—and my worry became the problem. The anxiety began as soon as I lay down (what if I can't get to sleep?); I felt myself recoil from it (as the question grew a hundred heads: what if I can't sleep for three nights? four? what if I can't sleep for a week? what if I never get to sleep again?) and then, no matter how tired I had been when I dragged myself up to bed, I felt wide awake. The question became a statement: I am not going to sleep.

It was on those nights that I began to ask the unanswerable questions. I had been raised in a religious household, taught that when I died I would go to heaven, but there—of all places—my troubles began. I knew that heaven was a wonderful place, that life there was endless bliss, but I just couldn't imagine a life that never ended. You were exactly the same, the whole time? You just walked around or something? Wouldn't you be afraid that, no matter what anybody said, no matter what even God said, it really would end sometime, you would finally be annihilated? Maybe God wasn't actually in charge here. He thought He was (and to his credit, He'd had a pretty long reign), but there was another being above him, or behind him (how did you even say this?) who wasn't such a nice guy, who would come in one day and wipe everybody out, God included. Almighty my ass! Where's your one and only son now, buddy?

Even if you were absolutely convinced that life never ended, no doubts whatsoever, wouldn't it finally start to wear on you, all that time, with no ending, ever? Time did seem to have a weight; I could feel it on my chest as I lay in bed with such thoughts. It could crush the life out of you. I felt the same way about endless space. How could space not have an end? You go on and on and it never ends. You never come to the border. (Or if you do, what's on the other side?) If there was no end to space, it seemed to me, there was really no such thing as location, because location was defined in terms of borders. So you were never really anywhere. The thought was dizzying. It almost made me sick. It was terrifying.

I would stay in bed with these thoughts as long as I could, but sooner or later I would go to my parents' room and tell them I couldn't sleep. The first night they laughed, maybe the first two, but as the nights wore on there was some concern in their laughter, and maybe a trace of annoyance: this kid just doesn't quit. The unwritten rule was that, once they had gone to bed, if you really couldn't sleep, you could get into bed with them, but I seemed to be straining this policy to the breaking point. Night after night, tromping into my parents' room with weary frightened eyes.

Finally one night, when I came in before my father had gone to bed, I tried to tell him my fears. I don't know how I put it, that I was afraid of the dark bedroom, or the black night outside; I was afraid of dying, of not being. Unfortunately, I was also afraid of living forever. I think I tried to describe what I actually feared. The crushing weight of eternal time. The dizzying spaces of infinity. I remember he laughed a little as I brought these things up. So big a subject for such a little kid. I was embarrassed too. I didn't know why I was thinking such things.

My father was a big man, six feet tall, two hundred pounds. He was a big hugger, a warm and affectionate man, and I sat with him in his chair, snuggled against him, as I told him my fears.

I have pondered that conversation ever since we had it. Sometimes what he said to me has seemed as mysterious as the thought of endless time and space. Sometimes it has seemed perfectly straightforward. Sometimes I have thought that he gave a perfect answer to my questions, sometimes that he didn't address them at all. I do think he gave me the answer he had. If he'd believed, for instance, that there was no God, I think he'd have told me that.

What he said was that when we were young, when we were infants, we thought the whole world revolved around us. It all just existed for our benefit. As we grew older, we began to grow away from that sole concern with ourselves, toward God. The process of living was a process of growth. Our life was a growing toward God.

I don't think I made any sense of his words at the time. They weren't any particular comfort to me (the comfort was in resting there against him, listening while he spoke). But I have always remembered them, or at least their import, through all these years. No doubt their import has changed, as I have changed. Maybe the words have too. We'll never know.

What has always haunted me about that night is that, six years later, when my mother told my brother and me that our father had leukemia (he would die roughly five months later), she said they had known about his illness for six years. I have always wondered if I was asking him those questions at the worst possible moment. I have even wondered if I'd had those fears just because he'd discovered his illness, if there was some mystical connection between us, he'd passed his anxiety on to me. My mother described his long silences in the days after he'd found out, his painful sighs. She'd finally had to ask him what was wrong. He hadn't been able to tell her.

I am an older man now than my father was when he said those words to me, almost the age he was when he died. I probably have less of an understanding of what I mean by the word God than I ever have in my life. It doesn't seem to matter. The name that can be told is not the true name. But if it makes any sense to say that God speaks to human beings, I believe he was speaking to me on those nights when I lay sleepless. It wasn't what I would have expected. It isn't necessarily what I'd expect now. But if God has ever spoken to me, he was speaking to me then. He was speaking from within my fear.

III

At a nine-day meditation retreat that I recently attended in Barre, Massachusetts, we awakened every morning at 5:15, began sitting at 5:45, and—except for a one hour work period and a couple of breaks after meals—alternated sitting and walking meditation throughout the day. We were not permitted to speak, or communicate in any way, through gesture or eye contact; we were not to read, or even to write. We spent the whole day just inhabiting our consciousness.

The mornings generally went well for me; my work period, chopping vegetables in the kitchen, was from 7:15 to 8:15, and I was fresh for the sittings. The main meal of the day was at noon, and we didn't sit again until 2:00, so I would always take a walk after lunch, on a three-mile loop that many of the meditators used, and head back to my room after the 2:00 sitting for a nap. I never missed a sitting, but was more relaxed about the walking periods.

That moment after the 2:00 sitting was always a difficult one. My room, a small cubicle with a cot, was not a haven for me, but a place of considerable torment. The year before, at the same retreat, I'd suffered from extreme insomnia, and though I was sleeping better this year—four hours or so per night—there was still anxiety about returning to my room after the last sitting; I was afraid I would lie sleepless all night, facing my fears alone. As I headed back to my room in the early afternoon, I experienced the flip side of that feeling, the daytime side. It was still light, bright sunny daylight sometimes, or at least (in the blustery Massachusetts spring) cloudy daylight, but the afternoon stretched endlessly in front of me, nothing but sitting and walking, sitting and walking. The evening meal, at 5:00, was a light tea, and broth was served around 9:30; there was a talk at 7:00, so for 45 minutes we would get to hear the sound of a human voice. But even in the midst of that talk night was falling; following the last sitting, I'd return to my room with the same heavy foreboding I'd had when I trudged up the stairs at the age of ten. And in the afternoon, that stretch of time between 3:00 and what wasn't really the end of the day for me, just a new and more difficult beginning, seemed unbearable, utterly empty and impossibly heavy at the same time. The next day the same, and the day after that, and I could clearly see that, when I got home, though I would sprinkle my days with a patina of supposedly worthwhile and important activity, beneath it lay this emptiness, waiting to swallow it up. Emptiness was the basis of everything, and if I couldn't embrace that there would be no peace for me, afraid of the night and dreading the day; afraid of time itself, which is the ocean we swim in; afraid of the present moment, which is eternity. There was no end to this, no beginning and no end: this was it, this was all there was.

My feelings were raw on retreat, and the slightest thing would set me off. I would lie on my bed and sob, afraid, sick of my fear, frustrated at feeling it again, tired of being the person I'd been all my life.

This was the same thing, I'd think, that I'd been afraid of when I was ten years old. It wasn't really death, or what happened after. It was life. I was afraid to live.

I was already in heaven. I had been all along.

The Halo

•

Michael McFee

When Jesus was born, I thought he had a caul; but with
his first cry, it began to glow. That was the halo—always in the
way, poking my breast when he nursed, nicking Joseph when
he'd bend to kiss the boy good night. But if we reached to take
it off, somehow it wasn't there: it was a mirage, a shadow, a
little golden cloud we couldn't quite touch.

Jesus could remove it, though. He'd fly it like a kite, the sun
on a string. He'd skip it across the lake and it would always
return. He'd even work it into his juggling routine, pieces of
fruit landing on a dazzling plate, ta-dah!

Joseph was embarrassed. Maybe the halo reminded him of
what he wasn't. So he built it a fine cedar box, and made Jesus
take it off and lock it inside and bury it out back under the fig
tree and promise not to dig it up. Joseph told him he could have
it back one day, when he was a man.

And so Jesus grew up a normal boy, and everybody forgot
about the halo.

But last night I dreamed that a couple of thieves dug up the
box. And when they opened it, the fig tree burst into golden
fruit, hundreds of sweet halos and not a snake in sight.

Jailhouse Religion

•

Mary E. Lynn Drew

This morning I am clearing my desk. Overstuffed boxes form a circle around me. It is a teacher work day, students are locked down on the hill, and I face retirement philosophically, wiser than I was when I unpacked these same weary boxes. Gifts and good-by dinner are over. My last good-by is in this desk jammed with folders, state Christmas cards, disciplinary forms, letters, Valentines, and poems mostly plagiarized.

I pull the heavy drawer open, the one with the built-in vertical file, and jammed under a folder is a religious hate-comic book that a self-named chaplain from somewhere in Texas sends to prisons. The cover on the comic book headlines groups who are oppressed by the whore, meaning the Catholic Church. I toss the comic into the trash box.

Religion here means a Protestant chaplain with guest preachers, some "called" and some ordained, each taking part in the Sunday service with a born again piano player from Atlanta. Volunteer preachers eager for converts fill in to teach Bible study, and home missionaries who visit inmates regularly bring small gifts from the church, the Word from God, and hope from Jesus Christ. A Catholic priest covers Saturday evenings.

Any of the different kinds of holy books used here are grounded in the certainty that there is a right and a wrong. A scared, adolescent, 15 to 21, who has done anything from possession of one joint to matricide, knows that somewhere in one of those books is a statement concerning his incarceration and that if he believes, really believes, he can make it out of here. How long will religion last once they get that state issue suit, a bus ticket and $25.00 in cash? Staying with any religion is hard on inmates. They put so many restraints on themselves when they join a church it is almost impossible to stay with their vows. But which God and what rights and wrongs had everything to do with the interpretation of the holy word.

Corey, tall and saffron, walked lightly and carried his Christian Bible everywhere. Claude, short and rusty-brown, who had converted to Islam and had taken the name Abdul Kareem Muhammed, fasted, prayed, and abstained from pork-eating. Claude wrote his mother about his new name.

"What did she say?"

"She say, 'I like Claude'."

Even after I was there three years, my students still tried personal questions which could get them expelled.

"Have you got a husband?" To cover quickly, they added, "Because we would like to invite you both to chapel— "Uh, the reason we ast you is because the choir is having a Christmas program and we'd like you and your husband to come and that's why we said that—" They nodded vigorously, "Drones, here, he has a solo. Corey, too." I said I'd come.

Visitors were rare. I was the only one going through the administration building with a security escort. Drones peered at me through the bars at the end of the hall. He looked like a pale prisoner I had known from somewhere, instead of a person in my class who joked and drew murals.

"You came," as the officer slid the accordion gate open.

"You sound surprised."

"I didn't think you would."

I had done the right thing, but he hadn't expected it.

He had been "fronting" for three weeks, assuming that I would find an "out" at the last minute, and he would accept that. But he checked with the chaplain, and he and Drones, others in my class, more inmates from other dormitories, and the security officer escorted me to the chapel. It was a security custom for visitors to go in early and sit in front.

"I am blessed," Drones confided walking over the choppy lawn. "I have never been so blessed. I have been moved to a better dorm, I am in trade school learning upholstery, and I heard from a couple in North Carolina who will help me when

I get out. I have been saved, and today is the anniversary of my first year in Christ."

I was seated down front just behind the choir in the large yellow brick chapel. Suddenly it was flooded with several hundred inmates to the back and all around me. It crossed my mind that they were on decaffeinated coffee and I wondered if that would be enough should any agitation stir them up. In my dark suit among the dark jackets of the inmates, I had hoped for anonymity. Three Protestant ministers were on hand, including the prison chaplain who gave the sermon. One minister gave a short talk at the beginning inviting those, who wished, to come forward to speak for Christ.

Drones did. He thanked the Lord for himself, ". . . for the big crowd here today, for the ministers, and for my visitor." I had been at that prison school long enough to know there is no anonymity, just forgot.

"Yes," said the minister, "I want to recognize the visitor, too, and your name is — ?"

I croaked out my name, and had to repeat it after throat-clearing, whereupon I was greeted by the entire front section. They rose on signal, turned, reached and gripped like a flock of birds rising, tipping wings, and settling once again.

Our class choir members filed up from the front row to the stage, about a dozen of them, and stood facing us in a semicircle, shifting feet, adjusting their space. Drones stood with his hands out from his body, not knowing what to do with them as he sang in a surprisingly sweet, "country" baritone. Corey sang, too, summoning all his courage for the Lord.

The group sang bravely and loudly. Afterwards, they blessed one another, and thanked the free-world volunteer choir master. The choir shook my hand one at a time. Even seeing me out of the school, my students felt it was right. It is right to go to church.

* * *

I reach for a folder, an early one and am struck by the coincidence. There is a Christmas card, provided by the state from Donnie found on my desk several Christmases ago. "I wish you a blessing Xmas and I know you have seen many a one," it read. Along with it was a sheet of blue notebook paper with a blue ink heart and everyone's signature. When Donnie said, "Sign the card," they signed the card. The prison came through those holidays that year without a lasting incident.

Holidays were special. We were decorating for Valentines Day. After they had gotten over the first embarrassment of Halloween, we decorated for everything. They can't have scissors, so I cut out. I like cutting-out, and I took orders.

"We need more white chains." "We need more small red hearts."

As they worked. they talked. I learned that right or wrong might depend on where it happened. Whipple said he had robbed the church poor box. "In front of everybody?" they asked.

"No, it was a country church. They never locked it. I was going to give it back."

"Sure. Glue, please."

"The other ones with me never came forward."

"What'd you get?" meaning his sentence.

"Five do two, maybe." Whipple meant he would be out in two years with his earned time in school and with good behavior.

I did not want to know their crimes. During my training to teach in a prison school, instructors told our class that it was not our job to punish inmates, we were there to teach them. They were already being punished. I stuck to that.

"Hand me that strip. Please." Whipple said.

Two students stayed at the back happy with their Bibles. Lee marched around holding his folder, grumbling. He made waves when discussion went to crimes. He put his folder down and slapped his pencil on top. He was taking a self-test in his workbook.

"I do not see why they ask the same questions over and over, making you answer when they already have the answer in their book. They know what the answer is." Lee did not smile,

216

but sometimes I could see a row of small, rounded baby teeth. At a loss for what to say next, he added, "Did you get over the flu?"

"Oh yes. I never told this but—" they always stopped and when I prefaced with that, "I can do anything," I said, "I am Wonder Woman's mother."

"Aw, you ain't that old," Lee said. They nodded in agreement and went back to work.

They talked about how sick everybody was, that it was an "appendemic," and talked about the tunnel.

"When you die in here, don't nobody know it. They carry your body to the tunnel and hang it on the wall hooks down there, until they can bury you on the other side of the road in the grave yard."

I had been told that inmates believed that. Some creative guard's tale, I thought.

"They ain't no graveyard, is they, over there, Miz Drew?"

"Yes, but—"

When the highway went through the grounds separating the laundry, or something, from the main buildings, they dug a tunnel for access, but filled it in later. The graveyard just happened to be there. They heard what they wanted to hear. They thought about death and punishment, and where you died. Beside separation from loved ones, from everyone, inmates suffer fear of dying before they get out. Sickness or delay in paper work could, at the least, postpone a discharge, so if a parole or discharge is imminent, they won't go to the hospital, or cough, or even complain. They are also afraid others will die before they get out. An ex-student of mine kept coming back, "Don't die," he told me. I am old, and he is a lifer.

Claude feared that his whole family will be killed. His grandmother, who raised him, and grandfather, have died since he has been inside. His little brother was stabbed, and almost died, trying to break up a drunken fight. His big brother ran over the stabber with his car and put the stabber in a wheel chair. He was not charged. "There is a war going on," he told me, lifting his eyes from a letter. "Can you imagine what my mother is going through?"

217

This normal free-world observation shook me. It was then I decided that fate was keeping him in prison to be spared while he grew, while he changed.

Claude came in the next day with a letter. He had got another lady pregnant.

"From here?" I was amazed.

"No," he laughed, "before I came."

"Well?"

"She was married at the time. She has a child to support and now is divorcing her husband and moving south to find me to support her and the child."

That was the gist of what he said. It took him many words, backing away and starting over to get anything said.

"You are Muslim," I told him, "maybe you can take two wives."

This short, learning disabled person with one lazy eye, had some kind of charm that kept them coming. He was my steady, dependable philosopher.

"How did you get into this mess?" I asked meaning women.

Claude laughed and shook his head. "I don't know," he showed me the woman's business card. She was a mortician.

"Oh, that's the one you—?"

"Yeh—"

"—and shouldn't have—"

"Yeh."

Claude also corresponded with a young woman who sang in an Atlanta church choir which was on television Sundays at 6:00 a.m. He had the advantage in this relationship: he could see her but she couldn't see him. The young woman wrote that she couldn't see him but she knew he was a sensitive person because he wrote beautiful poetry.

Claude was never mean, never lied, only his friendships, and letter writing, and an occasional original poem copied straight from the Holy Koran kept him in trouble. His spoken-language disability held him back. Islam gave him self-respect as a black man, and also told him what to eat, and when to fast, and when and how to pray.

"Right" is also what is proper. Tiller said, "I have to use the rest room. I am really tight." Words they chose to use, and ones considered improper changed when they saw the need. Whipple had not approved of another inmate. I asked what was wrong with him. He thought about it and said, "He is an anus." They decided that "getting it out" and "getting off," though in general use in the free world, were not to be used in the classroom. "Even though there were not no bad words in them," one inmate said. "Log" was not acceptable because used in the dorm it meant ones male member, so they kept a journal, but never logged anything. How to turn a swear word around for class, parlor, or church, and not get expelled from school? Easy, I told them. With the SH-word, use sugar. SSHHuhggah. We practiced. They had never heard of son-of-a-biscuit-eater.

* * *

I give up. So many memories are in this old desk. I look at my watch. Lunch time. Lunch I bring to eat in the lounge because of the food-preparation-in-the-cafeteria stories. I resolve to move faster with packing afterward. It doesn't happen. McReady's dusty ragged cassette tape in a shoe box of paper clips, and Band-Aids puts a stop on my resolution when I return.

McReady was a black, bedrock, fundamentalist Baptist. His claim as a religious authority, besides his ironbound belief in his interpretation of the Bible, was his father who came to grips daily with God's presence in his line of work. McReady was training with him to be an undertaker. Stories like the time he and his father went to the train wreck and collected people in bags commanded respect from any silent slackers. He could not quote scriptures, though, so he stayed out of Corey's way, whom I suspect was working on a nondenominational approach from his Bible, for his church that he would have some day.

When an inmate went home he willed the marigold he was raising in an Styrofoam cup to McReady who promptly drowned it. I said that he did it so he could do the funeral. "They'd be too wet for cremation," he grinned.

219

McReady had a baby he had never seen, born while he was in prison. He asked me, "How long is a baby when it is newborn?" I showed him with my arm. He told me about a "lady who had a baby half that size. Born early. We bury them in a shrift."

He often surprised me with his quick knowing laugh. He recognized any old tunes I play on my "jam box" at the end of the school day. He would say softly that his mother used to play them. And she left us, he would add.

We did a unit on History of Gospel Music, and we studied tribes of Africa like the Masai, who bled their cattle and mixed the blood with urine and milk for food.

"Oh sure," said McReady, "they call that a 'bloody milky'." It was my turn to laugh.

After a movie on religions of the world, we talked about original sin. "You mean that a new baby coming into the world has sin on it?"

"Oh yes," McReady.

"Why?" I asked.

"Because of what his Mama done."

"What did she do?"

He hesitated, not planning to go this far. Surely, he was thinking, she knows this much.

"You mean what she done, did to get the baby?" I asked again.

"Yes," relieved.

Only Corey was shaking his head. He looked up when I asked if the father was in sin, too. There was mixed reaction. Someone suggested that the father couldn't help himself and everyone felt better. McReady looked puzzled and was probably wondering how such a smart, funny lady on some things could be so mixed up on others.

McReady had unloaded box cars that morning. We had an after-test conference. He had failed it, and all I could tell him was that now that he knew how the testing went, he would do better next time, and that even if he never did better on the test he was so smart where it really mattered, that he could hire people to do the school stuff. It didn't help. Another time we talked about women. His religious comments laid most of the world's troubles on women, as did most inmates, needing something to blame for being in this place.

Except for Claude, who was sort of ahead of the rest, the class was still trying to reconcile the fact that if women are the root of all evil why did they have the desire to own one of them. The premise that most of them had reached, was that there are good women and there are bad women. This was a start.

Something was said about letting nice women work in a prison. "If you mean me, I like the money, and if you mean inmates talk about us, men talk about women everywhere. Women are doing the same thing." I told them.

They disagreed.

"Have you ever walked by a group of girls who suddenly laugh? Why do you think they do that?"

"Is you going to give us bubble gum to chew when we play in the tournament?" Spinney asked. And that took care of that.

Discussion after a 1930's Garbo, Anna Karenina film prompted me to ask, "How could a woman in those days earn a living if she were on her own?"

"She getting paid." Claude knew.

"Right. What do you think? Should she have left the husband?"

"She was in too much hurry." Almost pleading in sincerity. "They could have worked something out." A lot of nods.

On prostitution. "Is it wrong?"

"Yes."

"For which one? The one who is paying?"

McReady pushed back stretching his legs. "Oh, I think a man ought to do what he want with his money."

"Should a woman?"

"Yes."

"Should she, or he, do what they want with their body to get money?"

"Depends."

"Suppose they don't want to, but are made to."

"Wrong. Wrong." Consensus.

The next day, after an obvious dorm session that night, they told me, "Society makes them do it."

"Some say society puts you in jail," I observed. "Who was forced in here." No answer. "A man might steal to survive."

"Right." They agreed.

"A stereo?"

"No."

"Bread?"

"Yeh."

"Drugs?" No answer.

"How many in here stole dough-bread for his family?"

No one was in there for stealing bread.

Even music was wrong once because one little black and tan fellow sat with a stiff back to the class for educational movies, and for music he stopped his ears, even a history unit on gospel music. I asked why. It was against his religion, he said. The Christian Comic Books religion.

It seemed like a good time for religious class experience. We ran slides from our library on world's religions daily for a week, discussed each viewing, then individuals presented talks on tenets of their religion.

Claude went first and after the slides no one was amazed at his pronouncements about the holy Koran or his Arabic spelling of the word. Five pillars of Islam . . . submission to God's will. . . . (A whisper was heard on hearing God mentioned), a Muslim is one who submits. . . . (Several heads hit desks to try for an after lunch nap). No God but Allah . . . fast during Ramadan . . . all except ill, old, pregnant, and soldiers . . . no sex neither (Heads up) . . . Muslims have no control over their destinies, he concluded. And, accepting Allah's will, will get you into paradise.

"What is Christmas to a Muslim," students asked him.

"Another day, just another day," said Claude from South Georgia.

Up to this point in the speech no one shared his belief on Christmas, however, hearing new facts from a "scientific document" quoting doctors and ministers on pork-eating was an attention grabber. The following facts included: Hog meat is more difficult than most other kinds, that means that the biological value (BV) is therefore low . . . Hog is by choice a dirty, filthy animal; it follows the cattle and other animals on the farms to eat their droppings.

I interrupted telling him that I knew a little about the habits of hogs—but the next pronouncement was a stunner.

"It has been reported by Dr. ____ that many people who eat carnivorous animals tend to be vicious, are ready to kill others without reason, and some are even known to eat the meat of other people . . . We have seen that the hormone diethylstil-besterol injected into calves was passed on to humans who ate the meat of the calves and increased the ratio of homosexuality in men.   Therefore, eating the flesh of the hog may affect the individual by increasing immorality, including homosexuality, lesbianism, adultery, and prostitution. Incidence of looting, killing, stabbing, shooting, sniping, strangling, robbing, and stockpiling of arms cannot be tolerated any more."

Those who were against homosexuality were now mulling over pork and stockpiling and just about everybody was into a good reason not to eat prison pork, served several times a week.

I was determined that the next unit after religion was going to be questioning the written (and spoken) word.

But, we were not out of it, yet. Kenneth, of the Christian Comics, confided that nuns and priest make babies, kill them, and hide the babies under the Vatican.

I told him, "Never mind what you feel about Catholics, that's not their style. Think about it. They would raise them in the Catholic faith, not kill them off."

His jaw was stone.

"You heard this, right?" I hissed in the conference corner of the classroom.

"No! I read it! And I will show it to you, and prove it!"

We were into each others faces. Assuredly not one of my better days.

Kenneth would not share his comics with the class but let me have them overnight. I photocopied some, along with

Claude's pork-eating scientific document.

The next day Kenneth and I talked again.

"I couldn't find the one on the babies," he said.

"Never mind." I gave him the comics.

There was one cover. "The Godfathers," showing popes in tall hats with pointed, satanic faces. Among people betrayed by them were listed as, ". . . poor Nazis, Jews, KKK's, Masons, Communists, and a statement, 'God help them to have the strength to come out of her (the church).'" There was another cover depicting the Biblical Creation with a violent Adam blaming God for giving him a woman and spoiling it all. Several scripture quotes were sprinkled throughout giving the impression that it was "all in the Bible."

"It's all in the Bible! I know what I see! I can read!" My poor student controlled his voice if not his emotion.

As long as all hope for me as a professional person was gone anyway, I reasoned that I might as well give it one last try.

"Since black people were first on earth, if you believe the archeologists, and there was an Adam and Eve, if you believe the creationists, they must have been black. Adam and Eve *must have been black, right?"*

He was nodding carefully.

"*Now.* I'll just bet you *cannot even picture* one of my black sisters taking the blame for the world being run out of paradise!"

I was exhausted. I let them have free-reading.

* * *

I am exhausted, now in my desk chair, just thinking about it. You can only teach them how to question. I hear that the academic part of the school will be phased out. I wonder if that will stop the religious comic books and the other hate material. No one knows how lasting jailhouse religion is, or education for that matter, when inmates leave. To Corey, McReady, and Claude, and the others: May you keep searching. I told them, like I told them all when they left, that I never, ever, wanted to see them again. And for what it is worth, I never did.

Naufrage and Diapason

•

Joe Ashby Porter

Johnny John Hawk fingers aside the pitiful thin curtain his ex ran up from a patchy dishtowel. Johnny stretches his big head into the niche at the end of his bunk. Through a Plexiglas window, scarred as if it had been to the moon and back and not much bigger than a spaghetti box, Johnny can see what the begrudging cold purple means dawning over the new snow and totem poles and the bay where his *Lorna* bobs at anchor like a red toy. Trouble is what that sky means. Bad squalls and worse.

Snuggle back into the sleeping bag and hibernate a week more? In these Alaskan waters this early in the spring it's only fifty-fifty you'll even locate salmon. Plus nephew Elmo perking coffee at the other end of the trailer is too green for weather like this, ought to be back at Ketchikan Middle School learning a trade, not hanging with a hand-to-mouth trawler uncle pushing forty squatting here on this lost bay. Elders say the cove had honor once. Now, with the remains of a fishing camp that never got built, it looks like a frozen train wreck on a landfill. Plus a hangover aching from one temple to the other like Frankenstein rods.

Plus . . . But Johnny shakes his head and lets the curtain spread back into place. He unzips his mummy bag and rolls out of the bunk. The sockeye should be running. Except . . . What was it a moment ago in the sky, a shade north of the tall totem, wheeling behind a precipice of cloud, an eagle?

When Elmo hears Johnny slump to the john and pee, he films a black skillet with bear grease and cracks in six eggs. By the time he has shaken out and divided an omelette filled with roe,

225

meanwhile toasting bread over the second gas ring in a vintage four-sided holder with hinged sloping sides, Uncle Johnny himself has taken his place at the eating table and is praying the way he does before he eats anything or even tastes the BC fizzing in his toothbrush glass. Elmo sets the food and coffee on the table.

Elmo's mother, Johnny's ex's younger sister, told Elmo he could lay out of school two weeks in May here, on two conditions. One is, apply himself when he gets back, which means more study, less firewater, condoms. Elmo expects to finesse that condition, but he's not so sure about the other, which is to talk to Johnny about maybe coming to Ketchikan and getting on welfare, maybe signing on as night watchman at the cannery or custodian at the high school. Last night near midnight, when they stumbled out to view the auroras, Elmo had almost broached the subject. Maybe today? Or maybe never. The dude's life is shot, so how much good could leaning on a broom handle do? Still, maybe today all the same. There's television in Ketchikan, monthly social dancing.

Johnny sometimes prays to the Great Spirit or the Blessed Virgin, but now he's studying how to say no if Elmo asks for money or some other kind of help. Maybe Elmo could handle the truth that Uncle Johnny's at the end of his rope. Cash for *Lorna* payments and alimony ran out in October, and cash for hooch and groceries won't last through May. Johnny's been squatting and living off the land, but any day now the marshall will show up with repo papers and maybe a warrant.

Johnny looks up and unfolds his hands. Ice cracks and thunks into snow outside. Johnny tells Elmo he'll take the *Lorna* out alone today for a shakedown trawl through a near passage and be back before dark. He asks Elmo to fill a thermos.

Okay, says Elmo. But you know I was thinking. Us Tlingits, we ought to open us up a casino and kick back, forget salmon.

Lest I forget my love for thee, sings Johnny.

Down at the pier icy froth scumbles around pilings and against the wooden dory. Casting off, Johnny takes Elmo's hand and says, stroke the thunderbird pole with that same hand for me on your way back up to the trailer. Me, I forgot.

Check, but it doesn't seem like you, Johnny. We must've partied you too hard last night. So look lively out there.

No, says Johnny as he pushes off with an oar. Truth is, I stopped myself from touching that pole. My hand went out automatically but then some devil got into me and I said fuck it. But now I'm having second thoughts. You carry the touch back up and it should be the same.

Don't worry, says Elmo. When he reaches the pole he pushes his open hand hard against the frozen wood, back and forth until down on the water Johnny has anchored and boarded the *Lorna* and turned to wave, and Elmo can wave back with his other hand.

Through the day Elmo listens to short wave and writes half a letter to his girlfriend and naps and listens to the radio some more. Going on three he loses the signal in spumes of interference. A little later a deep whistle sounds from the harbor, from a strange boat. Ahoy, ahoy, rattles the ship-to-shore set. It's a fisherman from Wrangell come to tell Elmo his mother's in the hospital with a burst gall bladder. Elmo leaves Johnny a note under the salt shaker and locks up, more against bears than people. At the helm, the captain with walrus moustaches says the hospital transmitter bounced word off a satellite, an operation scheduled for twenty minutes ago. Good odds, the surgeon's supposed to have said. Maybe on the way out to a clear channel they'll glimpse Johnny heading in. Dusk, a ribbed sky, frozen ribbed water with black umbrellas opening in it, squalls.

Zrr, zrr. The twenty-three-year-old white woman with lank reddish hair, granny glasses, and braces, whose name is Frieda Wakeland, slides piecework left, right, out, and back. I never got asked to a sock hop, Frieda told Maudie Roberts, who shares her piecing table, so I guess that's why I hop these treadles in my sock feet. How 'bout yourself? Maudie said she'd got asked to an ice cream supper in the churchyard, the night dead Bobby popped the question and she accepted, but sock hops were more in her children's time and maybe the grandchildren's. At work Maudie's always preferred tartan fleece-lined house slippers for her bunions, or maybe it was a hammertoe she'd mentioned last week at lunch.

Frieda's worked in the riverfront Carolina hosiery mill since she was nineteen. Her pa, an upstanding Crittenden deacon and lay minister, had aimed for her to enroll for a church-related nursing degree out in southern Indiana, either that or learn tap for real at the Crittenden Academy of Dance behind the drygoods store so she could bring home more than the miniature plastic trophies lined up on her dresser, maybe a contract from one of the televangelists she could send a videotape audition to. When Frieda couldn't see her way clear to go along with either plan, Pa sent her down the street to let her rethink priorities working minimum wage in the hosiery mill, no benefits, with seven other local women, mothers and grandmothers, widows.

At the time, Frieda hadn't wanted to go off to nursing or television because she didn't want to leave Crittenden. Not that she cared much for the country backwater near nothing except the impassable river that provided nothing except alewives each spring and power for the mill. Frieda hated Crittenden, really. What had kept her there at first was love, at least that's what she called it, for Eddie Thorne, six years her senior. He'd tried to scrape a living with sugar beets on the farm he inherited from the auntie who raised him, south on the county road, beets then tobacco and then boo that landed him in the pen where he went bad and stopped even writing, and then so had Frieda. Eddie'd always worn rubbers, and the subject of marriage had never come up, so that was okay.

Like meringue on the baked Alaska Maudie turned out of her cast-iron stove a hundred years ago to snag her dead Bobby with, fabric ripples and billows, sliding to the sewing food, each blend wrinkling in its own way, rayon-polyester, rayon-cotton-polyester, each with its own name, Lureen, Softex, Lureen Twill. Once, Frieda goes, which is your favorite? Maudie goes, blends pshaw, before you was born, sugar, we used to sew pure goods, even linen.

Is an interloper a kind of deer, Frieda remembers asking Pa after grace at breakfast. She was nine and Ma had been gone only a year. A schoolmate's mother had explained that since Ma was an interloper you could see how she might prance back out of Crittenden one fine day, as she did. Pa hasn't remarried. He keeps busy lettering and sign-painting, and with his ham radio and of course the church, and his health seems to be holding for the moment. Says he doesn't know Ma's whereabouts or desire to.

Muzzle up for the race, cracked Frieda this morning before the whistle, because of the Bakelite breath-filter masks the crew wears to protect against textile dust, and she was recalling a science show about dog races. Greyhounds muzzled but not huskies in the Iditarod (not Izod), the opposite of what you'd expect, really. Frieda wears earplugs too, against the noise. You learn to read lips. While Frieda sews she runs stories in her mind that unfold and settle like cloth.

Pa is lettering a blue roadsign for the Herring Shack down river when over his ham set comes a bulletin, escaped convicts camped in the wildwood. Planning to blast their way into Crittenden, two whites and a halfbreed, beating drums and singing. One of the whites rumored to be lovelorn for a Crittenden spitfire who spurns him. Pa swishes his lettering brush in thinner and shakes dry the bristles. Moments later in the den he secretes his wedding ring and billfold behind a trick board. Now he kneels, humming the doxology.

Zrr, zrr. The livid sun seems to hang motionless in the freezing heavens as the tormented western horizon rises to it. Loaded with sockeye and some coho, the *Lorna* trundles through a high chop and wind stiffening to gale force.

Overdue caulking, the *Lorna* seems to have sprung a leak. In the hold the salmon are swimming again, bumping each other in the dark, trailing tackle like Mail Pouch from their cruel underslung mouths. Above at the wheel, Johnny estimates he will have time to spare. The cannery should buy most of the catch, and Johnny thinks, why not ship a nice fish to the new President's little girl, for her salmon hair. Maybe one for Arthur

Godfrey and all the little Godfreys too, that Johnny's ex-mother-in-law used to like on Ketchikan radio. Something in the engine or the drive sputters. Johnny gears down and slips on the ship-to-shore.

Frieda snips the thread. She pushes the nightie over the edge onto a conveyor belt that will move it past finishing and inspection. As she taps the counting machine she checks her liquid crystal wristwatch for the first time since lunch. As she hooks up the next batch of piecework out of the tumbrel beside her folding chair, she steals her first glance since lunch at the fly-specked skylight. Were she Alice with the giraffe neck, she might nudge it open and peer around in the foolish sunshine while her hands stayed busy.

The ship-to-shore fails to respond. Johnny tries again. No dice, dead catheters or something. The *Lorna* is sideslipping and yawing. Johnny keys a different map onto his screen and plots a different course, to the nearest docking. He shifts back into full forward. The engine hums as if considering. Then it retches and gives up the ghost. Through his legs Johnny feels a shudder as the *Lorna* begins to founder.

Johnny thinks what it will be like to go down in these icily sloshing dark waves of ocean sea, with a life unspooling before his eyes. Water will fill his lungs. He'll empty them and fill them again with water.

Two days later at lunch hour Elmo gets through to a maritime warden who's swung by Johnny's cove and seen neither hide nor hair of him. Thoughtfully chewing a stick of pemmican, Elmo saunters back to the bleachers. He has a funny feeling, he tells his girlfriend. He says the same thing that evening to his ma and her boyfriend at the kitchen table over red flannel hash. When his ma calls her sister for her birthday the second week of June she says, thanks for the carnations when they did my gall bladder, Lorna. By the way, looks like your Johnny's shipped out for parts unknown, but I know you already gave up hope for alimony checks.

Months pass and years. Elmo moves to Nome. Once at his

mailbox he thinks maybe he'll find a picture postcard from Johnny. After a while Elmo forgets his uncle. He sells Toyotas, opens his own dealership in Yessum, marries, raises two children, dies during an earthquake. His aquamarine class ring gleaming in the rubble leads investigators to the body. Tough luck, says the captain, dusting off her viscose coverall. The lieutenant shrugs, snaps open her gas mask, and says he had a rich full life probably. One of Elmo's children assumes the dealership.

Maudie reaches across the table and taps Frieda with a yardstick. When Frieda pulls out an earplug Maudie says, my Junie needs a sitter Monday week if your neighbor's girl wants pin money. Alaska, chirps Frieda. She stuffs the plug back in. Zrr, zrr. The piece yoke she slides off the table billows like a liquid map.

A widowed society dentist planning to summer in Crittenden seeks a hygienist trainee between twenty and twenty-five years of age. Running the tip of her tongue against her braces, Frieda tastes waterpack salmon, an impulse purchase from the Piggly Wiggly. Frieda wanted to be able to say she'd tried it at least once in her life.

Now the prison escapees have Pa hostage and they're barricading themselves. Helicopters buzz in from Charlotte, and armed Hovercraft ascend the river. In a skirmish the desperadoes are recaptured. Unharmed, Pa testifies in their behalf on national television, before the sheriff herds all three into his paddy wagon and whisks them back for more decades in the slammer.

What is a life after all but a piece of stretched meat? The story ratchets along regardless. In a sci-fi Frieda rented last Sunday for her birthday, this gob will settle on your face and you can't pry it off any more than you can pry off the world. That's right, Frieda thinks. Zrr, zrr. People find themselves at dead ends all the time, up a creek. Pa and Frieda have widescreen in the den, hordes succumb daily. So what else is new? And yet . . .

Johnny has swum out the pilothouse and risen toward the

dim choppy surface, almost free, until a part of the superstructure has caught his ankle, and it is too late now to struggle. Johnny goes feet first into the green black. His arms trail above his upturned face, his poor fingers already frozen. The *Lorna*'s hull collapses. One by one, sockeye and coho nose through the rupture out into the depths and away toward western rivers.

Rumors

•

MariJo Moore

It was rumored that Addy May Birdsong would sneak into your house, touch your forehead with her fingers while you were sleeping, and change the course of your dreams. I had heard this rumor for the first time when I was about thirteen. Lydia Rattler, who sat next to me in Home Room, told me this because she had heard that Addy May was related to me.

"So what?" I had said back to her. "Everybody's related to everybody on this reservation." I had never liked Lydia much because she had ugly teeth that stuck way out and because she wanted to gossip all the time like an old woman. But she sat next to me that whole school year and I learned to endure her gossip, if not her buck teeth.

When I had asked my mama about the rumor, she said that lots of things were said about Addy May because she was different than most.

"What do you mean, different?" I asked in total sincerity. It seemed to me that almost every adult I knew back then had some sort of strangeness about them - mostly caused from alcohol, or from running out of it.

"Well," my mama had said thoughtfully as she scratched her chin the way she often did when she was trying to explain something in terms that she thought I might understand, "Cousin Addy May just has a way of stirring up people. She looks all the way into their souls with those black pitted eyes of hers and it makes people wonder if she knows what they've been up to." I had to agree with the part about the black pitted eyes. They reminded me of a tunnel a train had just gone through.

"But you don't pay any mind to what you hear about her. She's your cousin and she's had a hard life, harder than most on this reservation, and so she deserves to be a little stranger than most if she wants."

I forgot about my "stranger than most" Cousin Addy May and all the rumors about her until one night it was so hot I was having trouble sleeping and decided to crawl out the bedroom window to get some fresh air. I was careful not to wake my younger twin sisters. Course I loved them with all my heart, but they could be quite bothersome when I wanted some time alone.

The night air was so cool and refreshing I pulled my braids on top of my head and let it touch the back of my neck. It made me feel so good, I decided to take a walk down the road that led up the mountain to our house. The two other families that lived on the road were at least two miles away, so I felt like I had the road all to myself. I had walked for about ten minutes, staring up at the stars and the full moon, feeling proud that I was so brave to be out by myself that late at night when I saw Addy May standing there in the middle of the road with the moon shining down on her head like a flashlight. Her hair was long and loose, not braided as usual, and I remember thinking that it looked like a thick, black waterfall flowing down her skinny back. I was totally shocked to see someone standing there in the middle of the night and grateful that she hadn't heard me coming down the road.

She had her back to me, so I stepped into the darkness of the brush beside the road so I could watch her. She was wearing a long cotton skirt that was probably dark blue but looked purple in the moonlight, and a shawl of many colors was draped loosely around her thin shoulders. I watched quietly as she swayed her body back and forth, waving both hands above her head. The more I watched her, the faster my heart beat. And when she starting singing, I felt like it would bust right out of my chest. Her voice was beautiful, high pitched and full of rich guttural tones. Over and over she sang her song, swaying there in the moonlight. I could hear her words distinctly:

"First I was woman
    then I was mother

Now I am woman again."

Mesmerized by her presence and her voice, I had no idea what her song was about, but I knew the words came from way down deep inside her. From the same place my moon time had begun flowing several months back when Mama had told me that I had become a woman. Addy May's words came from the connecting source to the earth that every woman has inside her, and my stomach burned way down deep in that spot as I listened.

I must have stood there in the brush for at least half an hour, watching her, listening to her singing, and feeling my heart trying to jump up into my throat. Then something happened that I never would have believed if someone else had told me about it. There were two female spirits come down from the sky and stood right next to Addy May's swaying body. One was real old and the other a young girl just a little older than me. With quick, jerky movements, they began to dance around Addy May, looking kind of like the white curling smoke that dances around a red hot fire, and chanting in Cherokee. I couldn't understand all of what they were saying because I don't speak my native language proper, but I heard a few words I could recognize and realized the gist of their song had to do with sorrow and grief.

As I stood there, squinting my eyes trying to figure out what was in the bundles each spirit woman carried in her arms, and muster up enough courage to stay and see what would happen next, Addy May turned and looked directly at me. I swear she looked directly at me and smiled right into my eyes, never missing a beat to her swaying or a word to her song. When she did that, I ran back home as fast as I could and didn't tell a soul what I had seen that night. Not even my mama. As a matter of fact, I kind of forgot about the incident for a while because my thoughts were on other things. Mostly my new boyfriend, Roger. That is until I heard from Lydia Rattler that Addy May had been arrested for stealing a baby boy.

She had gone into John and Amanda Wolfe's house late one night and taken their baby right from his crib. The baby hadn't cried or made any noise or anything, so the parents didn't know he was missing until his mama woke up the next morning and went to check on him. He was only six months old but he was big for his age. I had seen him in front of the Spirits on The River with his mama the week before Addy May stole him. Amanda had gone in there to apply for a job and asked me and my cousin Lenny, who happened to be walking by at the time, to hold him for her while she went in the restaurant to get an application. It was really curious to me that I had actually held that same baby in my arms just a week before Addy May stole him.

She hadn't tried to hide him or anything, and that's why they found out so quick that she had him. She had just taken him home with her, and when Mavis Rose had passed by Addy May's house on her way to the Tribal Offices as she did every weekday morning, she had seen Addy May sitting there on her front porch in an old rocking chair, holding him. Mavis said later that she thought it was kind of odd, Addy May sitting there on her front porch with a baby and all, but didn't know how odd until she arrived at work and was told that the Wolfe baby was missing. Of course she told all of them at the Tribal Offices what she had seen and they called the Wolfes who had Addy May arrested. The baby wasn't hurt or anything, so the Wolfes didn't press it. The authorities let Addy May go after a good talking to because they didn't know what else to do with her, I guess.

Mama said she probably needed some kind of professional help cause she had never got over the death of her two babies who had burned to death that past winter. One was a girl, about a year and a half old, and the other a boy, six months old. Her old mobile home had caught fire because of bad wiring or something, and she hadn't been able to save them.

I cried after my mama told me that story. I cried like I had never cried for anybody before because I felt close to Addy May somehow. So I went to visit her about a week after that. I just stopped by her house on my way home from school one day to tell her I was her cousin and just to see how she was doing. She didn't talk much, just nodded her head, and gave me some water from her well to drink. I can still taste that water now, all fresh and cool and sweet from that dipper gourd she used. I stayed for about an hour I guess, just sitting there on her front porch with her, not talking. And that was OK with me cause I felt like I just needed to be there for her. She never mentioned that night I had seen her in the road, swaying and singing, but I knew she knew. And I knew she knew that I cared about her.

I didn't go back to visit her again, but I did see her at different times, walking around, mumbling to herself. She got real crazy after the Wolfe baby incident and people just kind of left her alone and made up more rumors about her to entertain themselves. She wasn't a real threat to anybody, and the Crowe Sisters who lived down the road from her always made sure she had something to eat.

I guess I just grew up and forgot about her for several years. There were my two kids and a husband to worry over, and I hadn't thought about her for a while until Mama told me that Addy May had died. She had got the flu or pneumonia or something, and passed away in her sleep one night.

"She's probably better off," Mama had said. I quietly agreed cause deep inside I knew that Addy May was with those two spirits who understood the song she was singing that night there in the middle of the road. The night she was swaying and singing in the moonlight, and I stood in the darkness of the brush, quietly watching and listening.

Chang & Eng—A Love Story

•

Maudy Benz

I could not find a babysitter the last weekend in July, so I packed my children into the station wagon and we all headed for White Plains, North Carolina. They asked enough questions to last the two-and-a-half-hour trip up the interstate to the Bunker reunion.

"How did they go to the bathroom?"

Together.

"How did they sleep?"

Usually face to face, I answered—and all of a sudden I felt melancholy, as I thought of my own partnerless nights.

"Did they ever get cut apart?"

No, they couldn't be separated and live through it, not back then.

Eng and Chang Bunker shared a liver that passed through a ligament. They could wear regular shirts and just leave a button undone for the ligament. They always dressed alike but you could tell Chang from Eng—Chang was usually on the right of the photo (their left), and he was shorter, his body tipped in toward his brother's at the chest and away at the shoulders and neck. Chang tilted, Eng didn't—postures that mirrored their different temperaments.

"Will they really be there?" my seven-year-old son asked, his voice tremulous with excitement.

Only in spirit, I said.

A set of fraternal twins named Eng and Chang, great-grandsons of Eng, would be there. They had been featured as children in *Life* magazine (they are now grown men). Of course my son thought they were joined together. He would not give up his vision of seeing living Siamese twins. "Are there lots of twins in the family?" my twelve-year-old daughter asked. I said there were six sets of twins in the families of the descendants, who now numbered in the thousands. But no twins were conjoined. "No fair," my son said.

The first year I was in Chapel Hill, North Carolina (having moved there from Michigan in an attempt to escape all reminders of my first heartbreak), my roommate Darcy and I dressed up as Siamese twins for Halloween. We wore one giant turtleneck and one huge skirt with a cummerbund. We moved our inside legs in step down Franklin Street, to the rhythm of the Crystal Gale song we sang all evening: "Don't it make our brown eyes blue."

I have always been fascinated by the closeness of twins. With a twin, you would feel comforted and certainly less alone.

It was only after having lived in Chapel Hill for ten years — after having been married and, just recently, separated — that I learned that Eng and Chang Bunker, the "original" Siamese twins, had lived a good part of their lives in North Carolina during the mid-1800s. It occurred to me that a day as a fly on the wall in Eng and Chang's home would've shed some light on how to live with someone (and saved me plenty in divorce lawyers' fees).

As the second part of my life begins, I realize that if I am ever going to have a relationship that works, there are some things I'm going to have to learn. So when I heard that a family reunion of Eng and Chang's descendants was scheduled for July in White Plains, North Carolina, the twins' American home, I knew I had to go.

Eng and Chang were born in Siam (now Thailand) in 1811. Conjoined twins existed before them, of course, most notably brothers who entertained on musical instruments in the Scottish court in the 1500s. But because Eng and Chang spent years (1829-1839 and 1860-1870) touring during a time when sideshows of human curiosities drew large crowds, their fame eclipsed all others.

When they were thirteen years old, the twins were sighted

swimming in the Mekong River by a British merchant named Robert Hunter who immediately thought of exhibiting them in a sideshow. When he visited the twins' home, their mother Nok told him how, at their birth, the King of Siam had been advised to execute them—otherwise they might bring about the end of the world. She also told how several doctors had suggested brutal methods of separating them.

Hunter visited the twins and their mother often. He finally convinced Nok (for a price) to let her sons travel with him, but he could not at first persuade the King of Siam to allow it because the king was using them to accompany a group of ambassadors to China (he was negotiating a trade agreement at the time). Finally, Captain Abel Coffin, Hunter's new partner, was able to persuade the king to let the twins go abroad with them.

In the spring of 1829, the twins landed in America and toured Boston and New York for two months. Meanwhile, Hunter was in England drumming up interest for an English tour, on the theory that if the twins could succeed internationally, then glorious success in even the smallest U.S. towns would follow. So the twins sailed to London in November and for two years they performed before large crowds in the British Isles.

When they returned to America in January of 1831, Hunter told them that he had sold his end of the partnership to Captain Coffin. They liked and respected Hunter (and corresponded with him to the end of their lives) but by the spring of 1832 the twins were fed up with Coffin, whom they suspected of skimming profits, and so they ended their relationship with him. Coffin confronted Eng and Chang and heatedly accused them of impropriety. His intimidation, however, did not take and the twins became their own men: free, aged twenty-one, in America.

Before going to the reunion I decided to meet with Dr. H. G. Jones, retired curator of the University of North Carolina's Wilson Library. The Library houses a collection of more than 100,000 books and 75,000 pamphlets—as well as maps, journals, photographs, broadsides, and audiovisuals—all linked to North Carolina (it is the largest collection in the country that is devoted to one state). In his clerestory room above the vaults that hold much of the material, he told me, among other things, that in 1990 a film troupe from Thailand filmed a movie in North Carolina about the twins and that the man and woman filming the movie fell in love. At the close of the project, Dr. Jones said, they got married.

Later, when I looked back at my meeting with Dr. Jones, I got the impression that he was hinting at the existence of a spell—a love spell, I'd guess you'd call it—that the twins could cast on those who came close.

By 1839, Eng and Chang had toured a total of ten years throughout Europe and America. One night Dr. James Calloway, a Yankee-educated physician from North Carolina, saw the twins in a show at Peale's New York Museum and was fascinated by their intelligence and personalities. At the end of the show, he made his way to their dressing room and invited them to consider moving to his native Wilkesboro. He described clear rivers, cool, pure air, a variety of wildlife, and good farmland. Dr. Calloway assured them the town would welcome them not as freaks, but as people.

Eng and Chang were twenty-eight years old that evening. A year later, they took Dr. Calloway up on his offer and settled in Wilkesboro. They became American citizens and took the surname Bunker. (In New York City, Chang had fallen in love with Catherine Bunker, a young woman from a family with whom the twins were on very cordial terms. Years later, after his death, lawyers discovered that in his first will Chang had left most of his estate to Miss Bunker.)

It is possible that no other conjoined twins (left unseparated), before or after them, ever accomplished such full lives. This is not to say they didn't want to be separated. They twice begged doctors to operate on them, despite the possibility that they'd die in the process. Once they asked in hopes it would help them get married, and, later, sheerly out of a desire to flee the daily suffocation of joined life. The story goes that Chang

241

pulled a knife on Eng one night. In desperation, Eng begged Dr. Hollingsworth, their physician in Mt. Airy, to separate them. Dr. Hollingsworth informed them that any operation would likely cause their deaths.

So they were never to be parted, although the plan was for the doctor to rush over at the death of either twin, and free the living one from the other.

In the Main Exhibit Gallery of the North Carolina Collection, an electronic eye recorded my arrival and gallery keeper Neil Fulghum emerged from the back to greet me. A display case of artifacts from the life of Eng and Chang was close by and as I headed for it I noticed that Neil Fulghum was beside me.

Some of the things I saw were: a brown, worn, pocket-sized copy of *The Psalm of David*, which reminded me that the twins had married into a Baptist community in the mountains and that they were literate in both Chinese and English (Eng, the milder of the two, often read poetry aloud, including Pope, who had even written a poem about famous Hungarian twins, sisters who were joined at the back and shared one pair of legs); a ledger of expenses which described, among other things, a trip they made through Chapel Hill where they had to hire an extra horse to pull their wagon out of the mud; a delicate French water color on ivory (circa 1838) that shows the twins in fancy black frock coats—their interior arms looped around one another's back in their characteristic embrace; a flyer; an engraved portrait; an embroidered cigarette case; visiting cards of the twins and their wives.

Neil Fulghum led me to one of the collection areas that held more artifacts. Together we gazed upon a delicate brass hammer. "The twins probably used the hammer in a private Buddhist ceremony they conducted while traveling," he explained. He then showed me photographs of Chang's home, and the twins' families. Children were everywhere in the photographs.

I realized it was time to pick up my own children from camp. "I have to go," I said, and began gathering my notes. We somehow wedged in five more minutes of talk. He told me that, like me, he was divorced and that, like me, he had two children—a girl and a boy.

I said I'd be back the next day.

"Will you have time for lunch tomorrow?" he asked.

I answered yes, but my hands were sweating.

The next day I wore a Jane Austen-style dress to lunch. Neil and I talked nonstop. We discovered that we both loved to travel and that we both loved New York City. We both loved art. He painted. I wrote. But he had once written journalism and I had once exhibited paintings. He said he wanted to visit the Seven Wonders of the World. I told him that Eng and Chang had been described by one writer in the 1840s as the Eighth Wonder. I almost asked him if he had heard of the twins' love spell from his boss, Dr. Jones.

I also spoke on the phone with Ruth Minick of the Mt. Airy Historical Society who said she "fell in love with the Siamese twins" while growing up in their landscape. Mt. Airy is only a few miles from White Plains and Ms. Minick described it as having a "sophistication that played into the acceptance of the twins." It was a community founded in the mid-1700s as a trading center, where different kinds of people met often for commerce. "Industrialists who started textile mills in the area would always say the same thing," Minick continued. "They said, 'These people up here are different.'"

How so? I asked.

"Well, they would come to work a honest day's work, but if you didn't treat them right, they wouldn't say a thing, they just didn't come to work again."

The twins, who valued hard work and privacy, possibly saw themselves reflected in these independent, taciturn people who, like them, would not tolerate abuse. On their sideshows, the twins had always reacted angrily to touches by onlookers, to demands that they take off their shirts and prove that they were really joined. Several times, altercations with audience members came to blows. It was Chang who usually played out his anger, with Eng dragged along into the conflict.

Occasionally, the twins' own relationship ruptured and they punched each other.

"Up here they call it the Bunker Temper," Ms. Minick explained.

In White Plains the first thing we noticed was the air: cool and lighter than at home, it rushed into our lungs. We barely had to breathe it. We headed for the twins' grave at the White Plains Baptist Church. In the distance over Mt. Airy the mountains rose soft and bluish against the sky, like the backs of whales against the sea. We asked for directions at a convenience store. When I mentioned the twins, the teenaged clerk said she knew of them. "They're buried up there in the churchyard," she said, "but I really never thought much more about it." I hoped a similar nonchalance had welcomed the twins.

A historical marker on the road in front of a peeling, white clapboard church simply stated that the original Siamese twins had lived in the community and were buried close by. There was no mention of fame or freak shows. No mention of the wives or the twenty-two children.

But, down the center of its small expanse, the graveyard held many Bunkers. The air was heavy and quiet, with only the cawing of distant crows filtering in. The twins' grave did not dominate the way it seemed it should have. Instead, it stood surrounded by the others—just the way they had lived.

I read the name of the Yates sisters on nearby tombstones. Sarah and Adelaide Yates first met Eng and Chang when the twins briefly owned a store in Wilkesboro, right before they bought their first farm, Trap Hill. Chang courted Adelaide for years. They would visit the Yates home often, and play their flutes for the family. Adelaide returned Chang's flirtations; and Eng and Sarah's affections followed.

The Yates sisters lived in an era when women lacked the legal rights to own land or vote. Yet they made their desire to marry the twins known. Their parents objected—not because they were a curiosity, the story goes, but because they were foreign. The twins, however, believed it was their joined condition that the parents objected to and they went to Philadelphia to schedule a dangerous operation. The sisters followed them and stopped the surgery. The four then planned an elopement.

When they heard that an elopement was in the works, Sarah and Adelaide's father, a farmer and lay preacher, and their mother, a five-hundred-pound housewife, finally gave in.

The couples' wedding gifts included slaves.

The twins and Yates sisters were granted marriage licenses by Wilkes County, an amazing event when you learn that in the 1930s, Daisy Hilton of the famous Hilton sisters—gorgeous joined twins who were very successful in vaudeville—was refused a license by twenty-three states before she was able to get one, because of the sexual impropriety in such a union. (Ten days after the marriage, Daisy's husband Don left her.)

The Bunkers and the Yates sisters were married at the Yates' home on April 13, 1843. The only other successful marriage of conjoined twins was that of the Godino twins, Catholic Filipinos who likewise married sisters in 1929. But unlike the Bunkers, who would have twenty-two children between them, the Godinos did not have families.

Because of her girth, Mrs. Yates couldn't pass through the doors of her own home unaided and was herself something of a human curiosity. I recalled that in the New York show—the night Dr. Calloway first saw the twins—they had appeared with Deborah and Susan Tripp, obese sisters dubbed "The Incredible Fat Children."

In later years Sarah and Adelaide would become near behemoths themselves. Their pictures in the North Carolina Collection show stern, large women in starched dresses. They seemed almost to be twins, alike in posture and demeanor, not to mention gender and blood. I imagined the intimacy of the Yates sisters, who must have seen each other naked often during childhood. They would have accepted the oddity of their bedroom arrangement better than most women not because they were kinky, but because they were kin.

"They did it the same way anyone else does it," Milton Haynes, great-grandson of Chang, said of the twins' connubial maneuverings. They "did it" the same way others do, for sure, but unlike most of us, they always had an audience. Some people find it titillating to speculate on the aspects of such a union, but Eng and Chang, like other Siamese twins, learned to block out the actions of the other during sex. The uninvolved twin would simply trance himself out.

My daughter started to cry in the car on the way to the reunion. "We're not related," she said. "How can we go in? Will everyone but us look Siamese?"

Probably not, I said.

I stopped at a run-down country store for directions to the White Plains Recreational Building, where the reunion would be held. "You're going to the Bunker reunion," the clerk said. "Which one are you?"

I wanted to say, Both, I'm both—family of both. But I just said, I'm a writer who's fascinated by them.

"Well, of course you are," said the clerk.

In the car I told my daughter that not all the descendants looked Asian—I had just been mistaken for a Bunker.

The cars in the Recreational Building lot were, for the most part, big, American-made, family cars, and I felt momentarily as if I were back in my Michigan hometown. Inside the simple brick building we wrote out our names on cards and family members signed into a ledger where they were designated as belonging to either Eng or Chang. I met Chang, the great grandson, right off. He's a retired Air Force man with a Cheshire cat smile, who, though it's forty years later, still resembles his picture in the *Life* magazine article. I let my eyes scan over the sea of faces. The differences in appearances astounded me. Some people clearly looked Asian, with olive skin color and Asian features. But others looked like white suburbanite Americans, the genes of the later generations having mixed with Irish and English and Scotch blood. The Asian appearance was strongest in Dennis Bunker, ninety-one, and Nan Atkins, eighty-one, two grandchildren of Eng.

Of the one hundred people at the reunion, Eng's family vastly outnumbered Chang's, and the reason behind this, I was told, was that it wasn't until 1990, when the film troupe from Thailand was in the area, that members of Chang's family had even attempted to mingle with Eng's family. There had been tension between the two families, but the film had somehow caused an easing of it. Harry Bryant, who grew up in White Plains and married Eng's great-granddaughter Jessie, said Chang's family "had an uppity streak in them, and kept to themselves" and that this explained why the families had not really gotten along before this. As a boy, Harry hauled lumber for Albert Bunker, Chang's son. Harry said that back when the sons of the twins squabbled they would pull aside the log bridge that spanned the creek between the houses until the spat ended. Later Chang's daughters moved into Mt. Airy, where they didn't talk to anyone about the twins for years.

Chang's daughters had kept an account of the twins' life written by Judge Jesse Franklin Graves in a trunk. Finally, the family gave it to Ms. Minick who was helping in the research for *The Two,* a book about the twins written in 1978 by Irving and Amy Wallace. "They were ashamed, I guess," Ms. Minick said the daughters' reserve. "But now more of Chang's family has started coming to the reunion. Why, Jim Haynes — who's running the meeting this year — his father wouldn't say a word about the twins."

Chang, always the more stubborn of the two, had produced a family of strong-willed folks who left White Plains and dispersed across the states. Chang's reputation for drinking and fighting may have added to the family's reluctance to claim him. Eng's family stayed on in White Plains as successful farmers. Around us bobbed the heads of their kin: babies from Kansas and old folks from Siler City, North Carolina, and newcomers from California, all sitting down to eat. A century-and-a-half ago, and a mile away, Eng and Chang would have been sitting down to dinner at one of their White Plains houses. After they had eleven children between them and their wives had grown unhappy living in one house in Wilkesboro, they built two homes almost within shouting distance of each other in White Plains. The agreement was that they stayed at each house for three-day spans. At Chang's house, Chang was complete master of their lives, and Eng fell silently into the shadows. Chang would drink. At Eng's house, Eng would play poker and read poetry aloud. Chang could have been a statue attached. But their relationships with their wives improved, and they adhered to this plan even through Chang's final illness.

At dinner Milton Haynes's wife, Chase, told me about a man she thought I should meet, a restauranteur and writer in Durham. She encouraged me to call him when I got back to Chapel Hill. There went another Bunker love dart. On our drive up to White Plains, we had stopped in Winston-Salem at a fast-food restaurant and a man dressed garishly in cashmere and silk had gone out of his way to give me his place in line. He asked me why I was going up to the mountains so I told him about the twins. On our way out he stopped by his Jaguar to get his business card (he was a lawyer) and asked me to send him this article. I wasn't wearing makeup at the time, and I had pinkeye, so something else—possibly the love spell of the twins—was at work.

When Chase began talking about her friend I recalled Plato's idea of sexual love as an attempt to recreate a broken twinship. Humans, he said, had been created by Zeus with two identical faces and four arms and four legs and two genders. Zeus commanded Apollo to sever them down the center. Forever after, they searched for their former state of completeness by uniting with others in sexual love.

Jim Haynes, Milton Haynes's second cousin, made the opening remarks at the reunion and he was followed by Hershell Bunker of Pilot Mountain, great-grandson of Eng, who told humorous stories of his own long marriage. One day while riding in the car, after he and his wife had fought, he saw a donkey in a field. "Some of you might call it an ass," he said to the audience. "But I said to my wife, 'A relative of yours?' 'By marriage,' she said." He told me later that he had wanted to loosen people up; one of his stories was deliberately off-color. One family member remarked that last year the introductory remarks had focused, in an almost defensive manner, on the dignified lives the twins had lived. This year they wanted to have more fun with Eng and Chang.

Patricia Cooper Erhardt from California stood up to tell the group this was her first reunion. When asked if she were from Eng or Chang's side, she first said, "Chang," then hesitated, smiled, and said, "I mean—Eng. I always get the Siamese twins mixed up."

The twins themselves were known to joke with train conductors about who was who and whether it was necessary that they buy two tickets (they usually rode on one). Nearly all the books I read on them had misidentified Eng and Chang at least once. As if to confound the problem, early daguerreotype photography transposed images. Even the painting in the North Carolina Collection showed Eng and Chang on the wrong sides.

The blurring of their boundaries went deeper. Eng and Chang signed their names as such, but also at times as "Chang-Eng," one entity. In their letters they moved from "I" to "we" fluidly. Their tax listing in 1862 in Mt. Airy cited them as two people. But the census in Surrey County in 1950 listed them as a single item, number 538, with their wives under their names in alphabetical order, not in order of relationship, followed by their children, not designated as belonging to one or the other, but to both.

Their distinct temperaments and the two separate homesteads were important in defining their individuality and in giving them some freedom. After the reunion, we decided to drive past the homesteads.

Eng's house speaks almost entirely of the present. Nan Atkins had told me how sad it was to see the new I-77 and Highway 52 interchange running across the back lot; the grading for the project has been finished; all that's left is putting in the asphalt.

"It's just not the way it used to be," Nan said. Where the creek once separated the homesteads, Highway 601 and the new interchange bifurcate the land. At first the connector was going to go right through the corncrib in Eng's backyard, the only original structure left standing after the house burned down in the 1950s. But once the consultants working on the project learned of the history of the land they would develop, they changed their plan.

"Since we could avoid going through existing structures, we did," Dana Brantley, Manager of Planning for DeLeuw, Cather and Co., engineers to the project, told me. "The Siamese twins made the project so much more interesting. I love the twins. I bought a copy of *The Two* from a used bookstore while we were working on the project."

As much as Eng's homestead pulled us into modern life, Chang's homestead took us back to the 1800s. Nested beneath a surging line of mountains, misted and looking far off, the home was only visible for seconds as we passed it on Highway 601. We had to drive in the driveway, park, and open the windows to get a feel of the place. We let the cicada songs whir in our ears. The large, white house looked relaxed in the landscape. It was cushioned, almost protected, by surrounding hardwoods. And it was not at all imposing like an antebellum mansion you might visit for a fee, but instead it looked like an old house you could imagine your own moderately well-off relatives living in.

A vision of children running through the yard flashed in my mind. Then I saw slaves working the land, and remembered reading that the twins sometimes whipped their slaves. The cicadas quieted. It was the quiet of the church graveyard again. The quiet of history.

In 1860 they began to feel the financial crush of taking care of two houses and a bundle of children so they fell back on their old occupation of touring (they had not been on stage since 1839). And then the Civil War came and hurt the twins even more, just as it did many Southerners.

Their most valuable investment had been slaves. When the slaves were freed, Eng lost $17,000 and Chang $9,500. In addition Eng and Chang had been money lenders, and their debtors repaid them after the war with Confederate currency which had no value, even though it was considered legal payment.

So they toured. And in 1870, while returning from shows in Europe, Chang suffered a stroke which paralyzed his right arm and leg. From then on, Eng helped Chang walk by holding onto the ends of a long leather strap that was wrapped around Chang's right foot. Chang was also forced to lean heavily on Eng's shoulders. Unfortunately, with these new miseries Chang began drinking a lot and the drinking affected him adversely: he sometimes broke furniture in tirades Eng could only endure. On January 17, 1874, when they were sixty-two-years old, Chang died of a cerebral clot. A few hours later, and before Dr. Hollingsworth could arrive and attempt a separation, Eng died — in the doctor's words — "of great shock and terror."

Individual passions could be kept alive in a relationship, along with interdependence and acceptance. That was the center of their story as I saw it. And the second time around in love I might let ourselves be more ourselves: I'd just imagine an invisible ligament linking my beloved and me. I'd tell myself, when he was a jerk, to tolerate him. When I'd have to, I'd learn to blank him out a little bit. Maybe we'd fight. So? The twins did. And then I could stand by my man without giving up my identity and my own depth of emotion. If given a go at another relationship, I'd let me be me and him be him even if it meant we had to put up with each other when one of us was being a pain in the ass. I'd be Eng to his Chang, and he'd be Eng to my Chang.

And we'd not be parted.

Moschovitz and Pasternak

•

James Steinberg

An older Jewish man stands sideways four people in front of me in line at a polling place in Chapel Hill. He waits and watches with a patience and curiosity no other early morning voter matches. He has a pleasant face with eyes still fresh and clear, observant and interested. I watch their small dark pupils dance around the room and decide the old man will talk with anyone. But this crowd is impatient and inward, as if to remain aloof will hurry the procession through lines and registration tables and voting booths to cars and freeway journeys. Like the others, I came here enclosed in my own cocoon, incubating myself for the daily rebirth of my work face. I want to complete this task and be on my way, but watching someone who seems to be here so agreeably changes that. I wonder if age explains him and if I'll become as patient and observant. I wish I were closer.

His eyes push out a bit too far from their sockets in a way I notice in some fellow Jews. In a way, I say to myself, because that caveat makes me more comfortable with my stereotype. I'm a Jew, I say to myself, I am entitled to recognize another Jew by his features. But I laugh at myself for this excuse that works for only one stereotype. I have others and enjoy them, too.

The old man is pleasant and warm and handsome, but more is going on here. Surely I stare as much at his Jewishness as his welcoming face. I feel a connection so strong and present it unsettles me, and I know why. I have always been ambivalent about identifications that connect me with some and separate me from others. But here in the American Legion Hall, in line with so many strangers, I assure myself no harm can come, and give in to the connection.

I decide to give myself a generous allowance for sentimentality. The old man's eyes contain a smile, a welcome he can not escape offering. His bright pupils are mobile stations looking up from under the surface of still white ponds, periscopes from the bottom of his well. They move slowly about, waiting to greet. Shalom, they want to say. To anyone. They wait for contact, but in its absence are nearly as content with watching.

Two lines crawl forward through the doors of the building in replication of the clogged highways everyone hopes to be riding soon. "A through L" seems bottle-necked and slow to divide for the two registration stations reserved for it at the tables. By comparison, "M through Z" breezes by. The occupants of the slow lane express envy and disbelief.

"Same mistake every year," says one. "You'd think they'd learn."

"Splitting the population right down the middle of the alphabet clearly doesn't work in this precinct," says another. She shakes her head.

A few more remarks, some half-smiles and light laughter, a few nodding heads. The stress of these folks seems to lessen, and they become more sociable. The old Jew begins a slow circle, trying I think, to seize the opportunity for conversation.

Some Jews speak of a tribal identity. We are Members Of The Tribe, it goes. I've done little of this over the years, I haven't approved. In my judgment "The Tribe" elevates, separates, creates unbridgeable distance. I forget the centuries of experience that can force a group in on itself behind circled wagons. Yet I pick from the crowd another Jew, though everyone in the room and waiting outside the door all the way to the parking lot is responding to a call that should bind us all together. My connection to this polity pales next to the bond I feel with one stranger with whom I will probably never speak. Is he a stranger, or are we seeds from a single tree with roots in the ancient past, surviving in small scattered groves all over the world? We are, but this should not be emphasized, I think, so many can say something like this. And if you look at all of history, you must see the separation and distance that cultural and ethnic and religious and national identity bring, the centuries of hate and warfare and persecution that are their bastard children. It makes a shame of this.

But I like staring at this handsome old man, and I like that he is a Jew. I don't want a self-inquisition denying me this feeling of belonging that I don't get enough of from the places where I think I should. I don't want to soil it with doubt. Whatever it is rises inside me like a spring welling up from some deep unreachable source at the base of a wooded bluff. Though I may never know this source, I want to feel the welling up. This is knowledge as in getting to know, becoming better acquainted. Felt knowledge, so strong a sixth sense should be added to the list of five.

I ask myself how I can read so much into eyes?

Or a nose. His crags downward like an eagle's, pointing first to a little mouth that moves about with the slightest touch of impatience (more for lack of contact, I think, than for hurry, because our line is moving well), then beyond to a little cleft in his square chin, a real Kirk Douglas dimple, a mark I've always associated with active men. He scrapes his perfect lower teeth against his upper lip, then purses his lips together, the tip of his tongue occasionally protruding, making a slow arc from side to side, a touch of impatience now. But he's not hurrying to work, not in that knit short sleeve shirt, those Khaki shorts, that windbreaker tossed over his shoulder, those running shoes. He's headed for tennis or racquetball, the spa or the golf course. He's finished with freeways. I envy him.

His body supports the inference that he is no aging couch potato. He is small but athletically built and postured. Straight-backed, trim in the belly, he stands at ease with legs apart, one hand clasping the other wrist behind his back. He rocks lightly back and forth from heel to toe, a referee on a basketball court waiting for the end of a timeout. Now he folds his arms in front and trades his rocking for twisting at his waist to the ends of his range of motion. His broad shoulders have no forward bend at all, his arms still have visible muscle, he has been doing something healthy most every day, swinging a racket or a golf club, using his trim legs to carry him as often as a car has. I want to look like that in twenty years.

His face is ruddy and tanned soft leather, a topography of smooth shallow valleys, no rough wrinkles packed together. His hair is pure snow drifting back from a high forehead, a glacier melting from warm eyes that carry the satisfaction of his years. The neat little creases radiating from the corners of those eyes are from focusing his periscopes as he looks for places to land.

I realize this is how I want him to be. I am giving him an identity and wishing it for myself. Yet I think it's true.

He is chatting now with a few complainers from "A through L" and doesn't notice "M through Z" splitting as it approaches the volunteers who will verify our registration. In two steps I am next to him. He sees me and smiles and returns to rocking forward and back ever so slightly. I see him davening in an Orthodox synagogue or at the Wailing Wall in Jerusalem, where I've never been. The smile continues through the rocking.

Recognition. A silent shalom without a question. He is as certain of me as as I am of him.

"Are you a native?" he asks.

"No, a St. Louisan by way of Colorado and California." My standard short-form answer.

"New York by way of Cleveland."

I recognize the faint nasal edge, a remnant under flat Midwestern.

"I can hear New York, just a bit."

He smiles. "I don't mind it's still here. What brings you here?"

The line is too short for more than a footnote. I give him highlights of my zig zag route to Chapel Hill through regions and careers. He smiles in recognition.

"Like my son. You'd tell me more if you had time."

An invitation, I think. "What brings you to Chapel Hill?"

"The city next door, Durham, the City of Medicine."

"You must work at Duke Medical Center."

"Not at my age." He smiles. "My wife's doctor does. A fine young man, about your age. Forty, forty-five."

"Fifty, thank you." I return the smile.

"A saint, this doctor. I love him. He keeps my wife alive and well. No small accomplishment. You would love him for that, right?"

"Absolutely."

"I love him so much he keeps us from Florida. That's where we thought we'd retire. But a doctor keeps your wife alive and well, you stay. Besides, Chapel Hill is better. A very nice place. But a person sees things differently when he has a good reason. You know?

"Yes, I know. We came here for my wife to go to school. It was her turn to make a change."

"Good, very good." He is nodding from the shoulders again. I can almost feel mine begin. We fall silent and move forward, only two left between us and the tables.

"He keeps my wife with me, this doctor," he repeats, his voice deep in appreciation. "For this I love him."

I slide to the left, avoiding the right branch of the split, and am still beside him. A voice over his shoulder asks, "Sir, could you give me your name and address?"

As he turns I see another volunteer waiting for me, a woman topped with a small blue-gray beehive, blue-tinted bifocals, blue eye shadow. A blue woman. I move toward her.

"I'll spell it for you," the old man says. "M-o-s-c-h-o-v-i-t-z, Saul, 1808 South Lake Shore Drive."

"I'll spell it for you," I say to the blue woman before she can ask. The old man, ballot in hand, looks over at me. He waits.

"P-a-s-t-e-r-n-a-k, Louis," I say. "2478 Foxwood Drive." We are practically neighbors. The blue woman peers through the bottom half of her bifocals and flips pages till she finds my name.

"Your ballot, sir," she says. "Thank you for voting."

"Thank you," I say. The old man waits, watches. I think of my father who didn't get to grow old, who never seemed particularly like a Jew, my agnostic, totally assimilated, urbane, sophisticated father. For a flash I miss him terribly again. This man feels every bit as modern, yet more a Jew. For a moment I am a Member Of The Tribe. I don't remember wanting this before. I decide to like it.

"Shall we?" Saul asks. We are going to do this together.

256

"After you," I say. His smile broadens.

Once again, Saul rocks forward and back. I say to myself he rocked like that on many a Saturday morning at an Orthodox or Conservative synagogue where a cantor sang to the ancient rituals in the ancient tongue, no watered down Sunday morning ceremony at a Reform temple like the one I stopped attending as soon as I could, for want of feeling. (I may be wrong now, it has been years, and I was a kid.) He had Bar Mitzvah, I only confirmation. Though in all likelihood I would have tired of his synagogue as I tired of my temple, one thing is sure: I have not been to the spring, nor drunk there, like Saul has.

He turns slowly to the left and walks the fifteen feet to the row of black-curtained booths. I follow him till we are side-by-side at two that are empty. He goes to the left, I to the right. At the same moment our left hands reach forward and part the curtains. We turn toward each other and nod a simple acknowledgement. I feel the warmth, but this time from within me as much from him.

He extends a hand.

"Moschovitz," he says with a knowing smile.

"Pasternak," I answer. I reach for his hand, squeeze it firmly, hold it a few moments too long, then let go slowly. With a final nod, almost a bow, we disappear into our booths.

I read the instructions on the ballot and follow them, connecting lines this time instead of punching holes. There is so much to vote on, so many ballot measures to properly identify. I try to hurry.

When I come out, Saul is gone. I think about going after him, but decide against it. Had he wanted more, he would have remained.

Now the place seems empty, or not a place at all.

Outside I look toward the parking lot, search for him, see him in the distance walking briskly past the long slow-moving line. His white hair shines in the morning light. He turns his head to the side and waves at someone without breaking stride. I think I can see his hooking beak pointing down toward his broad smile.

Shalom.

Paths of Glory

•

Hal Crowther

Once upon a time there were three coaches, upon whom fortune smiled. The oldest coach was so successful that he became a national institution. A huge blue arena was built as a monument to his achievement, and powerful men traveled great distances to sit at his feet. In the fullness of his years, he enjoyed his greatest triumph, and celebrated at the White House with the president of the United States.

The second coach achieved equal success, even more rapidly than the first, and a giant corporation rewarded him with an enormous pot of gold, more money than any coach had ever seen.

The third coach was blessed with great charm as well as coaching ability. He won the highest prize when he was still a young man, and all the riches and power that went with it. But then fortune turned her back on this coach. He was accused of misdemeanors. The press hounded him and the public turned against him; his reputation was tarnished and he lost his job. His friends said he was run out of town. Then he was diagnosed with a dreadful disease and died, still young, just 10 years after his most famous victory.

Down here where I live, there's no need to attach any names to these brief biographies. Basketball rules in North Carolina, and coaches speak with the authority of archbishops. Now that our local universities have won three national championships in a row (and five of the last 12), it would take a pretty feisty partisan from Indiana or Kentucky to deny that North Carolina's Triangle, the cradle of Michael Jordan, is the center of the basketball universe.

But it was just at the moment of our greatest glory, while President Clinton embraced Carolina's Dean Smith and the Nike sneaker tycoons embraced Duke's Mike Krzyzewski, that the Triangle was forced to pause and observe the horrible public death of the third coach, Jim Valvano.

Maybe the pause will count for something, for some overdue self-examination. I didn't know Jim Valvano, actually. I met him twice and liked him. Most people liked him. What happened to his career wasn't fair. What happened to his life wasn't fair.

He was saying just that in his interviews, toward the end — "Hey, who ever said life was fair?" But we can't walk away from it like that, as if it had been the death of a man whose brakes failed or whose next-door neighbor went trigger-happy. As if fate just rolled the dice and they came up snake-eyes for the Italian wise guy.

How about some guilty consciences? If you never acknowledged that Valvano got a raw deal until you heard that he had cancer, you should hang your head. If you had a hand in running him out of Raleigh, maybe you should apologize to his family. There's a certain editor, now retired, who should have been the first to apologize. I hope he found the strength.

A lot of people still don't get it. A columnist in Texas wrote that Valvano "came to exemplify much of what has gone wrong with big-time college athletics. He got greedy."

That's not fair. Jim Valvano was the product and the victim of a corrupt system that he finally failed to understand, at least in the form that has evolved here in the basketball capital of America. He was a professional basketball coach who was hired to compete successfully against the high-powered programs at UNC and Duke. When he succeeded beyond N.C. State's gaudiest expectations, he became the Prince of the City in Raleigh.

His employers turned out to be adoring fans who would give him anything he wanted. He took what he thought he needed. He never grasped the pathological side of the Tar Heel basketball frenzy — the dogged hypocrisy, the desperate hunger to pretend that these transient mercenaries in size 16 shoes are still "scholar-athletes" descended from the teams that Daddy played on back in the '30s and '40s.

According to some of the best Southern writers, it's a powerful capacity for denial, more than anything else, that sets Southerners apart from their countrymen. The South is the place where ministers of God stood in the pulpit and conferred the blessings of Jesus Christ on Jim Crow. It's where agrarian dreamers still contend that the antebellum South was a balmy Eden of enlightened gentleman farmers and cheerful darkies singing in the fields.

With such a rich legacy of denial, it's almost comprehensible that people could talk about a basketball program's "graduation rates" and "academic standards" without expecting anyone to laugh. Jim Valvano was from up north, where they barely pay lip service to basketball's Big Lie. He didn't understand that some people down here cherish their illusions as much as they cherish their championships. He gave them victories. He recruited Chris Washburn, with a 470 on his SATs and the willpower of a six-year-old. When a network news crew came to film some Wolfpack players in class, Valvano neglected to warn his scholars, and the truant players were filmed clowning with their girl friends in a parking lot.

Some of the "fans" who were married to the Big Lie turned out to be sportswriters, editors, politicians. Valvano failed to respond to the urgent needs of their denial. They cut his heart out. I was in Seattle when I read about the "scandal" at N.C. State. But to this date there has been no scandal. None of the NCAA violations — minor ones — involved the coach in any way. *Personal Fouls*, the book by Peter Golenbock that proved so damaging to Valvano, was one of the most careless, malicious, unreliable manuscripts ever compiled by an individual who had the temerity to call himself a journalist. It contained hundreds of errors no editor had ever attempted to correct.

Personal Fouls was a cut-rate generic expose that could have described almost any successful program in Division I. But there were only a few coaches with profiles high enough to sell the book. Coach Valvano, charismatic and careless, was the perfect guy to take the fall.

It might make us all proud if we could bury this great millstone of hypocrisy along with the coach who was crushed by it. But it's the coaches who profit most from the myth of the student athlete, and they're not about to let it die. The worst hypocrites of all become the darlings of the NCAA, that shameless pack of pimps that runs a prosperous whorehouse and pretends to be the vice squad. I guess Dean Smith is so eminent now that he can just run his program and let other people feed the fools what they want to hear. But the fellow over at Duke is saying things that make me grind my molars to stumps.

Never mind that Mike Krzyzewski has the meanest rabid-rodent courtside sneer this side of Gene Keady. The man can coach, as they say, as if that makes up for anything. But lend an ear to his latest sermon in the *New York Times*:

"I believe college sports, as an extension of what we do and learn in the classroom, is an invaluable facet of higher education."

What is he talking about, this pompous little guy who teaches a dozen itinerant gland cases how to set picks? Why wasn't a Duke education and the bonding, sharing experience of playing on a national championship team enough to keep Billy McCaffrey in Durham? Did Vanderbilt offer him a better choice of electives in European history? Players transfer from Duke, which has one of the best academic reputations in Division I, for the same reason they transfer everywhere. For more playing time, which is critical to any professional player who's trying to showcase himself for the NBA.

Playing time is the main thing that matters to these kids, the same as it matters to the Boston Celtics. If you can deny that, you've got a denial problem I couldn't dent with a diamond drill. An actual "scholar-athlete" — a quality player who masters serious courses and works toward a serious post-graduate profession in spite of his coach's ridiculous demands on his time and energy — occurs only accidentally among these boy professionals, and about as frequently as a homosexual or a Buddhist or a munchkin like Muggsy Bogues.

And the teaching, character-building, citizen-molding function of the coach, as described by Krzyzewski? I seem to recall a player named Christian Laettner, who had something to do with Duke's success. After four years of character-building under Coach K, it took Laettner about a week to establish himself as the most immature, obnoxious player in the NBA.

Krzyzewski is a fountain of self-righteous nonsense. But I used to give him the benefit of the doubt. What if he believed this stuff? There were people who believed that David Koresh was Christ.

The multi-million-dollar shoe deal ought to silence most of Coach K's defenders. A million-dollar bonus and a 15-year contract worth $6 million to switch his kids from Adidas to Nike sneakers? Remember when Valvano was denounced for his greed?

I'm sure there's some major difference between Krzyzewski's bonus and a simple bribe, but so far it hasn't been explained to my satisfaction. And then immediately we read about Krzyzewski's $250,000 donation to the athletic building fund, "in honor of Duke's student body."

That's what we call "a Hill and Knowlton bequest," an image-repairing ploy by an individual who knows he's been caught red-handed. Like Mike Milken's famous burst of post-indictment charity. But it only makes things worse. Krzyzewski is always calling himself a teacher. How many of his colleagues on the Duke faculty are making bequests that amount to $400,000 before taxes? It would be like signing over half of everything a professor grossed between tenure and retirement.

The sneaker scandal exposes the atrocious double standard in force at the NCAA, which trashed Jim Valvano because some of his players sold their sneakers for pizza money. It shows the cynical, venal side of this myth of the student athlete. Maybe there's a doomed idealistic side, too. But this is the side that says the coach can collect millions because he's a professional and his team gets nothing because they're college students.

Somewhere there must be an ex-Duke player who really needs his share of this treasure. You explain to me why he shouldn't have it. His coach is always talking about sharing.

Tell us about "the true purpose of college sports," Coach K. Tell us why you were a role model while Jim Valvano was a hustler. At least the phonies won't have Jimmy V to kick around anymore. He was a good guy, and gifted. Wouldn't it be nice to think that he's coaching in a league where the hypocrites don't always win in the end.

Sports: Family Style

•

Kat Meads

My brother, eight years older, had his own regulation-height hoop tacked to a pine tree; I had another, half the height, tacked to the tree beside it. A good brother, Craig let me shoot hoops alongside him even at the runty stage when I lobbed the basketball from between my knees.

As a family we often played HORSE, each missed shot counting as a letter. My mother, a high school star with the photo album to prove it, made a specialty of the two-handed chest heave. With no one in front of her defending the basket, she got quite a momentum going until we got her giggling. Then her style went all to pieces. My father played with his cap on and never worked up a sweat. He took impossible shots from beyond the official playing court. Sometimes he climbed on top of the picnic table and threw over the clothes line and our heads. He kept shooting from those outer reaches, shooting and grinning, exasperating my mother, until the arc of the ball lined up perfectly with the nylon net and "swished." Still, it was my brother who won nine of ten matches. Dubby was wedded to trick shots, my mother rattled easily, and my basket percentage was poor at best. Craig relied on non-flashy jump shots from either side of the dirt court or free throws from a foul line he dug with his heel.

We recreated as a family, nuclear and extended. Every Sunday of every season the Meads clan gathered at my grandmother Dora's, and once conversation lagged, we moseyed outside for games of croquet, badminton, horse shoes, softball, hardball, basketball and tennis on a root-gnarled court beneath the sycamore tree. Player age ranged from five to fifty-five; everyone participated except Dora, who oversaw events with a kind of put-upon smirk, as if she were baby-sitting two generations of rambunctious, yappy children.

"Look, Ma. Home run," Aunt Madeline might say as the ball headed for swamp muck.

And then perhaps Dora would reply: "About time."

My father's prime sport was baseball. A left-handed pitcher, he'd been good enough in high school to win a baseball scholarship to Wake Forest College. People said he'd had a chance at the minor leagues, but if that were an aspiration, the war ended it. With his brothers scattered in Europe, Dubby was the son who came home to farm. He didn't complain. War was war; family obligations, family obligations. And if you carried a drop of Meads blood in you, the obligation on Sunday afternoon was to play hard, play fair and never, never whine.

When I whined, blaming the size of the bat (too heavy), the color of the croquet mallet (too green), Dubby said: "Get out there and play and quit fussin'." If my brother ever whined, he stopped before I came along. I stopped before I graduated to the regulation-size hoop. You miss a shot, try again. You fall down, get up. Hurt yourself? Throw a Band-Aid on the wound and keep going.

It wasn't a terrible code to play or live by, but sometimes it was a tough one to keep.

During my mother's heyday, gymnasiums were the luxury rather than the rule. She and her high school teammates played the bulk of their games on cement slabs outdoors. Deeply offended by "glory grabbers," she had a stash of cautionary tales about swell heads who hogged the ball and lost the game. Play team, not individual, she drilled into my brother and me. Take the shot if you have it, but don't run over the rest of the pack attempting to shine.

Even without hogging the ball, my brother shone. For six years he held the high school record for points scored in a single game (twenty-eight), that glory achieved the same season his team won the tournament trophy. For tournament games, our conference, composed of small county high schools, played in the city gymnasium, an awesome place. The backboards there were fiberglass, not wood; the court was blond, not brown; smooth, not pitted; the bleachers rose to the ceiling. County fans usually cheered from a couple of rough benches designated "Home" and "Visitor."

To win anywhere was thrilling, but to win in that swank arena was the pinnacle of success. Victory night for my brother's team, as the tournament officials arranged the trophies and Craig and his flushed buddies lined up to receive their due as champions, I couldn't restrain myself. I made a beeline across the court. He was seventeen; I was nine. It was his big moment; I was his goofy kid sister. But when I grabbed his waist and squeezed, mortified or not, he didn't flinch or turn away. He hugged me back.

My basketball career officially began in seventh grade. First game out, I scored the team's first basket. After that, the opposing coach sicced his finest guard on me, and in four quarters I never got off another shot. Still, we won. We almost always won in those days and entered high school expecting the trend to continue. Currituck County had a reputation for excellent basketball teams, male and female.

As a high school freshman, I got to play with my cousin Linda, my pal Sharon and the legendary Alice Gregory who'd been a starter on three championship teams. At that stage of women's basketball, only two on the team could cross the center line and play both offense and defense. Smart coaches chose the fastest two, and one of them was Linda. Slower and bigger, I played stationary forward; as such, my prime contribution was supposed to be points. After Alice shook hands with the opposing captain, the game buzzer buzzed, and we took to the court, I was also responsible for the opening tip-off (Linda was too short). But if I gained control of the tap, I always batted the ball in my cousin's direction. With little or no head start, she could usually outdistance the pack for an uncontested lay-up.

We started losing early in the season, despite the stellar Alice. Once Alice graduated, we lost more frequently, and whenever we lost, I cried. To my recollection, Linda never did, keeping me and my misery company. Against the Creswell Wildcats, Linda scored three of the first four field goals and wasn't at all happy. I was supposed to be the shooter; why wasn't I *shooting*? Her bangs had already sweated into pitchforks; my face had already gone splotchy. We had expected to win against Creswell, a team ranked even lower than us in the conference standings, and their competitiveness surprised us.

"*Quit holding back!*" Linda screamed at me at the onset of the third quarter, after which I did begin to shoot more. Still, we lost. At the final buzzer, when no amount of effort could undo the defeat, my crying erupted mid-court. We must have been quite the sight: the little squirt of a girl comforting the lummox.

"Numskull," she hissed. "You think you lost it all by yourself?"

I felt fairly sure I had, but I appreciated the contradiction. Since it came from Linda, I almost accepted it as truth.

Although we practiced hard, ran our laps, charged the goal, dove for loose balls, shot foul shots and executed passing drills, instead of victories, we racked up an even more stunning string of defeats. The fans soon deserted us, trickling in for the boys' match only. The game Craig saw, his sister couldn't hit the side of a barn. A yearbook photograph preserves my father's disappointment. Among a conglomeration of other fathers, Dubby sits, chin in hand, solemnly watching his girl child commit a grievous foul, my elbow lodged in a guard's neck.

Whenever an elbow knocked out one of Sharon's contacts, the referees stopped the game and both sides dropped to the floor to search for the lens. We usually found it—a green dot among hightops—and after licking it a couple of times, Sharon popped it back in her eye and the game resumed. But as our losing streak continued, she considered playing blind to see if a vision swag would help. We were all feeling desperate by then and very, very frustrated. Even my glory moment against Columbia brought no lasting joy. Seconds left, the ball in my hand and no time to get it to anyone else, Linda again screamed "shoot" and I did, using Mom's two-handed technique. The ball cannon-balled toward the basket, slammed hard against the backboard and by sheer luck bounced in. We were euphoric! Tied score! We could still win in overtime!

Could have, but didn't. That game we lost by a single, tear-jerking point.

After Linda graduated, the year Sharon and I became seniors, a new coach, female this time, took over the disastrous girls' team. Traditionally, co-captains got to choose their uniforms first; a small privilege, but coveted. The new coach called one, then two, then several players into the locker room before Sharon and me. By the time we were summoned, only the dregs were left. It could have been an oversight, and for a while we tried to believe it was. But the slights just kept multiplying. Team meetings convened without us; Monday mornings we heard about scrimmage sessions held the Saturday before. As the season wore on, with victories still few and far between, Sharon and I became known as "the lead butts"—a joke and not a joke. During a late-season pep rally, our coach announced to the school at large how much she looked forward to "next season" when her team could get down to "playing ball" after the "big shots" had graduated.

No one expected her to like losing—God knows, we didn't—but neither did Sharon and I expect to take full blame for the disappointment. Linda wrote "buck up" letters from college, urging me, in the spirit of family tradition, to ignore the jabs, play hard. My parents stoically sat through loss after loss. At home, after practice every day, I shot lay-ups by porch light until bedtime. If you shoot lay-ups on a goal tacked to a pine tree, you learn to feint and swerve.

For the final road game of that miserable year, we travelled to Hatteras. Hatteras had a strong team, offensively and defensively, led by the Dillon sisters who played to win but expected at least the appearance of a good fight. Sharon sat out the game because of a sprained ankle. By the end of the first quarter she must have been grateful for the injury; it spared her a whole new level of humiliation. I scored eight points, set up two other shots, even grabbed a rebound and got benched without explanation after three minutes of play.

As the second quarter moved into the third, the Dillon sisters mimed "What Gives?" in my direction. Winning by a landslide, they had time to inquire. I was glad Dubby wasn't there; I wished my mother had stayed home too. I would have preferred an entire gymnasium of strangers to one half-filled with everyone I knew. Five seconds showing on the game clock, our coach called a time out and sent me back in. I remember Sharon's curse, the outrage that broke through my mother's public mask, the too bright lights, my billion-pound resistant body. I remember our scorekeeper looking up from the check-in desk with a kind of startled, wondering pity that helped me to understand I inhabited one of those pivotal moments wherein I could act by the "code" or listen to my gut. My gut wanted blood, of course, but I wasn't my parents' child for nothing. I took my place on the court, "played" those remaining five seconds. I kept my mouth shut, head up. No whining aloud/allowed.

Obviously our team carried home no trophies at tournament time. Even if I'd had a kid sister to rush across the court, I wasn't part of any victory to inspire the trip. I did win a couple of personal citations for conference and tournament play, voted on by other coaches and players. So, in a way, by sticking out the season and refusing to quit, I won a modicum of revenge. But winning those two gold-plated miniature basketballs felt a lot like sacrificing the war for the battle. All that persevering left a permanent smear on the pastime. I no longer associated competitive sports with fun. Basketball, in particular, I associated with the stringent test: "Who Will Buckle First?"

One day many years later, while Linda and I chatted on the porch, Dubby and two of her sons played HORSE on the old backyard goal. At nine, Linda's oldest was a quiet fellow: a little clumsy, eager to please. His younger brother was the opposite: a frenetic sassy pants. For a time the game proceeded along the usual lines—shouts, dribbles, a vibrating backboard. Then the tone changed. The sassy pants started in with excuses: unfair, foul, he tripped me, I'm taking that shot over.

"Get back over here and play and quit your fussin'," Dubby advised.

But that go-around he wasn't talking to a son or even a grandson, and his opinion carried less weight. It was left to Linda to reform the behavior of the quitter who kicked his way past us. Doing so, she seemed more my father's daughter than I did. Barely turning her head, she drawled:

"Go on then. Good riddance to you."

I watched the spoilsport glance back again and again, turning full around at his great-grandmother Dora's birdbath, waiting for and wanting someone to call him back. No one did. Dubby and the whiner's brother had returned to playing HORSE, his mother to her conversation with me. He had gone against the family code, and when he did, because he did, the family said: go, go on, good riddance.

Wallpaper

•

Sally Buckner

The Fosters were coming to town! All of them—feisty
Aunt Naomi, merry Uncle Claude, fifteen-year-old
Angela—whom I adored—and Nancy, at almost-four the
perfect playmate for my baby sister Leigh Anne. Furthermore,
they were coming not just for one of those annual two-week
visits from Pennsylvania to North Carolina. No, they were
moving permanently, they'd already bought a house on the
other side of town, less than ten minutes from our home.

At the prospect, I was dizzy with delight. This was an
answer to prayers—no, it was better, because I'd never
presumed to pray for such a gift. It was beyond expectations,
beyond wishes. My life, I felt certain, would be forever changed.

I was right.

By the time this announcement was made, I was accustomed
to assorted relatives moving to Scotshaven. Since we had come
there ourselves in 1936, two other branches of the family had
established themselves nearby: since 1937, Aunt May had
taught piano lessons in a small house on the next block; the
following year Aunt Lola and Uncle Richard arrived, moved
even closer—just two houses down and across the street.

And now, in September, 1939, the Fosters were coming.
"Every year somebody from our family moves to our town," I
observed. "Gosh, they'll all be here soon,"

"Quenn, you know better than to say 'gosh,'" Mama
admonished me. "It's not fit language for a nine-year-old girl.
And," she added, "we're a long way from getting all the family
here. A whole passel of folks would have to tear up deep roots

for that to happen. Besides, Scotshaven wouldn't have jobs for everybody."

And, indeed, jobs had been the drawing card. Despite the fact that Scotshaven was a small town with only two industries — agriculture and textile mills — somehow we and three sets of our relatives had managed to find work there in the job-scarce era of the late Depression.

I was especially excited about the Fosters' impending arrival. During their yearly visits, they mostly stayed with Grandpa Clayborn and Miss Ellie on the family farm sixty miles away, but almost every year they also reserved two or three days for us. (Aunt Naomi declared she couldn't stand but just so much of being out in the country, that she'd had enough country her growing-up days to last several lifetimes.) Those days were among my most cherished each summer. Aunt Naomi always set us upon some day-long expedition to someplace intriguing, someplace we'd never been before. Uncle Claude could entertain us children for hours with card tricks and an unending supply of jokes. And Leigh Anne and I savored each moment when Nancy and Angela, our favorite cousins, would be right there, day and night, under our own roof.

When they moved to Scotshaven, the Fosters broke the patterns established by Aunt May and the Wallaces: they didn't *have* to find new work and they didn't live with us for several weeks before getting their own place.

What happened was, one morning during their annual visit Uncle Claude went with Daddy to see the new project he was engaged in — installing the plumbing in a new wing on Tabernacle Baptist Church. When Daddy mentioned that Uncle Claude was a bricklayer, the construction foreman remarked that it sure was hard to find skilled bricklayers, that he was short two right now and looking for substantial help. Picking up a trowel, Uncle Claude did a short demonstration right that minute. One thing led to another, and within an hour he'd headed home to tell Aunt Naomi that they'd have to start packing, that he had a new job.

I've always wished I had been in the room when he

delivered that news, because in all the years I knew her, right up until she died six years ago at ninety-four, it was seldom that anybody *told* Aunt Naomi anything that directly concerned her. You asked or you proposed or you wondered if, but you sure didn't *tell* Aunt Naomi. And it seemed to me that Uncle Claude was even more skittish than most people about dealing with Aunt Naomi. If a troublesome matter arose, he either gave in, tried to make a joke, or turned very, very quiet.

I never heard how that announcement was received, but certain factors may have rendered it easy for Uncle Claude to proclaim the news: he was offered what for that time was a substantial raise—30 cents an hour—to come to Scotshaven, and the foreman assured him that his company had months of good work already lined up after Tabernacle Baptist was completed. We had also heard Aunt Naomi complain at length that their Pennsylvania house was in bad shape, that some night it was going to collapse around their feet if Uncle Claude didn't get around to repairs. Mama surmised that both of them were also tired of living up North, that Aunt Naomi didn't like the winters and they both wanted to be closer to their families.

At any rate, they stayed long enough to find a place to live, then headed back to Pennsylvania to pack. Three weeks later Daddy and Mama were helping them move furniture into their new home on the other side of town. I had to spend most of the day keeping Leigh Anne and Nancy out of the way. Angela helped me some, but mostly she was preoccupied with fixing up her own room—"My *own* room!" she kept exclaiming in wonder whenever she came downstairs to pick up a box.

Each time she uttered those words I felt a sharp pang of envy. Ever since I'd discovered that some children, unlike Leigh Anne and me, claimed individual rooms with their own things securely stashed away from the meddlesome fingers of siblings, I'd coveted one for my very own self. The bedroom off the living room at the front of the house was designated the "company bedroom," though we seldom had overnight company. Whenever I'd asked if I couldn't move into that front room—adding that I'd be glad to share it with any company that came—Mama talked about the expense of heating it year round and explained Leigh Anne's need for her big sister to be nearby. Her attitude made it clear that this was not a negotiable matter. I'd long since given up the request, but not the desire.

The minute Leigh Anne and Nancy finally went down on folded quilts for naps, I ran upstairs—and was dazzled. Although Angela's room was quite small—just big enough for twin beds, a narrow dresser-with-mirror between them, and a chair—it had personality. For one thing, the ceiling slanted upward from one outside wall; I'd never seen anything other than flat ceilings before except in church. For another, the walls were lined in floral wallpaper: pale blue with cabbage-sized pink and cream-colored roses entwined with ivy. The fact that the pattern was fading on one wall and shredded on another was unimportant; wallpaper seemed as exotic to me as the frescoes or hand-stitched tapestries I'd seen in an art book in the library.

Another asset: the room was bathed in sunlight from dormer windows on the two outside walls, each with a window seat, and each offering a special opportunity. From one, looking out over the apple orchard, a garden space, and thick woods, you could gaze far, far into the horizon. Sitting there, you could forget that you were anywhere near town, and your imagination could soar to all sorts of unusual settings. The other window was brushed by the leaves from a sturdy tulip poplar limb—one, Angela pointed out, that was strong enough to bear your weight if you decided to climb outside. Whirling, she shook her mop of dark curls and rolled her eyes. "We could make a quick getaway," she exulted. "We could *escape*."

I had no idea where we could escape to or what circumstances might compel our flight, but I was thrilled at her use of *we*, and the whole notion was too adventuresome to resist. I wanted to test out the escape route right away, but when I started to raise the window, Angela grabbed my arm and shushed me. "We mustn't let them know," she said in the hoarse whisper of a conspirator.

I've said that the Fosters didn't live with us before finding their own place. At the time I would have loved for them to move in, no matter how their presence might have crowded us, because I admired Angela beyond words. At fifteen—a wonderfully appealing age, I thought—she was pretty as Aunt May, though in a radically different way. Whereas Aunt May was willowy, Angela was shorter and amply curved—sort of like Rita Hayworth. Whereas Aunt May's hair swirled in easy, honey-colored waves, Angela's was a thick tangle of dark auburn curls. Aunt May was graceful and gracious, all harmony—a soft, flowing waltz. Angela was activity and energy and dissonance—a clamorous, merry polka.

May, with her winsome smile and musical talent, was the woman I very much wanted to be when I was "getting on towards forty," as Mama put it. Angela was the girl I wanted to be on the way to becoming May.

Whenever our families were together, Leigh Anne and Nancy, happy playmates, kept their distance from us older sisters As the months passed, the surprising thing was that Angela, who immediately established herself as one of the popular set at Scotshaven High, *didn't* keep her distance from a mere nine-year-old. Those first visits she let me help her decorate her room: gluing tatters of wallpaper back in place to form a smooth, almost-unblemished surface; hanging pink gingham curtains at the dormers; stuffing old feather pillows into pink gingham cases to make comfortable seating at the dormers.

Later she would invite me into that enchanting room, where we sprawled on the beds or folded ourselves into the dormers while she regaled me with tales of the exciting world of high school. She let me watch while she practiced using makeup and rouge and lipstick or experimented with new hair styles. She even applied her cosmetics to my yearning face, and we both admired the dramatic results in the mirror before washing everything off so that our mothers wouldn't suspect. And she included me on shopping trips—well, window-shopping trips, we rarely bought anything—during which she educated me on the fine points of style and accessories.

Wonder of wonders, she also sometimes included me when her oh, so mature and sophisticated friends—both girls and boys—came to the house to listen to records and eat popcorn.

Because she treated me just as one of them, so did her companions, sharing jokes with me, letting me hear their stories. On each of those occasions I felt so adult and beautiful that if lightning had struck, I would have died happy.

Meanwhile, although Mama had always been eager to see Naomi during the yearly visits, she wasn't nearly as happy about her oldest sister's move to Scotshaven as I would have expected. One night just before the Fosters returned from Pennsylvania with all their worldly goods, as I dozed on the sofa I overheard her express her qualms to Daddy.

"This is all happening mighty fast, Walter," she noted. "I'm not sure they're ready for such a big move."

"They'll be all right," Daddy said placidly. Daddy expected most things to turn out all right.

Mama probably wanted to believe him. "Maybe it will be good for Claude to get away from his drinking buddies," she murmured.

"I'm not sure those buddies are the main things spurring him to drink," Daddy hinted—about what, I couldn't tell, but Mama's next comment gave me a clue.

"I know Naomi's not easy to live with," she sighed. Daddy laughed. "Well, all right, she's *hard* to live with. She's as feisty as my pa ever has been and she never held her temper in her life." A pause, then emphatically, "Well, I told her she's got to hold one thing—her tongue—that she's got to clean up her language, that she can cuss around her own girls if she wants to, but I'm not going to have her doing so around mine."

"Good for you," Daddy said approvingly.

"Lord knows where she learned to cuss! She sure didn't hear that language when we were growing up—not in Pa's presence. I can't stand it." Another pause. "And that temper. Much as I hate liquor, if I had to live with that kind of screeching day and night, I might take to drinking myself."

After the Fosters arrived, when I wasn't indulging in private sessions with Angela, I watched carefully for signs of the behavior I'd heard Mama and Daddy discussing. Aunt Naomi's feistiness was of course always evident: she walked in a semi-trot, she spoke in italics, she worked—housecleaning, housepainting, canning, gardening,—in a roaring fever; she probably *slept* feisty. But she never used any swear words in my presence. However, sometimes if I was outside, one or another of those terms which Mama called "bad words" and which some of the naughtier boys at school liked to use when the teacher was out of earshot, would explode through the kitchen window. My favorite was her own personal variation on the old words: "God D-Double-Dammitall to Hell!" After she yelled that, a door might slam, like an exclamation mark.

I never saw Uncle Claude drunk or even drinking. Or if he had been drinking, I usually couldn't tell it. Sometimes his face was more flushed than at other times and he laughed more readily. But he was a naturally ruddy man who worked outdoors, and he was usually quite cheerful, so I couldn't attribute those signs to liquor. The only times I suspected he'd been drinking were when he'd lean close to tease me and I'd smell something sour on his breath.

He was apparently doing fine at his new job. Daddy said he had a reputation as an exceptionally able bricklayer, industrious and reliable. One afternoon Aunt Naomi observed that with all their skills Daddy (a plumber) Uncle Claude (a bricklayer) and Uncle Richard (an electrician who changed jobs every few months) ought to form a partnership and go into construction themselves so somebody else wouldn't be making profit off their labor. Mama just said, "It's a good thing we all got hardworking men," and changed the subject quickly. At supper that night she repeated Naomi's comment to Daddy, adding, "I can't imagine anything riskier than going into business with one man who drinks too much and another who's liable to quit you any time you look cross-eyed at him."

Now and then Aunt Naomi and Uncle Claude left town to visit friends or kin; once they went away together for a weekend at the beach. On those occasions Angela and Nancy stayed with us. That arrangement was always just fine with Leigh Anne and me; Leigh Anne and Nancy would play with dolls long past their usual bedtime before going to sleep in our room. Angela and I would take the company bedroom where, after we had turned out the lights, we'd share our dreams for the future.

I was thinking about being a cowgirl like those in the Saturday night westerns which our family regularly attended. Cowgirls had exciting adventures and got to ride beautiful horses, and they always ended up cozying up to a handsome fellow with a wide hat, a white horse, a ready smile, and sometimes even a guitar. Furthermore, they helped the handsome fellows confound the plans of the wicked: together they broke up train robberies, rescued elderly widows from robbers who rode heedlessly down the center of the dusty Main Street, rid their serene little towns of crooked and ugly outlaws. When the screen went black, virtue was triumphant—and all because of handsome cowboys, aided by sweet-faced cowgirls.

Angela would listen patiently to my plans, even encourage me, then drift into her own, which were much larger. She was going to be a movie star or a model, she wasn't sure which. But she'd already decided that as soon as she graduated from high school she'd get her portrait made in a variety of glamorous poses, compile the results in a portfolio, and light out for Hollywood or New York. In our darkened bedroom she'd whisper about New York City, where her parents had taken her once years ago—how it was like fairyland, lights shimmering in every color you could imagine. And, for her, no more cotton prints or dirndl skirts which Aunt Naomi whipped up in an afternoon on her treadle sewing machine, some of the seams crooked and the hem not always even—no, she'd be draped in velvet and organdy and satin. As she talked, I could envision her, as lovely as any of the actresses whose smoky, heavy-lidded eyes gazed at us from posters at the Alameda Theater. Her dream seemed to me entirely achievable—for her, maybe even inevitable.

In preparation, Angela had already tried out for and won a major role in the spring play at Scotshaven High. She'd also decided that it was important to learn to smoke. A woman looked so sophisticated with a cigarette between her fingers, she declared, especially if she used a long, trim holder. A cigarette gave you a prop, she added, something to punctuate your conversation. You could breathe smoke into rings and watch them float lazily to the ceiling while your companion wondered what was on your complicated mind—or you could blow smoke into his face and turn sharply on your heel, leaving him choking as you marched away. You could tap the ash, firmly but delicately with your scarlet-nailed finger—or let it grow until some gallant fellow leapt forward with an ash tray to catch it.

Listening to Angela's detailed descriptions, I decided she must have already tried cigarettes, although I knew that Aunt Naomi, like Mama, thought nobody but Fast Girls smoked, so I was sure that she prohibited Angela from doing so. I also decided that if I were to become glamorous, I would have to take up the habit myself. I started to ask Angela about drinking cocktails—something else which looked exotic in the movies and in Four Roses magazine advertisements—but, figuring that liquor might be a touchy subject in her family, I refrained.

Whenever she took one of her out-of-town jaunts, Aunt Naomi told Mama she'd be happy to swap favors, that she'd look after Leigh Anne and me while Mama and Daddy enjoyed a little vacation. Mama always found excuses: she and Daddy were too busy to leave, she had to help me get ready for the school chorus concert, Leigh Anne had been having lots of earaches. I wasn't sure that those were the real reasons. I thought that maybe she didn't believe she and Daddy should "squander" money on a pure pleasure trip, or maybe she just didn't care for the family being separated, even for one night. But I also sort of suspected that she didn't like the idea of our being in the care of Aunt Naomi, who cussed, and Uncle Claude, who drank.

However, fate had its own ideas. One grey February day we got word that Grandpa Bradley had the flu and while Grandma Bradley was trying to take care of him, she had slipped off the back porch and sprained her ankle. Everyone was concerned, of course, especially when we considered Grandpa's near-miss with pneumonia two years before. Daddy's sister Aunt Evelyn took off two days from her job to be with them, but felt that she just had to go back to work, and Aunt Lola had a bad case of strep throat herself, so she couldn't do them any good. Of course the men in the family couldn't leave their jobs. That left Mama, who wanted to help, but was hesitant about leaving us.

Aunt Naomi ended the hesitation. She came right over, all business, and started packing our things herself. "Now you just stay as long as you need to, Rachel, you know these young'uns are in good hands. Walter can have meals with us and make sure Quenn gets to school on time, and either him or Claude can pick up Quenn in the afternoon. And Nancy and Leigh Anne will just have themselves a fine old time keeping each other company. In fact you'll be doing me a favor letting them stay. Nancy just about drives me crazy wanting attention all day long." She was so insistent that it seemed clear that she felt the need to clear her debts with Mama and Daddy.

I was sorry that my grandparents were ailing, but I was almost beside myself with delight at the prospect of staying with Angela in her wallpaper-covered boudoir. I promised Mama that I'd help look after Leigh Anne, that I'd dry dishes every night for Aunt Naomi and make up my bed and do homework without being reminded.

And I did. Then the first night, after Angela and I had both finished our homework, we lay in our beds and told ghost stories. Hers, of course, were much more elaborate than mine, and more than sufficiently fearsome; when Aunt Naomi called us to get on to sleep, I was glad to see that the garage light reflected in our window, taking the edge off the darkness.

The next night, we shared our future plans again. By this time I was considering becoming either a concert pianist or a singer. To perform music and then receive applause from thousands of adoring fans in the audience — that scenario seemed the ultimate in fulfillment. Besides, pianists and singers got to wear glittering gowns, and after they finished performing, ushers dashed down the aisles with armloads of flowers. What more could one want?

Angela was giving even more thought to her acting career. She couldn't decide whether to train as a dancer, so she could appear in musicals with Fred Astaire, or work towards serious roles in costume drama. She was leaning towards the latter. *Gone With the Wind* was sweeping the country, and she'd saved her lunch money so that she could see it not once, but three times. Mama wouldn't hear of my going to such a film, but I had seen the ads, with Vivian Leigh looking sumptuous and daring in an off-shoulder dimity dress with a wonderfully wide ruffled skirt. Angela assured me that the glamour of the movie lived up to the glamour of the ads. "And Clark Gable," she breathed into the dark room. "Imagine kissing Clark Gable! And being paid to do it!"

We both giggled at that. We giggled a lot that night as we indulged in our wildest, sweetest dreams. Aunt Naomi finally stuck her head in the door and told us to stop that foolishness and get to sleep, that Daddy would be over just after sunrise to take me to school the next morning.

I slept soundly for several—I don't know how many—hours before I was awakened by voices downstairs. Blinking awake, I wondered why anyone was still up. Then I remembered that Uncle Claude had gone out after supper. Aunt Naomi had looked particularly grim as she watched his Plymouth rolling down the road.

Straining my ears, I could identify the voices as those of my aunt and uncle. So Uncle Claude's safely back home, I thought, and, reassured, turned over to go back to sleep. But the voices got louder. What had begun as just murmurs changed to normal speaking voices—and then, in Aunt Naomi's case, to yelling. I lay very still and listened, wide eyes straining against the dark.

"My God, look at you!" she was shouting. "You're a disgrace to the human race."

Uncle Claude rumbled something I couldn't hear, then she continued. "Drunk as a fish, drunk as a pig—and you look like a pig and smell like a pig—like pig shit." Another undistinguishable rumble, then a sharper shriek. "And it's not just liquor either—who's the woman?"

"What woman?" His voice sounded like it was clambering through a fog. "No woman, no woman."

"Damn you, *damn* you, don't you lie to me! Even through all that liquor I can smell perfume. Cheap perfume at that. Goddamn you, what little floozy are you picking up? Got a sweetie on the side? Or are you paying for her services? Where'd you find your little whore? And what are you getting that you can't get in your own bed, tell me that! What the hell is she giving you?"

Still more rumbling. And then a tirade that seemed to last forever, all about women and liquor and spending money like it was water, spending it on women and liquor and not caring for his family, Angela needed nice clothes in high school and Nancy was growing like a weed, she was outgrowing everything she had, and not caring for his house, the goddamn roof needed fixing and the goddamn back screen was about to fall off the hinges, and there he was running after women and liquor, and she'd thought things would change back down South away from his stupid Yankee friends, but no, here he was, right back to his old God-D-Double-Dammit-all-to-Hell tricks.

The spiel went on and on and on, generously peppered with those phrases Mama didn't want me to hear. Every once in a while Uncle Claude would manage to get in another unintelligible rumble, but I'm not sure Aunt Naomi ever heard his protests, for her words were spilling in a torrent. Finally she paused — by this time she was sobbing and the words were nearly indistinguishable — and Uncle Claude spoke up louder, though still in a slurry voice. "For God's sake, Naomi, tone it down. Think of the children. You want to wake them up? You want Nancy shaking all night again and Angela crying? You want Quenn and Leigh Anne scared half to death?"

Whether Uncle Claude's words took effect or whether Aunt Naomi was too worn out to continue, I don't know, but the yelling stopped. I could hear her still sobbing, then there were the sounds of someone stumbling up the stairs and going into the bathroom, slamming the door. There were more noises for a little while, moving-about noises both upstairs and down, creaking noises from the bed across the hall, then silence — a thick, hot silence.

I was lying on my right side, turned away from Angela's bed. My eyes were open, and I was drawing shallow, imperceptible breaths as I lay motionless as a stone, stifling any urge to twitch, as if I feared movement would start the uproar going again. After a few quiet, but tremulous minutes, I heard

Angela turn over and her voice tentatively pronounce my name: "Quenn?"

I didn't know what to do. I felt a strong urge to jump from the bed, to leap across the narrow space between us, to grab her in a tight hug, to say, as Mama probably would say, "It's all right, Angela, it's all right." But in the first place, it seemed presumptuous for me to take the comforting role; that was the business of grownups. Besides, I knew perfectly well that this wasn't all right, and certainly that no words of mine would make it so. I also briefly considered just asking, "What?" to see what would happen. Would Angela talk about what we had just heard, explain it? Or would she rage about her parents' behavior? Or—this seemed likely and most frightening to me—would she burst into tears?

So I just lay still, now breathing long and deeply—playing possum, as Daddy would say. And eventually I wasn't playing; eventually, against my will or expectations, I fell into deep, dreamless sleep. When I woke the next morning, Angela was not in the room, and Daddy was bending over me. "Okay, sleepyhead," he teased, "you better hurry on down and eat your breakfast before Aunt Naomi throws it to the chickens."

Groggily I followed him downstairs. All the Fosters except Uncle Claude were in the kitchen, Nancy with a mouthful of oatmeal, Angela toying with a piece of toast and hardly looking up, Aunt Naomi at the range. As I ate my oatmeal, I watched for unusual behavior. Aunt Naomi seemed quieter than usual. Her eyes looked empty, like those of a doll, with no life in them. Angela left the kitchen soon after I entered it, mumbling that she had to get a bath. After a few minutes, Uncle Claude came in, still in pajamas, very rumpled; what little hair edged his round face was tousled and his eyes seemed red and tired. But he grinned at me, and he had a quick rejoinder when Daddy teased him about being a slug-a-bed. "Better a slug-a-bed than a slug at work. I'll put in my eight hours or so, then beat the dickens out of you in a game of checkers." Aunt Naomi's mouth grew tighter.

Back upstairs, as I gathered school clothes from my suitcase

I glanced around the room. Thin February light coming from the clabbered sky outside made the pale wallpaper paler than ever; the blue background was almost grey, the pink roses no longer blushed brightly, the cream-colored ones looked merely sallow. I saw that the shreds Angela and I had so carefully glued in place near the ceiling were once again curling from the wall, displaying mildewed stains beneath. When I turned on the light, the colors brightened some, but the stains looked even dingier.

Angela came in then, and we dressed silently. Once, while she was trying to tame her mop of curls, she caught me looking at her image in the mirror and asked, "Quenn, did you hear any noises last night?"

"Noises?" I raised my eyebrows innocently.

"Yeah, anything wake you up?"

I paused, then nodded. The sight of Angela's face at my nod demolished any notion of telling the truth. "I was just falling asleep when I heard some shots—or I guess they were shots. Sounded like they came from way off."

Angela's face eased. "Probably somebody coon-hunting down in the woods," she said. "Or possum-hunting. They do that lots of nights."

"Oh," I said, "I thought maybe somebody was shooting off firecrackers. But it's not the Fourth of July or anything." I was surprised at how quickly the falsehoods leapt to my lips; evidently, in spite of all Mama's admonitions and my Sunday school training, lying came naturally to me.

"There's some fools don't need a holiday for an excuse to shoot off firecrackers." Angela said. There was a bitter edge to her voice as she added, "Or do other kinds of stupid stuff."

I felt tense, crammed full of secrets that wanted to spring out. I'd always been so happily open with Angela that it seemed weird to play-act around her. Pretending took a lot of energy, and I was glad when Daddy called to urge me downstairs so I wouldn't be late for school.

Cushioned by school routine, by mid-morning I fell back into my own self. I was still in a good mood when Uncle Claude came to pick me up from school. But at the sight of him, grinning and beckoning to me from his dusty Plymouth, memory of the night before returned like a slap. I smiled, hoping to look natural, but as we rode home, I drew deep breaths, trying to smell either cheap perfume or alcohol. The only scent I could discern was that of sweat. Uncle Claude was in a fine mood, singing sea songs like "A Capital Ship" and "Sailing, Sailing" in a rollicking voice that made it seem that he really did know and love the sea. When we got to his house, Aunt Naomi met me at the kitchen door with peanut-butter cookies and milk, but her smile was tight and fleeting, her questions more remote.

I took the cookies and milk upstairs, saying I was going to start my homework, but mostly I just looked into the distant woods and remembered the night before. A lot that had been said didn't make sense to me. What did it mean to be running after women—and why would anybody do it? Sounded like a silly thing for adults to do. What would a woman be giving Uncle Claude in bed? I guessed that it had something to do with hugging and kissing, if perfume got on his clothes—but why would they be in bed? What was a whore? What would he be paying for? And was Uncle Claude really not taking care of his children? Angela always looked pretty to me, and I couldn't see that Nancy was popping out of her clothes. It was all a mystery.

That night when Daddy came, he didn't stay for supper. He was jubilant with good news. Grandma Bradley was hobbling around now and Grandpa was out of bed, even able to do some light chores, and they'd gotten a neighbor boy to help him with the heavy stuff, so Mama would be coming home. In fact, Daddy was going straight to their house that minute, would have supper and spend the night there, then he and Mama would head back at sunrise. "We'll be here by the time you've got your clothes on," he told me and Leigh Anne.

"Let us go with you," I pled. "We want to see Mama, too, and Grandpa and Grandma."

"No, you'd be up too late on a school night. Just you get a good night's sleep and we'll be here before you can finish your cereal."

"Well, don't eat breakfast before you come. I'll have a big

one ready when you get here," offered Aunt Naomi.

"Oh, Walter'll eat both times," Uncle Claude joshed.

Daddy grinned broadly. "Why pass up such an opportunity? Be sure you got plenty of bacon."

That night Angela and I attended to our homework silently, without our usual complaining to each other about long, dumb assignments or my asking for help. After we climbed into bed, we were still both wordless. Finally I asked, just to break the stiff atmosphere, perhaps to get back the old Angela again, "You got any more ghost stories, Angela?"

"No." Her voice was dim, weary. "I told you all I knew."

I strained to think of something that might cheer her up, but I couldn't come up with a single idea. I was just starting to drowse when she suddenly said, almost in a whisper, but firmly, "I've got to go away. A long way."

"Yes," I said quietly. "That will be nice."

"New York." Her voice was urgent.

"Or Hollywood?"

"Yes. Maybe Hollywood." And those were the only words spoken.

The next morning I was pouring Wheaties into a bowl when we heard Daddy's Chevrolet come up the drive. Leigh Anne and I both jumped from our chairs and, despite the sharp winter cold, I ran outside without even grabbing a coat just as Mama and Daddy were emerging from the car. Leigh Anne was laughing and yelling as she ran to Mama's arms. To my utter surprise, as well as that of both Mama and Daddy, I broke into tears — no, not just tears, but hard, hurting sobs that shook my whole body.

"What in the world?" Mama asked, astounded, as she hugged me tightly with one arm — she held Leigh Anne in the other.

"You sure did miss your Mama, didn't you?" Daddy said, reaching over to pat my shoulder.

I couldn't answer. I just nodded and lay my head against Mama's bosom, feeling Leigh Anne reach her fingers into my hair. At the same time I grabbed Daddy's hand, squeezing it as tightly as my fingers could manage. I stood there, not caring who saw me or who thought what, just holding onto and being held by those beloved forms, firmly substantial and reliable.

Getting Mitch

•

Barbara Presnell

The problem is that Mitch has decided to come home for the weekend, to nestle into their britches like chiggers, as Lyn says, and leave them squirming for days after he is gone. He feels the need to come only twice a year at most—once at Christmas and one more time when something turns his mind to them, some misplaced sense of responsibility, Lyn calls it. It angers her that Mama always says, "Come on," always straightens his room, changes his sheets, cooks food enough for Lyn's entire graduating class, and on top of that, lets him turn their lives upside down as though they are no more than empty beer cans. They are doing just fine without Mitch, Lyn says.

But, he is there, in the kitchen, his muddy Reeboks clodding the linoleum floor Mama waxed just because he was coming.

"Lyn said she was going out with a friend." Mama is thinning tomato seedlings with a pencil, sticking the lead between plants then lifting each one gingerly from the soil with her fingers. She doesn't look up. "I simply didn't bother to ask who."

Lyn props her hip against the counter top and folds her arms like weapons across her chest. "No reason for her to ask. It's always Silas on Saturdays."

"Mama, you let her do this every Saturday?" Mitch says. "Jesus God. I bet you let her smoke heroin and swim naked in Memorial pool."

"To my knowledge, she doesn't do either one of those. Oh, Betty," Mama curses. "I pulled the roots right off of that one." Her hair is sprouting wildly from the red bandanna she's tied it in and knotted at the back like a tuberous root. It reminds Lyn of the women she sees in the grocery store or the post office, limp, sad things like worn-out clothes, with their hair in rags or, worse, rowed with pink curlers as though the contraptions are some new wave fashion.

"Who has time to fool with their hair?" Mama said when Lyn complained. She was digging in the garden, planting purple and burgundy pansies whose richness and color made Mama's plainness even more apparent. She'd scratched a spider from her forehead that left a patch of soil streaking across her head from left to right. "Anyway, I think it becomes me."

"Just please don't wear it out."

"Who's going out?" Mama said.

No, Mama wasn't going anywhere then, but now. . . Now. Lyn thinks perhaps it is time to bring it up again when the two of them are alone.

Mitch leans back on two legs of his chair and says, "Does he come in the house every Saturday?"

"Not to my knowledge," Mama replies.

Mitch pulls a cigarette from a pack of Merits on the table and lights it with a lighter he takes from the pocket of his jeans. Smoke from its tip curls green over his head like Mama's sage, but the puff he blows from his mouth is gray as the exhaust from the textile mills that hangs in the air on weekday afternoons. Lyn fakes a cough and waves the air with her hand.

"We don't allow smoking inside the house, do we, Mama? Chokes the plants."

Mama doesn't answer. She pushes her glasses up from her nose where they have slipped, and squints at the dirt.

"Since when?" Mitch asks.

"Since you left."

He is wearing a green Hawaiian shirt with palm trees and flowers like wild poinsettias winding from front to back and climbing uncontrollably along the sleeves. The collar is folded across his shoulder blades, exposing a thick jungle of dark hair.

"You look like Magnum, P.I.," Lyn says. "Is that how they dress in Georgia?"

Mitch glares at her, and exhales a stream of smoke from the corner of his mouth, but doesn't speak.

She opens the refrigerator and pulls a can of Diet Coke from a six-pack. "What was I supposed to do, anyway? His car was overheating, spewing radiator fluid all over the driveway, for Chrissake."

"Don't say 'Chrissake,'" Mama says. "It sounds like you're swearing."

Mitch taps his cigarette against the speckled blue ashtray Mama made at ceramics two years ago. "You'd have done what any decent girl would have done," he says. "Left him outside and made the call for him." He inhales. "But then any decent girl wouldn't have him sitting in her driveway in the first place."

"You wouldn't know a decent girl if she was wearing a sign on her forehead." Lyn pops the top of her can and gulps her Coke like it is water and smooth as rain.

"Children, now." Mama turns, holding her hands in mid-air. Her glasses have slipped again to the spread of her nose, and she peers over them. "He'll only be here a few days, Lyn. Why don't you just avoid subjects you disagree on."

"Mama, if you want my help with her, you're gonna have to tell me this kind of stuff that's going on," Mitch says. He crushes his cigarette in the ashtray and wipes his hand across his mouth.

"Who needs your help?" says Lyn.

When Daddy died almost eight years ago, Mama made the mistake of saying to Mitch, "You're the man of the house now." Mitch was in college then, and slipped into his new role with a stern jaw and a sudden voice of authority leveled like a shotgun on Lyn. He'd see to it Daddy would be proud of the girl, he said, but the problem was he was two hundred miles from home and never came back to stay any longer than the week it took to bury his father. Lyn liked to say that his authority was in remission, that every so often it would flare up and need to be treated with a dose of — who else? — them.

"I've met Silas." Mama dips her fingers back into the soil. "He's a sweet, well-mannered boy."

"That's not the point."

"Then what is?" Lyn says.

Mitch holds the bent filter of his cigarette, rolls it between his thumb and finger, and little crumbs of burnt tobacco sprinkle onto the table. He sighs and tosses the scraps of his butt into the ashtray. "Okay. Tell me about Silas. You have lunch with him every Saturday?"

Lyn looks to her mother with a face that says "Do I have to?" but Mama's eyes are buried like seeds in the dirt she works in. Lyn traces the letters of her can with her finger.

"I do his English homework," she says. "He owes me."

"Ha!" Mitch says. "And he'll graduate that way, I guess. I wonder how many of 'em. . ."

"You know who he is, Mitch," Mama says. "You used to run around with his older brother, Frank."

"I didn't 'run around' with him. He worked at the station with me. We hardly knew each other."

"Frank was always so smart, you remember?" Mama says. "I heard just recently what he is doing now, but I can't recall it right this minute."

Mitch continues. "So he takes you out every Saturday?"

"He's in advanced English. It's a lot of work."

"You know I think Silas is going be just as smart as Frank ever was," Mama says. "Maybe more so."

"It took me over a month to do his term paper," Lyn says.

"Jesus God." Mitch pulls another Merit from the pack. He taps the filter end on the table.

Lyn smiles. "He made an A on it."

Mitch flicks the flame of his lighter and holds it in the air, staring into it as though there are pictures inside, movies, Lyn thinks as she watches him, perhaps cigarette commercials or porno shows. What is he seeing? She knows so little about him now. She remembers falling off his bicycle when she was too small to be riding it, falling over a brick wall into a gravel driveway, cracking her front teeth and making Mama cry nonstop for the rest of the afternoon. Even now, she can picture him standing above her on top of the wall, hands in his pockets, staring down, expressionless. But more than anything else, she remembers the promise he made to her when she was eleven, when he put his arm around her shoulders like Daddy had always done, and he said, "Don't worry, kid. I'll take care of

291

you." Well, that was a joke if she ever heard one. She laughs out loud.

Mitch puts the flame to his Merit, sucks in smoke, then pops the lighter off. "I don't want you to go out with him anymore," he says, punctuating his words with spurts of smoke.

Lyn's smile folds into her face. Her mouth opens slightly then closes.

"Now, Mitch," Mama says.

"It's not right, Mama. It can only lead to trouble."

Lyn slams her empty Coke can onto the counter top.

"I'll do what I damn well please," she says to Mitch.

"Don't say 'damn well,'" Mama speaks to the tomatoes.

"I ought to wash your mouth," Mitch says. "I ought to move back here and straighten you out."

Lyn's eyes narrow and she looks straight into his glazy brown ones. "Oh, yeah? Then why don't you?"

Mitch's glare meets hers. "I just might."

"You're chicken."

Mama sighs, but her eyes still do not leave the dirt.

"Jesus God." Mitch stares at his sister a half-second more then turns away. He sits back in his chair, his face tight as elastic, and inhales.

"I remember now what Frank is up to," Mama says. "He's vice-president at Peoples Bank. He took old Mr. Harvey's place. Isn't that smart?"

The telephone rings in the living room, and Lyn moves like a reflex to answer it. In a few moments, she returns, prancing like a filly, rolling her hips slightly, and she speaks in a falsetto voice. "It's for you, Mama."

Mama turns, her face surprised, almost panicked. "Is it. . . ?" She touches her red bandanna, wipes her hands on her shorts.

"He wants 'Martha,'" Lyn says, and bumps her mother's hip with her own. Mama returns the bump, smiles, then skirts from the room.

"He?" Mitch looks up, but his mother is out of sight.

Lyn hops onto the counter beside Mama's mess of dirt and limp plants. She smiles at Mitch's scowl. Maybe with some luck, she thinks, they can run him out of town before the weekend is over, and she and Mama both can be in peace again. But he stays in that chair like he is glued to it. Like a statue whose only moving parts are the arms that bring the cigarettes to the mouth that won't stop talking.

Mama comes back. "That was Mr. Macon," she says, looking at neither of them. Her hands fidget from her shorts to her arms to her face, now spotted with dirt. "He'll be over in fifteen minutes to take me to get some azalea bushes. Oh, Betty, I've got a peck of dirt under each fingernail."

"You look just fine, Mama," Lyn says. "He'll give you time to clean up before dinner."

"Dinner?" Mitch says. "Who's Mr. Macon?"

"Just an acquaintance," Mama says. She is scrubbing her hands in the kitchen sink, lathering with Ivory soap and picking under her nails with the scrub brush.

"Mama's new boyfriend," Lyn says.

"I met him at the feed and seed," Mama says. "He's helping me re-landscape the yard."

"What's wrong with the yard?"

"Things can always use improvement."

Mitch's complexion turns the color of his smoke, and a look of horror settles on his face.

"You're dating this man, this whatsisname?"

"We're friends, dear." Mama dries her hands with a towel. "Would you mind cleaning this up for me, Lyn, honey?" she says. "I'll finish later."

"But what about Daddy?" Mitch says.

"It's been a long time, dear," Mama says. "It's all right."

"But, Mama, you can't."

Mama simply pats his green-flowered shoulder and says, "It's all right, honey. Really, it is." Then she hurries from the room, and as she does, Lyn sees her yank the red bandanna from her head and let her wild hair fall where it may.

There is utter silence in the kitchen. With one hand, Lyn brushes the crumbs of dirt from the counter top into the other palm, then she tosses them into the sink. Mitch smokes, stares through air. The refrigerator cuts off and the silence is almost painful to Lyn. She tries to hold her breath so she won't disturb it. When she sprays water into the sink and turns on the garbage disposal, the noise is like the intrusion of a dozen low-flying planes.

Mitch speaks. "How long has she been seeing him?"

Lyn cuts the disposal off. "A while."

"Do you think it's serious?"

She looks at Mitch who is lighting another cigarette, using the butt of the old one to ignite the tip of the second. She thinks she sees his hands trembling, having trouble making the two ends meet. He grinds his teeth.

"I couldn't say. I hope so."

A car horn honks like a goose, then honks again. Lyn peers over the sink out the window.

"It's Silas," she says. "The car must be fixed." She raises the window halfway and waves her hand.

"Be right there!" Lyn calls and closes the window, just as Mama steps into the kitchen. She has changed from her faded yellow shorts into the denim skirt Lyn gave her for her birthday, has traded ragged white tennis shoes for leather sandals.

"You look good, Mama," Lyn says.

"As long as he doesn't look under my fingernails."

"I thought you looked fine before," Mitch says.

Mama peers out the window. "There he is now. Lyn, did you know Silas is back?"

Mitch stands, pushing his chair slightly behind him. His Hawaiian shirt buckles at his waist.

"Mama, there is something I been wanting to say."

She kisses his cheek. "I'm sorry about lunch, honey. I was gonna make you a deviled ham sandwich with mustard like you used to eat."

Mitch steps toward her. "Mama, I really have been thinking about moving back here."

Mama stops, touches his arm, and smiles. "We'd love to have you, dear, for as long as you wanted to stay."

She throws her hand in the air as she turns her back, and calls in a lilting voice, "Don't wait up for me. Ta-ta." And then she is gone. Lyn watches out the window as her mother meets her new man coming down the sidewalk to greet her. He takes her elbow, kisses her on the cheek, holds her hand.

Mitch sees it too. He falls back into his seat by the table, his shoulders sagging into the hard back of the chair and disappearing in the over-size of his shirt. Lyn dries her hands on a paper towel and tosses it onto the counter. She turns. "See ya, Mitch."

He looks up, absently. "What? Yeah, okay."

As she is leaving the kitchen, Mitch calls behind her. "Hey." She looks back. "Don't be gone long." It is a strong voice, but the body she sees still slumps pitifully. Lyn takes a step toward Mitch, pauses a half-second beside him, then leans over and kisses him quickly on the cheek. His face is scratchy, and he smells stale like smoke and Old Spice. It's a familiar smell, something from a long way back. He looks at her, says nothing.

She turns away hastily. Silas is leaning with his elbow against the windshield of the Volkswagen, waiting. He waves. As Lyn steps onto the porch, she stops for a second, glances over her shoulder, and sees her brother's round face peering at her through the square window on the door. He quickly looks aside, but she is certain she sees, in the center pane, what even the garden of flowers can't conceal.

Touching What Remains

•

Virginia Holman

Neighbors we hadn't spoken to in years spilled onto their lawns the night the sheriff's department came for my mother. Not that she'd done anything unlawful. It's just that it was 1989, in Richmond, and if you were schizophrenic, that's how things were done.

For years, my father had tried to get my mother help. Her first signs of illness had blossomed in 1972, when I was six. We had no idea then that she needed to be forced into medical help, so the next seven years were spent trying to talk her into it.

When we did convince her, I was thirteen. Mother spent six weeks at the Medical College of Virginia and came home with a diagnosis and a bag full of pills. But the medicines that were supposed to restore the proper chemical balance in her brain failed. She still heard voices, still thought she was psychic, still believed the government had placed monitoring devices inside the TV set.

"Those voices you hear in your head aren't real," I would tell her with a fifteen-year-old's snotty authority. "You have to ignore them." I said this over and over, believing that she could stop listening if she tried hard enough. If she had a stronger will, a stronger character.

After one such dismissal of her pain, she pinned me against a wall and yelled into my face. "Am I not real to you? Can you not listen to me? Just try and turn me off, tune me out!" That moment never left me, because it was then I understood, however briefly, what it was like to be my mother, trapped in a world beyond control.

Her prescriptions only seemed to make things worse. She

became sluggish, suffered from facial tics and muscle spasms that contorted her neck and face with a crippling pain. Sometimes, not surprisingly, she refused her medication. The year I left to attend a local university, she stopped taking it altogether.

Three years later, my father and younger sister moved to an apartment in town. My mother was left in the house, alone. She was afraid to set foot outside. If we didn't bring her groceries, she couldn't get them herself.

We cared for her the best we could. Whenever we tried to solicit aid, we were told the situation was not bad enough to warrant outside intervention. As one social worker put it, "Unless she's cut you or herself, there's not much can be done."

That was our problem with mental illness and the law. You can't reason with someone whose brain isn't functioning properly, but until my mother attempted to hurt herself or someone else, we couldn't get her the long-term help she needed. She had violent outbursts, but never "dangerous enough" in the view of the authorities.

The night we finally got help was fourteen degrees. My father had gone to deliver Mother's groceries after work. When he stepped into the house it was dark. No lights would come on. Everything was still and cold.

Swallowing against the guilt of having left her alone, my father found my mother under piles of clothes. When he asked what had happened to the heat, she told him she had taken care of the wire taps. He got a flashlight from the utility room and saw live wires from the furnace on the concrete floor. He scanned the house, finding plaster dust and exposed beams in the walls where she had tried to remove every electrical outlet. He felt nauseating relief. Surely this was enough to get her help.

She could have electrocuted herself, he later told my sister and me. We bit our lips against the unspeakable thought: It might have been easier if she had just died.

***

That was the last day my mother spent in the house. After the

297

social workers agreed that she was legally dangerous, the sheriff's men took her to a private hospital in Richmond for a month of $20,000 treatment. She was one of the worst cases they had ever seen, with uncontrollable delusions. She believed she was an astronaut. She did not improve. And then her insurance coverage ran out.

My mother was given a week to get well enough to go to a halfway house or be transferred to Virginia State, a grim warehouse for people who are to be kept out of sight. After a few days — and several changes of medication — she grudgingly agreed to reside in what is basically a nursing home.

For a long time my father paid for her stay, out of pocket. Insurance won't cover you beyond so many thousands of dollars of mental-illness treatment, even if the illness is a brain disease. The reason for this inequity is not hard to imagine: Manifestations of an illness such as schizophrenia are anything but socially acceptable. If you're schizophrenic, it's because you can't get it together, because you're an inferior human being — that's the message. Doesn't matter if it's a legitimate illness; it's still an illness with a stigma.

Few people are up for the lifetime haul of schizophrenia — myself included. I couldn't bear to see my mother at the nursing home. Almost three years passed without a visit. I got a master's degree. Married my high-school sweetheart. Then I began to feel her absence everywhere. I saw women out of the corner of my vision who looked like my mother — women with wide, smooth faces and gapped front teeth. I'd hear her laugh across a restaurant. I felt haunted.

I asked my husband, who had lost both his father and his stepfather, how he'd survived their deaths, how he'd gotten on with the business of living. He talked about acceptance, family pictures, memories. And then he said very softly that I didn't have to do those things because, after all, my mother wasn't dead.

I decided to write her a letter. She responded in a palsied scrawl, making no sense, but I kept writing anyway. Then the doctor changed her medicines, and suddenly her handwriting and her thoughts became clearer. Though she was by no means well enough to take care of herself, my lost mother turned into a bit of a pen pal.

Still, it wasn't enough. I needed to visit her. I'd never done that during her first hospitalization, back when I was thirteen. I couldn't let it happen again.

***

All my adult life I have imagined conversations with my mother: what she might say, what I might say. I replay old family stories she told me as a child. It's how I keep her with me.

On the way to visit her, I am thinking about Mother as a teenager, about what her life was like. I remember her stories about the year my grandfather's back pain became crippling. His doctors could find nothing wrong with him, refused to give him anything for the pain except sugar pills. He drank, paid off the pharmacist to get paregoric, checked in and out of the Baptist Hospital in South Carolina.

The doctors did every test available at the time, but nothing was found. "There's nothing the matter with you," the specialists told him. "All in your head." One doctor told him that if his back was bothering him, he should stay out of the cathouses.

Eventually, a psychiatrist began making daily visits, helping himself each time to one of my grandfather's cigars. They talked about baseball, about the telescope my grandfather and his buddies at the shipyard had built to glimpse into the brothel across the way, about his imaginary pain.

But the pain worsened. One leg numbed. Finally, my grandfather convinced the doctors to do an exploratory surgery, to lay the matter to rest once and for all. My grandfather took bets. Even his surgeon bet on the side of the shrink. It was suppressed anger, they all said. An inability to trust.

Trust me, my grandfather told them.

I've seen the photo taken during his surgery: My grandfather laid open on the table, the pins holding his skin back, the doctors' gloved hands. Attached to the side of his backbone is a thin black tumor, like a semi-formed second spine.

My grandfather calmed after that, the story goes, though his right foot flopped awkwardly from nerve damage. He became proud and untouchable. You couldn't argue with him. That tumor was his jewel, the gift that proved to everyone that he was right, that his pain was real.

And what about the shrink? I ask the mother in my head.

He never came back so your grandfather could tell him off. But he did send him a bill for the visits, and do you know what your grandfather did? On the back of the psychiatrist's bill he wrote out a counter-bill for all the cigars that man smoked. No money ever changed hands.

Driving to the home, thinking about that story, I wonder: If I could reach a minuscule hand into the cells of my mother's brain and alter her tiny defect, would my love change from anger to acceptance? Someday doctors will do such things, I know, and people will understand the pain of people like my mother because they can be changed, because they can be cured. Because they will return and tell their own stories.

But even though I know my mother's illness is like that tumor, I am angry. What can I do, can doctors do, can she do? I want so much to see my mother's defect, to pluck it out and put it in a tiny Mason jar full of formaldehyde. Sometimes I think it would make all the difference.

***

I walk into the building where my mother now lives. Old people are arranged around the hot sitting room, doubled over in their wheelchairs, asleep. One young man screams that he wants his sister to come pick him up, *now*. The nurses just nod and wait for him to wear himself out.

On the elevator up to my mother's floor, a beautiful ashen man with one eye scarred like a marble looks at me. I say hello. He smiles and winks with his damaged eye.

There are worse places to be, I tell myself. But I know I never want to wind up in a place like this. I don't have the strength it takes for daily existence here.

I freeze when I locate the room. My visit is unexpected, and

I'm not sure what I desire from it. But I knock, finally, and my mother opens the door. The woman I talk with is not the one I lost and grieve for, but her smell, her likeness, our immediate wordless embrace make me grateful that she is not dead, that I can still touch what remains.

This Land is His Soul

•

Carole Boston Weatherford

During World War II when my father, Joseph Alexander Boston, Jr., enlisted in the Army, he discovered that his legal name was not the one his mother gave him, but Phillip, the name his grandmother registered when she applied for his birth certificate. Though my grandfather married my grandmother shortly after my father was born, Daddy didn't meet his namesake—Joseph Alexander Boston, Sr. until he was eight years old. For reasons I am now only beginning to understand, he spared me that detail of his life until I was an adult.

Despite a lifelong estrangement from his own father, Daddy is devoted to family. With my mother, his wife of 45 years, he gave me and my brother a home that he constantly customized and remodeled with his own hands. His carpentry, cabinetry, painting and gardening came to symbolize his wish to shelter us from harm and to give us a semblance of the life that anchored him as a boy.

Born in Baltimore in 1923, Daddy spent his early years in Copperville, a remote community bordering Leeds Creek on Maryland's Eastern Shore. Nestled amidst historic river plantations and a pink castle once owned by an alleged bootlegger and his showgirl wife, Copperville seems hopelessly stuck in the past.

For the most part, Copperville provided a peaceful existence. But occasionally tragedy struck. When Daddy was five, he saw his cousin's house burn to the ground. That is his earliest recollection. His cousin ran a general store out of that house and everyone suspected that the white man who owned

302

a nearby store had set the fire. The day after the fire, Daddy searched amid the ash and rubble and found an old photograph of a man with a bushy white mustache. It was his great grandfather, Phillip Moaney. An ex-slave, Phillip purchased a small farm during Reconstruction with money he and his wife Marena earned working for white folks and weaving corn-husk mats. When Phillip died, his youngest son James inherited the farm.

James and his wife Mary Ann raised my father after bringing up their own six children, all but one of whom migrated to the city. One son, Albert, a police officer up North, began calling my father "Bus." The nickname stuck. Big-city uncles came and went, but Bus vowed he would never abandon the farm, at least not of his own choosing. He loved the land too much to ever leave it for long.

And he idolized his grandfather. From dawn to dusk, Bus worked alongside him. He fetched the pail when it was time to milk the cows. He gathered the eggs while his grandfather fed the chickens and ducks. He looked on quietly while his grandfather shoed the mule and horses. He trailed behind as his grandfather plowed the fields. Together, they hoed the garden, religiously uprooting weeds that always seemed to grow back. When Bus was about eight, he planted a seed from a cantaloupe he'd eaten for breakfast. That seed bore what his family proclaimed was the sweetest melon they'd ever tasted; the first inkling that Bus had a green thumb. The next summer, beneath a relentless sun, he promised his grandfather he would one day run the farm.

Farm life was far from easy, but it was imminently rewarding, each year blessing the family with another harvest. In the fall, they slaughtered hogs, cured ham, and seasoned sausage. Long after the creek froze, the family savored the fruits of summer. Stored in the root cellar were potatoes, carrots, turnips and cabbage. The kitchen cupboard was filled with peaches, string beans, tomatoes and beets his grandmother canned. Though the family sometimes struggled to make ends meet, they never went hungry. Three generations had lived off the land. And for that, they were more than thankful.

Bus's grandmother saw him off to school each morning with a soft kiss on the forehead. He didn't have far to go; the one-room schoolhouse was just across the road. In its one classroom, the teacher taught first through seventh grades.

When Bus wasn't at school, he roamed tree-shaded roads that were paved with oyster shells. He scared up geese along the branch and taught himself to swim in the muddy creek. Crabbing from the wooden bridge, he saw perch dart beneath the pier. On a good day, he'd catch a dozen blue crabs large as a man's hand.

Summers were especially busy. Besides tending his grandfather's garden and livestock, Bus earned a little money picking vegetables on large white-owned farms. At his leisure, he combed the woods for wild blackberries to fill his grandmother's cobblers.

By evening, he was worn out. He climbed the steep, narrow stairs to his room and crawled into bed. His grandmother looked on as he kneeled in prayer and then tucked him snugly beneath a patchwork quilt. When growing pains woke him at night, he summoned her to his bedside. She rubbed his aching knees, and, in the still, dark night, told him stories that were written on her heart. She immersed him in the history of Wye House, the riverfront plantation where she was a servant. The place was famous she said, as were its owners, the Lloyds. The manor even boasted an orangery, a large hothouse used to grow citrus fruits. The plantation's fourth owner had more than 300 slaves. Young Frederick Douglass, slave to one of the Lloyds' employees, grew up there. John Copper, who founded Copperville had been a slave there, too. He bred the Lloyds' roosters for cockfights. Bus's grandmother went on and on. She was so wise. Her gentle voice cradled him and lulled him back to sleep.

When Bus turned 13, his grandmother could no longer postpone the inevitable. She believed he needed to be with his mother. Besides, the one-room school only went to seventh grade. And a boy needed an education to get by.

With a satchel of clothes, a box of ham biscuits, and all the wisdom his grandparents could give him, Bus, dreading his destination, boarded a ferry. The Chesapeake Bay may as well have been an ocean, for Baltimore seemed worlds away from Copperville. Its bustling harbor teemed with industry. Young men swaggered down concrete sidewalks as if they owned them. And rowhouses, like crops without spacing, were cramped between cobblestone streets and alleys. To Bus, not even marble stoops, the pride of every neighborhood, conveyed much of a welcome.

Thus, began his painful transformation from farm boy to man of the world. Bus longed for the country. Climbing ancient oak trees. Eating tomatoes fresh off the vine. Watching deer nibble soybeans in the field. Diving in the creek on hot summer days. Listening to his grandmother's stories by moonlight.

Bus came of age in a household where the electricity was frequently cut off for back rent. A better sugar daddy than family man, his father was sometimes gone for days. His mother, a domestic, occasionally let out anguished cries but usually took her husband's philandering in stride. After all, he was her children's father and he did have a good job. A red cap for the B&O Railroad, he got his son a job as a porter as soon as he was old enough to work. With his earnings, Bus bought natty, new clothes, a wardrobe his father virtually sold off his back to pay overdue bills. His father also pawned his trumpet. And when Bus returned home from military service in New Guinea and the Philippines, his father had spent the money he sent his mother to save for college. Today, Bus rarely discusses his father. That chapter of his life he would rather forget. But it is as much a part of him as the long silences that mute chronic anger; an unresolved cold war.

After World War II, Bus went to college on the G.I. Bill, and then became an industrial arts teacher at the Baltimore high school he himself attended. By the time he married my mother, Carolyn, his grandfather, whom I called Grandpa Moaney, was almost blind and too frail to work the farm. But the patriarch still dreamed of willing the land to future generations. During his last years that dream was confined to one dark room in his mind. After his wife died, he reluctantly sold five acres to a prominent white landowner. In 1956 — the year I was born — he

305

sold 13 more acres to the same man. The land was just about gone—reduced to the two acres where the house and outbuildings stood.

The verdure stayed vivid in retrospect. Grandpa Moaney passed his days in a rocker, trying not to lose sight of the dream the way he lost his land—piece by piece, as the stars left the night. Bus clung to the dream as well.

For years, I assumed that tiny patch of land was all there ever was of the family farm. The hollyhocks Daddy's grandmother planted still bloomed in the barnyard, and a lone peach tree bore fruit. Every season, Daddy took me and my brother to visit his boyhood home. As time wore on, old ways slowly, graciously bowed to progress. A gleaming white gas stove replaced the old blue wood stove. Indoor plumbing replaced the pump. Wind and rain obscured epitaphs on headstones in the cemetery beside the church that had closed forever. In the barn, antiquated tools and three-legged chairs hung from rafters. And weeds grew where a garden had once thrived. The down-to-earth pace seemed the only constant.

No matter how much changed, though, Daddy's memories did not fade. The long-ago promise he made to his grandfather still echoed in his mind. As Daddy neared his 50th birthday, he decided to make good on his promise. My mother lent her support. With a goal of planting a garden, he approached the wealthy white man who had bought the land from his grandfather, proposing to buy some of it back. As if the land were never meant to leave my family's possession, the man, now ailing himself, confessed he felt guilty about paying Grandpa Moaney so little for the property. He offered to sell it back at cost.

So, in 1972, my father brought a dozen acres back into the family.

That milestone gains added significance in view of alarming black land loss statistics. In the rural South, land is the most valuable resource in black hands. Yet, black farmers nationwide are losing land at a rate of 1,000 acres a day, ten times higher than the rate for whites. This trend has seen black-owned farmland decline from 15.6 million acres in the peak year of 1910 to less than 2.5 million acres at last count. In 1920, there were nearly a million black farmers. By 1982, however, almost 94 percent of all black-owned farms had been sold or lost.

My father's accomplishment alone is not enough to reverse black land loss. Yet it has had far-reaching implications for my clan. In reclaiming those 12 acres that once symbolized freedom for ex-slaves, Daddy recaptured the agrarian spirit and gave us a refuge from the urban rush and materialism.

He immediately set about reviving the farm. He repaired the chicken coop, painted the barn, tore down a dilapidated shed, and planted a small garden and an orchard. Each spring, he tilled the sandy loam, making furrows with his fingers just as his grandfather had done a century earlier.

He also equipped the farm with modern conveniences, most notably a modest house whose interior he himself finished. He enhanced our weekend home with annual building and landscaping projects: a split-rail fence, screened gazebo, enclosed patio and stocked pond. He tackled those projects with gusto belying middle age.

Daddy's love affair with the land not only produced bountiful harvests but priceless memories. One year, he and his cousin David bought a steer and hog. Daddy's face beamed like it must have when he was a boy. At that moment, his grandfather was probably smiling somewhere, too.

Daddy spent winters leafing through seed catalogs. In the process, he became well-versed in varieties. Each August, he picked his prized tomatoes, succulent, vine-ripened beefsteaks. And he plucked berries wearing the same straw hat that once shaded his grandfather's brow. "The blacker the berry the sweeter the juice," he mused as a thorn pricked his thumb. The juice of the ripe fruit rimmed his nail and met a fresh trickle of blood. He sucked the new wound, tasting both sacrifice and reward.

In his wisdom, Grandpa Moaney also grasped this bittersweet paradox. I still remember his strong hands. Long before his fingers became his eyes, soil embedded itself in his lifelines. His palms uplifted us and my Daddy's hands carried us over.

From the small farm my father saved, I gained a sense of my history. Like the geese that flock to the creek each autumn on their southern migration, I return to the farm each year to plow my past. Little is as it was when Daddy was a boy. But I am content to make my own memories. I take pride in seeing the soil that soaked up my forefathers' sweat once again bear fruit. I delight in seeing my own children pick blueberries and snap fresh-picked beans. I share my daughter's excitement as she reels in a snapping turtle rather than the bass she had hoped to bait. From the banks of the pond, my son skips stones across the still water. The ripples undulating from those pebbles remind me of my family, each circle, a generation, and this land at the very center.

Just as Daddy entrusted seeds to the Earth, he planted his progeny here as well. And today, the farm completes me, validating my values with evidence of my forefathers' strivings. They viewed each harvest as part of a continuum, linking what has passed with what is yet to come. This land is their legacy, handed down with faith that we would maintain it and it, in turn, would sustain us.

Though suffering from cancer, Daddy is still drawn to the family farm and its promise of tomorrow. He can no longer drive his tractor, so he surveys the field on foot. As I watch him I realize he's not just cultivating the land; he's preserving our roots.

"Where fruits are ever bearing and harvests always gold; gone on to Glory. This land is my soul." That could well be Daddy's epitaph.

Folks used to say "Land is the only thing God isn't making any more of." Well, God isn't making men like my daddy either.

I Stand Here Xeroxing

•

Ruth Moose

You call to say the Home cannot keep my mother any longer. Already I am tired. It is 9AM and the copy machine whirls paper in my face, a blizzard of shouting words. You say I have ten days to find her another Home or you will what? You are calling places that may take her. Homes that are not home. Homes that are waiting places for souls on hold. Homes of hand rails and wheel chairs, soft foods and Sunday School six days a week. On Saturdays everyone leaves them alone. No one comes to pray or sing or read them Bible stories. If they have not made their after life decision before coming here, it is too late now. If they pray, it is not for their sins, nor to forgive others, but to go. They want to go home, the home they left.

My mother complains of the bed. It has bars they put up at night like a crib. They say the bars keep her from falling out, breaking an arm or leg or hip. She says the bars are to keep her from *getting* out. They say she is to call when she wants up. She says she calls and they don't come or if they do come, it takes forever and she has wet her bed. She says she can crawl out between the rails and go to the bathroom herself and they never know. They do. They have called me and said if my mother does not stop climbing out of her bed, I will have to come get her.

The nurse told me if she gets out again, they will have to restrain her. "Tie her down?" I ask. "A straight jacket?" My mother is not crazy. She is only old. And not that old. She is 76, but had a stroke and cannot use her left side. Her left arm hangs limp as a flag. Her left leg can follow her right leg in the frame of a walker she uses. She holds bars and shifts right, left, right, left in front of her.

309

"Restraints," they repeat firmly, "we will have to use restraints."

My mother cannot bear to be tied to her bed. She will cry. She will beg me to take her home; to get her out of this place.

I can't take her to her home. She will fall. She must have someone with her to fix meals, bathe and dress her, wash and set her hair. Here at the home they have group showers they roll her through. She says some of the women scream. She says the water is warm and feels good. Sometimes she gets into the whirlpool bath and wants to stay. They will not let her stay longer than 20 minutes. There are others who need the treatment.

The Home has a beauty shop and twice a week she gets her hair shampooed and set. When she looks nice, her mood is better. All her life she did her own hair and that of others.

She did her sisters' hair and some of our neighbors, gave them home permanents on the screened porch in summer. Only after my father died did she allow herself weekly visits to the beauty shop. She was proud of having a "standing" appointment, of that constant in her life. The operator teased her hair two inches high and sprayed it to a luster. Here, at the Home, I write the girl a check, leave it in her box with a note saying how much it means that she helps my mother feel better. Mother thinks she pays for the beauty shop out of her money. The truth is, she has no money. She has the house, the small car she bought and learned to drive at age fifty five and that is all. Her savings went for the hospital and The Home the first month. Now she is on Medicaid. If she knew that she would be angry. She has never taken charity in her life. She has never lived "off the government." She has worked. All her life.

The first job she had was in a sock mill. Second shift. She went to work every afternoon at three, before I got home from school, left me a note on the table what to make my brothers for supper and other instructions. When she came in at midnight, I listened for her footsteps, soft and tired. Only then did I let myself sleep.

The mill closed and she worked in Ladies' Wear at a department store. She came home and made clothes for herself and me like ones she sold, only better and for a third the price.

Then my grandmother came to live with us. For thirteen years. Until she was ninety. Mother quit work to take care of her.

Soon after my grandmother died, my father began dying. Doctors gave him six months, but he took two years, and all that time my mother thought he'd live. She never learned to drive and toward the end, driving was all my father could do; drive her to work,come and get her until finally he couldn't get to the car. Still she didn't learn, thinking each day, he'd feel better and if he didn't, she couldn't bear that he see her replace him behind the wheel.

She didn't cry at the funeral, though the rain and wind tore at my eyes and hair and the Taps they played somewhere behind the hill nearly pulled me to the ground. You cry, she told me. You'll feel better.

Mother went back to school, trained as a nurses aide. She got a job in a private home, being paid for what she'd done so many years free. With a church group, she went on trips;to Canada, Amish Country, Nashville, New Orleans, DisneyWorld. She'd call when she came back from a trip telling me how the tour guide told them not to wear gold jewelry on the streets of New York nor their name tags on elevators in the hotel.

She'd tell me how many miles they rode on the bus and how their bus drivers were always named "Bubba." I gave her luggage for Christmas and travel sets for her birthday, sweaters and folding umbrellas for Mother's Day. I thought how my father never wanted to go anywhere. How we'd never had a family vacation.

So I saw my mother off on trips and each time said, "Enjoy, enjoy." And she did. She laughed and smiled and went to her class reunion with an old boy friend who was also alone.

She was the only one there who wasn't gray and was still working. She was the only one who had to.

Then came the HEADACHE. She fell, a neighbor found her. We carried her to the emergency room. Then we waited. It was a Sunday night. Halloween. Her doctor was not on call.

The one there didn't speak a lot of English, but smiled too

much and looked away when I asked questions.

I asked questions when her doctor came in and got no answers. For three weeks they did tests and we got no answers except one word; stroke. Her doctor said she could go home. I said there is no one at her home to help her.

He said take her to your home. I said there is no one at my home. I work. He said take her to work with you.

I said she can't sit in a wheel chair all day. I can't get her in and out of a car, office doors, bathrooms. I cannot be her nurse and do my job and turn my office into a hospital room. I have to work. The doctor left. He called from the hall she needed twenty-four hour care, but there was not an empty bed in a nursing home in the county.

I called nursing homes. I learned if one has unlimited funds, one can find an empty bed, plenty of empty beds. I found it would take more than I make in one month to pay for my mother to be in a Home. Yet, I cannot quit my job and take my mother in and be her nurse. I cannot help her in and out of bed. I cannot help her shower. I cannot give her physical therapy to help her relearn to use her arm and hand muscles, to retrain her legs to walk. If I give up my job, I have no health insurance, no retirement and I will be in the same room with my mother. So I sign her up for Medicaid. I find the deed to her cemetery plot, the space beside my father. I show them the deed for her house and that it can be rented and the rent go to the Home. I sign her Social Security check to go to the Home. My brother's wife asks who will tell Mother she's going to the Home? I will, I say. I do and she says she understands.

She is placed in a yellow room that overlooks a courtyard bare as a cemetery. There are no fountains, flowers nor outdoor furniture. No one here goes out to enjoy, weed or water or sit.

They get wheeled to the dining room and wheeled to chapel six days a week. Breakfast is brought to them.

You always wanted breakfast in bed, I tell my mother. And she did use to joke about it. Now it is no joke. She says the coffee is always cold. She can't understand it. She says she won't drink cold coffee. She says they bring her eggs every morning and she has never liked eggs. I say tell them you want cold cereal. She says I keep sending the eggs back and that ought to tell them I don't want eggs. She says the nurses eat her fruit and candy. They come in and use her hand and body lotion. They lose her panties and give her ones that are too big, not as nice. Ones that belong to somebody else. She says I don't talk back even when I want to.

I say please talk nice to Them and please call Them when you want to get up and please don't get out of bed by yourself again.

She says, "I will if I want to," and does not look at me.

"Promise me," I whisper and she does not answer.

So I am Xeroxing and waiting for the phone to ring. Each ring that is not for me I ask if I am closer or farther from a solution. I keep asking. I keep Xeroxing.

Pvt. McKinney Died in France July 9

•

Elizabeth Hunter

"The old black hen, which was frequently seen wandering in front of the courthouse and leisurely crossing the main street of Bakersville, is dead. She was run over by a streamlined '41 model car and so thoroughly squashed that there was nothing left but a handful of black feathers. She belonged to another era when a self-respecting and well-behaved chicken could stroll along the main street of any rural town and never come to harm. But now the old black hen and the times she represented are gone, with nothing to mark their passing but a few feathers blown away by the breeze."

So read a bold-faced, boxed, front page story in the Aug. 7, 1941, edition of the *Tri-County News.* I came upon the story of the hen's demise while researching the history of mica mining in the Toe River Valley in Western North Carolina, where I live. A woman had loaned me a complete set of the *News* from 1941-47, when the mica vein running through the weekly paper was rich indeed. Importation of the strategic mineral from India had been interrupted by the war, prompting a resurgence of local mica mining. Mica was big news—and a major source of income—in the Toe Valley during the war years.

Mica stories notwithstanding, nuggets like "Progress Overtakes the Old Black Hen" and other rich deposits—stories about construction of the Blue Ridge Parkway through the area, a fire sweeping through Spruce Pine's business district, plane crashes and blizzards—continually threatened to divert me. Mitchell County, one of the three counties the *News* served, has been my home for 20 years. The old newspapers illuminated its past like a flashlight beamed into the recesses of one of its abandoned mines.

Prospecting those papers was to produce more than mica — or diversions — I was soon to discover. As I dug my way through 1942, I became aware of an increasing preponderance of stories like one in the Sept. 10 issue, "Mrs. J.P. Martin Has Had Six Sons in Two Wars: Three Now Serving." In 1943, I started noticing the black stars. That was the way the *Tri-County News* highlighted stories of men killed in service to their country. Not all died in battle. More than one succumbed in stateside accidents. But as 1943 bled into the horrifying year of 1944, more and more often the stars appeared above stories of lives lost in France, Italy, and the Pacific.

The paper's editors weren't working from an official list; they had to rely on family members. A boxed, bold-faced story asked anyone with service news to call, write or bring it in. Front pages weren't laid out then the way they are now, with two or three big stories and a couple of shorter ones. Some of those old papers had 15-20 stories that began on page one. All the stories with the stars were there; most of them were nearly as brief as the accounts of soldiers wounded or missing in action.

By the summer of 1944, hardly a week passed without at least one front page star. Often there were two or three. Occasionally four. Frequently the black stars appeared over follow-ups of stories from a few weeks or months earlier, when their subjects had been reported as missing. The paper ran photographs of the young, unlined faces of soldiers like Cpl. Ray Glass and S/Sgt. Oval Willis, who wouldn't be coming home. Sometimes the photos ran with the death announcements, sometimes a couple of weeks later. Double stars appeared above a photo of Pvt. Jack Burleson and Pvt. Henry Burleson, standing side by side in uniform. Both died in Italy — Jack in February, Henry in June.

August, 1944, when the Burleson brothers' picture ran, was the worst month of all. There were two stars in the Aug. 3 edition; three on Aug. 10; two on the 24th; three more on Aug. 31. The stories with the stars were surrounded by others — of soldiers wounded, taken prisoner, missing. Still others told of medals awarded (including one about a Purple Heart presented to the four year old son of a dead soldier), of soldiers home on leave, of wounded men recovering and preparing to return to the front.

I found myself grieving for young men who'd died before they'd barely begun life, for families from whom a child had been untimely ripped. My growing interest in the war surprised me. I'd never given World War II much thought, nor understood others' fascination with it. I'd been born in its last year and had no first-hand memory of its terrible cost. The numbers it involved—more than a million U.S. casualties, including nearly 300,000 battle deaths; the extermination of 6 million Jews—were so huge as to be mind-numbing, incomprehensible.

Seeing the war through these old yellowed newspapers—working my way through the weeks and months and years it held sway over this little mountain county—was something altogether different. Here was a picture of Albert Canipe in his sailor uniform. I'd known Albert well during the years he was a county commissioner and I a newspaper reporter. He was a man who loved spinning a good yarn; until his death, at the age of 77, he'd told me plenty of them. He regaled me with tales of his youth, and with more than one war story. I'd always envisioned him, even in those stories, as the elderly man he'd become. Yet here was the young fellow he'd been talking about.

Albert had been one of the lucky ones, a participant in five invasions—North Africa, Sicily, Salerno, Southern France and Okinawa—who came through the war without a scratch. He returned home, ran a service station with his brother, served many terms as alderman and then as mayor of Spruce Pine, became a state senator, a Democratic county commissioner in a solidly Republican county. What might these others have become, the subjects of these stark, minimalist accounts, these privates and sergeants and lieutenants whose names appeared below black stars?

I once attended a writing seminar in which the instructor

described what must happen in a short story — something of such significance that the main character cannot return to the place he was when the story began, because he is no longer the same person he was at the beginning of the story. I believe that that is what happened to me reading those newspapers from 1944, the year before my birth. I can even pinpoint the turning point — the moment when a probing flashlight seeking mica history exploded like a grenade and became a floodlight illuminating a world.

It occurred as I read a story in the Sept. 7, 1944, issue, headed "Pvt. McKinney Died in France July 9." Below the headline was the usual black star; below that a photo of a young man in uniform, one hand on his hip, the other on the hood of a jeep. The story began the way most of them did, with the report received by Claude McKinney's mother of the death of her son. It had been her second loss of the summer. Her husband had died June 17, of injuries sustained in a fall from a cherry tree.

The story said Claude McKinney had volunteered for the service in January, 1941, and was one of the earliest inductees to leave the county. After two years stateside, he'd been sent overseas in January, 1944. There were no details about his death, not even the battle it occurred in, or the town. The list of surviving brothers and sisters was a long one: three siblings at home, six others who'd married and moved off. But this story ended the way most of the others did not, with Pvt. McKinney's last letter home. It was a condolence letter and a letter of advice, written to his mother.

"Dear Mamma," it read, "I know there is little I can say or do that will be of any comfort to you. But please, mamma, don't worry too much. I know you have troubles beyond my knowledge but worry will only make things worse. I know the tragedy was more a shock to you than anyone. But Dad is resting in a better world today, away from all troubles. We have to go sooner or later. Let's just live a life now where we can meet Dad again.

"If I was only home. I don't know what to tell you to do. You can't run the farm. I think I would sell everything but one cow. If you have out a very large crop, let someone work it on shares.

317

Please don't worry. Your loving son, Claude."

I see it all. A mountain farm in summer, the bees buzzing, the cows flicking away flies as they graze, the corn growing fast and green. It'll be knee high by the Fourth of July. High on a slope above the pasture, the blackheart cherries are ripening, attracting the birds and the squirrels and a 67-year-old farmer, who'll climb the tree—no dwarf this one—to pick the cherries for the jam his wife is planning to make. A branch he's putting his weight on will give, and he'll fall. They'll find him there in the grass, the broken man with the broken branch and the broken cherries. They'll transport him over unpaved roads to a hospital 35 miles away. He'll die there without ever regaining consciousness, on a Saturday night when the air is redolent with the smell of honeysuckle.

The morning Robert McKinney climbs the hill the sky is blue, with a few wispy high clouds. With the exception of the calling of the birds and the buzzing of insects, the day is very still. Halfway round the world, one of the farmer's sons is living and breathing under the same blue sky, though there it is obscured by smoke and wracked by the sounds of war.

In the farmhouse in the hollow below the hill, Maude McKinney believes she is preparing for an afternoon of jelly making. In point of fact, she's being prepared for a pair of shocks to her life, a life which will, before the summer is out, be scaled back to something she would have trouble recognizing this beautiful morning. She's a natural born worrier though, and later she'll wonder why she didn't sense an ill wind blowing.

Two cracks, neither of which she'll hear—one in an old, leaning, blackheart cherry far up a hillside she's looked at every day of her married life, the other on a hill she'll never see, in a country she'll never visit—are about to reverberate through her life. They will cleave the world she's grown so accustomed to she's barely noticed its beauty. The beauty of it will appear again as she grieves, not to soothe her, but to cleave her still further. She will read her dead son's last letter again and again. She will take his advice, which sounds portentous, because, while it's written simply, it comes from the pen of a young man who is about to die. She will sell all but the one cow. She will look for someone to work the crops on shares.

She will treasure the letter and the Purple Heart she's accepted in place of the beating one. She will fold the letter and the clipping from the Sept. 7, 1944, edition of the *Tri-County News*. She will place them in the family Bible where they will yellow and dry. She will put them with the obituary notice she's already clipped from the June 28 issue of the paper, the paper that lists Claude "of the U.S. Army" as one of the survivors of Robert V. McKinney, a "prominent farmer" of the Fork Mountain section of Mitchell County.

"If I was only home," Claude wrote. Her heart aches. So does mine. I'm reminded of a collection of letters I read a few years ago from a farmer from another section of Mitchell County. This farmer had left his young wife Sally in charge of their farm when he enlisted in the Confederate Army, 80 years before Claude McKinney went off to war. Like Claude, he did not come back. During the years between his departure and his death, he wrote out detailed advice to help Sally keep the farm going—how many bushels of corn she'd need to put by for the winter, how many cows to keep. His advice sounded a lot like Claude McKinney's. I believe Sally followed his advice, much as I believe Maude followed Claude's, though of course I do not know whether either did.

What I do know is this: during the 60 years between that Confederate soldier's death and his wife's, Sally made repeated and unsuccessful efforts to discover the location of his body and to bring him home. She is buried in a little hilltop cemetery in Rebel's Creek, a community a few miles down the road from where I live. I once visited her grave, and I have thought about her in the same concentrated way I am now thinking about Claude and Maude and Robert McKinney. I can see the McKinney family and the world they lived in, the world before World War II descended on Mitchell County, a world in which a well-behaved chicken and a farm boy from Fork Mountain could stroll along the main street of a rural town and never come to harm. But the times they lived in are gone, with nothing to mark their passing but some yellowed newspaper clippings in a family Bible and a few feathers blown away by the breeze.

Porch-Sitting as a Creative Southern Tradition

•

Trudier Harris

I have recently been reflecting on the significance of the porch in the South, on what that space allows and what it means. I have been thinking about the history of sharing and interaction that characterizes porch space in southern culture, about the voices that bring the space to life, about what this space meant historically and creatively to almost everyone in the deep South. Before proceeding, however, a definition is in order. Throughout this discussion, the word "porch" refers to the physical attachment that protrudes from the *front* of the *first level* of many houses and business establishments in the South. I emphasize front and first level because I do not wish to identify wrap-around porches, or verandas, or balconies with the activities I describe; I am concerned with those spaces that face *directly* toward the street, with an unobstructed view of traffic along the road or walkway or, later, sidewalks. Such porches were certainly a phenomenon of the nineteenth century, but I am primarily concerned with the time period in the first five or six decades of the twentieth century, where yards might have been a solid expanse of dirt and where walkways would probably not have been paved. This space is usually not enclosed, though it may be screened in, and it is covered by an extension from the roof of the house, with appropriate supporting joists. Frequently, owners of the houses include swings suspended by chains from the overhead beams, accordingly called "porch swings." In addition to swings, rocking chairs and straight-backed chairs are the usual furniture, and of course people can sit on the porch steps.

"Porch-sitting" is an activity in which people can participate from early morning until late at night. All they have to do is plop their bodies down, engage someone in conversation, and the *activity* is on. I emphasize activity because I interpret "porch-sitting" to be dramatically different from "porch-staring"; a single individual can sit on a porch and stare at the world passing by, and obviously lots of people have done that. However, "porch-staring" lacks the interactive quality that I believe is key to "porch-sitting." Keep in mind, however, that "porch-staring" can be upgraded to "porch-sitting" immediately when a second person joins the first person on the porch, or when that person interacts with people on other porches or with those who are passing by the porch. For example, when I was about twelve, I was sitting on my front porch steps early one morning, just staring—elbows on knees, legs gaped wide apart—when I heard this voice from the porch across the street, up the hill, saying, "[she used my nickname], sit according to your family." (I always wanted to use that line in a lecture or an article.) That was the voice of Aunt Nance Ann, and she, like every other woman in the neighborhood, had the right to chastise any child in the community. So, I straightened up immediately. More recently, when I was home in Alabama on the Fourth of July in 1994 and out about 7:00 A.M. doing my walking-jogging routine, I passed a porch-starer—just sitting there, watching the grass grow. He gained porch-sitting status when he yelled out at me, "Out mighty early this morning." "Yea," I responded, "gotta keep that fat off." "You gon cook out today?" "Naw, that's just more fat to work off." "Well, don't you get too hot out there." "I won't." Now, these are examples of porch-sitting at its minimalist range and briefest of interactions. The activity is obviously more appropriate to warmer months, but since the South is so temperate, there can be extended seasons of clinging to the porch.

The *activity* of porch-sitting can involve a great variety of things. Porches are where southern women have traditionally removed at midmorning to shell their peas or make other such preparations for dinner (that meal we southerners eat about 1:00

321

P.M.), to do some of their sewing or other portable work, or to visit with each other at any time of day. For children, especially during the summer months, porches offer an inviting space for entertainment that ranges from imaginative play to toys to hiding out beneath the floor. For older nonworking men, such as the one I encountered, porches might be the preferred space all day—either at their own homes or at neighborhood gathering places. They gather to play checkers, talk politics, reminisce, discuss crops, weather, and anything else that lures their imaginations. For working men, porches are where they retire after they have had their evening bath as they wait, with their families and sometimes their neighbors, for the houses to cool off sufficiently for everyone to go to bed in peace. These evening sessions can provide the most fruitful opportunities for traditional storytelling; folk characters such as Brer Rabbit and the mythical slave John make their entrances along with jokes, ghosts, and plain old gossip.

In 1982 I explored this evening phenomenon in a lecture called "Southern Black Folklore in the Twentieth Century: Can Brer Rabbit Kill Television?" In this talk I generally lamented the fact that television, video games (remember Pac Man?), and other more enticing forms of entertainment were supplanting the evening sessions on porches. That development, along with the advent of air conditioning in every nook and cranny of the South, is transforming and threatening with extinction the porch-sitting tradition, especially the evening portion. Today, there are certainly signs that the tradition still exists. But it is obviously not as strong now as it was when I was growing up, and it was probably not as strong then as it was for my mother and her siblings growing up in the 1920s and 1930s. This change and potential loss is all the more reason to consider what this activity is and what it offers participants.

The location of the porch is crucial. It is that (some critics would say) liminal area between private (inside the house) and public (the street) space. It is the natural squatting space for people you might like well enough but wouldn't particularly want in your house. And since notions of southern hospitality would not allow turning them away, you can always invite them to sit on the porch. It is the space where housedresses or bathrobes can be worn with impunity; if a person so dressed were to step into the street, neighbors would probably raise their eyebrows. It is the space where the person sitting can control what is going on in the house even though he or she is not physically inside the house; in other words, it's good hollering space, as in a mother calling out "Joann, check the water in them beans!" or "John, you done made up that bed yet?"

More important, perhaps, than the glimpse—figurative or literal—inside the house is the window the porch provides on the world. That window allows for observing any and everything that comes into view. Let me give you a couple of examples. I spent my formative years in Tuscaloosa, Alabama, at 2513 Fosters Ferry Road. That house, now no longer in existence, was at the bend of a dirt road with a full view of the other houses. (Imagine a boomerang with my house at the outer curve.) That formation gave my family, especially my brothers and sisters and me, a great view of what was happening "up the road" toward town or "down the road" toward the country. Periodically, there would be a car chase through our neighborhood, which usually meant that the police were chasing a black man who thought his car could outrun theirs. I remember witnessing several such chases from our porch. It was like walking into a theater for five minutes in the middle of a drama in a foreign language. You could observe the sword fight that was going on, but you had no idea what had caused it or how it would end. But that five minutes' worth of drama could stimulate porch conversation for days.

I also remember witnessing fights between Monkey and Lida Mae. They lived down toward the country, but they came to Miss Gert's, the bootlegger's house, two doors away from mine to get their daily shots of alcohol. Again, we were spectators to dramas that, from our perspective, began *in medias res*. All we knew was that Monkey and Lida Mae would occasionally come out of Miss Gert's house fighting. Remember, I said fighting, not wife-beating. They would curse and scream at each other, engage in fisticuffs, back off, curse some more,

323

then the fisticuffs again. Neither was sober nor strong enough to inflict serious damage on the other. They simply fought. Surprisingly, the fighting never interrupted overly much their progress toward home, so we had a steady show for three or four blocks. We watched and commented on this from the porch because that is where my mother insisted that we remain during this turmoil. What we considered — and what *was* — entertainment was the bane of this Christian neighborhood. We never thought about the implications of violence between people who presumably loved each other. We never passed judgment on the woman who sold liquor to these people who obviously could not handle it. We never thought about the vantage point from which we watched. We simply watched — from our porch window on the world — and, as Zora Neale Hurston would say, chewed up the lives of those people with our gossipy responses to their actions.

We also watched one of my male classmates put on his mother's stockings and high-heel shoes, dresses, and make-up and parade up and down the street. While we all considered it unusual, we never considered it abnormal. And nobody registered any objections. This was another of the watching events that were available to us from our porch window. Unlike the police car chases or the drunken fights, where participants did not care one way or another about our watching, my classmate paraded up and down the street precisely because he wanted an audience; we could call out to and interact with him, and he could do the same with us. He turned our window on the world into his public stage. And we who were busily watching were in turn being watched and evaluated by the performer for our assessments of his performance. Mirror on mirror — it was an interesting dynamic.

Looking in. Looking out. Offering comments either way. The porch was and is a two-way mirror. It is easy to combine the viewing with work. I remember those occasions on which we had bushels of corn to shuck or peas to shell in midsummer for immediate eating as well as for freezing or canning for the winter's food supply. In August it would be peaches — seemingly tons and tons of peaches — that would be frozen, canned, or, if we were lucky, layered with sugar in a crock jar to become peach brandy in the winter months. The women would shuck, shell, peel, and talk. Fingers or knives moved as fast as the conversation, and children big enough to be helpers could learn a lot about people and activities in the neighborhood. It was here that I learned of the impending marriage of a couple of my neighbors. Getting married was routine; what made this one interesting was that she was *older* than he was. Buzz. Buzz. We watched from our porch as they came home after the wedding—to the house across the street and up the hill from us (the same one in which Aunt Nance Ann resided). And it was announced throughout the neighborhood that they had fried chicken, rice, and gravy for their first meal in that house. Porch-sitters, I'd like to think, were perhaps the original grapevine.

Quilting always elevated porch-sitting a notch or two. People passing by were always curious about the quilt. And it was quite a feat to get those quilting horses positioned just right if the porch was smallish. Fingers and stitches vied with tongues as tales were related about who wore what among the many patches that were being sewed into the quilt. I think of the vividness with which William Ferris captures that tradition as passing shots of local color in two of his films, *Two Black Churches* and *Made in Mississippi: Black Folk Art and Crafts*. And I think of the quilting venture that Mama Day and her sister Abigail engage in as they sit sewing on Abigail's porch in Gloria Naylor's *Mama Day* (1988), making a double-ringed wedding quilt for Cocoa and George. Family history and personality inform their sewing as engagingly as they informed the sewing traditions on our porches in Tuscaloosa. Black women created art out of the pieces of fabric as they created art out of words. The Porch became their "wordshop" as assuredly as Paule Marshall's kitchen served the same function for the Bajan women among whom she grew up.

Children could claim porch-sitting as their own activity anytime the women did not need the porch for something they were undertaking. Playing in the swing, challenging its endurance. Rocking away in the rocking chair. Performing for adults in the evening. My nieces and I, on those occasions when I vacationed with my older sister in the country, would on a rare evening stand in front of the porch and sing for adults seated there. "Will the circle be unbroken? By and by, Lord, by and by." "That sounds good," my Uncle Dexter would say. (No, I can't sing worth two cents.) More frequently, if there was trouble to be gotten into on the porch in Tuscaloosa, we would find it. But we also had to pay the consequences on the porch, for it was there that we would be switched for all the world to see. Switching was bad enough, but we shared with large numbers of southern children the humiliation of having to go out and find our own switches. And if we dared to get ones that adults judged to be too small, they simply sent us back for larger ones. Punishments that today would probably reap a gaggle of social workers screaming child abuse were routine in those days, and none of us is particularly worse for wear. After all, one of the challenges of porch-sitting was to see how much devilment you could get into before some adult caught you pulling other children's hair, or pinching them, or taking some favorite toy away from them.

Things usually settled down in the early evening, and the porch became an extension of the house in another way. It was here that, after running around barefoot in the dust all day, we washed our feet in an appropriately named "foot tub." This was the era, remember, when children did not bathe every night because there was no indoor bathroom with a gleaming white bathtub. This was the heat-your-own-water-and-pour-it-into-a-metal-tub-to-bathe era. Since feet were the most abused and dirtiest parts of the body, they had to be washed every night. After all, in the absence of electric washers and dryers, cleaning dirt from sheets by boiling them in a cast-iron washing pot was hard work indeed. The nightly foot washing at least cut down on a portion of that work. Thus "cleaned," we could settle down and listen to the adults take over the porch-sitting routine.

The psychic zone that the porch occupies is the realm of creativity, which, with its intense interactive engagement, is the epitome of porch-sitting. In storytelling sessions, whether during the day or in the evening, porch space signals license — license to exaggerate, to lie, to enter into verbal contest with family and neighbors. Porch space is the border between the "real" world and the world of storytelling, an invitation to audiences to put aside their daily cares and go where the storyteller takes them. The active tradition bearer who begins a tale thus steps onto yet another stage. Not only is he or she on stage performing the tale — verbally as well as with gestures and dramatization — for the listening audience, but he or she is also on stage in being evaluated for quality of performance. A stage for subject matter and its quality of presentation. A stage for performer and his or her quality of performance.

Jokes and funny stories were favorite forms of narrative interaction on our porch, especially when my sister Hazel and her husband John would arrive to sit for a couple of hours with us. John liked to tell jokes, but he could barely get himself through a single one without balling up in laughter, tears streaming down his face. I think I remember those sessions so well because his laughter was as entertaining as the stories and the jokes. Somehow, there always seemed to be a story floating around about bare feet or about tennis shoes — you know, the plain white cloth ones (we polished them for gym class) or the high-top black ones ("buddies," we used to call them). In one tale the mythical slave John prays to God to take him to heaven because he's tired of dealing with white folks. "God" comes in the form of Old Massa in a white sheet, and John discovers that he really does not want what he prayed for. "God" insists that he come with him, however, and John "obeys" by taking off running down the road, with "God" chasing him. When John's children begin crying, their mother tells them that "God" cannot catch their father because he is barefoot. Tales abounded about black men in tennis shoes outrunning cars to escape some kind of trouble. When I later heard Bill Cosby's routine on tennis shoes, it was like *déja vu*. Porch-sitting in the evening allowed black folks to wrap themselves in laughter even as they were wrapped in darkness, watching fireflies buzz around and keeping mosquitoes away by smoking rags in a bucket.

Porch-sitting could also be applied to courting relationships, for the swing was usually reserved for the courting daughter

327

and her beau on Wednesday and Sunday nights. At times, other family members could join them there for the usual storytelling or other interactive sessions, but more often than not they could be left alone — under the watchful, behind-the-curtain eyes of parents, of course. Younger children, ever eager to interrupt the courting process, usually had to be driven from the scene under threat of whippings from parents or worse from the daughter. Hand-holding and polite kissing were allowable, but woe be unto the young man and woman who tried anything else.

Such courtships have found their way into southern literature again and again. One of the most striking instances occurs in a scene from Margaret Walker's classic novel, *Jubilee* (1966). While entertaining her beau and several other young people, the daughter of the owner of the plantation (where the heroine, Vyry Brown, is enslaved) inadvertently belches and breaks wind on the veranda after a dinner party one Sunday evening. Now that is something that pedestalized southern white ladies simply cannot do. The embarrassed southern belle escapes inside the house, but southern gentility must be upheld. Her mother insists upon some rectification and enlists the aid of one of the enslaved young black men, who is a "dumb-wit," in her effort to restore the status quo. The height of the absurd occurs when, on the porch on the next courting night, the young black male stands silent before the guests, and, when recognized, takes claim for the previous Sunday night's offense. Picture this: "Evening to yall. I come around here to take that fart on myself what Miss Lillian farted last week."[1]

Porch-sitting at business establishments is endemic to southern history as well as to southern literature. In my home neighborhood in Tuscaloosa today, Mr. Adell owns a little grocery store comparable to the one Miss Vera owned when I was growing up. It usually stocks a few staples for those occasions on which people may run out of something, but mainly it stocks things few people need but everybody likes — candy, cake, sodas. Its primary customers, therefore, are the children who shop there during weekdays, but especially before and after Sunday school and church. Its primary porch-sitters are male. They are the men who cultivate the sizable field behind the store, from which Mr. Adell supplies just about everybody who wants them with fresh collards, corn, turnips, and okra as each is in season, or they work elsewhere and just pause on the porch for resting space. They occupy the four or five chairs available and always seem to be engaged in earnest conversation when I pass by.

This 1990's manifestation is not unlike Hurston's description of one of the most famous literary porches in America. The porch in front of Jody Starks's store in the fictional Eatonville, Florida, in *Their Eyes Were Watching God* (1937) shares much with historical and literary barbershops in that it is a talker's paradise. It is the space where reputations can be made or nipped in the bud, where talkers engage each other for the sake of entertainment or to stimulate their own argumentative imaginations. Contest is foremost, and that contest, unlike historical porches, defines a male world. Two of Hurston's male characters, for example, engage in a lengthy discussion of the virtues of nature versus caution. All the lines are familiar to the crowd gathered to take in the discussion, amen good points made, and egg on the contestants to outperform each other. What is ever new is the performance, and listeners judge the quality of that by which contestant is most up to the task on a given day.

Just as men earn reputations for talking, in Hurston's world they also shape reputations for women. Budding sexuality and seasoned femininity get equal applause from the men who watch the women passing by. Sometimes the women join the porch-sitters, joke with them, or playfully act out courtship rituals; other women select their outfits on these occasions especially to evoke verbal applause. Consider one of Hurston's interactive exchanges:

> But here come Bootsie, and Teadi and Big 'oman down the street making out they are pretty by the way they walk. They have got that fresh, new taste about them like young mustard greens in the spring, and the young men on the porch are just bound to tell them about it and buy them some treats.

"Heah come mah order right now," Charlie Jones announces and scrabbles off the porch to meet them. . . . "Gal, Ah'm crazy 'bout you," Charlie goes on to the entertainment of everybody. "Ah'll do anything in the world except work for you and give you mah money."

The girls and everybody else help laugh. They know it's not courtship. It's acting-out courtship and everybody is in the play. The three girls hold the center of the stage till Daisy Blunt comes walking down the street in the moonlight.

Daisy is walking a drum tune. You can almost hear it by looking at the way she walks. She is black and she knows that white clothes look good on her, so she wears them for dress up. She's got those big black eyes with plenty shiny white in them that makes them shine like brand new money and she knows what God gave women eyelashes for, too. Her hair is not what you might call straight. It's negro hair, but it's got a kind of white flavor. . . .

"Lawd, Lawd, Lawd," that same Charlie Jones exclaims rushing over to Daisy. "It must be uh recess in heben if St. Peter is lettin' his angels out lak dis. You got three men already layin' at de point uh death 'bout yuh, and heah's uhnother fool dat's willin' tuh make time on yo' gang."

While most of this banter is disinterested, it can indeed become sexual. Consider Toni Morrison's "up South" version of this phenomenon in *Sula* (1974). Young teenagers Nel and Sula, on their way to Edna Finch's Mellow House for ice cream, pass by men who "drape themselve on sills, on stoops, on crates and broken chairs," waiting to be distracted, particularly by women. The girls pass by precisely because they want male attention. When Ajax calls out "pig meat," they get what they want. Their budding sexuality and potential attractiveness have been recognized by one of the most desirable men in the Bottom. It will be many years later before Sula actually sleeps with Ajax, and the lingering memory of that porch acceptance probably informs her spontaneous reaction to him as much as her own fully mature sexual desire.[2]

In the most devastating verbal contest that takes place on the porch in *Their Eyes Were Watching God*, Jody and his wife Janie play the dozens about the effects of aging. Usually passive and silent when Jody shames her in front of the porch audience (made up primarily of men), Janie retaliates in front of that same audience. The incident is certainly not planned, but it is no less devastating. In a space where Jody has watched reputations be bolstered, especially sexually, he must now see his own sexual reputation severely damaged if not destroyed. When Janie cuts a plug of tobacco unevenly, Jody uses the occasion to comment on her getting old and incompetent: "I god almighty! A woman stay round uh store till she get old as Methusalem and still can't cut a little thing like a plug of tobacco! Don't stand dere rollin' yo' pop eyes at me wid yo' rump hangin' nearly to yo' knees!" It is a serious mistake for Jody to mix up Janie's abilities with her physical looks. Since she is considerably younger than Jody, she quickly straightens him out: "Naw, Ah ain't no young gal no mo' but den Ah ain't no old woman neither. Ah reckon Ah looks mah age too. But Ah'm uh woman every inch of me, and Ah know it. Dat's uh whole lot more'n *you* kin say. You big-bellies round here and put out a lot of brag, but 'tain't nothin' to it but yo' big voice. Humph! Talking 'bout *me* lookin' old! When you pull down yo' britches, you look lak de change uh life."[3] A man of Jody's pomposity cannot take this humiliation, and it is embarrassing even for the listening audience. Nonetheless, the scene illustrates that if one elects to act out a drama on this stage of competition, then one is liable to suffer the consequences. If the porch has not been kinder to lesser men, then why should it bow to Jody just because he owns that space?

In another manifestation of liminality, the porch in front of businesses historically was the place where black and white people could pass or linger with each other legitimately before the segregation of service inside the stores or the segregation of society beyond the store porch. In an interesting literary representation, Lewis Nordan creates a store porch in *Wolf Whistle* (1993), a novel based on the 1955 murder of fourteen-year-old Emmett Till in Money, Mississippi. Here, black people sit on the front porch of the white-owned grocery store and white people sit inside. Blacks and whites pass each other freely on the porch, but inside the store blacks are served only after all whites have been attended to. Of interest is the fact that blacks and whites listen to the blues music that one of the black porch-sitters plays. It is on the porch and inside the store (the porch's mirror image) that the shock of the Till character's comment to a white woman is discussed briefly and interpreted before all the black folks disappear. The porch space itself has not represented a violation of southern norms, but the remark the young black man makes is outrageously beyond the norm. Sexuality that can be applauded on Hurston's porch serves as the impetus to murder when uttered from the porch of the white business establishment.[4]

Transitions in architecture and demography have had a profound impact upon the tradition of porch-sitting. In the former village environments in the South, where few people in a community owned automobiles, or if they did, they did not have a garage for them, people could easily amble by each other's porches and interact freely. Then, builders or owners began to devalue traditional porches — as more and more southerners retreated to their air-conditioned houses — and created instead those little overhangs that barely protect you in the rain before you can get into the house. Another architectural transition resulted in carports and garages taking up the space once allotted to porches. A few stalwart souls tried to move the site of porch-sitting activity from the front/center of the house to the front/end of the house. Porch-sitters retired to their carports. That is all that remains of a porch at the new house to which my family moved in 1970. My mother, now eighty, sits there intermittently all during the day, engaging her neighbors and scores of relatives in conversation, reminiscing about growing up, and watching every bit of activity that goes on in the neighborhood.

Together with these architectural transitions, southerners discovered suburbs.[5] Sidewalks disappeared or were so far from the houses that few people could talk across that space. Houses were set back, sometimes by hundreds of feet. Dwellers hid themselves behind lush shrubbery and curving driveways. There was little reason to sit on a porch—if the owners had one built—because you could only engage the folks in conversation who actually made the trek to your space. An overwhelming desire for privacy supplanted interaction and openness, and that impact upon the tradition of porch-sitting is still being felt.

This desire for privacy has led to the latest manifestation of the transformed porch-sitting space, that phenomenon known as "the deck." Its location, at the back of most houses, is a primary signal that its function is antithetical to the traditional porch. It exudes privacy. More frequently than not, it looks out over woods or over someone else's equally private backyard. It sports railings and can be too high off the ground to encourage uninvited entry—even if someone were to go to the back of the house. It says that the owners want to get away from everything interactive—except with the people they specially invite to share that space. The deck, in other words, is control, privacy, and lack of access writ large. It is one of the latest invasions of the South in that ever-increasing standardization of American culture. Everywhere in America must look like everywhere else in America, and southerners are slowly giving in to the deck part of the look-alike-ness.

I like to think, though—and I admit that this is pure unadulterated romanticism—that there are pockets of communities in the South where porch-sitting has survived whole, as Alice Walker would say. Where during the day as well as in the evening, people can engage themselves and their neighbors in the exchanges that reflect a way of life, a relational way of being, one that ties people to their families and their neighbors as well as to passersby. Where to "sit according to your family" is as much a cultural and creative imperative as a behavioral one. Where interaction is the norm. Where "staring" might be boring, but where "sitting" is joy.

Notes

1. Margaret Walker, *Jubilee* (1966; rpt., Bantam, 1969), 91.
2. Zora Neale Hurston, *Their Eyes Were Watching God* (1935; rpt., Harper and Row, 1990), 63–64. Hurston includes

comparable scenes in *Mules and Men* (1935) as well as in her autobiography, *Dust Tracks on a Road* (1942). Toni Morrison, *Sula* (Knopf, 1974), 49, 50.

3. Hurston, *Their Eyes Were Watching God,* 121, 122–23.

4. Lewis Nordan, *Wolf Whistle* (Algonquin Books, 1993), 22–39.

5. I am grateful to fellow southerner Alex S. Jones, who was one of my fellow residents at the Rockefeller Study and Conference Center in Bellagio, Italy, in October of 1994, for raising this point.

The Bufords

•

Elizabeth Spencer

There were the windows, high, well above the ground, large, full of sky. There were the child's eyes, settled back middistance in the empty room. There was the emptiness, the drowsiness of Miss Jackson's own head, tired from tackling the major problems of little people all day long, from untangling their hair ribbons, their shoelaces, their grammar, their arithmetic, their handwriting, their thoughts. Now there was the silence.

The big, clumsy building was full of silence, stoves cooling off, great boxy rooms growing cool from the floor up, cold settling around her ankles. Miss Jackson sat there two or three afternoons a week, after everybody else had gone, generally with a Buford or because of a Buford: It was agreed she had the worst grade this year, because there were Bufords in it. She read a sentence in a theme four times through. Was it really saying something about a toad-frog? Her brain was so weary—it was Thursday, late in the week—she began to think of chipmunks, instead. Suddenly her mouth began to twitch; she couldn't stand it any longer; she burst out laughing.

"Dora Mae, *what* are you doing?"

The truth was that Dora Mae was not doing anything. She was just a Buford. When she was around, you eventually laughed. Miss Jackson could never resist; but then, neither could anyone. Dora Mae, being a Buford, did not return her laugh. The Bufords never laughed unless they wanted to. She drew the book she was supposed to be studying, but wasn't, slowly downward on the desk; her chin was resting on it and came gradually down with it. She continued to stare at Miss Jackson with eyes almost as big as the windows, blue, clear, and loaded with Buford nonsense. She gave Miss Jackson the tiniest imaginable smile.

Miss Jackson continued to laugh. If someone else had been the teacher, she herself would have to be corrected, possibly kept in. It always turned out this way. Miss Jackson dried her eyes. "Sit up straight, Dora Mae," she said.

Once this very child had actually sewed through her own finger, meddling with a sewing machine the high school home-economics girls had left open upstairs. Another time, at recess, she had jumped up and down on a Sears Roebuck catalogue in the dressing room behind the stage, creating such a thunder nobody could think what was happening. She had also shot pieces of broken brick with her brother's slingshot at the walls of the gym, where they were having a 4-H Club meeting. "Head, Heart, Hands, and Health," the signs said. They were inside repeating a pledge about these four things and singing, "To the knights in the days of old, Keeping watch on the mountain height, Came a vision of Holy Grail, And a voice through the waiting night." Some of the chunks of brick, really quite large, came flying through the window.

Dora Mae, of course, had terrible brothers, the Buford Boys, and a reputation to live up to—was that it? No, she was just bad, the older teachers in the higher grades would say at recess, sitting on the steps in warm weather or crossing the street for a Coke at the little cabin-size sandwich shop.

"I've got two years before I get Dora Mae," said Miss Martingale.

"Just think," said Mrs. Henry, "I've got four Bufords in my upstairs study hall. At once."

"I've had them already, all but one," said Miss Carlisle. "I've just about graduated."

"I wish they weren't so funny," said Miss Jackson, and then they all began to laugh. They couldn't finish their Cokes for laughing.

Among the exploits of Dora Mae's brothers, there always came to mind the spring day one of them brought a horse inside the school house just before closing bell, leading it with a twist of wire fastened about its lower lip and releasing it to wander right into study hall alone while the principal, Mr. Blackstone, was dozing at his desk.

The thing was, in school, everybody's mind was likely to wander, and the minute it did wander, something would be done to you by a Buford, and you would never forget it. The world you were dozing on came back with a whoosh and a bang; but it was not the same world you had dozed away from, nor was it the one you intended to wake up to or even imagined to be there. Something crazy was the matter with it: a naked horse, unattended, was walking between the rows of seats; or (another day altogether) a little girl was holding her reader up in the air between her feet, her head and shoulders having vanished below desk level, perhaps forever. Had there actually been some strange accident? Were you dreaming? Or were things meant to be this way? That was the part that just for a minute could scare you.

The Bufords lived in a large, sprawled-out, friendly house down a road nobody lived on but them. The grass was never completely cut, and in the fall the leaves never got raked. Somebody once set fire to a sagebrush pasture near their house—one of *them* had done it, doubtless—and the house was threatened, and there were Bufords up all night, stamping the earth and scraping sparks out of the charred fence posts and throwing water into chicken wallows, just in case the fire started again.

When any of the teachers went there to call, as they occasionally had to do, so that the family wouldn't get mad at the extraordinary punishment meted out to one of the children at school—Mr. Blackstone once was driven to give Billy Buford a public whipping with a buggy whip—or (another reason) to try to inform the family just how far the children were going with their devilment and to implore moral support, at least, in doing something about it—when you went there, they all came out and greeted you. They made you sit in a worn wicker rocking chair and ran to get you something—iced tea or lemonade or a Coke, cake, tea cakes, or anything they had.

Then they began to shout and holler and say how glad they

were you'd come. They began to say, "Now tell the truth! Tell the truth, now! Ain't Billy Buford the worse boy you ever saw?" . . . "Did you ever see anybody as crazy as that Pete? Now tell me! Now tell the truth!" . . . "Confidentially, Miss Jackson, what on earth are we ever going to do with Dora Mae?"

And Dora Mae would sit and look at you, the whole time. She would sit on a little stool and put her chin on her hands and stare, and then you would say, "I just don't know, Mrs. Buford." And they would all look at you cautiously in their own Buford way, and then in the silence, when you couldn't, couldn't be serious, one of them would say, very quietly, "Ain't you ever going to eat your cake?"

It was like that.

There had once been something about a skunk that had upset not just the school but the whole town and that would not do to think about, just as it didn't do any good, either, to speculate on what might or could or was about to happen on this or any future Halloween.

Was it spring or fall? Dreaming, herself, in the lonely classroom with Dora Mae, Miss Jackson thought of chipmunks and skunks and toad-frogs, words written into themes on ruled paper, the lines of paper passing gradually across her brow and into her brain, until the fine ruling would eventually print itself there. Someday, if they opened her brain, they would find a child's theme inside. Even now she could often scarcely think of herself with any degree of certainty. Was she in love, was she falling in love, or getting restless and disappointed with whomever she knew, or did she want somebody new, or was she recalling somebody gone? Or: Had someone right come along, and she had said all right, she'd quit teaching and marry him, and now had it materialized or had it fallen through, or what?

Children! The Bufords existed in a haze of children and old people: old aunts, old cousins, grandfathers, friends and relatives by marriage of cousins, deceased uncles, family doctors gone alcoholic, people who never had a chance. What did they live on? Oh, enough of them knew how to make enough for everyone to feel encouraged. Enough of them were clever about money, and everybody liked them, except the unfortunate few who had to try to discipline them. A schoolteacher, for instance, was a sort of challenge. A teacher hung in their minds like the deep, softly pulsing, furry throat in the collective mind of a hound pack. They hardly thought of a teacher as human, you had to suppose. You could get your feelings hurt sadly if you left yourself open to them.

"Dora Mae, let's go," Miss Jackson suddenly said, way too early.

She had recalled that she had a date, but whether it was a spring date (with warm twilight air seeping into the car, filling the street and even entering the stale movie foyer—more excitement in the season than was left for her in this particular person) or whether it was a fall date (when the smell of her new dress brought out sharply by the gas heater she had to turn on in the late afternoon, carried with it the interest of somebody new and the lightness all beginnings have)—which it was, she had to think to say. At this moment, she had forgotten whether she was even glad or not. It was better to be going out with somebody than not; it gave a certain air, for one thing, to supper at the boardinghouse.

Even the regulars, the uptown widows and working wives and the old couples and the ancient widower who came to eat there, held themselves somewhat straighter and took some degree of pride in the matter of Miss Jackson's going out, as going out suggested a progress of sorts and put a tone of freshness and prettiness on things. It was a subject to tease and be festive about; the lady who ran the boardinghouse might even bring candles to light the table. In letting Dora Mae Buford out early, Miss Jackson was responding to that festiveness; she thought of the reprieve as a little present.

She recalled what she had told a young man last year, or maybe the year before, just as they were leaving the movies after a day similar to this one, when she had had to keep another Buford in, how she had described the Bufords to him, so that she got him to laugh about them, too, and how between them they had decided there was no reason, no reason on earth, for Bufords to go to school at all. They would be exactly the same whether they went to school or not. Nothing you told them soaked in; they were born knowing everything they knew; they never changed; the only people they really listened to were other Bufords.

"But I do sometimes wonder," Miss Jackson had said, trying hard to find a foothold that had to do with "problems," "personality," "psychology," "adjustment," all those things she had taken up in detail at teachers' college in Nashville and thought must have a small degree of truth in them — "I wonder if some people don't just feel obligated to be bad."

"There's something in that," the young man had answered. (He had said this often, come to think of it: a good answer to everything.)

Now the child trudged along beside Miss Jackson across the campus. Miss Jackson looked down affectionately; she wanted a child of her own someday — though hardly, she thought (and almost giggled), one like this. It went along on chunky legs and was shaped like cutout paper-doll children you folded the tabs back to change dresses for. Its face was round, its brow raggedly fringed with yellow bangs. Its hands were plump — meddlesome, you'd say on sight. It wore scuffed brown shoes and navy-blue socks and a print dress and carried an old nubby red sweater slung over its books.

"Aren't you cold, Dora Mae?" said Miss Jackson, still in her mood of affection and fun.

"No, ma'am," said Dora Mae, who could and did answer directly at times. "I'm just tired of school."

Well, so am I sometimes, Miss Jackson thought, going home to bathe and dress in her best dress, and then go to the boardinghouse with the other teachers, where, waiting on the porch, if it was warm enough or in the hall if it was not, sitting or standing with hands at rest against the nice material of her frock, she would already be well over the line into her most private domain.

"I don't really like him all that much," she would have confided already — it was what she always said. "I just feel better, you know, when somebody wants to take me somewhere." All the teachers agreed that this was so; they were the same, they said.

What Miss Jackson did not say was that she enjoyed being Lelia. This was her secret, and when she went out, this was what happened: she turned into Lelia, from the time she was dressing in the afternoon until after midnight, when she got in. The next morning, she would be Miss Jackson again.

If it was a weekday.

And if it wasn't a weekday, then she might still feel like Miss Jackson, even on weekends, for they had given her a Sunday School class to teach whenever she stayed in town. If she went home, back fifty miles to the little town she was born in, she had to go to church there, too, and everybody uptown called her "Leel," a nickname. At home they called her "Sister," only it sounded more like Sustah. But Lelia was her name and what she wanted to be; it was what she said was her name to whatever man she met who asked to take her somewhere.

One day soon after she had kept Dora Mae Buford after school, she went back into the classroom from recess quite late, having been delayed at a faculty meeting, and Dora Mae was writing "LELIAJACKSONLELIAJACKSONLELIAJACKSONLELIAJACKSON" over and over in capital letters on the blackboard. She had filled one board and had started on another, going like crazy. All the students were laughing at her.

It became clear to Miss Jackson later, when she had time to think about it, that the reason she became so angry at Dora Mae was that the child, like some diabolical spirit, had seemed to know exactly what her sensitive point was and had gone straight to it, with the purpose of ridiculing her, of exposing and summarizing her secret self in all its foolish yearning.

But at the moment she did not think anything. She experienced a flash of white-faced, passionate temper and struck the chalk from the child's hand. "Erase that board!" she ordered. A marvel she hadn't knocked her down, except that Dora Mae was as solid as a stump, and hitting her, Miss Jackson had almost sprained her wrist.

Dora Mae was shocked half to death, and the room was

deadly still for the rest of the morning. Miss Jackson, so gentle and firm (though like to get worried), had never before struck anyone.

Soon Dora Mae's mother came to see Miss Jackson, after school. She sat down in the empty classroom, a rather tall, dark woman with a narrow face full of slanted wrinkles and eyes so dark as to be almost pitch black, with no discernible white area to them. Miss Jackson looked steadfastly down at her hands.

Mrs. Buford put a large, worn, bulging black purse on the desk before her, and though she did not even remove her coat, the room seemed hers. She did not mean it that way, for she spoke in the most respectful tone, but it was true. "It's really just one thing I wanted to know, Miss Jackson. Your first name is Lelia, ain't it?"

Miss Jackson said that it was.

"So what I mean is, when Dora Mae wrote what she did on the blackboard there, it wasn't nothing like a lie or something dirty, was it?"

"No," said Miss Jackson. "Not at all."

"Well, I guess that's about all I wanted to make sure of."

Miss Jackson did not say anything, and Mrs. Buford finally inquired whether she had not been late coming back to the room that day, when Dora Mae was found writing on the board. Miss Jackson agreed that this was true.

"Churen are not going to sit absolutely still if you don't come back from recess," said Mrs. Buford. "You got to be there to say, 'Now y'all get out your book and turn to page so-and-so.' If you don't they're bound to get into something. You realize that? Well, good! Dora Mae's nothing but a little old scrap. That's all she is."

"Well, I know," said Miss Jackson, feeling very bad.

At this point, Mrs. Buford, alone without any of her children around her, must have got to thinking about them all in terms of Dora Mae; she began to cry.

Miss Jackson understood. She had seen them all, her entire class, heads bent at her command, pencils marching forward across their tablets, and her heart had filled with pity and love.

Mrs. Buford brushed her tears away. "You never meant it for

a minute. Anybody can get aggravated, don't you know? You think I can't? I can and do!" She put her handkerchief back in her purse and, straightening her coat, stood up to go. "So, I'm just going right straight and say you're sorry about it and you never meant it."

"Oh," said Miss Jackson, all of a sudden, "but I did mean it. It's true I'm sorry. But I did mean it." Her statement, softly made, threw a barrier across Mrs. Buford's path, like bars through the slots in a fence gap.

Mrs. Buford sat back down. "Miss Jackson, just what have we been sitting here deciding?"

"I don't know," said Miss Jackson, wondering herself. "Nothing that I know of."

"Nothing! You call that nothing?"

"Call what nothing?"

"Why, everything you just got through saying."

"But what do you think I said?" Miss Jackson felt she would honestly like to know. There followed a long silence, in which Miss Jackson, whose room this after all was, felt impelled to stand up. "It's not a good thing to lose your temper. But everyone does sometimes, including me."

Mrs. Buford rose also. "Underneath all that fooling around, them kids of mine is pure gold." Drawn to full height, Mrs. Buford became about twice as tall as Miss Jackson.

"I know! I know that! But you say yourselves—" began Miss Jackson. She started to tremble. Of all the teachers in the school, she was the youngest, and she had the most overcrowding in her room. "Mrs. Buford," she begged, "do please forget about it. Go on home. Please, please go home!"

"You pore child," said Mrs. Buford, with no effort still continuing and even expanding her own authority. "I just never in my life," she added, and left the room.

She proceeded across the campus the way all her dozen or so children went, down toward their lonely road—a good, strong, sincere woman, whose right shoulder sagged lower than the left and who did not look back. From the window, Miss Jackson watched her go.

Uptown a lady gossip was soon to tell her that she was

known to have struck a child in a fit of temper and also to have turned out the child's mother when she came to talk about it. Miss Jackson wearily agreed that this was true. She could feel no great surprise, though her sense of despair deepened when one of the Buford boys, Evan, older and long out of school, got to worrying her — calling up at night, running his car behind her on the sidewalk uptown. It seemed there were no lengths he wouldn't go to, no trouble he wouldn't make for her.

When the dove season started, he dropped her. He'd a little rather shoot doves than me, she thought, sitting on the edge of the bed in her room, avoiding the mirror, which said she must be five years older. It's my whole life that's being erased, she thought, mindful that Dora Mae and two of her brothers, in spite of all she could do, were inexorably failing the fourth grade. She got up her Sunday School lesson, washed her hair, went to bed, and fell asleep disconsolate. . . .

Before school was out, the Bufords invited Miss Jackson for Sunday dinner. Once the invitation had come — which pleased her about as much as if it had been extended by a tribe of Indians, but which she had to accept or be thought of as a coward — it seemed inevitable to her that they would do this. It carried out to a T their devious and deceptively simple-looking method of pleasing themselves, and of course what she might feel about it didn't matter. But here she was dressing for them, trying to look her best.

The dinner turned out to be a feast. She judged it was no different from their usual Sunday meal — three kinds of meat and a dozen spring vegetables, hot rolls, jams, pickles, peaches, and rich cakes, freshly baked and iced.

The house looked in the airiest sort of order, with hand-crocheted white doilies sprinkled about on the tables and chairs. The whole yard was shaggy with flowers and blooming shrubs; the children all were clean and neatly dressed, with shoes as well, and the dogs were turned firmly out of doors.

She was placed near Mr. Tom Buford, the father of them all, a tall, spare man with thick white hair and a face burned brick-brown from constant exposure. He plied her ceaselessly with food, more than she could have eaten in a week, and smiled the gentle smile Miss Jackson by now knew so well.

Halfway down the opposite side of the table was Evan Buford, she at last recognized, that terrible one, wearing a spotless white shirt, shaved and spruce, with brown busy hands, looking bland and even handsome. If he remembered all those times he had got her to the phone at one and two and three in the morning, he wasn't letting on. ("Thought you'd be up grading papers, Miss Jackson! Falling down on the job?" . . . "Your family live in Tupelo? Well, the whole town got blown away in a tornado! This afternoon!") Once, in hunting clothes, his dirt-smeared, unshaven face distorted by the rush of rain on his muddy windshield, he had pursued her from the post office all the way home, almost nudging her off the sidewalk with his front fender, his wheels spewing water from the puddles all over her stockings and raincoat, while she walked resolutely on, pretending not to notice.

From way down at the foot of the table, about half a mille away, Dora Mae sat sighting at her steadily through a water glass, her eyes like the magnified eyes of insects.

"'Possum hunting!" Mr. Tom Buford was saying, carving chicken and ham with a knife a foot long, which Miss Jackson sometimes had literally to dodge. "That's where we all went last night. Way up on the ridge. You like 'possum, Miss Jackson?"

"I never had any," Miss Jackson said.

Right from dinner they all went to the back yard to see the 'possum, which had been put in a cage of chicken wire around the base of a small pecan tree. It was now hanging upside down by its tail from a limb. She felt for its helpless, unappetizing shapelessness, grizzly gray, with a long snout, its sensitive eyes shut tight, its tender black petallike ears alone perceiving, with what terror none could know though she could guess, the presence of its captors.

"Don't smell very good, does it?" Billy Buford said. "You like it, Miss Jackson? Give it to you, you want it." He picked up a stick to punch it with.

She shook her head. "Oh, I'd just let it go back to the woods. I feel sorry for it."

The whole family turned from the creature to her and examined her as if she were crazy. Billy Buford even dropped the stick. There followed one of those long, risky silences.

As they started to go inside, Evan Buford lounged along at her elbow. He separated her out like a heifer from the herd and cornered her before a fence of climbing roses. He leaned his arm against a fence post, blocking any possible escape, and looked down at her with wide, speculative, bright brown eyes. She remembered his laughing mouth behind the car wheel that chill, rainy day, careening after her. Oh, they never got through, she desperately realized. Once they had you, they held on—if they didn't eat you up, they kept you for a pet.

"Now, Miss Jackson, how come you to fail those kids?"

Miss Jackson dug her heels in hard. "I didn't fail them. They failed themselves. Like you might fail to hit a squirrel, for instance."

"Well, now. You mean they weren't good enough. Well, I be darned." He jerked his head. "That's a real good answer."

So at last, after years of trying hard, she had got something across to a Buford, some one little thing that was true. Maybe it had never happened before. It would seem she had stopped him cold. It would seem he even admired her.

"Missed it like a squirrel!" he marveled. "The whole fourth grade. They must be mighty dumb," he reflected, walking along with her toward the house.

"No, they just don't listen," said Miss Jackson.

"Don't listen," he said after her with care, as though to prove that he, at least, did. "You get ready to go, I'll drive you to town, Miss Jackson. Your name is Lelia, ain't it?"

She looked up gratefully. "That's right," she said.

Blues Devil

•

Yusef Salaam

The Devil sho' is a crafty thang
Well–well, just calls ya and ya come
Said yeah–yeah, the Devil is a crafty thang
Ummmmmmmmmm–call ya and ya come
Promise you the key to heaven, man
Don't you know he's lyin', son

Once upon a time there was a fellow named William Leroy Thompson Jones the Third down here in Carolina (North, that is), in Lumberton, a small town in Robeson County. We called him Sugar Ray Willie; naw, didn't have nothing ta do with his skills in lovin' the ladies. Now, the ladies liked him well enough alright, that's the truth 'cause he was a champion. And you see, womenfolks they love a winner, the whole world does, doesn't it?

He was nicknamed Sugar Ray Willie 'cause like Sugar Ray Robinson, the famous prize fighter, Willie wasn't nothin' but pure brown sugar. His pugilist moves was slick, smooth, and sweeter than honey fresh out of the hive with bees still hangin' on. Sugar Ray Willie's hands was faster than a blink. He and a fellow named Snookie was sparrin' one time. Just standin' there, one-to-one, bobbin' and weavin', punchin' at each other real light like. Sugar Ray betted Snookie that he could hit'em twice and the naked eye wouldn't be able ta pick up on the second punch. He told Buddy ta shout "double punch" every time he see Sugar Ray pop Snookie with "two straight hits. Buddy didn't shout not one time. He swore that all he saw (and we all bore witness) Sugar Ray do was throw single right hands ta Snookie's chest and a 'casional left hand to the shoulder. But

Snookie 'clared that the single right hand thrusts that we all testified ta was actually double and triple flickers that had escaped our eyes. He said that he didn't see them either, but he'd sho' nuff felt them.

Ta show how sweet Sugar Ray was, listen to how he outboxed fellows who double-teamed and sometimes triple-teamed him. Sometimes he'd put on exhibitions, surround himself with two or three men who was good with their hands. Each man's job was ta punch at Sugar Ray, ta hit him. "Don't hold back," he'd tell'em. "Give it all ya' got." It was a beautiful thang ta see that boy in the midst of that circle, duckin' and blockin' punches. On his toes dancin', left jabs poppin' out like a frog's tongue snappin' in dragon flies. A blur of right hands ta the chest. A mongoose dodgin' the strikes of a cobra. Silk smooth, no herky-jerky moves, not a wrinkle in his style. Hands like octopus tenacles checkin' and neutralizin', fists flying at him from everywhere. Then Sugar Ray would hold his hands behind his back and never budge from that spot in the circle. The harder and faster the fists flew, the more presence of mind Sugar had ta duck'em. He'd stoop lower ta the ground than a snake's belly, swingin' and swayin' ta a rhythm in his lionish heart, duckin' so that the opponents were hittin' each other.

See, now, them was the days when menfolks were men. If a fellow had a problem with another man and they couldn't talk it out, they'd duke it out like men 'sposed ta, chest to chest. Wasn't like these punks today who can't fist fight. All they know how ta do is shoot ya. If a man got a bone to pick with another man, he don't go man-to-man; naw, he gots ta go and git his gun and kill the man. Not only that, mind you, he blows aways innocent bystanders, little children and all. Back in the old days, a man was a man. If a man got whupped by the other man, he just took it like a soldier. He didn't go draggin' his tail cryin' and come back shootin' up everything.

Now Ray, he could take a whuppin' as well as give it. One night the fellows were hangin' out at Pretty Pearl's place down in the Bottom. Negroes down there would damn-near kill themselves with weekend fun like drinkin', gamblin', and cuttin'. When the fire of that stump-hole liquid exploded in their bellies, they'd raise hell 'till the rooster crowed or the law come. And the lawmen always took their time about comin', hopin' the ruckus be over by the time they got there. Let me tell ya that when them white folks did show (sometimes they didn't 'till the next day), they usually come five-to-six car loads, shot guns and pistols at the ready. Them was some deadly colored folks in the Bottom. The women down there was dangerous, too. Most of 'em carried razors or ice picks in their bosoms.

Soldiers from nearby Fort Bragg in Fayetteville used to hang out at Pretty Pearl's. Our gals seemed to really love themselves some soldier boys. They didn't have nothing going no more than we homeboys, except their army outfits and they spent more money. Had some nice wheels, too. Some of 'em acted like they were better than we homeboys and were real possessive with the girls, too; fight ya over'em quicker than a cat'll stratch ya eyes out over messin' with her new-born kittens. That's how Sugar Ray got in a fight with a sergeant over Lillie Mae. She was a real tender-roni. Her complexion was the color of blackberry wine. Her eyes, milk white with chocolate kisses in the middle, twinkled like a galaxy of stars. Lillie Mae's smile showed pearls with a tiny gap in the middle carved by nature. Those full lips were delicious clusters of grapes that put nibblin' on a man's mind. Her hair was short, a jeweled wooly crown. And when the woman got ta swingin' on the dance floor with what the good Lord gave her, the juke box sounded like a live band playin' just for her.

Now, Lillie Mae was the sergeant's (we all called him Sarge) woman. He guarded her like a rooster does his favorite hen. Reckon the man was just trying ta make sure he was the only one roosterin'. Anyway, one Saturday night down at Pretty Pearl's, Sugar Ray sauntered over and asked Lillie Mae for a dance. It wasn't no big deal ta Lillie Mae for her homeboys ta ask her ta dance. The way she saw it, she didn't come out ta have fun by sittin' in Sarge's lap all night. She came ta kick up her heels, flirt a little, too. Sarge didn't mind his sweet thing enjoying herself neither. But he didn't like her dancin' with Sugar Ray Willie. You see, about three years back, Lillie Mae used ta go with Sugar Ray for their whole four years of high school. After graduation, Lillie Mae moved ta Detroit ta stay with her aunt for a year. When she came back, she and Sugar tried ta rekindle the fire, but time had doused the flames to a flicker. Sugar Ray, who was workin' at the post office by now, worked hard ta make the flicker flare but he was too slow. Sarge jumped all over opportunity like white on snow. Lillie Mae was tryin' ta hold him back at first, waiting to see what Sugar was going ta do. She had opened Sarge's nose wide enough ta park a tractor trailer. He followed that gal around like an ant on a sugar trail. Sarge wasn't no hummin' and hawwin' man like Sugar Ray. He popped that engagement ring on Lillie Mae's finger six months after he met her. Everybody knew, though, that deep inside of the kernel of her heart, Lillie Mae loved herself some Sugar Ray Willie. Sarge knew it, too. He wasn't no fool—you couldn't pee in his face and tell him that it was rainin'. That's why he didn't like Sugar Ray dancin' with Lillie Mae, but he put up with it because he didn't want ta upset his Lillie Mae, and he didn't want ta show weakness in front of his fellow soldiers by makin' a fuss over Sugar and Lillie Mae dancin'.

The juke box was jumpin' with Jackie Wilson shoutin' jubilantly on his hit record, "Baby, Work Out." Sugar and Lillie Mae danced like—how the Bible say it?—like they "knew" each other. Their feet moved in perfect rhythm. When he twirled her out and back, she rolled into his arm like it was the bosom of Abraham. He held her there for a few seconds on his chest. That musta've been an eternity ta Sarge. Their buttocks bounced ta the shake of their tambourine hips. Jackie was shoutin' like a preacher, Sugar's and Lillie Mae's feet and arms flyin' every which way but loose. Bodies swingin', spinnin'. Two bodies become one, then two again. Sweat and gaspin' breaths. Jackie hit with that last high-pitched shout, then a numbin' silent joyful noise from Ray and Lillie. Gone from here, they were, ta a space where they could no longer hear the music, no longer could see the other dancers, or Sarge's scowlin' face. Eyes only for each other.

Well-well, said the Devil is a crafty thang
He just call ya and ya come
In-deeeeed! the Devil is a crafty thang!
Ummmmmmmmmm, just call ya and ya come
When ya all tangled up in trouble
No need ta call Mr. Fork Tongue!

Sarge sat there blue in the face. His teeth fronted a smile that masked a sneer that made him look like a big tobacco worm. He stood gunslinger-style, his eyes aimed at Sugar Ray. He gulped down the remains of a pint of stump-hole and teetered across the dance floor where Ray and Lillie Mae was talkin' after they'd finished dancin'. He pushed Ray so hard that he crashed inta the juke box. He grabbed Ray in a bear hug. Ray managed ta wiggle out. By now, a crowd had circled the two men. Voices urged, "Put something on his ass, Ray!" Lillie cried for both of them ta quit. Pretty Pearl stepped from the kitchen, her finger on her double-barrelled shotgun, and threatened ta drop both of them. "Take ya shit outside in the street," she ordered. Everyone knew that that high yella gal would shoot ya (she done done a year for shootin' her brother), so the crowd followed Sarge and Ray outside. Sarge had been a welterweight champion a few months before he'd made sergeant and had fought on army bases around the country and overseas. He was competin' in the Olympics tryouts when a butt ta the eye unhinged something, forcin' him ta quit boxin'.

Sugar's speed was too much for Sarge at first. Soon, though, the turtle walked the rabbit down. Sarge was in good shape for the long haul. Sugar had never really trained ta stay in shape because he could always depend on his natural stuff. Sarge the bull was gougin' the matador with both fists. Sugar Ray was suckin' air. He was flat footed, no longer on his toes. The soldier stabbed him with right hands that busted inta his ribs like cannon shots. Sugar dragged backwards. His arms hung down like broken wings. Sarge trailed him, his fists like knives ta Ray's kidneys. He hit Sugar Ray Willie everywhere—his legs, knees, thighs. Fifteen minutes later, though, Ray found a second wind. He was back on wheels again. Sarge couldn't catch him.

351

He hit air every time he swung. He fell three times trying ta catch Sugar with roundhouses. He cussed up a storm, demandin' that Ray stand still and fight like a man. His cussin' didn't hurt Ray none, but Ray's hooks-off-the jabs sho' hurt Sarge plenty. Finally, Ray put out his lights with an overhand right ta the chin.

> Yeah–Yeah the Devil is a crafty thang
> My–My just call ya and ya come
> Ya know the Devil is a crafty thang
> Lord–lord–lord just call ya and ya come
> Whisper in ya ear and slips away, mister
> Makes ya think ya the invincible one

Ray was a changed man after dukin' it out with Sarge. Started braggin' about how great he was. How fast he was with his hands and on his feet. He musta've given a hundred or more braggin' lectures and demonstrations on the street corners on how he demolished Sarge, a champion United States Army boxer. He stopped sparrin' with the fellows, said they were too small time for him. He went over ta Fort Bragg where Sarge was and challenged a fellow who was training ta fight in Germany for the World Army Welterweight Championship. "I'm the greatest fighter, pound-for-pound, in Robeson County," he announced in the boxin' gym full of soldiers. They said he pointed at Sarge, who was skippin' rope (and was married to Lillie Mae by now) and boasted, "Ask that man over there how I smoked his head like a Vagin'a ham." Sarge didn't say nothin', just under-eyed Ray. They strapped the gloves on Ray and they say he gave that German-bound contender for the world championship a boxin' lesson. Ray really bragged after that.

"I'm the best boxer, pound-for-pound, in North Carolina and the whole South."

The children, they loved Sugar Ray Willie. He used ta teach them boxin' moves. But now he didn't have time for 'em. Was real mean ta 'em, talkin' about he didn't sign autographs. Shucks! They wasn't askin' for no autographs. They just wanted him ta play-box with him like he used ta do before he got too big for his britches.

One Saturday afternoon when the sun was spittin' fire like a dragon drunk off stump-hole, Sugar Ray announced ta the fellows on the basketball court at the recreation center that he planned to be the Welterweight Champion of the World. Now, here we were in the middle of a game and he stops dribblin' and holds the ball ta broadcast his boxin' career plans. "That's right!" he shouted to everyone's amazement, as if ta dispute anyone who might doubt his ambition. "I'm going ta have millions of fans. Kings, queens, and presidents will honor me. I'm the greatest, the baddest in the world, the whole universe. Hell fire and all its host can't beat me. I'm God of boxin'." Pee-Wee, the littlest thing on the court—and in town—with the biggest mouth—decided it was time ta do a little preachin'. He quipped, "Negro, ya ain't no God of nothin'. God is the God of boxin' and everything else. It was Him who gave ya your talent, your speed and everything." Ray pushed Pee-Wee, who looked around for one of us ta back him up, which somebody always did. But nobody moved this time. "Punk, God ain't got a goddamn thing ta do with it. I'm the one in that ring throwin' punches and knockin' lames out, not God." The fellows sort of distance themselves from Ray after that. Seems like he was gettin' crazier, walkin' around braggin' ta himself like he was punch drunk. Bobbin' and weavin' in the streets like a piston, throwin' furious combinations, back pedallin' from a ghost nobody saw but him. His eyes got real red like folks say eyes do when ya eat raw meat drippin' with blood and all. His mouth foamed white at the corners when he talked a lot.

Well, one day—a Saturday evening, it was—a stranger came to town. Rented a room in Rev. Dorothy Carter's three-story house. Rev. Carter said that if it had been left up ta her, she wouldn'a rented ta him, but her husband rented the stranger the room while she was at a Baptist conference in Raleigh. Daeman—that was the stranger's name—seemed alright. He said he had a job in Fairmont, a nearby town. Rev. Carter said that he always paid his rent. Daeman didn't bother nobody. He hung out in the pool hall and juke joints like the average fellow.

One thing he liked doin' that got on a lot of people's nerves (and made some people laugh) was playin' pranks on people. (He enjoyed tellin' nasty jokes, too). Rev. Carter said that there was "somethin' funny" about Daeman. "No, not funny like them pranks he pulls; personally, I think they're disgustin'," she told the widow, Miss Clara Bell McCrae, one mornin' while they was shellin' peas on her porch. "The good Lord done showed me the first time I laid eyes on him." She said that Daeman was as clean as a dead man lyin' in a casket in a new store-bought suit. "He's full of yes m'ams and no m'ams,' polite and mild-mannered as he can be, handsome like Sidney Poitier, but the soul of my eyes sees the maggots in his heart," she testified. The saved-and-filled-with-the-Holy-Ghost-Reverend looked heavenward and whispered somethin' in Holy Ghost language. "Clara Bell, I tell ya he ain't nothin' but wood with clothes on," she sighed, tossin' a handfull of peas in a bucket.

Daeman had a bag of tricks that didn't have no bottom. He almost gave Betty Sue Simmons a heart attack when he offered her some peanuts and a mechanical mouse popped out of the bag. One night he placed a real funky stink bomb in Pretty Pearl's place. Folks, coughin', cryin', and holdin' their noses, fled the joint. Pearl had ta shut down business for a week to air the funk of dyin' skunks outta her place. She barred Big Mac from comin' there because she thought he farted up her joint.

Daeman loved scarin' people by screwin' up his face inta ugly masks. The old folks and children were 'specially scared of him. He'd buck his eyes, roll them up in the top of his head. The pupils switched from a wild, icy blue to a murky brown. He'd peel his lips back up ta his nose. He could flatten his nose like a plate, squishin' out hairs from his nostrils. Then, his hair would jerk straight up his head like porcupine quills. He'd stretch his tongue four times its normal size, then he'd pop it out and catch flies. His complexion changed colors—a dull, dried-up black to a pale, dead white, accordin' ta the horror he was trying ta put in ya. Every time Daeman scared someone out of his shoes, he'd laugh until tears streamed down his face, which really made him look like he'd been whupped with a ugly stick.

Daeman played one of his tricks on Sugar Ray one time. Ray

had just finished his evenin' road work. He'd started a trainin' routine after that battle with Sarge. He was doin' stretches in the school yard when Daeman offered him some candy in a box. Ray didn't eat candy, but he reached for the box anyhow. He knew that Daeman was a joker, had seen him pull tricks on folks. But he figured that there was no way that Daeman would try ta make a fool out of Sugar Ray Willie, soon-ta-be, one day, the Welterweight Champion of the World. He figured that Daeman had heard of his awesome fightin' reputation and would snatch the box back before the trick in the box could be sprung. Or suffer for bein' fool enough ta mess with Ray. Sugar's hands rested on the lid of the box like he was givin' Daeman a chance ta pull it away. Daeman grinned, pointed ta a button that would open the lid. Ray pushed it and a boxin' glove, curled inta a fist, jumped out. Ray leaned ta the left and the glove whooshed by his chin. Ray popped Daeman upside his head with an open hand. "Don't be playing with me like that, sucker!" he warned. The box crashed ta the ground. He slapped Daeman side the head again. Daeman grinned. "So, you think you're bad, huh, William Leroy Thompson Jones the Third," Daeman said, soundin' like a judge about ta sentence Ray to time on the chain gang. "That's right and you better respect that!" Sugar spat, wonderin' how Daeman knew his real name. "We heard you say that you are greater than the Chief of hell and better than the Boss of paradise," Daeman continued.

"Right again, mister. You'd rather walk through hell in gasoline drawers than mess with me." Daeman grinned when Sugar said that. "We have permission ta test you, but we can't hurt you. Can't put you in any pain." Sugar laughed. "You the one who's gonna be in pain, my man, if you don't get outta my face, real quick, fast, and in a hurry." Daeman raised his pinkie finger. He pointed it impishly at Sugar like it was a sword. "See this here finger. I'm going to beat you with just this one little finger." Sugar chuckled, grunted as he swung at Daeman. He ducked and wiggled his pinkie in Ray's upper rib. A faint smile quivered around Sugar's mouth. Ray jabbed, Daeman moved, then stepped in and rubbed the finger in Ray's lower rib and Ray laughed slightly like Daeman might have said somethin' comical. The sugar man shuffled cautiously taward this new, kinda strange, opponent. He flickered three steamin' jabs, but Daeman scooted under them and tucked his finger in Ray's navel area, churned it, and Ray giggled. Daeman followed up with quick tickles ta Sugar's neck and he yelped like a hyena. Daeman's finger danced up and down the funny bones in Sugar Ray Willie's back and the boy spooked. He fell on the ground in tears, kickin' and cacklin'. Daeman was on him like sweet on sugar. He worked that finger like he knew every tickle spot on Ray's body. He snatched off the man's shoes and socks and started playin' one-finger piano on the poor man's feet. You could hear Sugar's whoops 32 miles up in Fayetteville. Ray moaned and pleaded for mercy. Daeman's eyes locked inta Ray's and Ray started sweatin' so 'till his clothes was wringin' wet.

Ray struggled ta pull his eyes away but his will was sapped. His teeth started chatterin' and he folded up like a baby in the womb, shiverin' like it was below zero. Daeman had on his Sidney Portier smile like he was posin' for a picture. His eyes looked alright normal ta us, but Sugar Ray saw somethin' in 'em that had him laughin', babblin', and cryin' all at the same time. "Please, I don't want ta go! I don't want ta go!" he kept whimperin'. Didn't look like he was goin' nowhere but crazy ta us. The ticklin' kid kept fingerin' like he done gone fool 'til Sugar Ray kicked one last time and fainted.

After that, Sugar Ray Willie was a changed man. He became quiet-like, didn't have much to say ta nobody. Just look at ya with blank eyes when ya said somethin' ta him. He clean gave up boxin', joined Rev. Carter's church. A year or so later, he got himself together enough to start courtin' and married a gal from Elizabethtown. They had a passel of children, five boys and four girls in all.

Daeman, seems like he just vanished in thin air. Left his clothes (expensive stuff, too), shoes and everything in the closet, and the week's rent on the dresser drawer. Rev. Carter said that he'd gone back ta the underground. When her husband suggested she give Daeman's clothes ta the Salvation Army, she said she wasn't givin' nothin' evil ta folks ta wear. The Reverend said she was goin' ta send 'em ta hell where they belong, so she burnt 'em, and lit musk oil candles in that room for seven days and nights.

> The Devil/the Devil is a slick-tricky-sly old thang
> Calls ya and ya come
> The Devil, he be/he be a craf-f-f-f-tee thang
> Calls ya/calls ya/calls ya
> and ya come/on the run
> He ain't satisfied/ain't happy till ya down
> yown-yown-and done
> Said he's a liar and the truth ain't in him
> Lord have mercy, ya ain't gotta come when he calls
> He be (help me sing it somebody)/he be/he be a low
> down dirty . . .

After Revelation

•

Fred Chappell

1

Then one evening I woke from a nap to find the door of my cell open and I walked out. Simple as that. The other cells were empty and the compound was empty and the big gate flung wide. I walked out of the deserted stockade, no one to stop me.

I'd been sentenced for practicing science. Our customary history has it that civilization twice destroyed itself by means of science, and they were going to prevent my doing it to them again. So they hauled me up on charges and tried me, what a farce.

This was the village council. I had known every one of the old buzzards since I was a child, and they knew me, too. They didn't scare me. The last new thought that any of them ever had was the discovery that girls are different from boys—and most of them were too old to remember that one.

"What is science?" I said. "You tell me what science is and I'll tell you whether I've been practicing it or not. Then we can all go home."

"Now, George, you know what it is as well as we do. The council is not going to waste its time quibbling over terms. We all realize how clever you are with words." This was Stavros, the council elder. He spent a lot of his valuable time trying to look the part of a sage. Long white hair cut severely at the shoulders, a grave expression on his wrinkled face, measured speech—maybe he deceived a few backward adolescents. Nobody else.

"Tell you what," I said. "I'll go down to the stockade and turn myself in. The council can stay here and formulate a definition of science. When you finish that little job, come and get me. Then we'll have a trial."

"Now wait, George," Stavros said. There are procedures—"

"Goodbye, geniuses," I said, and stalked out of the chamber.

During this time I was smitten with the widow Larilla. I used to sit holding her hands in mine and gazing into her lovely brown eyes by the hour. I wrote bad canzones in praise of her midnight-colored hair and her gull-wing eyebrows. So I went by her house to tell her I was headed to jail, but she wasn't home. I left a note.

At the stockade I told Bert, the gatekeep, to let me in. "I'm a dangerous bad man, Bert. You'd better put me away. I'm out to destroy civilization."

"Again?" he said. "What have you been doing, George?"

"Practicing science," I said. "Do you know what kind of crime that is?"

" No."

"Well, in my case it amounts of collecting wildflowers."

"Oh," he said, with a careful lack of interest.

"Anybody else put away here?"

"Croya's here. Charged with black magic."

"That means she's been peddling her aphrodisiacs again. You ever try any of her potions, Bert?"

"No."

"Well, don't bother," I said. "They don't work."

He took me to a cell and I went in and stayed three days. I was going to stay there forever if I had to. The council was either going to apologize or they were going to try me publicly. In order to try me, the old geezers would have to define science, and I was looking forward eagerly to hearing that marvel of intellectual endeavor.

2

But then I woke to find my cell door open, the stockade deserted, and I came out. Everything had changed in three days. The village had changed; the whole world was different from what it had been before.

I knew something had happened, but I didn't know what. I could feel the changes in the air about me and it seemed there were different smells; all sorts of sensations I had never felt before.

For one thing, there were few people in the village. It was just at that late twilight hour when we first light the lamps, but now only twelve scattered lights shone in the houses. And no last excited shouts of children before they are ordered in at night, and no stir and mutter of preparing meals. No dogs barking. Only four lonesome smokes out of the chimneys.

The tavern was closed but Sylvia sat on the bench in front of it, her guitar across her lap. Sylvia is the village's blind ballad singer. Long gray-blond hair down to her waist, clear blue sightless eyes. A wicked way with her songs. I'd once paid her handsomely to stop singing her scurrilous ballad about Larilla and me. Then I realized how fine a song it was and felt I missed hearing it and had to pay her again to sing it anew.

"Good evening, Sylvia," I said.

"George?" A voice like the tingling of spider-thread.

"It's me. What's been going on? Everything seems different."

"Everything *is* different."

"Well, tell me about it, please. I haven't heard anything. I've been in jail. Do you want to know why I was in jail?"

"You haven't heard anything?"

"Not a thing," I said, a bit miffed that she wasn't interested in my story.

"The Owners have arrived," she said.

"What Owners?"

"The people that own men."

"What men?"

"Mankind," she said. "The people that own the human race."

"I didn't know that anybody owned the human race."

"None of us knew," she said. Her voice became more intimate, more silvery; she might have been talking to herself. "But hadn't you always wished that somebody did? Hadn't you hoped that there was someone who knew how to take care of you?"

Well . . . no. Maybe back in the furthest reaches of my mind I'd entertained this wistful fancy, but I'd never thought about it directly. Now that I did, the notion was as repulsive as it was attractive. In the first place, why would anyone want to own that tedious, quarrelsome rodent, mankind? "I don't know," I said.

"Now they've arrived," she said. "That makes it all different. Everything."

"Where did they come from?"

"Down from the sky, some say. Others say they came up out of the rivers."

"Nobody knows, then."

"Nobody knows much of anything."

" How do we know they own us?"

"Because that's something you don't mistake," she said. "That fact was clear as soon as they showed up. You'll know it, too, George. You like troublesome questions; you like to make fun of what people believe. But this is simple truth."

"It doesn't sound simple. Anything but. And where," I asked, "is everybody? The village is almost empty."

"They went north, south, east, and west," she said. "Following rumors, making pilgrimages."

I could believe that. When people are faced with new situations, they run around in circles. "What about you?" I asked. "Why are you sitting here in front of the tavern?"

"I'm waiting for an Owner to come," she said. "Then I'll know what to do."

"You're just going to sit here by yourself? It's getting dark, Sylvia."

"Yes, George, it's getting dark. I'm blind, I'm not stupid."

"Do you want me to leave you sitting here?"

"Yes," she said.

3

I went to Larilla's house, and there I saw one of the Owners.

The only light was in her bedroom, so I stepped round to the back of the house and peeped in at the window. Larilla was sitting before her mirror, brushing out her lovely long black hair. She crooned a little melody as she brushed and it tugged at my heart. I'd heard it a hundred times; often I heard it in memory when I was away from her. Does this detail say something about my passion for Larilla? After we met, I never saw the hour I didn't think of her.

The Owner was seated in a chair in a corner, watching her. He watched with a delicate but keen interest the long, leisurely strokes and the hair sifting down in skeins as the brush let go.

Sylvia was right. Easy to know that here was a personage who deserved to own mankind, if that was his desire. There was about him a full but unimposing awareness and a deep, whole calm. I felt certain as I looked through the window that he knew of my presence there, that the fact of my presence interested him as much as Larilla did, and that he was prepared to acknowledge me and understand. He possessed a serenity so profound and secure that it could not even be described as benevolent; benevolence would be an accidental quality of his personality.

He was a tall man; even sitting down he looked to be imperially tall. His features were grandly straightforward: a wide forehead under his ivory-blond hair, a fine straight nose, and large gray eyes as clear and cool as water. He wore a plain gray tunic and white linen trousers and sandals. Now it seems to me that except for his height there was little extraordinary in his physical appearance. But the attitude in which he held his body—easy, open, willing, and yet dignified—invited respect. And the poised, attentive attitude of his mind imposed deference, but without seeming to impose.

In short, he was epitome of what an Owner should be, and what I suppose the Owners are, though he is the only one I have seen as yet.

The Owners are, I believe, those who can pay full attention to someone else.

I withdrew from the window and walked in the road, heartsick. I wasn't jealous; that was too silly. The world was changed entirely; jealousy was one of those dispositions, like greed, that had no place anymore. I looked in myself for jealousy and found only longing, an intense longing to be near an Owner who would give me his calm attention, who would shed that broad and deep serenity over my troubles, who would bring peace the way a lamp brings a warm and pleasant glow into a dark room.

It had come to me, as I looked in the bedroom window, that there must be a single Owner for each person. That seemed right, inevitable; and it explained why the villagers had departed. Each was looking for his Owner—except for those few like Sylvia who were waiting for an Owner to come to them.

I found that I could not wait. Perhaps no one would come for me. I was stricken with grievous longing and driven on the roads under the starry night. I, too, must leave and go as a pilgrim; and even as I realized that fact and began to see a little of what lay before me, I thought, Wherever I roam tonight I shall see the slow strokes of Larilla's brush and hear her little song.

I walked to the edge of the village and looked back. I could see it all in my mind: the warm sleepers and the many empty beds, the clothes hanging on pegs, the shoes and chamber pots beneath the beds. I could see the dying coals in the ovens and the meats and vegetables and spices in the jars. I could smell the fatty oil lamps burning and the mouse droppings inside the walls and the gray cat's fur where it napped in the ingle.

My village has been like a nest of little birds waiting to learn to fly, I thought, and I walked away from it then. Midnight moved beside me on the road, a silent companion walker, and a yellow star on my left-hand side kept winking a message, but I could not make out the meaning.

4

I had not gone a mile or so before I saw firelight fitful behind the bush and trees beside the road. I slipped down off the road and toward the light, toward a mutter of elder voices. I hid in the bushes at the edge of a small clearing and peeped, to see what I could see.

Who should it be but the village council out in the midnight woods? The old ones stood warming themselves by the fire and talking. I felt a twinge of pity for them. When things were normal, this council had been an ignorant and helpless bunch of fools. Now that everything had changed, now that the Owners had arrived, they must feel perfectly useless, without hope or purpose. What was the point of a village council when there was no longer a village?

Old Stavros asked the questions for all of them. He paced in the firelight, rubbing his chin and appearing to muse wisely, while they sat in a semicircle on the ground.

"Shall the council also desert the village?" he asked, and they said nothing and only stared into his shadow as it crossed against the fire. "Shall we protect the secret manuscripts? They have become so fragile that they crumble almost at a touch."

All right, I had suspected as much. There were secret manuscripts remaining from the old days. They were full of science, no doubt. Always tyrannic old men try to keep the rest of us ignorant for what they conceive to be our own good. But now the piddling little secrets they had guarded meant nothing to anyone.

Science meant nothing now, either, whatever science was. I had always surmised that science was merely a separate mode of knowledge not so far removed from our customary white magic. The reputation of science had been unjustly blackened when it had been linked to the two earlier failures of civilization that we knew about. But it takes more than a way of knowing things to bring about such momentous collapse. Science, I thought, would be harmless in itself, but perhaps it could be misapplied. You can knock a man's brains out with a lute, but that's not the purpose the lute was designed to fulfill. In my case, I had been gathering wildflowers and comparing their colors, roots, and the shapes of their leaves and petals. Could not our society withstand such a dire enterprise?

Stavros stopped pacing and turned to look into the dark woods. "I do not know," he admitted, "whether we stand in a deep abyss or on the peak of a mountain. I cannot say if there will continue to be a village for us to counsel. Perhaps we no longer are useful to give advice, perhaps our time is past."

He surprised me with that remark. I wouldn't have thought him capable of owning up to the facts. The world had obviously changed even more than I realized.

I rebuked myself. Why had I been so supercilious toward the old men; why did they always bring out that streak of cynical rebellion in me? Just look at them here, harmless elderly uncles and grandfathers, trying not to cling to their old ways, to their specious authority. Think of all those years they had guarded their precious secret manuscripts in which, no doubt, they could not understand a single word. They must have had anxieties, bad dreams I had never guessed at. Now the world had been transformed by the arrival of the Owners and the council was trying to adjust, trying to give up its oppressive habits. Could I not give up my resentment against these stranded anachronisms?

Yes—but not entirely. I would still remember my grievances, but without rancor. My former way of life, and the life of our whole village, now seemed quaint and remote, as delicately remote as a dried flower pressed in a schoolgirl's book of poems. Let me keep my old defiance in mind, then, as a remembrance of days gone by.

I slid out of the undergrowth and climbed back to the road and walked along until I came to an abandoned slaughterhouse. I sat by the slaughterhouse until the late moon rose. I was still different, I thought, from the old men of the council. They were still trying, however falteringly, to make plans for the future. But there was no point in making plans. When our past went away, the future disappeared, too. It was important to keep in mind that the future had died.

The risen moon outlined in the treetops the intricate lodgments of squirrels. Who knows? Tomorrow the trees may consider squirrels their pets and naturally put forth these nests to entice them. Maybe this has already taken place. That's what the future is, the purposes of things becoming apparent too late.

5

I sat by the slaughterhouse till sunrise, then rose refreshed and began walking the road again. I wasn't tired or hungry or even thirsty; I felt I could walk a thousand miles. The air was bright and cool, ringing with bird song. In my youth I had set out like this many times, marching blithely to the river, going to see the morning on the water. I would watch for hours the damselflies over still pools, darting and hovering, drawing angular designs in air. I had been careless in those days.

On the road a long procession approached from behind and I sat on a big white rock to let it go by. A hooded white-robed priest trudged before a coffin borne by six men from my village. A troop of silent mourners shuffled behind the coffin.

I fell in with the procession, and plucked Tonio by the sleeve. "Who has died?" I asked.

His eyes were hot and dry. "The widow Larilla," he answered.

I staggered then as from a blow with a cudgel. "That is not possible," I said. "Only last night she was well. She was brushing her hair and singing her little song. It cannot be Larilla who died."

"Nevertheless it is she," he said. "She died of happiness."

I grasped Tonio's arm and pulled him to the ditch. The procession went on by, and he looked at it fretfully. At first I could not speak, the anguish hard in my throat. I flapped my arms and sputtered bits of words.

Tonio eyed me unmoved. "Yes, I know," he said. "You were in love with her, perhaps. But we were all fond of Larilla.

And there were others truly in love with her also." He looked away. "Yet we are not sad that she died."

"How —?"

He began to talk with a sudden urgency. "Listen, George, have you ever been happy? Completely happy, I mean, so that there was no other thought or feeling in you but happiness?"

"I don't know."

"Then your answer is no. . . . Larilla was with the Owner. Her happiness was too much for her. She simply spilled out of her body, that's all. That's why we are not weeping." He looked down into the dust. "I think," he said, "we are envious of her."

"But she was young and beautiful —"

· "And happy," he said. "Now she is young and beautiful and happy forever."

"The Owner is responsible. It's his fault. It's terrible."

"Maybe he told her things we know nothing of," he said. "Perhaps he made love to her. Whatever happened, it was her greatest joy."

"Where is he? I have to talk to him."

His voice became melancholy. "He must have gone away. We looked and couldn't find him."

I began to weep then, but Tonio pressed my hand in his. "No tears," he said. "She was happy."

He drew me into the road and we fell in at the end of the procession, walking along until we came to a grove of bright poplars. We paced on the path through the grove into the homely small graveyard beyond.

They lowered the coffin into the grave and the priest said some words I didn't listen to. Her tombstone was set at the head of the grave, with the epitaph already carved. *Fulfilled*, it said. I noticed that the stone was old and weather-eaten and lichenous; only Larilla's name and the other single word were new.

Then the others went away while Tonio and I remained. I looked down there a long time, but the blank box of yellow pine told me nothing. Finally Tonio led me away. "Let's go back to the village," he said, and we did so. I could not say what I felt as we walked along; I didn't know what to feel.

He led me straight to Larilla's deserted cottage. It was in

immaculate order; the village women must have visited in order to clean and straighten. He set me on a stool before the well-scrubbed table and placed a loaf of oat bread before me and poured a cup of water from the pitcher. "Rest," he said. "Eat. Remember. I'll be back in a while to talk with you."

"There are things you haven't told me. Isn't that true?"

"They're not important right now. Just now you'll want to be alone."

"Yes," I said.

Tonio went away and I sat and stared at the walls for a long time, still not knowing what to feel. I broke the loaf of bread and it was full of bright red and yellow sparks. The sparks flew round and round the room like wasps and made a musical sound that was the same as Larilla's crooning when she brushed her hair. I became dizzy and steadied myself by holding on to the edge of the table. Then the humming swarm of sparks flew up the chimney and disappeared.

The world, you see, was still changing. The Owners had not finished with it yet. That is why I did not know what emotions to feel or what signals to observe in the world about me. A great deal has been revealed to us, but it is revelation so pure that our minds and senses cannot interpret it. We are not ready.

I decided then, sitting at the table in Larilla's quiet cottage, that I would start again on my journey. I would join the great army of nameless pilgrims; it was no good sitting in a room and waiting for the answers to rise from inside myself. Probably there were no answers in pilgrimage, either, but I was so bewildered and so filled with longing that I could not stay still. Everything had been revealed to us, and yet . . .

After revelation, what then?

About the Authors

Lavonne Adams is a former recipient of a grant from the North Carolina Arts Council. She currently teaches at the University of North Carolina at Wilmington.

Ellyn Bache is the author of three novels: *The Activist's Daughter* (Spinster's Ink, 1997), *Festival in Fire Season* (August House, 1992), and *Safe Passage* (Crown, 1988), which was made into a 1995 film starring Susan Sarandon and Sam Shepard. Her collection of short stories, *The Value of Kindness* (Helicon Nine Editions, 1993) was awarded the Willa Cather Fiction Prize. A native of Washington, D.C., she came to North Carolina to attend The University of North Carolina at Chapel Hill, then left the state for more than 20 years before moving to Wilmington in 1985, where she lives with her family.

Rebecca Baggett was born in Wilmington, raised at Carolina Beach and in Garner, and educated at Salem College in Winston-Salem, North Carolina. Her fiction, essays, and poems have appeared in numerous journals and anthologies, including *North American Review, New England Review, and Ms.* Her poetry chapbook, *Still Life with Children,* was published in 1996 She lives with her husband, Elmer Clark, and their daughters, Morgan and Emma Baggett-Clark, in Athens, Georgia.

Jeff W. Bens teaches at the North Carolina School of the Arts. "Ten Rabbis Eat Cake" received the 1996 Writers Conferences and Festivals Fiction Award and was originally published in *Vignette.*

Maudy Benz is a graduate of the Bennington College MFA program, where she studied with Alice Mattison and Jill McCorkle. She is also a performance artist and gives one-woman shows based on her fiction. She teaches memoir writing

369

in the Duke Short Courses Program. Her first novel, *Oh Jackie,* is scheduled for publication in 1998.

Sally Buckner writes poetry, fiction, and plays when she isn't teaching at Peace College, where she is Alumnae Distinguished Professor of English, or enjoying her family and garden. She is the author of a collection of poetry (*Strawberry Harvest,* St. Andrews Press, 1996) and editor of *Our Words, Our Ways: Reading and Writing in North Carolina* (Carolina Academic Press, 1991, 1995), an anthology of North Carolina literature used to accompany the history studies in middle and high schools.

Fred Chappell is the author of many books of fiction and poetry. His *The Fred Chappell Reader* is published by St. Martin's Press.

Kelly Cherry has published five books of fiction, five of poetry, and two of nonfiction. Her most recent title is *Death and Transfiguration,* a collection of poems published by Louisiana State University Press in 1997. She received her MFA from the University of North Carolina at Greensboro and now teaches at the University of Wisconsin, Madison.

Michael Chitwood was born and raised in the foothills of the Virginia Blue Ridge and is now a free-lance writer living in Chapel Hill, North Carolina. His poetry and fiction have apepared in *Poetry, Ohio Review, The Southern Review, Threepenny Review, Virginia Quarterly Review, Field,* and numerous other publications. Ohio Review Books has published two books of his poetry--*Salt Works* (1992) and *Whet* (1995). He is a regular commentator for WUNC-FM and a columnist for *The Independent* in Durham, North Carolina.

Kim Church lives in Raleigh, North Carolina.

Jim Clark is a freelance writer and author. He teaches at Barton College in Wilson, North Carolina.

Hal Crowther was born March 26, 1945, in Halifax, Nova Scotia, of American parents. He is a graduate of Williams College (B.A., English) and the Columbia University Graduate School of Journalism, Class of 1967. He was a staff writer at *Time* and an associate editor at *Newsweek*, where he was television critic and editor of the Media section. At the *Buffalo News* he was a media columnist and a film and drama critic. He began writing his syndicated column for *Spectator* magazine in 1981, and was executive editor there from 1986 to 1989. Since 1989 his column has originated in *The Independent Weekly* of Durham. In 1992 it received the *Baltimore Sun's* H. L. Mencken Writing Award, the first weekly column so honored. A collection of his essays, *Unarmed But Dangerous*, was published in 1995 by Longstreet Press of Atlanta. He is married to novelist Lee Smith. They live in Hillsborough, North Carolina.

Mary E. Lynn Drew was born in Pettersburg, Virginia. She is a lecturer on and consultant in learning abilities. She has received a grant from the North Carolina Humanities Council for an oral histories series, *Heroic Women of the Southern Highlands.*

Charles Edward Eaton was born in Winston-Salem, North Carolina, and was educated at the University of North Carolina, Princeton, and Harvard, where he studied with Robert Frost. He taught creative writing at the Universities of Missouri and North Carolina and was American vice-consul in Rio de Janeiro for four years. His work in poetry and prose has appeared throughout the English-speaking world. Eaton has been included in such standard anthologies as *O. Henry Prize Stories* and *Best American Short Stories*. Recognition for his four collections of short stories and thirteen volumes of poetry include the Ridgely Torrence Award, The Golden Rose from the New England Poetry Club, The Alice Fay di Castagnola Award, an Arvon International Poetry prize, and a Kansas Quarterly/Kansas Arts Commission Short Story Award. The North Carolina Award for Literature was presented to the author by the governor in 1988.

Allan Gurganus is the author of *Oldest Living Confederate Widow Tells All* and a volume of short stories, *White People.*

David Guy is the author of four novels, most recently *The Autobiography Of My Body.* He lives in Durham.

Trudier Harris is J. Carlyle Sitterson Professor of English at the University of North Carolina at Chapel Hill. She earned her B.A. from Stillman College (1969), Tuscaloosa, Alabama. She has lectured and published widely in her specialty areas of African American literature and folklore. Her authored books include *From Marries to Militants: Domestics in Black American Literature* (1982), *Exorcising Blackness: Historical and Literary Lynching and Burning Rituals* (1984), *Black Women in the Fiction of James Baldwin* (1985, for which she won the 1987 College Language Association Creative Scholarship Award), *Fiction and Folklore, The Novels of Toni Morrison* (1991), and, most recently, *The Power of the Porch: The Storyteller's Craft in Zora Neale Hurston, Gloria Naylor, and Randall Kenan* (1996). She edited *New Essays on Baldwin's Go Tell It on the Mountain* (1996) for Cambridge University Press and co-edited The *Oxford Companion to African American Literature* (1997). Two other volumes for which she has served as co-editor, *Call and Response: The Riverside Anthology of the African American Literary Tradition* and *The Norton Anthology of Southern Literature*, will also be published in 1997. During 1996-97, she is a resident fellow at the National Humanities Center in Research Triangle Park, North Carolina.

Virginia Holman received an emerging artist grant from the Durham Arts Council in 1992. She has worked at *New Virginia Review* and *The Greensboro Review* and was Chief Copy-editor for Algonquin Books until 1993. She is currently a freelance book editor and teacher.

Elizabeth C. Hunter, a native New Englander, is a resident of the Bandana Community of Mitchell County, and a contributing editor and columnist for *Blue Ridge Country Magazine.* Her personal essays have appeared in *The Christian Science Monitor,* and she has written many articles for state and regional magazines. In 1996, she received a travel grant from the East Tennessee State University Center for Appalachian Studies and Services to underwrite research into the history of mica mining in the Toe River Valley; "Private McKinney Died in France July 9" is an outgrowth of that research. A longtime newspaper reporter and feature writer for local weeklies and regional dailies in Western North Carolina and East Tennessee, she is also an avid hiker, gardener and observer of the natural world.

Richard Krawiec is the editor of a previous anthology of North Carolina writing, *Cardinal*. His two novels are *Time Sharing* and *Faith In What?* (Avisson, 1996). He lives in Raleigh, North Carolina.

Rebecca McClanahan is the author of three books of poetry (most recently *The Intersection of X and Y* from Copper Beech Press) and a book of essays and lectures. She has received a Pushcart prize, the Carter prize for the essay from *Shenandoah*, the J. Howard and Barbara M. J. Wood Prize from *Poetry*, and a P.E.N. Syndicated Fiction Award. Her work has appeared in *Georgia Review, Gettysburg Review, Southern Review,* and *Kenyon Review,* and has been aired on NPR's "The Sound of Writing". McClanahan has taught writing workshops at Kenyon College, Queens College, Davidson College, Ashland Unviersity, the University of North Carolina, and other institutions.

Michael McFee has published five books of poetry, most recently *Colander* (Carnegie Mellon University Press, 1996), and edited a poetry anthology, *The Language They Speak Is Things to Eat: Poems by Fifteen Contemporary North Carolina Poets* (University of North Carolina Press, 1994). He teaches creative writing at UNC-Chapel Hill.

Erstwhile librettist and occasional playwright, **Melissa Malouf** is also the author of two works of fiction, *No Guarantees* (Morrow, 1990) and *It Had to Be You* (Avisson, 1997). She teaches literature and creative writing at Duke University.

Kat Meads is the author of a collection of creative nonfiction, *Born Southern and Restless* (Duquesne University Press), which includes "Sports: Family Style". She has also published a collection of poetry (*Filming the Everyday*) and a chapbook of short fiction (*Wayward Women*). She grew up in eastern North Carolina and received her MFA from UNC-Greensboro.

MariJo Moore is of Eastern Cherokee, Dutch and Irish ancestry. Her published works include *Returning To The Homeland – Cherokee Poetry And Short Stories, Stars Are Birds, Crow Quotes,* and *Spirit Voices of Bones.* Her writings have appeared in numerous publications. She is a staff writer for *Indian Artist* magazine and *News From Indian Country.* The recipient of several literary awards, she travels widely to present lectures and literary readings, and to teach workshops on the Spirituality of Creative Writing. She resides in Asheville, North Carolina.

Ruth Moose has published two short story collections, *The Wreath Ribbon Quilt* and *Dreaming in Color* (August House, 1989). She has published individual stories in *Atlantic Monthly, Redbook, McCall's,* and other places. Moose has received three PEN Awards for Syndicated Fiction, as well as a North Carolina Writers Fellowship and a MacDowell Fellowship. She teaches Creative Writing at UNC-Chapel Hill.

Joe Ashby Porter is the author of the novel *Eelgrass* (New Directions) and the two collections *The Kentucky Stories* and *Lithuania: Short Stories* (both Johns Hopkins Press). His stories have appeared widely in periodicals and have been reprinted in *Best American Short Stories, The Pushcart Prize, Contemporary American Fiction,* and other anthologies. He has taught writing at the University of Virginia, Brown University, and Duke, and at the Sewanee Writer's Conference.

Barbara Presnell is a native North Carolinian who received her MFA from UNC-Greensboro. Her stories have been included in numerous journals. She teaches writing and literature at

Catawba College in Salisbury, North Carolina.

Yusef Salaam lives in Harlem, New York City. He (as Joseph Jones) was raised in Lumberton, North Carolina, where he attended J. H. Hayswood High School. "Blues Devil" is his third published short story. His most recent book is *Muslim Women Talk About Abuse, Love, and God-Consciousness.*

Lee Smith is the author of nine novels and several collections of short fiction. Her latest, *News of the Spirit,* a collection of short stories and novellas, will be published by Putnam in September 1997. She is affiliated with the writing program at North Carolina State University.

Elizabeth Spencer was born and brought up in Mississippi where she lived until 1953. After residencies in Italy and Montreal, she moved to Chapel Hill in 1986 with her husband John Rusher. She has published nine novels and three volumes of stories.

James Steinburg writes: "I am a fifty-year old writer who for nearly seven years has thrived on the intrinsic satisfaction of following the stories I discover. I've completed five and have roughly a dozen others in various stages of emergence. In spite of a rich family and professional life, inside a story is my preferred place to be.

. . . I have been a lawyer, dishwasher, blacksmith, gardener, truck driver, secondary school Language Arts and Social Studies teacher, father, stepfather, stone mason, some of these more than once, and probably a few others I've forgotten. None has given me more satisfaction than writing, but all have given me much to raise up from inside. I'd have it no other way.

Since 1992 I have been running a police academy at Durham Technical Community College, teaching law in the college's Criminal Justice Associate Degree Program, and gathering from this "next career" more material for stories. That seems to be the purpose of my employment odyssey, the last chapter of which I hope will be purely writing."

Carole Boston Weatherford is the author of *The Tan Chanteuse*, a prizewinning poetry chapbook, and *Juneteenth Jamboree*, the first children's book about the emancipation holiday. Her essays and articles have appeared in *Christian Science Monitor*, *Washington Post* and *Essence*. The recipient of a North Carolina Arts Council Writers Fellowship, she holds an M.F.A. in creative writing from the University of North Carolina at Greensboro and an M.A. in publications design from the University of Baltimore. A native of Baltimore, she resides in High Point, North Carolina.

Susan Weinberg was a 1989-91 Stegner Fellow in fiction at Stanford University, where she served as a Jones Lecturer in Creative Writing from 1991-94. She currently teaches in the creative writing program at Appalachian State University.

Richard Zimler is a freelance writer of African American heritage who currently works and lives in Portugal. He has published two novels in Europe, *The Last Kabbalist of Lisbon,* and *Unholy Ghosts.* He earned a bachelor's degree in Religion from Duke.